WORKING MEN'S COLLEGE.

LIBRARY REGULATIONS

The Library is open every week-day evening, from 6.30 to 10 o'clock, except on Saturdays. when it closes at 9.

This book may be kept for three weeks, If not returned within that period, the borrower will be liable to a fine of one penny per week.

If lost or damaged, the borrower will be required to make good such loss or damage.

Only one book may be borrowed at a time.

Works by the Same Author

ALEXANDER HAMILTON (**An Essay on American Union**).

LIBRARY EDITION. Demy 8vo. 6s. net. Messrs. Constable & Co., London.

LIBRARY EDITION. 8vo. $1.50 net. Messrs. G. P. Putnam's Sons, New York.

POPULAR EDITION. Fcap. 8vo. Cloth, 1s. net; Leather, 2s. net. Messrs. Thos. Nelson & Sons.

FEDERALISM AND HOME RULE (**Letters of Pacificus**). Demy 8vo. Cloth. 2s. 6d. net.

THE ALTERNATIVES TO CIVIL WAR. Demy 8vo. Paper. 6d. net.

WHAT FEDERALISM IS NOT. Demy 8vo. Paper. 6d. net.

Mr. JOHN MURRAY, London.

ORDEAL BY BATTLE

MACMILLAN AND CO., Limited
LONDON · BOMBAY · CALCUTTA
MELBOURNE

THE MACMILLAN COMPANY
NEW YORK · BOSTON · CHICAGO
DALLAS · SAN FRANCISCO

THE MACMILLAN CO. OF CANADA, Ltd.
TORONTO

ORDEAL BY BATTLE

BY

FREDERICK SCOTT OLIVER

With that they looked upon him, and began to reply in this sort: SIMPLE said, *I see no danger*; SLOTH said, *Yet a little more sleep*; and PRESUMPTION said, *Every Vat must stand upon his own bottom.* And so they lay down to sleep again, and CHRISTIAN went on his way.

The Pilgrim's Progress.

MACMILLAN AND CO., LIMITED
ST. MARTIN'S STREET, LONDON
1915

COPYRIGHT

First Edition June 1915
Reprinted twice June 1915
July 1915

TO

THE MEMORY OF

HUGH DAWNAY

COMMANDING THE 2ND LIFE GUARDS

WHO WAS KILLED AT ZWARTELEEN ON THE 6TH OF NOVEMBER 1914

AND OF

JOHN GOUGH, V.C.

CHIEF OF THE STAFF OF THE FIRST ARMY

WHO FELL NEAR ESTAIRES ON THE 20TH OF FEBRUARY 1915

THEY WERE BROTHER-OFFICERS OF THE RIFLE BRIGADE

AND THOSE WHO KNEW THEM BOTH

WILL ALWAYS THINK OF THEM TOGETHER

PREFACE

PREFACE.

The purpose of this book.

It is hardly necessary to plead, in extenuation of those many faults which any impartial reader will discover in the following pages, the impossibility of discussing events which are unfolding themselves around us, in the same detached spirit as if we were dealing with past history. The greater part of this volume has been written in haste, and no one is more alive to its shortcomings than the author himself.

Faults of style are a small matter, and will be easily forgiven. It has not been the aim to produce a work of literary merit, but solely to present a certain view of public affairs. It is to be hoped that actual errors of fact are rare. Inconsistencies however—or apparent inconsistencies—cannot be altogether avoided, even by careful revision. But the greatest difficulty of all is to keep a true sense of proportion.

In Part I.—*The Causes of War*—an attempt has been made to state, very briefly, why it has hitherto proved impossible to eliminate the appeal to arms from human affairs; to set out the main incidents which occurred at the opening of the present European struggle; to explain the immediate occasions, as

The purpose of this book.

well as the more permanent and deep-seated causes, of this conflict; to consider some of the most glaring miscalculations which have arisen out of misunderstanding between nations.

In Part II.—*The Spirit of German Policy*—an attempt has been made to understand the ambitions of our chief antagonist, and to trace the manner in which these ambitions have been fostered, forced, and corrupted by a priesthood of learned men. The relations which exist between this Pedantocracy and the Bureaucracy, the Army, the Rulers, and the People of Germany have been examined. It would appear that under an academic stimulus, healthy national ambitions have become morbid, have resulted in the discovery of imaginary grievances, and have led the Governing Classes of Germany to adopt a new code of morals which, if universally adhered to, would make an end of human society. On the other hand, it would also appear that the German People have accepted the policy of their rulers, without in any way accepting, or even understanding, the morality upon which this policy is founded. It is also important for us to realise the nature of the judgment—not altogether unjustified—which our enemies have passed upon the British character, and upon our policy and institutions.

In Part III.—*The Spirit of British Policy*—our own political course since the beginning of the century has been considered—the difficulties arising out of the competition for priority between aims which are

The purpose of this book.

not in themselves antagonistic: between Social Reform, Constitutional Reform, and Imperial Defence —the confusion which has resulted from the inadequacy of one small parliament, elected upon a large variety of cross issues, for dealing with these diverse needs—the lowering of the tone of public life, the depreciation in the character of public men, which have come about owing to these two causes, and also to a third—the steadily increasing tyranny and corruption of the party machines.

The aim of British Foreign Policy has been simply —Security. Yet we have failed to achieve Security, owing to our blindness, indolence, and lack of leadership. We have refused to realise that we were not living in the Golden Age; that Policy at the last resort depends on Armaments; that Armaments, to be effective for their purpose, must correspond with Policy. Political leaders of all parties up to the outbreak of the present war ignored these essentials; or if they were aware of them, in the recesses of their own consciousness, they failed to trust the People with a full knowledge of the dangers which threatened their Security, and of the means by which alone these dangers could be withstood.

The titles of Parts II. and III. are similar—*The Spirit of German Policy* and *The Spirit of British Policy*; but although the titles are similar the treatment is not the same. Confession of a certain failure in proportion must be made frankly. The two pieces do not balance. German Policy is viewed

The purpose of this book.

from without, at a remote distance, and by an enemy. It is easier in this case to present a picture which is clear, than one which is true. British Policy, on the other hand, is viewed from within. If likewise it is tinged with prejudice, the prejudice is of a different character. Both Parts, I fear, diverge to a greater or less extent from the main purpose of the book. Mere excision is easy; but compression is a difficult and lengthy process, and I have not been able to carry it so far as I could have wished.

In Part IV.—*Democracy and National Service*—an attempt has been made to deal with a problem which faces us at the moment. Democracy is not unlike other human institutions: it will not stand merely by its own virtue. If it lacks the loyalty, courage, and strength to defend itself when attacked, it must perish as certainly as if it possessed no virtue whatsoever. Manhood suffrage implies manhood service. Without the acceptance of this principle Democracy is merely an imposture.

I prefer 'National Service' to 'Conscription,' not because I shrink from the word 'Conscription,' but because 'National Service' has a wider sweep. The greater includes the less. It is not only military duties which the State is entitled to command its citizens to perform unquestioningly in times of danger; but also civil duties. It is not only men between the ages of twenty and thirty-eight to whom the State should have the right to give orders; but men and women of all ages. Under conditions of modern warfare it is not only armies which need to be disciplined; but whole nations. The undisciplined nation, engaged in anything like an equal contest with a disciplined nation, will be defeated.

The purpose of this book.

This volume was in type before the Coalition Government was formed; but there is nothing in it which I wish to change in view of that event. This book was not undertaken with the object of helping the Unionists back into power, or of getting the Liberals out of power.

The Coalition Government.

The new Cabinet contains those members of the late one in whom the country has most confidence. Lord Kitchener, Sir Edward Grey, Mr. Lloyd George, and Mr. Churchill have all made mistakes. In a great crisis it is the bigger characters who are most liable to make mistakes. Their superiority impels them to take risks which the smaller men, playing always for safety, are concerned to avoid.

The present Ministry also contains representatives of that class of politicians which, according to the view set forth in the following pages, is primarily responsible for our present troubles. Lawyer-statesmanship, which failed to foresee the war, to prepare against it, and to conduct it with energy and thoroughness when it occurred, still occupies a large share of authority. Possibly ministers of this school

Ordeal by Battle.

will now walk in new ways. In any case, they are no longer in a position of dangerous predominance.

The Coalition Government.

The Coalition Government, having wisely refused to part with any of those men who rose to the emergency, and having received an infusion of new blood (which may be expected to bring an accession of vigour) starts upon its career with the goodwill and confidence of the People.

What has happened, however, is a revolution upon an unprecedented scale—one which is likely to have vast consequences in the future. The country realises this fact, and accepts it as a matter of course—accepts it indeed with a sigh of relief. But in other quarters, what has just happened is hardly realised at all—still less what it is likely to lead to in the future.

During the 'Cabinet Crisis' one read a good deal of stuff in the newspapers, and heard still more by word of mouth, which showed how far, during the past nine months, public opinion has moved away from the professionals of politics; how little account it takes of them; also how much these gentlemen themselves mistake the meaning of the present situation.

In political circles one has heard, and read, very frequently of late, expressions of regret—on the one hand that Unionists should have come to the assistance of a discredited and bankrupt administration—on the other hand that a government, secure in the confidence of the country, should, through a mistaken

The Coalition Government.

sense of generosity, have admitted its opponents to a share in the glory and prestige of office. One has read, and heard, cavillings at the idea of appointing this, or that, public character to this, or that, office, as a thing beyond what this, or that, party 'could fairly be expected to stand.' Reports have appeared of meetings of 'a hundred' perturbed Liberals; and very possibly meetings, though unreported, of equally perturbed Unionists have also been held. An idea seems still to be prevalent in certain quarters, that what has just occurred is nothing more important than an awkward and temporary disarrangement of the party game; and that this game will be resumed, with all the old patriotism and good feeling, so soon as war is ended.

But this appears to be a mistaken view. You cannot make a great mix-up of this sort without calling new parties into existence. When men are thrown into the crucible of a war such as this, the true ore will tend to run together, the dross to cake upon the surface. No matter to what parties they may have originally owed allegiance, the men who are in earnest, and who see realities, cannot help but come together. May be for several generations the annual festivals of the National Liberal Federation and the Union of Conservative Associations will continue to be held, like other picturesque survivals of ancient customs. When Henry VII. was crowned at Westminster, the Wars of the Roses ended; the old factions of York and Lancaster were dissolved, and

The Coalition Government.

made way for new associations. Something of the same sort has surely happened during the past month—Liberal and Conservative, Radical and Tory have ceased for the present to be real divisions. They had recently become highly artificial and confusing; now they are gone—it is to be hoped for ever.

Will the generation which is fighting this war—such of them as may survive—be content to go back to the old barren wrangle when it is done? Will those others who have lost husbands, sons, brothers, friends—all that was dearest to them except the honour and safety of their country—will they be found willing to tolerate the idea of trusting their destinies ever again to the same machines, to be driven once more to disaster by the same automatons? To all except the automatons themselves—who share with the German Supermen the credit of having made this war—any such resumption of business on old-established lines appears incredible. There is something pathetic in the sight of these huckstering sentimentalists still crying their stale wares and ancient make-believes at the street corners, while their country is fighting for its life. They remind one, not a little, of those *Pardoners* of the fourteenth century who, as we read in history books, continued to hawk their *Indulgences* with unabated industry during the days of the *Black Death*.

PREFACE.

The origins of this book.

It is necessary to offer a few words of explanation as to how this book came to be written. During the months of November and December 1912 and January 1913, various meetings and discussions took place under Lord Roberts's roof and elsewhere, between a small number of persons, who held widely different views, and whose previous experience and training had been as different as were their opinions.

Our efforts were concerned with endeavouring to find answers to several questions which had never been dealt with candidly, clearly, and comprehensively in the public statements of political leaders. It was clear that there was no 'national' policy, which the British people had grasped, accepted, and countersigned, as was the case in France. But some kind of British policy there must surely be, notwithstanding the fact it had never been disclosed. What were the aims of this policy? With what nation or nations were these aims likely to bring us into collision? What armaments were necessary in order to enable us to uphold this policy and achieve these aims? How, and when, and where would our armaments be required in the event of war? Assuming (as we did in our discussions) that our naval forces were adequate, was the same statement true of our military forces? And if it were not true, by what means could the necessary increases be obtained?

The final conclusion at which we arrived was that National Service was essential to security.

The origins of this book.

Under whatever aspect we regarded the problem we always returned—even those of us who were most unwilling to travel in that direction—to the same result. So long as Britain relied solely upon the voluntary principle, we should never possess either the Expeditionary Force or the Army for Home Defence which were requisite for safety.

It fell to me during the winter 1912–1913 to draft the summary of our conclusions. It was afterwards decided—in the spring of 1913—that this private Memorandum should be recast in a popular form suitable for publication. I was asked to undertake this, and agreed to do so. But I underestimated both the difficulties of the task and the time which would be necessary for overcoming them.

When we met again, in the autumn of that year, the work was still far from complete, and by that time, not only public attention, but our own, had become engrossed in other matters. The Irish controversy had entered upon a most acute and dangerous stage. Lord Roberts put off the meetings which he had arranged to address during the ensuing months upon National Service, and threw his whole energies into the endeavour to avert the schism which threatened the nation, and to find a way to a peaceful settlement. Next to the security and integrity of the British Empire I verily believe that the thing which lay nearest his heart was the happiness and unity of Ireland.

It is needless to recall how, during the ensuing

The origins of this book.

months, affairs in Ireland continued to march from bad to worse—up to the very day when the menace of the present war suddenly arose before the eyes of Europe.

During August 1914 I went through the old drafts and memoranda which had now been laid aside for nearly a year. Although that very thing had happened which it had been the object of our efforts to avert, it seemed to me that there might be advantages in publishing some portion of our conclusions. The form, of course, would have to be entirely different; for the recital of prophecies which had come true, though it might have possessed a certain interest for the prophets themselves, could have but little for the public.

Early in September I consulted Lord Roberts, and also such of my friends, who had originally worked with me, as were still within reach. Finding that their opinion agreed with my own upon the desirability of publication, I laid out a fresh scheme, and set to for a third time at the old task. But as the work grew, it became clear that it would contain but little of the former Memorandum, and much which the former Memorandum had never contemplated. So many of our original conclusions, laboriously hammered out to convince the public in the spring of the year 1913, had become by the autumn of 1914, the most trite of commonplaces. And as for the practical scheme which we had evolved—endeavouring to keep our demands at the most modest minimum—

ORDEAL BY BATTLE.

The origins of this book.

it was interesting chiefly by reason of its triviality when contrasted with the scale of warlike preparations upon which the Government was now engaged. Practically, therefore, the whole of the present volume is new—not merely redrafted, but for the most part new in substance.

The author's acknowledgments.

I wish to acknowledge my indebtedness to the friends with whom I have studied the problems of policy and defence for some years past. The responsibility for the contents and publication of the present volume is mine alone; but I have used their ideas without hesitation, and have drawn largely upon the notes and memoranda which they drafted for my assistance. I wish also to thank several others—one in chief—for the kindness with which, upon the present occasion, they have given me help and criticism as these pages were passing through the press.

There is also another source to which I wish here gratefully to confess my obligations. During the past five years there have appeared in *The Round Table* certain articles upon the relations of England with Germany [1] which have been characterised by

[1] *The Round Table* (quarterly Review). Macmillan & Co., Ltd. Of the articles referred to the chief are: 'Anglo-German Rivalry' (November 1910); 'Britain, France, and Germany' (December 1911); 'The Balkan War and the Balance of Power' (June 1913); 'Germany and the Prussian Spirit' (September 1914); 'The Schism of Europe' (March 1915). It is to be hoped that these and some others may be republished before long in a more permanent form.

The author's acknowledgments.

a remarkable degree of prescience and sanity. At a certain point, however, there is a difference between the views expressed in *The Round Table* and those expressed in the following pages—a difference of stress and emphasis perhaps, rather than of fundamental opinion, but still a difference of some importance. I have dealt with this in the concluding chapter.

I should like to make one other acknowledgment of a different kind. I have known the editor of *The National Review* from a date long before he assumed his onerous office—from days when we were freshmen together by the banks of the Cam. During a period of upwards of thirty years, I cannot remember that I have ever had the good fortune to see absolutely eye to eye with Mr. Maxse upon any public question. Even now I do not see eye to eye with him. In all probability I never shall. At times his views have been in sharp opposition to my own. But for these very reasons—if he will not resent it as an impertinence—I should like to say here how greatly I respect him for three qualities, which have been none too common among public men in recent times—first, for the clearness with which he grasps and states his beliefs; secondly, for the courageous constancy with which he holds to them through good and evil report; thirdly, for the undeviating integrity of his public career. Next to Lord Roberts, he did more perhaps than any other—though unavailingly—to arouse public opinion to the dangers

ORDEAL BY BATTLE. which menaced it from German aggression, to call attention to the national unpreparedness, and to denounce the blindness and indolence which treated all warnings with derision.

The author's acknowledgments.

Lord Roberts.

Lord Roberts's responsibility for the contents of this volume, as for its publication at the present time, is nil. And yet it would never have been undertaken in the first instance except at his wish, nor re-undertaken in September last without his encouragement. There are probably a good many besides myself who owe it to his inspiration, that they first made a serious attempt to study policy and defence as two aspects of a single problem. I also owe to him many things besides this.

The circumstances of Lord Roberts's death were befitting his character and career. The first great battle of Ypres was ended. The British line had held its own against tremendous odds of men and guns. He had no doubt of the ultimate result of the war, and during his visit to France and Flanders inspired all who saw him by the quiet confidence of his words and manner. After the funeral service at Headquarters a friend of his and mine wrote to me describing the scene. The religious ceremony had taken place in the entrance hall of the Mairie at St. Omer. It was a day of storms; but as the coffin was borne out "the sun

Lord Roberts.

'appeared, and made a magnificent rainbow on a 'great black block of cloud across the square; and 'an airman flew across from the rainbow into the 'sunlight."

If I were asked to name Lord Roberts's highest intellectual quality I should say unhesitatingly that it was his instinct. And if I were asked to name his highest moral quality I should say, also unhesitatingly, that it was the unshakeable confidence with which he trusted his instinct. But the firmness of his trust was not due in the least to self-conceit, or arrogance, or obstinacy. He obeyed his instinct as he obeyed his conscience—humbly and devoutly. The dictates of both proceeded from the same source. It was not his own cleverness which led him to his conclusions, but the hand of Providence which drew aside a veil, and enabled him to see the truth. What gave him his great strength in counsel, as in the field, was the simple modesty of his confidence.

He was a poor arguer; I think argument was painful to him; also that he regarded it as a sad waste of the short span of human life. It was not difficult to out-argue him. Plausible and perspicacious persons often left him, after an interview, under the firm impression that they had convinced him. But as a rule, he returned on the morrow to his old opinion, unless his would-be converters had brought to his notice new facts as well as new arguments.

ORDEAL BY BATTLE.

Lord Roberts.

He arrived at an opinion neither hastily nor slowly, but at a moderate pace. He had the gift of stating his conclusion with admirable lucidity; and if he thought it desirable, he gave the reasons for his view of the matter with an equal clearness. But his reasons, like his conclusion, were in the nature of statements; they were not stages in an argument. There are as many unanswerable reasons to be given for as against most human decisions. Ingenuity and eloquence are a curse at councils of war, and state, and business. Indeed, wherever action of any kind has to be determined upon they are a curse. It was Lord Roberts's special gift that, out of the medley of unanswerable reasons, he had an instinct for selecting those which really mattered, and keeping his mind close shut against the rest.

It is superfluous to speak of his courtesy of manner and kindness of heart, or of his unflagging devotion—up till the very day of his death—to what he regarded as his duty. There is a passage in Urquhart's translation of *Rabelais* which always recalls him to my mind:—*He was the best little great good man that ever girded a sword on his side; he took all things in good part, and interpreted every action in the best sense.* In a leading German newspaper there appeared, a few days after his death, the following reference to that event:—"It was not given to Lord Roberts 'to see the realisation of his dreams of National 'Service; but the blows struck on the Aisne 'were hammer-strokes which might after a long

Lord Roberts.

'time and bitter need produce it. Lord Roberts 'was an honourable and, through his renown, a 'dangerous enemy . . . personally an extraordinarily 'brave enemy. Before such a man we lower our 'swords, to raise them again for new blows dealt 'with the joy of conflict."

Nor was this the only allusion of the kind which figured in German newspapers 'to the journey of 'an old warrior to Walhalla,' with his final mission yet unaccomplished, but destined to be sooner or later accomplished, if his country was to survive. In none of these references, so far as I have been able to discover, was there the least trace of malice against the man who had warned his fellow-countrymen, more clearly than any other, against the premeditated aggression of Germany. This seems very strange when we recollect how, for nearly two years previously, a large section of the British nation had been engaged in denouncing Lord Roberts for the outrageous provocations which he was alleged to have offered to Germany—in apologising to Germany for his utterances—in suggesting the propriety of depriving him of his pension in the interests of Anglo-German amity. What this section has itself earned in the matter of German gratitude we know from many hymns and other effusions of hate.

ORDEAL BY BATTLE.

Hugh Dawnay and John Gough.

I have dedicated this volume to the memory of John Gough and Hugh Dawnay, not solely on grounds of friendship, but also because from both I received, at different times, much help, advice, and criticism—from the latter when the original Memorandum was in course of being drafted—from both when it was being reconsidered with a view to publication. Whether either of them would agree with the statement in its present form is more than I can venture to say, and I have no intention of claiming their authority for conclusions which were never seen by them in final shape.

In the first instance (November 1912–March 1913) Dawnay [1] and I worked together. His original notes and memoranda are to a large extent incorporated in Parts III. and IV.—so closely, however, that I cannot now disentangle his from my own. The calculations as to numbers and probable distribution of the opposing forces, were almost entirely his. I have merely endeavoured here—not so successfully as I could wish—to bring them up to the date of the outbreak of war.

Dawnay took out his squadron of the 2nd Life Guards to France early in August. Already, however, he had been appointed to the Headquarters General Staff, on which he served with distinction, until early in October, when he succeeded to the command

[1] Major the Hon. Hugh Dawnay, D.S.O., *b.* 1875; educated Eton and Sandhurst; Rifle Brigade, 1895; Nile Campaign and Omdurman, 1898; South Africa, 1899–1900; Somaliland, 1908–1910; 2nd Life Guards, 1912; France, August-November 1914.

Hugh Dawnay and John Gough.

of his regiment. He fell at Zwarteleen near Ypres on the 6th of November 1914—one of the most anxious days during the four weeks' battle.

His friends have mourned his death, but none of them have grudged it; for he died, not merely as a brave man should—in the performance of his duty—but after having achieved, with consummate skill and daring, his part in an action of great importance. On the afternoon of this day General Kavanagh's Brigade of Household Cavalry[1]—summoned in haste—dismounted, and threw back a German attack which had partially succeeded in piercing the allied line at the point of junction between the French and English forces. This successful counter-attack saved the right flank of Lord Cavan's Guards' Brigade from a position of extreme danger, which must otherwise, almost certainly, have resulted in a perilous retreat. The whole of this Homeric story is well worth telling, and some day it may be told; but this is not the place.

Dawnay was fortunate inasmuch as he lost his life, not as so many brave men have done in this war—and in all others—by a random bullet, or as the result of somebody's blunder, or in an attempt which failed. On the contrary he played a distinguished, and possibly a determining part, in an action which succeeded, and the results of which were fruitful.

He was not merely a brave and skilful soldier

[1] This Brigade was known during the battle of Ypres as 'the Fire Brigade,' for the reason that it was constantly being called up on a sudden to extinguish unforeseen conflagrations.

Hugh Dawnay and John Gough.

when it came to push of pike, but a devoted student of his profession in times of peace. The mixture of eagerness and patience with which he went about his work reminded one, not a little, of that same combination of qualities as it is met with sometimes among men of science.

Hunting accidents, the privations of Ladysmith followed by enteric, divers fevers contracted in hot climates, and the severity of a campaign in Somaliland, had severely tried his constitution—which although vigorous and athletic was never robust—and had increased a tendency to headaches and neuralgia to which he had been subject ever since boyhood. Yet he treated pain always as a despicable enemy, and went about his daily business as indefatigably when he was in suffering, as when he was entirely free from it, which in later years was but rarely.

Dawnay had a very quick brain, and held his views most positively. It was sometimes said of him that he did not suffer fools gladly, and this was true up to a point. He was singularly intolerant of presumptuous fools, who laid down the law about matters of which they were wholly ignorant, or who—having acquired a smattering of second-hand knowledge—proceeded to put their ingenious and sophistical theories into practice. But for people of much slower wits than himself—if they were trying honestly to arrive at the truth—he was usually full of sympathy. His tact and patience upon great occasions were two of his noblest qualities.

Hugh Dawnay and John Gough.

In some ways he used to remind me, not a little, of Colonel Henry Esmond of Castlewood, Virginia. In both there was the same hard core of resistance against anything, which appeared to challenge certain adamantine principles concerning conduct befitting a gentleman. On such matters he was exceedingly stiff and unyielding. And he resembled the friend of Lord Bolingbroke, and General Webb, and Dick Steele also in this, that he was addicted to the figure of irony when crossed in discussion. One imagines, however, that Colonel Esmond must have kept his countenance better, and remained imperturbably grave until his shafts had all gone home. In Dawnay's case the sight of his opponent's lengthening face was, as a rule, too much for his sense of humour, and the attack was apt to lose some of its force—certainly all its fierceness—in a smile which reminded one of Carlyle's description—'sunlight on the sea.'

The following extract from a letter written by one of his friends who had attended the War Service at St. Paul's gives a true picture: "A sudden vision 'arose in my imagination of Hugh Dawnay striding 'down the choir, in full armour, like St. Michael—'with his head thrown back, and that extraordinary 'expression of *resolution* which he always seemed to 'me to possess more than any one I have ever seen. 'His wide-apart eyes had more of the spirit of truth 'in them than almost any—also an intolerance of 'falsehood—or rather perhaps a disbelief in its 'existence. . . ." This is true. He was one of that race of men whose recumbent figures are seen in our old churches and cathedrals, with hands clasping crusaders' swords against their breasts, their hounds couching at their feet.

Hugh Dawnay and John Gough.

In physique and temperament Hugh Dawnay and John Gough [1] were in most respects as unlike a pair of friends as ever walked this earth; but we might have searched far before we could have found two minds which, on most matters connected with their profession, were in more perfect accord. Dawnay, younger by four years, had served under Gough in trying times, and regarded him (an opinion which is very widely shared by seniors as well as juniors) as one of the finest soldiers of his age. Though Dawnay was slender and of great height, while Gough was rather below the middle stature, broad and firmly knit, there was one striking point of physical resemblance between them, in the way their heads were set upon their shoulders. There was something in the carriage of both which seemed to take it for granted that they would be followed wherever they might chose to lead. In Lord Roberts, and also in a strikingly different character—Mr. Chamberlain—there was the same poise, the same stable equilibrium, without a trace in it of self-consciousness or constraint. It may be that the

[1] Brigadier-General John Edmund Gough, V.C., C.M.G., C.B., A.D.C. to the King; *b.* 1871; educated Eton and Sandhurst; Rifle Brigade, 1892; British Central Africa, 1896–1897; Nile Campaign and Omdurman, 1898; South Africa, 1899–1902; Somaliland, 1902–1903 and 1908–1909; France, August 1914–February 1915.

Hugh Dawnay and John Gough.

habit of command induces this bearing in a man; or it may be that there is something in the nature of the man who bears himself thus which forces him to become a leader.

Gough took no part in the preparation of the original Memorandum; but in March 1913 he discussed it with me [1] and made various criticisms and suggestions, most of which have been incorporated here. His chief concern with regard to all proposals for a National Army was, that the period of training should be sufficient to allow time for turning the average man into a soldier who had full confidence in himself. "When war breaks out"—I can hear his words—"it's not recruits we want: it's soldiers we 'want: that is, if our object is to win the war as 'speedily as possible, and to lose as few lives as 'possible." Under normal peace conditions he put this period at a minimum of two years for infantry; but of course he would have admitted—and did, in fact, admit when I saw him last December—that under the stress and excitement of war the term might be considerably shortened.

His chief concern in 1913 was with regard to shortage of officers. He criticised with great severity the various recent attempts at reforming our military

[1] At St. Jean de Luz, when he was endeavouring, though not very successfully, to shake off the after-effects of his last Somaliland campaign. He was then engaged in correcting the proofs of the volume of his Staff College lectures which was subsequently published under the title *Fredericksburg and Chancellorsville* (Rees)—a most vivid and convincing narrative. In the intervals of work and golf he spent much of his time in visiting Wellington's adjacent battlefields and studying his passage of the Bidassoa and forcing of the Pyrenees.

Hugh Dawnay and John Gough.

system, not only on the ground that we had chosen to rely upon training our national forces after war had actually broken out (in his view a most disastrous decision); but also because we had not taken care to provide ourselves against the very emergency which was contemplated, by having a reserve of officers competent to undertake the training of the new army in case of need.

I went to see him at Aldershot on the Friday before war was declared, and found, as I expected, that he regarded it as inevitable. He had undergone a very severe operation in the early summer, and was still quite unfit to stand the strain of hard exercise. It had been arranged that we were to go together, a few days later, to Sweden, for six weeks' shooting and fishing in the mountains. He was very anxious to return to England for the September manœuvres. His surgeon,[1] however, forbade this, on the ground that even by that time he would not be fit to sit for a whole day in the saddle.

He was in two moods on this occasion. He was as light-hearted as a boy who is unexpectedly released from school; the reason being that the Army Medical Officer had that morning passed him as physically fit to go abroad with Sir Douglas Haig, to whom he had acted as Senior Staff Officer since the previous autumn.

[1] Gough's many friends will ever feel a double debt of gratitude to that distinguished surgeon, Sir Berkeley Moynihan, who by this operation restored him, after several years of ill-health and suffering, almost to complete health; and who once again—when by a strange coincidence of war he found his former patient lying in the hospital at Estaires the day after he was brought in wounded—came to his aid, and all but achieved the miracle of saving his life.

Hugh Dawnay and John Gough.

His other mood was very different. The war which he had foreseen and dreaded, the war which in his view might have been avoided upon one condition, and one only—if England had been prepared—had come at last. I don't think I have ever known any one—certainly never any anti-militarist—whose hatred and horror of war gave the same impression of intensity and reality as his. Not metaphorically, but as a bare fact, his feelings with regard to it were too deep for words; he would suddenly break off speaking about things which had occurred in his own experience; in particular, about loss of friends and comrades. He was an Irishman, and had not the impassive coldness of some of the great soldiers. But most of all he hated war when it was not inevitable—when with foresight and courage it might have been averted—as in his opinion this war might have been.

In radium there is said to be a virtue which enables it to affect adjacent objects with its own properties, and to turn them, for a time, and for certain purposes, into things of the same nature as itself. Certain rare human characters possess a similar virtue; but although I have met with several of these in my life, there is none of them all who seemed to me to possess this quality in quite so high a degree as Gough. He was an alchemist who made fine soldiers out of all sorts and conditions of men, and whose spirit turned despondency out of doors.

The clearness of his instinct and the power of his

Hugh Dawnay and John Gough.

mind were not more remarkable than his swiftness of decision and indomitable will. There are scores—probably hundreds—of young officers who fought by his side, or under him, at Ypres and elsewhere, who years hence, when they are themselves distinguished—perhaps great and famous—and come, in the evening of their days, to reckon up and consider the influences which have shaped their careers, will place his influence first. And there are boys looking forward to the day when they shall be old enough to serve in the King's Army, chiefly from the love and honour in which they held this hero, with his winning smile and superb self-confidence.

He has left behind him a tradition, if ever man did. You will find it everywhere, among young and old—among all with whom he ever came into touch. Nor is the tradition which he has left merely among soldiers and with regard to the art of war, but also in other spheres of private conduct and public life. He had strong prejudices as well as affections, which made him sometimes judge men unfairly, also on the other hand too favourably; but he banished all meanness from his neighbourhood, all thoughts of self-interest and personal advancement. Duty, discipline, self-discipline, and the joy of life—these were the rules he walked by; and if you found yourself in his company you had perforce to walk with him, keeping up with his stride as best you could.

We value our friends for different qualities, and would have their tradition fulfil itself in different ways. Those of us who counted these two—'Johnnie' Gough and Hugh Dawnay—among our friends will wish that our sons may be like them, and follow in their footsteps.

PREFACE.

Hugh Dawnay and John Gough.

F. S. O.

CHECKENDON COURT, OXFORDSHIRE,
1st *June* 1915.

ORDEAL BY BATTLE

PART I

PART II

PART III

PART IV

TABLE OF CONTENTS

PART I

THE CAUSES OF WAR

CHAPTER I

PEACE AND WAR

CHAPTER II

THE OUTBREAK OF WAR

CHAPTER III

WHO WANTED WAR ?

CHAPTER IV

THE PENALTY OF NEGLIGENCE

CHAPTER V

PERSONAL RESPONSIBILITY

CHAPTER VI

GERMAN MISCALCULATIONS

CHAPTER VII

INTERNATIONAL ILL-WILL

PART II

THE SPIRIT OF GERMAN POLICY

CHAPTER I

THE BISMARCKIAN EPOCH

CHAPTER II

AFTER BISMARCK

CHAPTER III

THE GERMAN PROJECT OF EMPIRE

CHAPTER IV

THE NEW MORALISTS

CHAPTER V

THE STATECRAFT OF A PRIESTHOOD

CHAPTER VI

THE DEVIL'S ADVOCATE

CHAPTER VII

THE CONFLICTS OF SYSTEMS AND IDEAS

PART III

THE SPIRIT OF BRITISH POLICY

CHAPTER I

A REVOLUTIONARY PERIOD (JANUARY 1901–JULY 1914)

CHAPTER II

THREE GOVERNING IDEAS

CHAPTER III

POLICY AND ARMAMENTS

CHAPTER IV

THE BALANCE OF POWER

CHAPTER V

THE MILITARY SITUATION (AUGUST 1911)

CHAPTER VI

THE MILITARY SITUATION (AUGUST 1914)

CHAPTER VII

A TRAGEDY OF ERRORS

PART IV

DEMOCRACY AND NATIONAL SERVICE

CHAPTER I

THE BRITISH ARMY AND THE PEACE OF EUROPE

CHAPTER II

THE COMPOSITION OF THE BRITISH ARMY

CHAPTER III

LORD ROBERTS'S WARNINGS

CHAPTER IV

LORD KITCHENER'S TASK

CHAPTER V

MATERIAL OF WAR

CHAPTER VI

METHODS OF RECRUITING

CHAPTER VII

PERVERSITIES OF THE ANTI-MILITARIST SPIRIT

CHAPTER VIII

SOME HISTORICAL REFLECTIONS

CHAPTER IX

THE CRUCIBLE OF WAR

PART I

THE CAUSES OF WAR

Then *Apollyon* strodled quite over the whole breadth of the way, and said, I am void of fear in this matter, prepare thyself to die; for I swear by my infernal Den, that thou shalt go no further; here will I spill thy soul.

And with that he threw a flaming Dart at his breast, but *Christian* had a shield in his hand, with which he caught it, and so prevented the danger of that.

Then did *Christian* draw, for he saw 'twas time to bestir him: and *Apollyon* as fast made at him, throwing Darts as thick as Hail; by the which, notwithstanding all that *Christian* could do to avoid it, *Apollyon* wounded him in his *head*, his *hand*, and *foot*: This made *Christian* give a little back; *Apollyon* therefore followed his work amain, and *Christian* again took courage, and resisted as manfully as he could. This sore Combat lasted for above half a day, even till *Christian* was almost quite spent; for you must know that *Christian*, by reason of his wounds, must needs grow weaker and weaker.

Then *Apollyon* espying his opportunity, began to gather up close to *Christian*, and wrestling with him, gave him a dreadful fall; and with that *Christian's* Sword flew out of his hand. Then said *Apollyon*, *I am sure of thee now*: and with that he had almost pressed him to death, so that *Christian* began to despair of life. But as God would have it, while *Apollyon* was fetching of his last blow, thereby to make a full end of this good man, *Christian* nimbly reached out his hand for his Sword, and caught it, saying, *Rejoice not against me, O mine Enemy! when I fall I shall arise*; and with that gave him a deadly thrust, which made him give back, as one that had received his mortal wound: *Christian* perceiving that, made at him again, saying, *Nay, in all these things we are more than conquerors through him that loved us.* And with that *Apollyon* spread forth his Dragon's wings, and sped him away, that *Christian* for a season saw him no more.

In this Combat no man can imagine, unless he had seen and heard as I did, what yelling and hideous roaring, *Apollyon* made all the time of the fight; he spake like a Dragon. . . .

The Pilgrim's Progress.

CHAPTER I

PEACE AND WAR

CHAPTER I. — Peace and war.

It is a considerable number of years since the most distinguished Tory statesman of his time impressed upon his fellow-countrymen as a maxim of policy, that *Peace is the greatest of British interests.* There was an unexpectedness about Lord Salisbury's words, coming as they did from the leader of a party which had hitherto lain under suspicion of jingoism, which gave the phrase almost the colour of an epigram. The truth of the saying, however, gradually became manifest to all men; and thereupon a new danger arose out of this very fact.

As a nation we are in some ways a great deal too modest; or it may be, looking at the matter from a critical standpoint, too self-centred. We have always been inclined to assume in our calculations that we ourselves are the only possible disturbers of the peace, and that if we do not seek war, or provoke it, no other Power will dream of forcing war upon us. This unfortunately has rarely been the case; and those persons who, in recent times, have refused most scornfully to consider the lessons of past history, have now at last learned from a sterner schoolmaster the falseness of their favourite doctrine.

The United Kingdom needed and desired peace, so

Peace and war.

that it might proceed undistracted, and with firm purpose, to set its house in order. The Dominions needed peace, so that they might have time to people their fertile but empty lands, to strike deep roots and become secure. To the Indian Empire and the Dependencies peace was essential, if a system of government, which aimed, not unsuccessfully, at giving justice and fostering well-being, was to maintain its power and prestige unshaken. The whole British race had nothing material to gain by war, but much to lose, much at any rate which would be put in jeopardy by war. In spite of all these weighty considerations which no man of sense and knowledge will venture to dispute, we should have been wiser had we taken into account the fact, that they did not apply to other nations, that in the main they affected ourselves alone, and that our case was no less singular than, in one sense at all events, it was fortunate.

We did not covet territory or new subjects. Still less were we likely to engage in campaigns out of a thirst for glory. In the latter particular at least we were on a par with the rest of the world. The cloud of anxiety which for ten or more years has brooded over the great conscript nations, growing steadily darker, contained many dangers, but among these we cannot reckon such antiquated motives as trivial bravado, light-hearted knight-errantry, or the vain pursuit of military renown.

What is called in history books 'an insult' seemed also to have lost much of its ancient power for plunging nations into war. The Chancelleries of Europe had grown cautious, and were on the watch against being misled by the emotions of the moment. A sensational but unintended injury was not allowed to drive us

Peace and war.

into war with Russia in 1904, and this precedent seemed of good augury. Moreover, when every statesman in Europe was fully alive to the electric condition of the atmosphere, a deliberate insult was not very likely to be offered from mere ill-manners or in a fit of temper, but only if there were some serious purpose behind it, in which case it would fall under a different category.

Fear was a great danger, and everybody knew it to be so—fear lest this nation, or that, might be secretly engaged in strengthening its position in order to crush one of its neighbours at some future date, unless that neighbour took time by the forelock and struck out forthwith. Among the causes which might bring about a surprise outbreak of war this was the most serious and probable. It was difficult to insure against it. But though perilous in the extreme while it lasts, panic is of the nature of an epidemic: it rages for a while and passes away. It had been raging now with great severity ever since 1909,[1] and by midsummer 1914 optimists were inclined to seek consolation in the thought that the crisis must surely be over.

More dangerous to peace in the long run even than fear, were certain aims and aspirations, which from one standpoint were concrete and practical, but regarded from another were among the cloudiest of abstractions — 'political interests,' need of new markets, hunger for fresh territory to absorb the outflow of emigrants, and the like; on the other hand, those hopes and anxieties which haunt the

[1] The increase and acceleration of German shipbuilding was discovered by the British Government in the autumn of 1908, and led to the Imperial Defence Conference in the summer of the following year.

Peace and war.

imaginations of eager men as they look into the future, and dream dreams and see visions of a grand national fulfilment.

If the British race ever beheld a vision of this sort, it had been realised already. We should have been wise had we remembered that this accomplished fact, these staked-out claims of the British Empire, appeared to fall like a shadow across visions seen by other eyes, blotting out some of the fairest hopes, and spoiling the noble proportions of the patriot's dream.

There is a region where words stumble after truth, like children chasing a rainbow across a meadow to find the pot of fairy gold. Multitudinous volumes stuffed with the cant of pacifism and militarism will never explain to us the nature of peace and war. But a few bars of music may sometimes make clear things which all the moralists, and divines, and philosophers —even the poets themselves for the most part, though they come nearer to it at times than the rest—have struggled vainly to show us in their true proportions. The songs of a nation, its national anthems—if they be truly national and not merely some commissioned exercise—are better interpreters than state papers. A man will learn more of the causes of wars, perhaps even of the rights and wrongs of them, by listening to the burst and fall of the French hymn, the ebb and surge of the Russian, in Tschaikovsky's famous overture, than he ever will from books or speeches, argument or oratory.

Yet there are people who think it not impossible to prove to mankind by logical processes, that the loss which any great nation must inevitably sustain through war, will far outweigh any advantages which

Peace and war.

can ensue from it, even if the arms of the conqueror were crowned with victories greater than those of Caesar or Napoleon. They draw us pictures of the exhaustion which must inevitably follow upon such a struggle conducted upon the modern scale, of the stupendous loss of capital, destruction of credit, paralysis of industry, arrest of progress in things spiritual as well as temporal, the shock to civilisation, and the crippling for a generation, probably for several generations, possibly for ever, of the victorious country in its race with rivals who have wisely stood aside from the fray. These arguments may conceivably be true, may in no particular be over-coloured, or an under-valuation, either of the good which has been attained by battle, or of the evils which have been escaped. But they would be difficult to establish even before an unbiassed court, and they are infinitely more difficult to stamp upon popular belief.

It is not sufficient either with statesmen or peoples to set before them a chain of reasoning which is logically unanswerable. Somehow or other the new faith which it is desired to implant, must be rendered independent of logic and unassailable by logic. It must rise into a higher order of convictions than the intellectual before it can begin to operate upon human affairs. For it is matched against opinions which have been held and acted upon so long, that they have become unquestionable save in purely academic discussions. At those decisive moments, when action follows upon thought like a flash, conclusions which depend upon a train of reasoning are of no account: instinct will always get the better of any syllogism.

CHAPTER I.

Peace and war.

So when nations are hovering on the brink of war, it is impulse, tradition, or some stuff of the imagination—misused deliberately, as sometimes happens, by crafty manipulators—which determines action much more often than the business calculations of shopkeepers and economists. Some cherished institution seems to be threatened. Some nationality supposed—very likely erroneously—to be of the same flesh and blood as ourselves, appears—very likely on faulty information—to be unjustly oppressed. Two rival systems of civilisation, of morals, of religion, approach one another like thunder-clouds and come together in a clash. Where is the good at such times of casting up sums, and exhibiting profit-and-loss accounts to the public gaze? People will not listen, for in their view considerations of prosperity and the reverse are beside the question. Wealth, comfort, even life itself, are not regarded; nor are the possible sufferings of posterity allowed to count any more than the tribulations of to-day. In the eyes of the people the matter is one of duty not of interest. When men fight in this spirit the most lucid exposition of material drawbacks is worse than useless; for the national mood, at such moments, is one of self-sacrifice. The philosopher, or the philanthropist, is more likely to feed the flames than to put them out when he proves the certainty of loss and privation, and dwells upon the imminent peril of ruin and destruction.

The strength of the fighter is the strength of his faith. Each new Gideon who goes out against the Midianites fancies that the sword of the Lord is in his hand. He risks all that he holds dear, in order that he may pull down the foul images of Baal and build up an altar to Jehovah, in order that his race

Peace and war.

may not be shorn of its inheritance, in order that it may hold fast its own laws and institutions, and not pass under the yoke of the Gentiles. This habit of mind is unchanging throughout the ages. What moved men to give their lives at Marathon moved them equally, more than a thousand years later, to offer the same sacrifice under the walls of Tours. It is still moving them, after yet another thousand years and more have passed away, in the plains of Flanders and the Polish Marshes.

When the Persian sought to force the dominion of his ideals upon the Greek, the states of Hellas made head against him from the love and honour in which they held their own. When the successors of the Prophet, zealous for their faith, confident in the protection of the One God, drove the soldiers of the Cross before them from the passes of the Pyrenees to the vineyards of Touraine, neither side would have listened with any patience to a dissertation upon the inconveniences resulting from a state of war and upon the economic advantages of peace. It was there one faith against another, one attitude towards life against another, one system of manners, customs, and laws against another. When a collision occurs in this region of human affairs there is seldom room for compromise or adjustment. Things unmerchantable cannot be purchased with the finest of fine gold.

In these instances, seen by us from far off, the truth of this is easily recognised. But what some of our recent moralists have overlooked, is the fact that forces of precisely the same order exist in the world of to-day, and are at work, not only among the fierce Balkan peoples, in the resurgent empire of Japan, and in the great military nations—the French, the

CHAPTER I. — Peace and war.

Germans, and the Russians—but also in America and England. The last two pride themselves upon a higher civilisation, and in return are despised by the prophets of militarism as worshippers of material gain. The unfavourable and the flattering estimate agree, however, upon a single point—in assuming that our own people and those of the United States are unlikely to yield themselves to unsophisticated impulse. This assumption is wholly false.

If we search carefully, we shall find everywhere underlying the great struggles recorded in past history, no less than those which have occurred, and are now occurring, in our own time, an antagonism of one kind or another between two systems, visions, or ideals, which in some particular were fundamentally opposed and could not be reconciled. State papers and the memoranda of diplomatists, when in due course they come to light, are not a little apt to confuse the real issues, by setting forth a diary of minor incidents and piquant details, not in their true proportions, but as they appeared at the moment of their occurrence to the eyes of harassed and suspicious officials. But even so, all the emptying of desks and pigeon-holes since the great American Civil War, has not been able to cover up the essential fact, that in this case a million lives were sacrificed by one of the most intelligent, humane, and practical nations upon earth, and for no other cause than that there was an irreconcilable difference amongst them, with regard to what St. Paul has called 'the substance of things hoped for.' On the one side there was an ideal of Union and a determination to make it prevail: on the other side there was an ideal of Independence and an equal determination to defend it whatsoever

Peace and war.

might be the cost. If war on such grounds be possible within the confines of a single nation, nurtured in the same traditions, and born to a large extent of the same stock, how futile is the assurance that economic and material considerations will suffice to make war impossible between nations, who have not even the tie of a common mother-tongue!

A collision may occur, as we know only too well, even although one of two vessels be at anchor, if it happens to lie athwart the course of the other. It was therefore no security against war that British policy did not aim at any aggrandisement or seek for any territorial expansion. The essential questions were—had we possessions which appeared to obstruct the national aspirations and ideals of others; and did these others believe that alone, or in alliance, they had the power to redress the balance?

The real difficulty which besets the philanthropist in his endeavour to exorcise the spirit of war is caused, not by the vices of this spirit, but by its virtues. In so far as it springs from vainglory or cupidity, it is comparatively easy to deal with. In so far as it is base, there is room for a bargain. It can be compounded with and bought off, as we have seen before now, with some kind of material currency. It will not stand out for very long against promises of prosperity and threats of dearth. But where, as at most crises, this spirit is not base, where its impulse is not less noble, but more noble than those which influence men day by day in the conduct of their worldly affairs, where the contrast which presents itself to their imagination is between duty on the one hand and gain on the other, between self-sacrifice and self-interest, between their country's need and

CHAPTER I.

Peace and war.

their own ease, it is not possible to quench the fires by appeals proceeding from a lower plane. The philanthropist, if he is to succeed, must take still higher ground, and higher ground than this it is not a very simple matter to discover.

CHAPTER II

THE OUTBREAK OF WAR

CHAPTER II.

The outbreak of war.

WHEN war came, it came suddenly. A man who had happened to fall sick of a fever on St. Swithin's day 1914, but was so far on the way to convalescence four weeks later as to desire news of the outside world, must have been altogether incredulous of the tidings which first greeted his ears.

When he fell ill the nations were at peace. The townspeople of Europe were in a holiday humour, packing their trunks and portmanteaus for 'land travel or sea-faring.' The country people were getting in their harvest or looking forward hopefully to the vintage. Business was prosperous. Credit was good. Money, in banking phraseology, was 'cheap.' The horror of the Serajevo assassinations had already faded almost into oblivion. At the worst this sensational event was only an affair of police. Such real anxiety as existed in the United Kingdom had reference to Ireland.

We can imagine the invalid's first feeble question on public affairs :—'What has happened in Ulster ?'—The answer, 'Nothing has happened in Ulster.'—The sigh of relief with which he sinks back on his pillows.

When, however, they proceed to tell him what has happened, elsewhere than in Ulster, during the

CHAPTER II.

The outbreak of war.

four weeks while they have been watching by his bedside, will he not fancy that his supposed recovery is only an illusion, and that he is still struggling with the phantoms of his delirium ?

For what will they have to report ? That the greater part of the world which professes Christianity has called out its armies ; that more than half Europe has already joined battle ; that England, France, Russia, Belgium, Servia, and Montenegro on the one side are ranged against Germany and Austria on the other. Japan, they will tell him, is upon the point of declaring war. The Turk is wondering if, and when, he may venture to come in ; while the Italian, the Roumanian, the Bulgar, the Greek, the Dutchman, the Dane, and the Swede are reckoning no less anxiously for how short or long a period it may still be safe for them to stand out. Three millions of men, or thereabouts—a British Army included—are advancing against one another along the mountain barriers of Luxemburg, Lorraine, and Alsace. Another three millions are engaged in similar evolutions among the lakes of East Prussia, along the river-banks of Poland, and under the shadow of the Carpathians. A large part of Belgium is already devastated, her villages are in ashes or flames, her eastern fortresses invested, her capital threatened by the invader.

Nine-tenths or more of the navies of the world are cleared for action, and are either scouring the seas in pursuit, or are withdrawn under the shelter of land-batteries watching their opportunity for a stroke. Air-craft circle by day and night over the cities, dropping bombs, with a careless and impartial aim, upon buildings both private and public, both sacred and profane, upon churches, palaces, hospitals,

The outbreak of war.

and arsenals. The North Sea and the Baltic are sown with mines. The trade of the greater part of industrial Europe is at a standstill; the rest is disorganised; while the credit and finances, not merely of Europe, but of every continent, are temporarily in a state either of chaos or paralysis.

To the bewildered convalescent all this may well have seemed incredible. It is hardly to be wondered at if he concluded that the fumes of his fever were not yet dispersed, and that this frightful phantasmagoria had been produced, not by external realities, but by the disorders of his own brain.

How long it might have taken to convince him of the truth and substance of these events we may judge from our own recent experience. How long was it after war broke out, before even we, who had watched the trouble brewing through all its stages, ceased to be haunted, even in broad daylight, by the feeling that we were asleep, and that the whole thing was a nightmare which must vanish when we awoke? We were faced (so at least it seemed at frequent moments) not by facts, but by a spectre, and one by no means unfamiliar—the spectre of Europe at war, so long dreaded by some, so scornfully derided by others, so often driven away, of late years so persistently reappearing. But this time the thing refused to be driven away. It sat, hunched up, with its head resting on its hands, as pitiless and inhuman as one of the gargoyles on a Gothic cathedral, staring through us, as if we were merely vapour, at something beyond.

So late as Wednesday, July 29—the day on which Austria declared war on Servia—there was

CHAPTER II.

The outbreak of war.

probably not one Englishman in a hundred who believed it possible that, within a week, his own country would be at war; still less, that a few days later the British Army would be crossing the Channel to assist France and Belgium in repelling a German invasion. To the ordinary man—and not merely to the ordinary man, but equally to the press, and the great majority of politicians—such things were unthinkable until they occurred. Unfortunately, the inability to think a thing is no more a protection against its occurrence than the inability to see a thing gives security to the ostrich.

The sequence of events which led up to the final disaster is of great importance, although very far from being in itself a full explanation of the causes.

On June 28, 1914, the heir to the throne of Austria-Hungary, together with his consort, was murdered by a young Bosnian at Serajevo, not far distant from the southern frontier. The Imperial authorities instituted a secret enquiry into the circumstances of the plot, as a result of which they professed to have discovered that it had been hatched at Belgrade, that Government officials were implicated in it, and that so far from being reprobated, it was approved by Servian public opinion.[1]

On Thursday, July 23—a month after the tragedy—Austria suddenly delivered an ultimatum to Servia, and demanded an acceptance of its terms within forty-eight hours. The demands put forward were

[1] There is perhaps as much reason, certainly no more, for believing that an official clique at Belgrade plotted the Serajevo murders, as that an official clique at Vienna connived at them, by deliberately withdrawing police protection from the unfortunate and unpopular Archduke on the occasion of his visit to a notorious hotbed of sedition.

The outbreak of war.

harsh, humiliating, and unconscionable. They were such as could not have been accepted, as they stood, by any nation which desired to preserve a shred of its independence. They had been framed with the deliberate intention, either of provoking a refusal which might afford a pretext for war, or of procuring an acceptance which would at once reduce the Servian Kingdom to the position of a vassal. Even in Berlin it was admitted [1] that this ultimatum asked more than it was reasonable to expect Servia to yield. But none the less, there can be but little doubt that the German ambassador at Vienna saw and approved the document before it was despatched, and it seems more than likely that he had a hand in drafting it. It also rests on good authority that the German Kaiser was informed beforehand of the contents, and that he did not demur to its presentation.[2]

On the evening of Saturday, July 25, the Servian Government, as required, handed in its answer. The purport of this, when it became known to the world, excited surprise by the humility of its tone and the substance of its submission. Almost everything that

[1] Herr von Jagow "also admitted that the Servian Government could not 'swallow certain of the Austro-Hungarian demands. . . . He repeated very 'earnestly that, though he had been accused of knowing all the contents 'of that note, he had in fact no such knowledge."—Sir H. Rumbold at Berlin to Sir Edward Grey (White Paper, No. 18).

[2] "Although I am unable to verify it, I have private information that 'the German Ambassador (*i.e.* at Vienna) knew the text of the Austrian 'ultimatum to Servia before it was despatched and telegraphed it to the 'German Emperor. I know from the German Ambassador himself that he 'endorses every line of it."—British Ambassador at Vienna to Sir Edward Grey (White Paper, No. 95). (Cf. also White Book, Nos. 95 and 141; French Yellow Book, No. 87; Russian Orange Book, No. 41.)

"The German Ambassador (*i.e.* in London) read me a telegram from 'the German Foreign Office saying that his Government had not known 'beforehand, and had no more than other Powers to do with the stiff terms 'of the Austrian note to Servia."—Sir Edward Grey to the British Ambassador in Berlin (White Paper, No. 25). (Cf. also French Yellow Book, Nos. 17, 30, 36, 41, 57, and 94.)

CHAPTER II.

The outbreak of war.

Austria had demanded was agreed to. What remained outstanding was clearly not worth quarrelling about, unless a quarrel were the object of the ultimatum. The refusal, such as it was, did not close the door, but, on the contrary, contained an offer to submit the subjects of difference to the Hague Convention.[1]

The document was a lengthy one. The Austrian minister at Belgrade nevertheless found time to read it through, to weigh it carefully, to find it wanting, to ask for his passports, and to catch his train, all within a period not exceeding three-quarters of an hour from the time at which it was put into his hands.[2]

When these occurrences became known, the English Foreign Minister immediately made proposals for a conference between representatives of Germany, France, Italy, and Great Britain, with the object of discovering some means of peaceful settlement.[3] France and Italy promptly accepted his invitation.[4] Germany, while professing to desire mediation, did not accept it.[5] Consequently Sir Edward Grey's effort failed; and before he was able to renew it in any more acceptable form, Austria, acting with a promptitude almost unique in her annals, declared war upon Servia, and hostilities began.

It is unnecessary to enter here into an examination of the feverish and fruitless attempts to preserve peace, which were made in various quarters during the next four and twenty hours. They present a

[1] Last paragraph of Reply of Servian Government to Austro-Hungarian note.

[2] White Paper, Nos. 20 and 23.

[3] White Paper, No. 36.

[4] White Paper, Nos. 35, 42, and 52.

[5] White Paper, Nos. 43 and 71. Cf. also German White Book, Nos. 12 and 15.

most pathetic appearance, like the efforts of a crew, sitting with oars unshipped, arguing, exhorting, and imploring, while their boat drifts on to the smooth lip of the cataract.

CHAPTER II.

The outbreak of war.

Russia ordered the mobilisation of her Southern armies, alleging that she could not stand by while a Slav nation was being crushed out of existence, despite the fact that it had made an abject submission for an unproved offence.[1]

Subsequently, on Friday, July 31, Russia—having, as she considered, reasons for believing that Germany was secretly mobilising her whole forces—proceeded to do likewise.[2]

Germany simultaneously declared 'a state of war' within her own territories, and a veil instantly fell upon all her internal proceedings. She demanded that Russia should cease her mobilisation, and as no answer which satisfied her was forthcoming, but only an interchange of telegrams between the two sovereigns—disingenuous on the one side and not unreasonably suspicious on the other — Germany declared war on Russia on Saturday, August 1.

On Saturday and Sunday, war on a grand scale being by this time certain, the chief interest centred in questions of neutrality. Germany enquired of France whether she would undertake to stand aside—knowing full well beforehand that the terms of the Dual Alliance compelled the Republic to lend assistance if Russia were attacked by more than one power.

[1] White Paper, No. 113; Russian Orange Book, No. 77; French Yellow Book, No. 95.

[2] These suspicions were well founded. German mobilisation began at least two days earlier (White Paper, No. 113; French Yellow Book, Nos. 60, 88, 89, and 106).

CHAPTER II.

The outbreak of war.

Sir Edward Grey enquired of France and Germany if they would undertake to respect the integrity of Belgium. France replied in the affirmative. Germany declined to commit herself, and this was rightly construed as a refusal.[1]

While this matter was still the subject of diplomatic discussion the German Army advanced into the Grand Duchy of Luxemburg, and was correctly reported as having entered Belgian territory near Liège and French territory near Cirey.

On the evening of Sunday, August 2, the German Government presented an ultimatum to Belgium[2] demanding free passage for its troops, thereby putting its intentions beyond all doubt.

On the same day Italy issued a declaration of neutrality, making it clear that, although a member of the Triple Alliance, she did not consider herself bound to support her allies in a war of aggression.[3]

Meanwhile Germany had been making enquiries as to the attitude of England, and, startled to discover that this country might not be willing tamely to submit to the violation of Belgium and invasion of France, proceeded to state, under cross-examination, the price she was prepared to pay, or at any rate to promise, for the sake of securing British neutrality.[4]

On Tuesday, August 4, the British Ambassador at Berlin presented an ultimatum which demanded an assurance, before midnight, that the integrity of Belgium would not be violated. The answer was given informally at a much earlier hour by the

1 White Paper, Nos. 114, 122, 123, and 125.
2 Belgian Grey Book, No. 20; French Yellow Book, No. 141.
3 White Paper, No. 152; French Yellow Book, No. 124.
4 White Paper, Nos. 85 and 123.

bombardment of Liège; and shortly before midnight England declared war on Germany.[1]

CHAPTER II.

The outbreak of war.

Two days later Austria declared herself to be at war with Russia, and within a week from that date Great Britain and France issued a similar declaration against Austria.

[1] "I found the Chancellor very agitated. His Excellency at once 'began a harangue which lasted for about twenty minutes. He said that 'the step taken by His Majesty's Government was terrible to a degree: 'just for a word—'neutrality,' a word which in war time had so often been 'disregarded—just for a scrap of paper Great Britain was going to make 'war on a kindred nation, who desired nothing better than to be friends 'with her."—British Ambassador at Berlin to Sir Edward Grey (White Paper, No. 160).

CHAPTER III

WHO WANTED WAR ?

CHAPTER III.

Who wanted war ?

SUCH is the chronological order of events; but on the face of it, it explains little of the underlying causes of this conflagration. Why with the single exception of Italy had all the great naval and military powers of Europe, together with several smaller nations, suddenly plunged into war ? Which of the combatants wanted war ? . . . To the latter question the answer can be given at once and with certainty—save Germany and Austria no nation wanted war, and even Germany and Austria did not want *this* war.

Whatever opinion we may entertain of the Servian character or of her policy in recent times, it is at all events certain that she did not desire war with Austria. That she submitted to the very depths of humiliation in order to avoid war cannot be doubted by any one who has read her reply to the demands put forward by Vienna. Only a few months since, she had emerged from two sanguinary wars—the first against Turkey and the second against Bulgaria—and although victory had crowned her arms in both of these contests, her losses in men and material had been very severe.

That Russia did not desire war was equally plain.

Who wanted war?

She was still engaged in repairing the gigantic losses which she had sustained in her struggle with Japan. At least two years must elapse before her new fleet would be in a condition to take the sea, and it was generally understood that at least as long a period would be necessary, in order to carry through the scheme of reorganisation by which she hoped to place her army in a state of efficiency. Whatever might be the ultimate designs of Russia, it was altogether incredible that she would have sought to bring about a war, either at this time or in the near future.

Russia, like England, had nothing to gain by war. Her development was proceeding rapidly. For years to come her highest interest must be peace. A supreme provocation was necessary in order to make her draw the sword. Such a provocation had been given in 1909 when, ignoring the terms of the Treaty of Berlin, Austria had formally annexed the provinces of Bosnia and Herzegovina. But at that time Russia's resources were not merely unprepared; they were utterly exhausted. Menaced simultaneously by Vienna and Berlin, she had been forced on that occasion to stand by, while her prestige in the Balkan peninsula suffered a blow which she was powerless to ward off. Now a further encroachment was threatened from the same quarters. A Serb power which looked to St. Petersburg [1] for protection was to be put under the heel of Austria.

Nor can any one believe that France wanted war. It is true that for a year, or rather more, after the Agadir episode [2] the spirit of France was perturbed. But no Foreign Office in the world—least of all that

[1] The name of the Russian capital was not changed until after the declaration of war, and therefore St. Petersburg is used in this chapter instead of Petrograd.

[2] July-September 1911.

CHAPTER III.

Who wanted war?

of Germany—was so ill-informed as to believe that the sporadic demonstrations, which occurred in the press and elsewhere, were caused by any eagerness for adventure or any ambition of conquest. They were due, as every calm observer was aware, to one thing and one thing only—the knowledge that the Republic had come to the very end of her human resources; that all her sons who were capable of bearing arms had already been enrolled in her army; that she could do nothing further to strengthen her defences against Germany, who up to that time, had taken for military training barely one half of her available male population, and who was now engaged in increasing her striking power both by land and sea.

The cause of this restlessness in France was the fear that Germany was preparing an invincible superiority and would strike so soon as her weapon was forged. If so, would it not be better for France to strike at once, while she had still a fighting chance, and before she was hopelessly outnumbered? But this mood, the product of anxiety and suspense, which had been somewhat prevalent in irresponsible quarters during the autumn of 1912 and the early part of the following year, had passed away. Partly it wore itself out; partly popular interest was diverted to other objects of excitement.

France, during the twelve months preceding Midsummer 1914, had been singularly quiescent as regards foreign affairs. Her internal conditions absorbed attention. Various events had conspired to disturb public confidence in the fidelity of her rulers, and in the adequacy of their military preparations. The popular mood had been sobered, disquieted, and scandalised to such a point that war, so far from being sought after, was the thing of all others which France most wished to avoid.

Who wanted war?

It is unnecessary to waste words in establishing the aversion of Belgium from war. There was nothing which she could hope to gain by it in any event. Suffering and loss—how great suffering and loss even Belgium herself can hardly have foreseen—were inevitable to her civil population, as well as to her soldiers, whether the war went well or ill. Her territory lay in the direct way of the invaders, and was likely, as in times past, to become the 'cockpit of Europe.' She was asked to allow the free passage of the Germanic forces. She was promised restoration of her independence and integrity at the end of the war. But to grant this arrogant demand would have been to destroy her dynasty and wreck her institutions; for what King or Constitution could have withstood the popular contempt for a government which acquiesced in national degradation? And to believe the promise, was a thing only possible for simpletons; for what was such an assurance worth, seeing that, at the very moment of the offer, Germany was engaged in breaking her former undertaking, solemnly guaranteed and recorded, that the neutrality of Belgium should be respected? That the sympathies of Belgium would have been with France in any event cannot of course be doubted; for a French victory threatened no danger, whereas the success of German arms was a menace to her independence, and a prelude to vassalage or absorption in the Empire.

Neither the British people nor their Government wanted war. In the end they accepted it reluctantly, and only after most strenuous efforts had been made

CHAPTER III.

Who wanted war?

to prevent its occurrence. To the intelligent foreign observer, however unfriendly, who has a thorough understanding of British interests, ideas, and habits of mind this is self-evident. He does not need a White Paper to prove it to him.

It is clear that Austria wanted war—not this war certainly, but a snug little war with a troublesome little neighbour, as to the outcome of which, with the ring kept, there could be no possibility of doubt. She obviously hoped that indirectly, and as a sort of by-product of this convenient little war, she would secure a great victory of the diplomatic sort over her most powerful neighbour—a matter of infinitely more consequence to her than the ostensible object of her efforts.

The crushing of Servia would mean the humiliation of Russia, and would shake, for a second time within five years, the confidence of the Balkan peoples in the power of the Slav Empire to protect its kindred and co-religionists against the aggression of the Teutons and Magyars. Anything which would lower the credit of Russia in the Balkan peninsula would be a gain to Austria. To her more ambitious statesmen such an achievement might well seem to open the way for coveted expansions towards the Aegean Sea, which had been closed against her, to her great chagrin, by the Treaty of Bucharest.[1] To others, whose chief anxiety was to preserve peace in their own time, and to prevent the Austro-Hungarian State from splitting asunder, the repression of Servia seemed to promise security against the growing unrest and discontent of the vast Slav population which was included in the Empire.

[1] August 1913.

Who wanted war?

For something nearer two centuries than one the Austro-Hungarian Empire has been miscalculating and suffering for its miscalculations, until its blunders and ill-fortune have become a byword. Scheming ever for safety, Austria has never found it. The very modesty of her aim has helped to secure its own defeat. Her unvarying method has been a timid and unimaginative repression. In politics, as in most other human affairs, equilibrium is more easily attained by moving forward than by standing still. Austria has sought security for powers, and systems, and balances which were worn out, unsuited to our modern world, and therefore incapable of being secured at all. The more she has schemed for safety the more precarious her integrity has become. There are things which scheming will never accomplish—things which for their achievement need a change of spirit, some new birth of faith or freedom. But in Vienna change in any direction is ill-regarded, and new births are ever more likely to be strangled in their cradles than to arrive at maturity.

Distracted by the problem of her divers, discordant, and unwelded [1] races, Austria has always inclined to put her trust in schemers who were able to produce some plausible system, some ingenious device, some promising ladder of calculation, or miscalculation, for reaching the moon without going through the clouds. In the present case there can be no doubt that she allowed herself to be persuaded by her German neighbours that Russia was not in a position to make

[1] The total population of the Austro-Hungarian Empire, including Bosnia-Herzegovina, is roughly 50 millions. Of these 11 millions are Germans and 10 millions Magyars. About 24 millions are composed of a strange variety of Slav races. The remaining 5 millions consist of Italians, Roumanians, and Jews.

CHAPTER III.

Who wanted war?

an effective fight, and would therefore probably stand by, growling and showing her teeth. Consequently it was safe to take a bold line; to present Servia with an ultimatum which had been made completely watertight against acceptance of the unconditional and immediate kind; to reject any acceptance which was not unconditional and immediate; to allow the Government of King Peter no time for second thoughts, the European Powers no time for mediation, her own Minister at Belgrade time only to give one hasty glance at the reply, call for his passports, and catch his train. So far as poor humanity can make certain of anything, Austria, with German approval and under German guidance, made certain of war with Servia.

But the impression produced, when this matter first began to excite public attention, was somewhat different. Foreign newspaper correspondents at Vienna and Berlin were specially well cared for after the Serajevo murders, and when the ultimatum was delivered, they immediately sent to England and elsewhere accounts of the position which made it appear, that the Austrian Government and people, provoked beyond endurance by the intrigues of Servia, had acted impetuously, possibly unwisely, but not altogether inexcusably.

At this stage the idea was also sedulously put about that the Kaiser was behaving like a gentleman. It was suggested that Germany had been left very much in the dark until the explosion actually occurred, and that she was now paying the penalty of loyalty to an indiscreet friend, by suffering herself to be dragged into a quarrel in which she had neither interest nor concern. In these early days, when

Who wanted war

Sir Edward Grey was striving hopefully, if somewhat innocently, after peace, it was assumed by the world in general, that Germany, for her own reasons, must desire, at least as ardently as the British Foreign Minister, to find a means of escape from an exceedingly awkward position, and that she would accordingly use her great influence with her ally to this end. If there had been a grain of truth in this assumption, peace would have been assured, for France and Italy had already promised their support. But this theory broke down very speedily; and as soon as the official papers were published, it was seen never to have rested on the smallest basis of fact.

So far from Germany having been dragged in against her will, it was clear that from the beginning she had been using Austria as an agent, who was not unwilling to stir up strife, but was only half-conscious of the nature and dimensions of the contest which was bound to follow. It is not credible that Germany was blind to the all-but-inevitable results of letting Austria loose to range around, of hallooing her on, and of comforting her with assurances of loyal support. But it may well be believed that Austria herself did not see the situation in the same clear light, and remained almost up to the last, under the delusion, which had been so industriously fostered by the German ambassador at Vienna, that Russia could not fight effectively and therefore would probably choose not to fight at all.

But although Austria may have had no adequate conception of the consequences which her action would bring about, it is certain that Germany foresaw them, with the single exception of British inter-

CHAPTER III.

Who wanted war?

vention; that what she foresaw she also desired; and further, that at the right moment she did her part, boldly but clumsily, to guard against any miscarriage of her schemes.

Germany continued to make light of all apprehensions of serious danger from St. Petersburg; but at the eleventh hour Austria appears suddenly to have realised for herself the appalling nature of the catastrophe which impended. Something happened; what it was we do not know, and the present generation will probably never know. We may conjecture, however—but it is only conjecture—that by some means or other the intrigues of the war cabal at Vienna—the instrument of German policy, owing more fealty to the Kaiser than to their own Emperor—had been unmasked. In hot haste they were disavowed, and Austria opened discussions with Russia 'in a perfectly friendly manner,' [1] and with good hopes of success, as to how the catastrophe might still be averted.

On Thursday, July 30, we are informed, the tension between Vienna and St. Petersburg had greatly relaxed. An arrangement compatible with the honour and interests of both empires seemed almost in sight when, on the following day, Germany suddenly intervened with ultimatums to France and Russia, of a kind to which only one answer was possible. The spirit of the Ems telegram [2] had inebriated a duller generation. "A few days' delay," our Ambassador at Vienna concludes, "might in all

[1] White Paper, No. 161.

[2] A harmless and unprovocative telegram from the King of Prussia to Bismarck in July 1870 was, by the latter, so altered in tone that when published it achieved the intention of its editor and served as 'a red rag to the Gallic bull' and brought about the declaration of war by Napoleon III. —Bismarck's *Reflections and Reminiscences*, vol. ii. p. 100.

'probability have saved Europe from one of the 'greatest calamities in history."[1]

CHAPTER III.

Who wanted war?

As we turn over the official pages in which the British Government has set out its case, we are inclined to marvel—knowing what we now know—that our Foreign Minister should have shown so much zeal and innocence in pleading the cause of peace on high grounds of humanity, and with a faith, apparently unshaken to the last, that in principle at least, the German Government were in full agreement with his aims. The practical disadvantages of being a gentleman are that they are apt to make a man too credulous and not sufficiently inquisitive. Sir Edward Grey acted according to his nature. His miscalculation was one which his fellow-countrymen have not hesitated to forgive. But clearly he misjudged the forces which were opposed to him. He was deceived by hollow assurances. He beat hopefully, but vainly and pathetically, against a door which was already barred and bolted, and behind which (could he but have seen) the Kaiser, with his Ministers and Staff, was wholly absorbed in the study of war maps and tables of mobilisation.

Sir Edward Grey failed to prevent war, and in the circumstances it is hardly to be wondered at. But if he failed in one direction he succeeded in another. His whole procedure from first to last was so transparently disinterested and above board that, when war did actually come upon us, it found us, not merely as a nation, but also as an Empire, more united than we have ever been at any crisis, since the Great Armada was sighted off Plymouth Sound. English people felt that whatever else there

[1] White Paper, No. 161.

CHAPTER III.

Who wanted war?

might be to reproach themselves with, they at any rate went into the fight with clean hands. What is even more remarkable, the people of all neutral countries, with the possible exception of the rigid moralists of Constantinople, appeared for once to share the same opinion.

This was a great achievement; nearly, but not quite, the greatest of all. To have prevented war would have been a greater achievement still. . . . But was war inevitable? Or was M. Sazonof right, when he said to our Ambassador, on the morning of the day when Servia replied to the Austrian ultimatum,[1] that if Britain then took her stand firmly with France and Russia there would be no war; but that if we failed them then, rivers of blood would flow, and in the end we should be dragged into war?[2]

Sir Edward Grey refused to take this course. He judged that a pronouncement of such a character would appear in the light of a menace to the governments of Germany and Austria, and also to public opinion in those countries; that it would only stiffen their backs; that a more hopeful way of proceeding was for England to deal with Germany as a friend, letting it be understood that if our counsels of moderation were disregarded, we might be driven most reluctantly into the camp of her enemies. To this, when it was urged by our Ambassador at St. Petersburg, the Russian Minister only replied—and the words seem to have in them a note of tragedy and weariness, as if the speaker well knew that he was talking to deaf ears—that unfortunately Germany was convinced that she could count upon the neutrality of Britain.[3]

[1] Saturday, July 25. [2] White Paper, No. 17. [3] *Ibid.* Nos. 17 and 44.

Who wanted war?

The alternative was to speak out as Mr. Lloyd George spoke at the time of the Agadir crisis, 'to rattle the sabre,' and to take our stand 'in shining armour' beside the other two members of the Entente.

Sir Edward Grey believed that this procedure would not have the effect desired, but the reverse. Further, it would have committed this country to a policy which had never been submitted to it, and which it had never considered, far less approved, even in principle. The Agadir precedent could be distinguished. There the danger which threatened France arose directly out of treaty engagements with ourselves. Here there was no such particular justification, but a wide general question of the safety of Europe and the British Empire.

With regard to this wider question, notwithstanding its imminence for a good many years, the British Empire had not made up its mind, nor indeed had it ever been asked to do so by those in authority. Sir Edward Grey appears to have thought that, on democratic principles, he had not the right to make such a pronouncement as M. Sazonof desired; and that even if this pathway might have led to peace, it was one which he could not tread.

The one alternative was tried, and failed. We proffered our good offices, we urged our counsels of moderation, all in vain. That, at any rate, is among the certainties. And it is also among the certainties that, although this alternative failed, it brought us two signal benefits, in the unity of our own people and the goodwill of the world.

About the other alternative, which was not tried, we cannot of course speak with the same sureness. If Sir Edward Grey had taken the step which

CHAPTER III.

Who wanted war?

M. Sazonof desired him to take, he would at once have been vehemently opposed and denounced by a very large body of his own fellow-countrymen, who, never having been taken frankly into the confidence of the Government with regard to the foundations of British policy, were at this early stage of the proceedings almost wholly ignorant of the motives and issues involved. This being so, if war had ensued, we should then have gone into it a divided instead of a united nation. On the other hand, if peace had ensued, it must have been a patched-up ill-natured peace; and it is not improbable that Sir Edward Grey would have been driven from office by enemies in his own household, playing the game of Germany unconsciously, as on previous occasions, and would have brought the Cabinet down with him in his fall. For at this time, owing to domestic difficulties, the Government stood in a very perilous position, and it needed only such a mutiny, as a bold departure in foreign affairs would almost certainly have provoked among the Liberal party, to bring Mr. Asquith's government to an end.

As one reads and re-reads the official documents in our present twilight, it is difficult to resist the conclusion that on the main point Sir Edward Grey was wrong and M. Sazonof right. Germany, with her eyes wide open, had determined on war with Russia and France, unless by Russia's surrender of her prestige in the Balkans—a surrender in its way almost as abject as that which had already been demanded of Servia—the results of victory could be secured without recourse to arms. Germany, nevertheless, was not prepared for war with Britain. She was reckoning with confidence on our standing aside,

Who wanted war?

on our unwillingness and inability to intervene.[1] If it had been made clear to her, that in case she insisted on pressing things to extremity, we should on no account stand aside, she might then have eagerly forwarded, instead of deliberately frustrating, Austria's eleventh-hour negotiations for an accommodation with St. Petersburg.

No one, except Germans, whose judgments, naturally enough, are disordered by the miscarriage of their plans, has dreamed of bringing the charge against Sir Edward Grey that he wished for war, or fomented it, or even that through levity or want of vigilance, he allowed it to occur. The criticism is, that although his intentions were of the best, and his industry unflagging, he failed to realise the situation, and to adopt the only means which might have secured peace.

The charge which is not only alleged, but established against Austria is of a wholly different order. It is that she provoked war—blindly perhaps, and not foreseeing what the war would be, but at any rate recklessly and obstinately.

The crime of which Germany stands accused is that she deliberately aimed at war, and that when there seemed a chance of her plan miscarrying, she promptly took steps to render peace impossible. Among neutral countries is there one, the public opinion of which has acquitted her? And has not Italy, her own ally, condemned her by refusing assistance on the ground that this war is a war of German aggression?

[1] A proof of this is the outburst of hatred in Germany against England so soon as we ranged ourselves with France and Russia.

CHAPTER IV

THE PENALTY OF NEGLIGENCE

CHAPTER IV.

The penalty of negligence.

THE East has been drawn into the circle of this war as well as the West, the New World as well as the Old; nor can any man feel certain, or even hopeful, that the conflagration will be content to burn itself out where it is now raging, and will not spread across further boundaries. . . . It is therefore no matter of surprise that people should be asking themselves—"Of what nature is this war? Is it 'one of those calamities, like earthquake or tempest, 'drought or flood, which lawyers describe as 'the 'act of God'? Or is it a thing which, having been 'conceived and deliberately projected by the wit of 'man, could have been averted by human courage 'and judgment? Was this war, or was it not, in-'evitable?" . . . To which it may be answered, that no war is inevitable until it occurs; and then every war is apt to make pretensions to that character.

In old times it was the Fates, superior even to Zeus, who decreed wars. In later days wars were regarded as the will of God. And to-day professional interpreters of events are as ready as ever with explanations why this war was, in the nature of things, unavoidable. Whether the prevailing priesthood wears white robes and fillets, or rich vestments, or

CHAPTER IV.

The penalty of negligence.

cassocks and Geneva bands, or the severer modern garb of the professor or politician, it appears to be equally prone to dogmatic blasphemy. There is no proof that this war was pre-ordained either by a Christian God or by the laws of Pagan Nature.

One may doubt if any war is inevitable. If statesmen can gain time the chances are that they will gain peace. This was the view of public opinion throughout the British Empire down to July 1914. It was in a special sense the view of the Liberal party; and their view was endorsed, if not by the whole body of Unionists, at any rate by their leader, in terms which admitted of no misunderstanding.[1] It is also the point of view from which this book is written. . . . This war was not inevitable; it could have been avoided, but on one condition—*if England had been prepared.*

England was not prepared either morally or materially. Her rulers had left her in the dark as to the dangers which surrounded her. They had neglected to make clear to her—probably even to themselves—the essential principles of British policy, and the sacrifices which it entailed. They had failed to provide armaments to correspond with this policy. When the crisis arose their hands were tied. They had to sit down hurriedly, and decipher their policy, and find out what it meant. Still more hurriedly they had to get it approved, not merely by their fellow-countrymen, but by their own colleagues—a work, if rumour[2] speaks truly, of

[1] "I hear it also constantly said—there is no use shutting our eyes or 'ears to obvious facts—that owing to divergent interests, war some day or 'other between this country and Germany is inevitable. I never believe in 'these inevitable wars."—Mr. Bonar Law in *England and Germany.*

[2] Rumour finds confirmation in the White Paper; also in an interview with Mr. Lloyd George, reported in *Pearson's Magazine,* March 1915, p. 265, col. ii.

CHAPTER IV.

considerable difficulty. Then they found that one of the main supports was wanting; and they had to set to work frantically to make an army adequate to their needs.

The penalty of negligence.

But it was too late. By this time their policy had fallen about their ears in ruins. For their policy was the neutrality of Belgium, and that was already violated. Their policy was the defence of France, and invasion had begun. Their policy was peace, and peace was broken. The nation which would enjoy peace must be strong enough to enforce peace.

The moods of nations pass like clouds, only more slowly. They bank up filled with menace; we look again and are surprised to find that they have melted away as silently and swiftly as they came. One does not need to be very old to recall various wars, deemed at one time or another to be inevitable, which never occurred. In the 'sixties' war with the second Empire was judged to be inevitable; and along our coasts dismantled forts remain to this day as monuments of our fathers' firm belief in the imminence of an invasion. In the 'seventies,' and indeed until we had entered the present century, war with Russia was regarded as inevitable by a large number of well-informed people; and for a part of this period war with the French Republic was judged to be no less so. Fortune on the whole was favourable. Circumstances changed. The sense of a common danger healed old antagonisms. Causes of chronic irritation disappeared of themselves, or were removed by diplomatic surgery. And with the disappearance of these inflammatory centres, misunderstandings, prejudices, and suspicions began to vanish also.

The penalty of negligence.

Gradually it became clear, that what had been mistaken on both sides for destiny was nothing more inexorable than a fit of temper, or a conflict of business interests not incapable of adjustment. And in a sense the German menace was less formidable than any of these others, for the reason that it was a fit of temper on one side only—a fit of temper, or megalomania. We became fully conscious of the German mood only after the end of the South African War, when its persistence showed clearly that it arose, not from any sympathy with the Dutch, but from some internal cause. When this cause was explained to us it seemed so inadequate, so absurd, so unreal, so contrary to the facts, that only a small fraction of our nation ever succeeded in believing that it actually existed. We had been taught by Carlyle, that while the verities draw immortal life from the facts to which they correspond, the falsities have but a phenomenal existence, and a brief influence over the minds of men. Consequently the greater part of the British people troubled their heads very little about this matter, never thought things would come to a crisis, or lead to serious mischief; but trusted always that, in due time, the ridiculous illusions of our neighbours would vanish and die of their own inanity.

We listened with an equal wonder and weariness to German complaints that we were jealous of her trade and bent on strangling it; that we grudged her colonial expansion, and were intriguing all the world over to prevent it; that we had isolated her and ringed her round with hostile alliances. We knew that these notions were all entirely false. We knew that, so far from hampering German commerce,

CHAPTER IV.

The penalty of negligence.

our Free Trade system in the United Kingdom, in the Dependencies, and in the Indian Empire had fostered it and helped its rapid and brilliant success more than any other external factor.

For fully thirty years from 1870—during which period what remained of the uncivilised portions of the world was divided up, during which period also Germany was the most powerful nation in Europe, and could have had anything she wanted of these new territories almost for the asking—Bismarck and the statesmen of his school, engrossed mainly in the European situation, set little store by colonies, thought of them rather as expensive and dangerous vanities, and abstained deliberately from taking an energetic part in the scramble. We knew, that in Africa and the East, Germany had nevertheless obtained considerable possessions, and that it was, primarily her own fault that she had not obtained more. We assumed, no doubt very foolishly, that she must ultimately become aware of her absurdity in blaming us for her own neglect. We forgot human nature, and the apologue of the drunkard who cursed the lamp-post for its clumsiness in getting in his way.

The British people knew that Germany was talking nonsense; but unfortunately they never fully realised that she was sincere, and meant all the things she said. They thought she only half believed in her complaints, as a man is apt to do when ill-temper upsets his equanimity. They were confident that in the end the falsities would perish and the verities remain, and that in the fulness of time the two nations would become friends.

As to this last the British people probably judged correctly; but they entirely overlooked the fact, that if truth was to be given a chance of prevailing in the end, it was important to provide against mischief which might very easily occur in the meantime. Nor did their rulers, whose duty it was, ever warn them seriously of this necessity.

The penalty of negligence.

When a man works himself up into a rage and proceeds to flourish a loaded revolver, something more is necessary for the security of the bystanders than the knowledge that his ill-temper does not rest upon a reasonable basis. War was not inevitable, certainly; but until the mood of Germany changed, it was exceedingly likely to occur unless the odds against the aggressor were made too formidable for him to face. None of the governments, however, which have controlled our national destinies since 1900, ever developed sufficient energy to realise the position of affairs, or ever mustered up courage to tell the people clearly what the risks were, to state the amount of the premium which was required to cover the risks, and to insist upon the immediate duty of the sacrifice which imperial security inexorably demanded.

CHAPTER V

PERSONAL RESPONSIBILITY

Personal responsibility.

ALTHOUGH in a technical sense the present war was brought on by Austrian diplomacy, no one, in England at least, is inclined to rate the moral responsibility of that empire at the highest figure. It is in Germany that we find, or imagine ourselves to have found, not only the true and deep-seated causes of the war, but the immediate occasions of it.

Not the least of our difficulties, however, is to decide the point—Who is Germany? Who was her man of business? Who acted for her in the matter of this war? Who pulled the wires, or touched the button that set the conflagration blazing? Was this the work of an individual or a camarilla? Was it the result of one strong will prevailing, or of several wills getting to loggerheads—wills not particularly strong, but obstinate, and flustered by internal controversy and external events? What actually happened — was it meant by the 'super-men' to happen, or did it come as a shock—not upon 'supermen' at all—but upon several groups of surprised blunderers? These questions are not likely to be answered for a generation or more—until, if ever, the archives of Vienna and Berlin give up their secrets—and it would therefore be idle to waste too much time in analysis of the probabilities.

CHAPTER V.

Personal responsibility.

The immediate occasion of the catastrophe has been variously attributed to the German court, army, bureaucracy, professors, press, and people. If we are looking only for a single thing—the hand which lit the conflagration—and not for the profounder and more permanent causes and origins of the trouble, we can at once dismiss several of these suspects from the dock.

Men of learning and letters, professors of every variety—a class which has been christened 'the Pedantocracy' by unfriendly critics—may be all struck off the charge-sheet as unconcerned in the actual delinquency of arson.

In fact, if not in name, these are a kind of priesthood, and a large part of their lives' work has been to spread among German youth the worship of the State under Hohenzollern kingship. It is impossible of course to make 'a silk purse out of a sow's ear,' a religion out of a self-advertising dynasty, or a god out of a machine. Consequently, except for mischief, their efforts have been mainly wasted. Over a long period of years, however, they have been engaged in heaping up combustibles. They have filled men's minds to overflowing with notions which are very liable to lead to war, and which indeed were designed for no other purpose than to prepare public opinion for just such a war as this. Their responsibility therefore is no light one, and it will be dealt with later. But they are innocent at all events of complicity in this particular exploit of fire-raising; and if, after the event, they have sought to excuse, vindicate, and uphold the action of their rulers it would be hard measure to condemn them for that.

CHAPTER V.

Personal responsibility.

Nor did the press bring about the war. In other countries, where the press is free and irresponsible, it has frequently been the prime mover in such mischief; but never in Germany. For in Germany the press is incapable of bringing about anything of the political kind, being merely an instrument and not a principal.

Just as little can the charge of having produced the war be brought against the people. In other countries, where the people are used to give marching orders to their rulers, popular clamour has led to catastrophe of this kind more frequently than any other cause. But this, again, has never been so in Germany. The German people are sober, stedfast, and humble in matters of high policy. They have confidence in their rulers, believe what they are told, obey orders readily, but do not think of giving them. When war was declared, all Germans responded to the call of duty with loyalty and devotion. Nay, having been prepared for at least a generation, they welcomed war with enthusiasm. According to the lights which were given them to judge by, they judged every whit as rightly as our own people. The lights were false lights, hung out deliberately to mislead them and to justify imperial policy. But this was no fault of theirs. Moreover, the judgment which they came to with regard to the war was made after the event, and cannot therefore in any case be held responsible for its occurrence. This is a people's war surely enough, but just as surely, the people had no hand in bringing it about.

The circle of the accused is therefore narrowed down to the Court, the Army, and the Bureaucracy. And there we must leave it for the present—a joint indictment against all three. But whether these

Personal responsibility.

parties were guilty, all three in equal measure, we cannot conjecture with the least approach to certainty. Nor can we even say precisely of what they were guilty—of misunderstanding—of a quarrel among themselves—of a series of blunders—or of a crime so black and deliberate, that no apologist will be able ever to delete it from the pages of history. On all this posterity must be left to pronounce.

It is only human nevertheless to be curious about personalities. Unfortunately for the satisfaction of this appetite, all is darkness as to the German Army. We may suspect that the Prussian junker, or country gentleman, controls and dominates it. But even as to this we may conceivably be wrong. The military genius of some Hanoverian, Saxon, or Bavarian may possess the mastery in council. As to the real heads of the army, as to their individual characters, and their potency in directing policy we know nothing at all. After nine months of war, we have arrived at no clear notion, even with regard to their relative values as soldiers in the field. We have even less knowledge as to their influence beforehand in shaping and deciding the issues of war and peace.

This much, however, we may reasonably deduce from Bernhardi and other writers—that military opinion had been anxious for some considerable number of years past, and more particularly since the Agadir incident,[1] lest war, which it regarded as ultimately inevitable, should be delayed until the forces ranged against Germany, especially upon her Eastern frontier, were too strong for her to cope with.

In the pages of various official publications, and in newspaper reports immediately before and after

[1] July 1911.

CHAPTER V.

Personal responsibility.

war began, we caught glimpses of certain characters at work; but these were not professional soldiers; they were members of the Court and the Bureaucracy.

Herr von Bethmann-Hollweg, the Imperial Chancellor, comes upon the scene—a harassed and indignant official—sorely flustered—not by any means master of his temper—not altogether certain of his facts—in considerable doubt apparently as to whether things have not passed behind his back which he ought to have been told of by higher powers, but was not. He appears to us as a diligent and faithful servant,—one who does not seek to impose his own decisions, but to excuse, justify, and carry out, if he can, decisions which have been made by others, more highly placed and greedier of responsibility than himself.

Herr von Jagow, the Foreign Minister, is much affected. He drops tears—or comes somewhere near dropping them—over the lost hopes of a peaceful understanding between England and Germany. We can credit the sincerity of his sorrow all the more easily, for the reason that Herr von Jagow behaves throughout the crisis as the courteous gentleman; while others, who by position were even greater gentlemen, forget momentarily, in their excitement, the qualities which are usually associated with that title.

Then there is the German Ambassador at Vienna—obviously a firebrand—enjoying, one imagines, the confidence of the war parties in both capitals: also apparently a busy intriguer. The documents show him acting behind the back of the Berlin Foreign Office, and communicating direct with the Kaiser.

We gather very clearly that he egged on the

Personal responsibility.

statesmen of Vienna, with great diligence and success, to press Servia to extremes, and to shear time so short that peace-makers had nothing left to catch hold of. Russia, he assured them, would never carry her opposition to the point of war. Even if she did so, he argued with much plausibility, she would be negligible. For she stood midway in a great military and naval reformation, than which no situation is more deplorable for the purposes of carrying on a campaign.

When Prince Lichnowsky, the German Ambassador in London, took his departure at the outbreak of war, he probably left no single enemy behind him. A simple, friendly, sanguine figure, with a pardonable vanity which led him to believe the incredible. He produced what is called in the cant of the day 'an atmosphere,' mainly in drawing-rooms and newspaper offices, but occasionally, one conjectures, even in Downing Street itself. His artistry was purely in air and touched nothing solid. He was useful to his employers, mainly because he put England off her guard. He would not have been in the least useful if he had not been mainly sincere.

But though he was useful to German policy, he was not trusted by the powers in Berlin to attend to their business at the Court of St. James's except under strict supervision. What precisely were the duties of Baron von Kuhlmann, Councillor to the Embassy? He was always very cheerful, and obliging, and ready to smooth any little difficulty out of the way. On the other hand, he was also very deft at inserting an obstacle with an air of perfect innocence, which imposed on nearly every one—even occasionally on the editors of newspapers. For

CHAPTER V.

Personal responsibility.

some reason, however, very few people were willing to accept this plausible diplomatist's assurances without a grain or two of salt. Indeed quite a large number were so misled by their prejudices against him, that they were convinced his prime vocation was that of a spy—a spy on the country to which he was accredited and on the Ambassador under whom he served.[1]

We know more of the Kaiser than of any of these others, and we have known him over a much longer period. And yet our knowledge of him has never enabled us to forecast his actions with any certainty. British ministers and diplomatists, whose business it is to gauge, not only the muzzle-velocity of eminent characters, but also the forces of their recoil, never seem to have arrived at any definite conclusions with regard to this baffling personality. Whatever he did or did not do, they were always surprised by it, which gives us some measure of their capacity if not of his.

The Kaiser is pre-eminently a man of moods. At one time he is Henry the Fifth, at another Richard the Second. Upon occasions he appears as Hamlet, cursing fate which impels him to make a decision. Within the same hour he is Autolycus crying up his wares with an unfeigned cheerfulness. He is possessed by the demon of quick-change and restlessness. We learn on good authority that he possesses an almost

[1] Prussian policy appears to be modelled upon the human body. Just as man is endowed with a duality of certain organs—eyes, nostrils, lungs, kidneys, etc.—so Prussian policy appears to proceed upon the principle of a double diplomatic representation, two separate Foreign Office departments, etc., etc. It is no doubt an excellent plan to have a second string to your bow; but it is not yet clear how far this can be carried with advantage in delicate negotiations without destroying confidence in your sincerity.

Personal responsibility.

incredible number of uniforms which he actually wears, and of royal residences which he occasionally inhabits. He clothes himself suitably for each brief occasion, and sleeps rarely, if reports can be believed, for more than two nights together under the same roof. He is like an American millionaire in his fondness for rapid and sudden journeys, and like a democratic politician in his passion for speech-making.

The phenomena of the moment—those which flicker upon the surface of things—engage his eager and vivacious interest. Upon such matters his commentaries are often apt and entertaining. But when he attempts to deal with deeper issues, and with the underlying principles and causes of human action, his utterances immediately lose the mind's attention and keep hold only of the ear's, by virtue of a certain resonance and blatancy. When the Kaiser discourses to us, as he often does, upon the profundities of politics, philosophy, and religion, he falls instantly into set forms, which express nothing that is living and real. He would have the world believe, and doubtless himself sincerely believes, that he has plunged, like a pearl-diver, into the deeps, and has returned thence laden with rich treasures of thought and experience. But in truth he has never visited this region at all, being of a nature far too buoyant for such enterprises. He has not found truth, but only remembered phrases.

The Kaiser is frequently upbraided for his charm of manner by people who have come under its influence and been misled. One of the commonest accusations against him is that of duplicity; but indeed it seems hardly more just to condemn him for duplicity than it would be to praise him for sincerity. He is a man dangerous to have dealings with, but this

CHAPTER V.

Personal responsibility.

is owing to the irresponsible effervescence of his ideas. At any given moment he probably means the greater part of what he says; but the image of one moment is swiftly expelled and obliterated by that of the next. The Kaiser's untrustworthiness arises not from duplicity, so much as from the quickness of his fancy, the shallowness of his judgment, and the shortness of his memory. That his communications frequently produce the same effects as duplicity, is due to the fact that he recognises no obligation either to stand by his word, or to correct the impression which his hasty assurances may have produced in the mind of his interlocutor. The statesman who is won over to-day by his advocacy of an English alliance, is astounded on the morrow to find him encouraging an English pogrom.[1]

[1] A labour leader, highly impressed by the spectacle, gave a vivid description of an equestrian parade through the streets of Berlin after the declaration of war—the Kaiser in helmet of gold, seated on his white charger, frowning terribly, in a kind of immobility, as if his features had been frozen into this dramatically appropriate expression—following behind him in a carriage the Crown Prince and Princess, all vivacity and smiles, and bows to this side and the other—a remarkable contrast!

It is interesting to contrast the ornate and flamboyant being whom we know as Kaiser Wilhelm the Second with Carlyle's famous description of the great Frederick :—

"A highly interesting lean little old man, of alert though slightly stooping 'figure; whose name among strangers was King *Friedrich the Second*, or 'Frederick the Great of Prussia, and at home among the common people, 'who much loved and esteemed him, was *Vater Fritz*,—Father Fred,—a 'name of familiarity which had not bred contempt in that instance. He is 'a King every inch of him, though without the trappings of a King. 'Presents himself in a Spartan simplicity of vesture; no crown but an old 'military cocked-hat,—generally old, or trampled and kneaded into 'absolute *softness*, if new;—no sceptre but one like Agamemnon's, a 'walking-stick cut from the woods, which serves also as a riding-stick '(with which he hits the horse 'between the ears' say authors);—and for 'royal robes, a mere soldier's blue coat with red facings, coat likely to be 'old, and sure to have a good deal of Spanish snuff on the breast of it; 'rest of the apparel dim, unobtrusive in colour or cut, ending in high 'over-knee military boots, which may be brushed (and, I hope, kept soft 'with an underhand suspicion of oil), but are not permitted to be blackened 'or varnished; Day and Martin with their soot-pots forbidden to 'approach.

Personal responsibility.

When a violent convulsion shakes the world people immediately begin to look about them for some mighty and malevolent character who can be held responsible for it. To the generations which knew them, Cromwell, Napoleon, and Bismarck all figured as Antichrist. But in regard to the policy which produced the present war, of what man can it be said truly, either that he controlled that policy, or that he brought about the results which he aimed at? Which of the great personages concerned possesses the sublime qualities of the spirit of evil?[1]

It is conceivable, though very unlikely, that behind the scenes there was some strong silent man who worked the others like puppets on a string; but among those who have made themselves known to us in the pages of White Papers and the like, there is none whose features bear the least resemblance to our conception of Antichrist; none who had firm

"The man is not of godlike physiognomy, any more than of imposing 'stature or costume; close-shut mouth with thin lips, prominent jaws and 'nose, receding brow, by no means of Olympian height; head, however, is 'of long form, and has superlative gray eyes in it. Not what is called a 'beautiful man; nor yet, by all appearance, what is called a happy. On 'the contrary, the face bears evidence of many sorrows, as they are termed, 'of much hard labour done in this world; and seems to anticipate nothing 'but more still coming. Quiet stoicism, capable enough of what joy there 'were, but not expecting any worth mention; great unconscious and some 'conscious pride, well tempered with a cheery mockery of humour,—are 'written on that old face; which carries its chin well forward, in spite of 'the slight stoop about the neck; snuffy nose rather flung into the air 'under its old cocked hat,—like an old snuffy lion on the watch; and 'such a pair of eyes as no man or lion or lynx of that century bore elsewhere, 'according to all the testimony we have."—Carlyle, *History of Frederick the Great*, Bk. I. chap. i.

[1] A friend who has been kind enough to read the proofs of this volume takes exception to the rating of Antichrist. The Devil, he maintains, is not at all a clever or profound spirit, though he is exceedingly industrious. The conception of him in the old Mystery Plays, where he figures as a kind of butt, whose elaborate and painfully constructed schemes are continually being upset owing to some ridiculous oversight, or by some trivial accident, is the true Satan; the Miltonic idea is a poetical myth, not in the least borne out by human experience.

CHAPTER V.

control of events, or even of himself. There is none of whom it is possible to say truly that he achieved the results at which he aimed.

Personal responsibility.

It is clear that the war which the joint efforts of these great personages brought into existence was a monstrous birth, and that it filled those who were responsible for it with dismay, only a degree less than it shocked other people. For proof of this, it is unnecessary to look further than the miscalculations of the political kind which became recognised for such within a few weeks after war was declared.

CHAPTER VI

GERMAN MISCALCULATIONS

CHAPTER VI.

German miscalculations.

In the world's play-house there are a number of prominent and well-placed seats, which the instinct of veneration among mankind insists on reserving for Super-men; and as mankind is never content unless the seats of the super-men are well filled, 'the Management'—in other words, the press, the publicists, and other manipulators of opinion—have to do the best they can to find super-men to sit in them. When that is impossible, it is customary to burnish up, fig out, and pass off various colourable substitutes whom it is thought, may be trusted to comport themselves with propriety until the curtain falls. But those resplendent creatures whom we know so well by sight and fame, and upon whom all eyes and opera-glasses are directed during the *entr'-actes*, are for the most part not super-men at all, but merely what, in the slang of the box-office, is known as 'paper.' Indeed there have been long periods, even generations, during which the supposed super-men have been wholly 'paper.'

Of course so long as the super-men substitutes have only to walk to their places, to bow, smile, frown, overawe, and be admired, everything goes safely enough. The audience is satisfied and the

CHAPTER VI.

German miscalculations.

'management' rubs its hands. But if anything has to be done beyond this parade business, if the unexpected happens, if, for instance, there is an alarm of fire—in which case the example set by the super-creatures might be of inestimable assistance—the 'paper' element is certain to crumple up, according to the laws of its nature, being after all but dried pulp. Something of this kind appears to have happened in various great countries during the weeks which immediately preceded and followed the outbreak of war, and in none was the crumpling up of the supermen substitutes more noticeable than in Germany.

The thoroughness of the German race is no empty boast. All the world knows as much by experience in peace as well as war. Consequently, people had said to themselves: "However it may be with other 'nations, in Germany at all events the strings of 'foreign policy are firmly held in giant fingers." But as day succeeded day, unmasking one miscalculation after another, it became clear that there must have been at least as much 'paper' in the political high places of Germany as elsewhere.

Clearly, although this war was made in Germany, it did not at all follow the course which had been charted for it in the official forecasts. For the German bureaucracy and general staff had laid their plans to crush France at the first onset—to crush her till the bones stuck out through her skin. And they had reckoned to out-general Russia and roll back her multitudes, as yet unorganised—so at least it was conceived—in wave upon wave of encroaching defeat.

Having achieved these aims before the fall of the leaf, Germany would have gained thereby another

German miscalculations.

decade for the undisturbed development of wealth and world-power. Under Prussian direction the power of Austria would then be consolidated within her own dominions and throughout the Balkan Peninsula. At the end of this interval of vigorous recuperation, or possibly earlier, Germany would attack England, and England would fall an easy prey. For having stood aside from the former struggle she would be without allies. Her name would stink in the nostrils of Russia and France; and indeed to the whole world she would be recognised for what she was—a decadent and coward nation. Even her own children would blush for her dishonour.

That these were the main lines of the German forecast no man can doubt, who has watched and studied the development of events; and although it is as yet too early days to make sure that nothing of all this vast conception will ever be realised, much of it—the time-table at all events—has certainly miscarried for good and all.

According to German calculations England would stand aside; but England took part. Italy would help her allies; but Italy refused. Servia was a thing of naught; but Servia destroyed several army corps. Belgium would not count; and yet Belgium by her exertions counted, if for nothing more, for the loss of eight precious days, while by her sufferings she mobilised against the aggressor the condemnation of the whole world.

The Germans reckoned that the army of France was terrible only upon paper. Forty-five years of corrupt government and political peculation must, according to their calculations, have paralysed the

CHAPTER VI.

German miscalculations.

general staff and betrayed the national spirit. The sums voted for equipment, arms, and ammunition must assuredly have been spirited away, as under the Third Empire, into the pockets of ministers, senators, deputies, and contractors. The results of this régime would become apparent, as they had done in 1870, only in the present case sooner.

War was declared by the Third Napoleon at mid-July, by William the Second not until August 1; but Sedan or its equivalent would occur, nevertheless, in the first days of September, in 1914 as in 1870. In the former contest Paris fell at the end of six months; in this one, with the aid of howitzers, it would fall at the end of six weeks.

Unfortunately for this confident prediction, whatever may have been the deficiency in the French supplies, however dangerous the consequent hitches in mobilisation, things fell out quite differently. The spirit of the people of France, and the devotion of her soldiers, survived the misfeasances of the politicians, supposing indeed that such crimes had actually been committed.

It was a feature of Bismarck's diplomacy that he put a high value upon the good opinion of the world, and took the greatest pains to avoid its condemnation. In 1870, as we now know, he schemed successfully, to lure the government of Napoleon the Third into a declaration of war, thereby saddling the French government with the odium which attaches to peace-breakers.[1] But in the case of the present war,

[1] British public opinion in regard to that war was divided roughly according to party lines, the Conservatives favouring France on sentimental grounds, the Liberals favouring Germany as a highly-educated, peace-loving people who had been wantonly attacked.

which, as it out-Bismarcked Bismarck in deliberate aggressiveness, stood all the more in need of a tactful introduction to the outside world, the precautions of that astute statesman were neglected or despised. From the beginning all neutral nations were resentful of German procedure, and after the devastation of Belgium and the destruction of Louvain, the spacious morality of the Young Turks alone was equal to the profession of friendship and admiration.

German miscalculations.

The objects which Germany sought to gain by the cruelties perpetrated, under orders, by her soldiers in Belgium and Northern France are clear enough. These objects were certainly of considerable value in a military as well as in a political sense. One wonders, however, if even Germany herself now considers them to have been worth the abhorrence and disgust which they have earned for her throughout the civilised world.

In nothing is the sham super-man more easily detected than in the confidence and self-complacency with which he pounces upon the immediate small advantage, regardless of the penalty he will have to pay in the future. By spreading death and devastation broadcast in Belgium the Germans hoped to attain three things, and it is not impossible that they have succeeded in attaining them all. They sought to secure their communications by putting the fear of death, and worse than death, into the hearts of the civil population. They sought to send the countryside fleeing terror-stricken before their advance, choking and cumbering the highways; than which nothing is ever more hampering to the operations of an army in retreat, or more depressing to its spirits. But chiefly they desired to set a ruthless object-lesson before the

CHAPTER VI.

German miscalculations.

eyes of Holland, in order to show her the consequences of resistance; so that when it came to her turn to answer a summons to surrender she might have the good sense not to make a fuss. They desired in their dully-calculating, official minds that Holland might never forget the clouds of smoke, from burning villages and homesteads, which the August breezes carried far across her frontiers; the sights of horror, the tales of suffering and ruin which tens of thousands of starved, forlorn, and hurrying fugitives brought with them when they came seeking sanctuary in her territories.

But if the Germans gained all this, and even if they gained in addition the loving admiration of the Young Turks, was it worth while to purchase these advantages at such a price? It seems a poor bargain to save your communications, if thereby you lose the good opinion of the whole world.

What is of most interest to ourselves, however, in the long list of miscalculations, is the confidence of Germany that Britain would remain neutral. For a variety of reasons which satisfied the able bureaucrats at Berlin, it was apparently taken for granted by them that we were determined to stand out; and indeed that we were in no position to come in even if we would. We conjecture that the reports of German ambassadors, councillors, consuls, and secret service agents must have been very certain and unanimous in this prediction.

According to the German theory, the British race, at home and abroad, was wholly immersed in gain, and in a kind of pseudo-philanthropy—in making money, and in paying blackmail to the working-classes in order to be allowed to go on making money.

Our social legislation and our 'People's Budgets' were regarded in Germany with contempt, as sops and shams, wanting in thoroughness and tainted with hypocrisy.

German miscalculations.

English politicians, acting upon the advice of obliging financiers, had been engaged during recent years (so grossly was the situation misjudged by our neighbours) in imposing taxation which hit the trader, manufacturer, and country-gentleman as hard as possible; which also hit the working-class hard, though indirectly; but which left holes through which the financiers themselves—by virtue of their international connections and affiliations—could glide easily into comparative immunity.

From these faulty premisses, Germans concluded that Britain was held in leading-strings by certain sentimentalists who wanted vaguely to do good; and that these sentimentalists, again, were helped and guided by certain money-lenders and exploiters, who were all very much in favour of paying ransom out of other people's pockets. A nation which had come to this pass would be ready enough to sacrifice future interests—being blind to them—for the comforts of a present peace.

The Governments of the United Kingdom and the Dominions were largely influenced—so it was believed at Berlin—by crooks and cranks of various sorts, by speculators and 'speculatists,'[1] many of them of foreign origin or descent—who preached day in and day out the doctrine that war was an anachronism, *vieux jeu*, even an impossibility in the present situation of the world.

[1] 'Speculatists' was a term used by contemporary American writers to describe the eloquent theorists who played so large a part in the French Revolution.

CHAPTER VI.

German miscalculations.

The British Government appeared to treat these materially-minded visionaries with the highest favour. Their advice was constantly sought; they were recipients of the confidences of Ministers; they played the part of Lords Bountiful to the party organisations; they were loaded with titles, if not with honour. Their abhorrence of militarism knew no bounds, and to a large extent it seemed to German, and even to English eyes, as if they carried the Cabinet, the party-machine, and the press along with them.

'Militarism,' as used by these enthusiasts, was a comprehensive term. It covered with ridicule and disrepute even such things as preparation for the defence of the national existence. International law was solemnly recommended as a safer defence than battleships.

Better certainly, they allowed, if militarism could be rooted out in all countries; but at any rate England, the land of their birth or adoption, must be saved from the contamination of this brutalising idea. In their anxiety to discredit Continental exemplars they even went so far as to evolve an ingenious theory, that foreign nations which followed in the paths of militarism, did so at serious loss to themselves, but with wholly innocent intentions. More especially, they insisted, was this true in the case of Germany.

The Liberal party appeared to listen to these opinions with respect; Radicals hailed them with enthusiasm; while the Labour party was at one time so much impressed, as to propose through some of its more progressive spirits that, in the exceedingly unlikely event of a German landing, working-men should continue steadily at their usual labours and pay no heed to the military operations of the invaders.

German miscalculations.

In Berlin, apparently, all this respect and enthusiasm for pacifism, together with the concrete proposals for putting its principles into practice, were taken at their face value. There at any rate it was confidently believed that the speculators and the 'speculatists' had succeeded in changing or erasing the spots of the English leopard.

But in order to arrive at such a conclusion as this the able German bureaucrats must have understood very little, one would think, of human nature in general, and of British human nature in particular. Clearly they built more hopes on our supposed conversion to pacifism than the foundations would stand. They were right, of course, in counting it a benefit to themselves that we were unprepared and unsuspicious of attack; that we had pared down our exiguous army and stinted our navy somewhat beyond the limits of prudence. They were foolish, however, not to perceive that if the British people found themselves confronted with the choice, between a war which they believed to be righteous, and a peace which they saw clearly would not only be wounding to their own honour but ruinous to their security, all their fine abstract convictions would go by the board; that party distinctions would then for the time being disappear, and the speculators and the 'speculatists' would be interned in the nethermost pit of national distrust. . . . In so far, therefore, as the Germans reckoned on our unpreparedness they were wise; but in counting upon British neutrality they were singularly wide of the mark.

CHAPTER VI.

German miscalculations.

One imagines that among the idealists of Berlin there must surely have been a few sceptics who did not altogether credit this wholesale conversion and quakerisation of the British race. But for these doubters, if indeed they existed, there were other considerations of a more practical kind which seemed to indicate that Britain must certainly stand aside.

The first and most important of these was the imminence of civil war in Ireland. If Prince Lichnowsky and Baron von Kuhlmann reported that this had become inevitable, small blame to their perspicacity! For in this their judgment only tallied with that of most people in the United Kingdom who had any knowledge of the true facts.

In March an incident occurred among the troops stationed in Ireland which must have given comfort at Berlin, even in greater measure than it caused disquiet at home. For it showed in a vivid flash the intrinsic dangers of the Irish situation, and the tension, almost to breaking-point, which existed between the civil authorities and the fighting services.

It also showed, what in the circumstances must have been peculiarly reassuring to the German Government, that our Navy and Army were under the charge of Ministers whose judgments were apt to be led captive by their tempers. Although the Secretary of State for War did not remain in office for many days to encourage the hearts of the general staff at Berlin, his important post was never filled. It was only occupied and kept warm by the Prime Minister, whose labours and responsibilities—according to the notions of the Germans, who are a painstaking and thorough people—were already enough for one man to undertake. Moreover, the First

German miscalculations.

Lord of the Admiralty had not resigned; and it was perhaps natural, looking at what had just happened, to conclude that he would be wholly incapable of the sound and swift decision by which a few months later he was destined to atone for his recent blunder.

Moreover, although the Curragh incident, as it was called, had been patched over in a sort of way, the danger of civil war in Ireland had not diminished in the least by Midsummer. Indeed it had sensibly increased. During the interval large quantities of arms and ammunition had been imported by Ulstermen in defiance of the Government, and Nationalists were eagerly engaged in emulating their example. The emergency conference of the leaders of parties which the King, acting upon the desperate advice of his Ministers, had called together at Buckingham Palace ended in complete failure.

On Monday the 27th of July readers of the morning newspapers, looking anxiously for news of the Servian reply to the Austrian ultimatum, found their eyes distracted by even blacker headlines, which announced that a Scots regiment had fired on a Dublin mob.

How the bureaucrats of Berlin must have rubbed their hands and admired their own prescience! Civil war in Ireland had actually begun, and in the very nick of time! And this occurrence, no less dramatic than opportune, was a triumph not merely for German foresight but for German contrivance—like a good many other things, indeed, which have taken place of late. When the voyage of the good ship *Fanny*, which in April carried arms to the coast of Antrim, comes to be written, and that of the anonymous yacht which sailed from German waters, transhipped its

CHAPTER VI.

German miscalculations.

cargo in the channel, whence it was safely conveyed by another craft to Dublin Bay to kindle this blaze in July—when these narratives are set out by some future historian, as they deserve to be, but not until then, it will be known how zealously, benevolently, and impartially our loyal and kindly Teuton cousins forwarded and fomented the quarrel between Covenanter and Nationalist. What the German bureaucrats, however, with all their foresight, apparently did not in the least foresee, was that the wound which they had intentionally done so much to keep open, they would speedily be helping unintentionally to heal.

With regard to South Africa, German miscalculation and intrigue pursued a somewhat similar course, though with little better results. It was assumed that South Africa, having been fully incorporated in the Empire as a self-governing unit only twelve years earlier, and as the result of a prolonged and sanguinary war, must necessarily be bent on severing the British connection at the earliest opportunity. The Dutch, like the frogs in the fable, were imagined to be only awaiting a favourable moment to exchange the tyranny of King Log for the benevolent rule of King Stork.

In these forecasts, however, various considerations were overlooked. In the first place, the methods of incorporation pursued by the British in South Africa were as nearly as possible the opposite of those adopted by Prussia in Poland, in Schleswig-Holstein, and in Alsace-Lorraine. In many quarters there were doubtless bitter memories among the Dutch, and in some others disappointed ambition still ached ;

but these forces were not enough to plunge into serious civil war two races which, after nearly a century of strife and division, had but a few years before entered into a solemn and voluntary covenant to make a firm union, and dwell henceforth in peace one with another. What object could there be for Dutchmen to rise in rebellion against a government, which consisted almost exclusively of Dutch statesmen, and which had been put in office and was kept there by the popular vote ?

German miscalculations.

What German intrigue and bribery could do it did. But Dutchmen whose recollections went back so far as twenty years were little likely to place excessive confidence in the incitements and professions of Berlin. They remembered with what busy intrigues Germany had in former times encouraged their ambitions, with what a rich bribery of promises she had urged them on to war, with what cold indifference, when war arose, she had left them to their fate. They also remembered how, when their aged President, an exiled and broken-hearted man, sought an interview with the great sovereign whose consideration for him in his more prosperous days had never lacked for warmth, he received for an answer, that Berlin was no place for people who had been beaten to come whining, and was turned from the door.

In India, as in South Africa, Germany entertained confident hopes of a successful rising. Had not the Crown Prince, a shrewd judge, visited there a few years earlier and formed his own estimate of the situation ? Was there not a widely spread network of sedition covering the whole of our Eastern Empire, an incendiary press, and orators who openly counselled

German miscalculations.

violence and preached rebellion? Had not riots been increasing rapidly in gravity and number? Had not assassins been actively pursuing their trade? Had not a ship-load of Indians just been refused admission to Canada, thereby causing a not unnatural outburst of indignation?

How far German statesmen had merely foreseen these things, how far they had actually contrived them, we are as yet in ignorance; but judging by what has happened in other places—in Ireland, South Africa, Belgium, and France—it would surprise no one to learn that the bombs which were thrown at the Viceroy and his wife with tragic consequences owed something to German teaching. It is unlikely that German emissaries had been less active in fomenting unrest in India than elsewhere among the subjects of nations with which they were ostensibly at peace; while the fact that the Crown Prince had but recently enjoyed the hospitality of the Viceregal Court was only a sentimental consideration unworthy of the attention of super-men.

Moreover, it had for long been abundantly clear, on *a priori* grounds, to thinkers like Treitschke and Bernhardi that India was already ripe for rebellion on a grand scale. There are but two things which affect the Indian mind with awe and submission—a sublime philosophy and a genius for war. The English had never been philosophers, and they had ceased to be warriors. How, then, could a race which worshipped only soldiers and sages be expected to reverence and obey a garrison of clerks and shopkeepers? A war between England and Germany would provide an opportunity for making an end for ever of the British Raj.

CHAPTER VI.

German miscalculations.

The self-governing Dominions were believed to be affected with the same decadent spirit and fantastic illusions as their Mother Country; only with them these cankers had spread more widely, were more logically followed out in practice, and less tempered and restrained by aristocratic tradition. Their eloquent outpourings of devotion and cohesion were in reality quite valueless; merely what in their own slang is known as 'hot air.' They hated militarism in theory and practice, and they loved making money with at least an equal fervour. Consequently, it was absurd to suppose that their professions of loyalty would stand the strain of a war, by which not only their national exchequers, but the whole mass of the people must inevitably be impoverished, in which the manhood of the Dominions would be called on for military service, and their defenceless territories placed in danger of invasion.

It was incredible to the wise men at Berlin that the timid but clear minds of English Statesmen had not appreciated these obvious facts. War, therefore, would be avoided as long as possible. And when at a later date, war was forced by Germany upon the pusillanimous islanders, the Dominions would immediately discern various highly moral pleas for standing aloof. Germany, honouring these pleas for the time being with a mock respect, would defer devouring the Dominions until she had digested the more serious meal.

It will be seen from all this how good the grounds were on which the best-informed and most efficient bureaucracy in the world decided that the British Empire would remain neutral in the present war.

CHAPTER VI.

German miscalculations.

Looked at from the strictly intellectual standpoint, the reasons which satisfied German Statesmen with regard to Britain's neutrality were overwhelming, and might well have convinced others, of a similar outlook and training, who had no personal interest whatsoever in coming to one conclusion rather than another.

None the less the judgment of the Kaiser and his Ministers was not only bad, but inexcusably bad. We expect more from statesmen than that they should arrive at logical conclusions. Logic in such cases is nothing; all that matters is to be right; but unless instinct rules and reason serves, right judgment will rarely be arrived at in such matters as these. If a man cannot feel as well as reason, if he cannot gauge the forces which are at work among the nations by some kind of second-sight, he has no title to set up his bills as a statesman. It is incredible that Lincoln, Cavour, or Bismarck would ever have blundered into such a war as this, under the delusion that Britain could remain neutral even if she would. Nor would any of these three have been so far out in his reckoning as to believe, that the immediate effect of such a war, if Britain joined in it, would be the disruption of her empire. They might have calculated that in the event of the war being prolonged and disastrous to England, disintegration would in the end come about; but without stopping to reason the matter out, they would have known by instinct, that the first effect produced by such a war would be a consolidation and knitting together of the loose Imperial fabric, and a suspension, or at least a diminution, of internal differences.

CHAPTER VII

INTERNATIONAL ILL-WILL

Chapter VII.

International ill-will.

In the foregoing pages an attempt has been made to consider the series of events which immediately preceded the recent outbreak of war. But the most complete account of moves and counter-moves, and of all the pretexts, arguments, demands, and appeals which were put forward by the various governments concerned, with the object of forcing on, justifying, circumscribing, or preventing the present struggle, can never give us the true explanation of why it occurred. For this we must look much further back than Midsummer last, and at other things besides the correspondence between Foreign Ministers and Ambassadors.

Nobody in his senses believes that Europe is at present in a convulsion because the heir-presumptive to the throne of Austria was murdered at Serajevo on the 28th of June. This event was tragic and deplorable, but it was merely a spark—one of that cloud of sparks which is always issuing from the chimney-stack of the European furnace. This one by ill-luck happened to fall upon a heap of combustibles, and set it in a blaze.

Great events, as the Greeks discovered several thousand years ago, do not spring from small causes,

CHAPTER VII.

International ill-will.

though more often than not they have some trivial beginning. How came it that so much inflammable material was lying ready to catch fire?

To answer this question truthfully we need more knowledge of men and things than is given in those books, of varying hue, which the Chancelleries of Europe have published to explain their causes of action. The official sources provide much valuable information; but they will never explain to us why public opinion in Germany, ever since the beginning of the present century, has been inflamed with hatred against this country. Nor will they ever give us any clear idea as to what extent, and where, the practical aims and policies of that nation and our own were in conflict.

According to the state papers, it would appear that Russia was drawn into this war because of Servia, and France because of Russia, and Belgium because of France, and we ourselves because of Belgium; but it may well be doubted if even the first of this row of ninepins would have been allowed to fall, had it not been for the feelings which the German people and their rulers entertained towards Britain.

It is always hard for a man to believe in the sincerity, friendliness, and peaceful intentions of one against whom he is himself engaged in plotting an injury. German distrust of England was based upon the surest of all foundations—upon her own fixed and envious determination to overthrow our empire and rob us of our property. Her own mind being filled with this ambition, how could she be otherwise than incredulous of our expressions of goodwill? How could she conceive that we were so blind as not to have penetrated her thoughts, so deaf as not to have heard the threats which her public characters

International ill-will.

were proclaiming so openly? Consequently when British Statesmen uttered amiable assurances they were judged guilty of a treacherous dissimulation. . . . One can only shrug one's shoulders, marvelling at the nightmares and suspicions which a bad conscience is capable of producing even among intelligent people.

It has been the fashion for half a century or more to talk of the Balkans as the danger-point of European peace. In a sense this is true. The crust is very thin in that region, and violent eruptions are of common occurrence. But the real danger of upheaval comes, not so much from the thinness of the crust, as from the violence of the subterranean forces. Of these, by far the most formidable in recent times have been the attitude of public opinion in Germany towards England—the hatred of England which has been sedulously and systematically inculcated among the people of all ranks—the suspicions of our policy which have been sown broadcast—the envy of our position in the world which has been instilled, without remission, by all and sundry the agencies and individuals subject to the orders and inspiration of government. An obsession has been created, by these means, which has distorted the whole field of German vision. National ill-will accordingly has refused to yield to any persuasion. Like its contrary, the passion of love, it has burned all the more fiercely, being unrequited.

The fact which it is necessary to face, fairly and squarely, is that we are fighting the whole German people. We may blame, and blame justly, the Prussian junkers, the German bureaucracy, the Kaiser himself, for having desired this war, schemed

CHAPTER VII.

International ill-will.

for it, set the match to it by intention or through a blunder; but to regard it as a Kaiser's war, or a junkers' war, or a bureaucrats' war is merely to deceive ourselves. It is a people's war if ever there was one. It could not have been more a people's war than it is, even if Germany had been a democracy like France or England.

The Kaiser, as regards this matter, is the mirror of his people. The Army and the Navy are his trusted servants against whom not a word will be believed. The wisdom of the bureaucracy is unquestioned. In matters of faith the zealous eloquence of the learned men is wholly approved. All classes are as one in devotion, and are moved by the same spirit of self-sacrifice. Hardly a murmur of criticism has been heard, even from the multitudes who at other times march under the red flag of Socialism.

Although a German panic with regard to Russia may have been the proximate occasion of this war, the force which most sustains it in its course is German hatred of England. We must recognise this fact with candour, however painful it may be. And we must also note that, during the past nine months, the feelings against England have undergone a change by no means for the better.

At the beginning the German people, if we may judge from published utterances, were convinced that the war had been engineered by Russia, and that England had meanly joined in it, because she saw her chance of crushing a dangerous and envied rival.

Two months later, however, it was equally clear that the German people were persuaded—Heaven

International ill-will.

knows how or why !—that the war had been engineered by England, who was using France and Russia as her tools. Behind Russia, France, Belgium, Servia, and Japan—according to this view—stood Britain —perfidious throughout the ages—guiding her puppets with indefatigable skill to the destruction of German trade, colonies, navy, and world-power.

Confiding Germany, in spite of all her unremitting abuse of Britain, had apparently, for some reason, really believed her to be a friend and a fellow Teuton! Could any treachery have been blacker than our own in outraging these family affections? And for Britain to support the Slav and the Celt against the Teuton, was judged to be the worst treachery of all—race treachery—especially by the Prussians, who, having forgotten that they themselves are half Slavs, seemed also to have forgotten that the British are largely Celts.

Every Englishman, whether he be an admirer of Sir Edward Grey's administration of Foreign Affairs or not, knows these dark suspicions to be merely nonsense. He knows this as one of the common certainties of existence—just as he knows that ginger is hot i' the mouth. Every Englishman knows that Sir Edward Grey, his colleagues, his advisers, his supporters in Parliament and out of it, and the whole British race throughout the world, hated the idea of war, and would have done—and in fact did, so far as in them lay—everything they could think of to avert it. Yet the German people do not at present believe a single word of this; and there must be some reason for their disbelief as for other things.

Unfortunately the nations of the world never

CHAPTER VII.

International ill-will.

see one another face to face. They carry on their intercourse, friendly and otherwise, by high-angle fire, from hidden batteries of journalistic howitzers. Sometimes the projectiles which they exchange are charged with ideal hate which explodes and kills; at others with ideal love and admiration which dissolve in golden showers, delightful and amazing to behold. But always the gunners are invisible to each other, and the ideal love and admiration are often as far removed from the real merits of their objective as the ideal hate.

That there was no excuse, beyond mere fancy on Germany's part, for her distrust of British policy, no one, unless he were wholly ignorant of the facts, would dream of maintaining. During the years which have passed since 1870, our intentions have very rarely been unfriendly. Still more rarely, however, have we ever shown any real comprehension of the German point of view. Never have we made our policy clear. The last is hardly to be wondered at, seeing that we had not ourselves taken the pains to understand it.

On occasions, it is true, we have been effusive, and have somewhat overstepped the limits of dignity, plunging into a gushing sentimentality, or else wheedling and coaxing, with some material object—the abatement of naval expenditure, for example—showing very plainly through our blandishments. And as our methods at these times have been lacking in self-respect, it is not wonderful if they have earned little or no respect from others. Our protestations that we were friends, our babble about blood-relationship, were suspected to have their origin in timidity; our appeals for restriction of armaments, to our aversion from personal sacrifice and our senile penuriousness.

International ill-will.

Until lately these lapses into excessive amiability, it must be allowed, were not very frequent. The main excuse for German suspicion is to be found elsewhere—in the dilatoriness of our foreign policy—in its inability to make up its mind—in its changeability after its mind might have been supposed made up—in its vagueness with regard to the nature of our obligations towards other powers—whom we would support, and to what extent, and upon what pleas.

Irritation on the part of Germany would have been natural in these circumstances, even if she had not been in the mood to suspect dark motives in the background. From the days of Lord Granville to those of Sir Edward Grey, we had been dealing with a neighbour who, whatever her failings might be, was essentially businesslike in her methods. We, on the other hand, continued to exhibit many of those faults which are most ill-regarded by business men. We would not say clearly what regions came within our sphere of influence. We would not say clearly where Germany might go and where we should object to her going; but wherever she went, we were apt after the event to grumble and make trouble.

The delay and indecision which marked Lord Granville's dealings with Bismarck over the partition of Africa were both bad manners in the international sense, and bad policy. The neglect of Sir Edward Grey, after Agadir, to make clear to his fellow-countrymen, and to the world at large, the nature and extent of our obligations to France, was bad business. Next

CHAPTER VII.

International ill-will.

to the British people and our present allies, Germany had the best reason to complain of this procedure, or rather of this failure to proceed.

The blame for this unfortunate record rests mainly upon our political system, rather than on individuals. We cannot enjoy the benefits of the most highly developed party system in the world, without losing by it in various directions. A change of Government, actual or impending, has more often been the cause of procrastination and uncertainty than change in the mind of the Foreign Minister. There are people who assure us that this must always be so, that it is one of the inherent weaknesses of party government, and even of democracy itself. This is not altogether true. It is true, however, that whereas statesmen may be reticent and keep their own counsel under an autocracy, they are bound to be frank, and simple, and outspoken as to their aims, where their power is drawn directly from popular support.

The criticism against British foreign policy for upwards of a century, is that it has aimed at managing our international relations on a system of hoodwinking the people, which is altogether incompatible with the nature of our institutions. The evils which have resulted from this mistake are not confined to ourselves, but have reacted abroad. "With whom," we can imagine some perplexed foreign Chancellor asking himself—"with whom does power really 'rest in England? With the Government or with 'the people? With which of these am I to deal? 'To which must I address myself? As regards 'France there is little difficulty, for her policy is 'national, and agreed on all hands. But in England, 'so far as we can judge, the people have no idea of

International ill-will.

'being dragged under any circumstances into a 'European war; while on the other hand, the Government is obviously drifting, consciously or unconsciously, into continental relations which, in certain 'events, can lead to no other result. . . ." Nor is it surprising that under these conditions German diplomacy should have directed itself of late, with much industry, to the cultivation of public opinion in this country, and should at times have treated our Government with scant respect.

The fact is that the two nations, which had most to gain by clear-sighted and tactful foreign policy, were perhaps of all nations in the world the least well served in that particular. English relations with Germany have for many years past been more mismanaged than anything except German relations with England. In their mutual diplomacy the fingers of both nations have been all thumbs.

It is not to be wondered at that two characters so antagonistic in their natures and methods as English and German foreign policy should have come to regard one another as impossible. The aggressive personage who does know his own mind, and the vague, supercilious personage who does not, have only one point in common—that they understand and care very little about the feelings of other people. But although this is a point in common, it is anything but a point of agreement.[1]

[1] If we may offer a very homely simile—German policy may be compared to a rude heavy fellow, who comes shoving his way into a crowded bus, snorting aggressively, treading on everybody's corns, poking his umbrella into people's eyes, and finally plumping himself down without a word of regret or apology, between the two meekest and most helpless-looking of the passengers.

British diplomacy, on the other hand, bears a close resemblance to a nuisance, equally well known to the bus public, and no less dreaded. It

CHAPTER VII.

International ill-will.

The causes of what has happened will never be clear to us unless we can arrive at some understanding of the ideas, aspirations, and dreams which have filled the minds of the German people and our own during recent years. On logical grounds we must consider the case of Germany first, for the reason that all the warmth of enmity has proceeded from her side, and, until recent events suddenly aroused the Old Adam in us, the uncharitable sentiments of our neighbours were not at all cordially reciprocated over here.

As in romantic drama, according to the cynics, there is usually one who loves and another who allows itself to be loved, so in this case there was one who hated and another who allowed itself to be hated. The British nation could not understand why the Germans were so angry and suspicious. Nor would it trouble to understand. It was bored with the whole subject; and even the irritation which it felt at having to find huge sums annually for the Navy did not succeed in shaking it out of its boredom.

The most careful analysis of our thoughts about Germany would do little to explain matters, because, as it happened, by far the greater part of our thoughts was occupied with other things. Indeed we thought about Germany as little as we could help thinking; and although we regretted her annoyance,

---

reminds us constantly of that dawdling, disobliging female who never can make up her mind, till the bus has actually started, whether she wants to go to Shepherd's Bush or the Mansion House. If she has taken a seat she insists on stopping the conveyance in order to get out. If she has remained gaping on the pavement she hails it in order to get in. She cares nothing about the inconvenience caused thereby to other passengers, who do know whither they want to be conveyed, and desire to arrive at their destination as quickly as possible.

our consciences absolved us from any responsibility for it.

International ill-will.

It was entirely different with Germany. For many years past she had been more occupied with her grievances against Britain, and with the complications and dangers which would beset any attempt at redress, than with any other single subject; or indeed, so it would appear, with all other subjects put together.

It is important to understand the German point of view, but it is difficult. For at once we are faced with the eternal obstacle of the foreigner, who sets out in search of a simple explanation. The mind of the ordinary man, like that of the philosopher, is hypnotised by a basic assumption of the One-ness of Things. He wants to trace all trouble to a single root, as if it were a corn and could be extracted. But in an enquiry like the present we are confronted at every turn with the Two-ness of Things, or indeed with the Multiplicity of Things.

We have only to read a few pages of any German book on England to see that the other party to the dispute is confronted with exactly the same difficulty. We are amazed, and perhaps not altogether chagrined, to discover that, to German eyes, British policy appears to be a thing of the most rigorous consistency. It is deliberate, far-sighted, and ruthless. It is pursued with constancy from decade to decade—nay from century to century—never faltering, never retreating, but always going forward under Whig and Tory, Liberal and Conservative alike, to the same goal. And we of course know, if we know anything, that this picture, though very flattering to our political instinct, is untrue.

CHAPTER VII.

International ill-will.

If Englishmen know anything at all, they know that the foreign policy of this country during the last fifty years—under Lord Beaconsfield, and Mr. Gladstone, Lord Salisbury, and Mr. Asquith—has been at times a series of the most eccentric wobbles and plunges, like a kite which is drawn at the wrong angle to the wind. Nay, even as regards our participation in this very War—which in the German White Book is asserted to have been preconceived and undertaken by us with a craft and coolness worthy of Machiavelli himself—we can see from our own White Paper that the final decision wavered this way and the other, from day to day during the critical week, neither the Cabinet nor public opinion being clear and unanimous as to the course which ought to be pursued.

Vacillation in national policy usually appears to hostile observers in the light of perfidy. And it must be admitted that there is good excuse for the mistake, seeing that weakness in such high matters is quite as likely to injure everybody concerned as wickedness itself.

Assuredly no sensible person who was required to make a defence of British foreign policy, either during the century which has passed since the battle of Waterloo, or in the much shorter period since the death of Queen Victoria, would ever dream of doing so on the ground that its guiding principles have been consistency and singleness of purpose. These, indeed, are almost the last virtues he would think of claiming for it. And yet these are the very qualities which foreign nations are inclined to attribute to British statesmen, by way of praise or blame. Our failures are apt to be overlooked by outside

International ill-will.

observers; our successes on the other hand are plain and memorable. Other nations assume that because we have happened to achieve some particular result, we must therefore have deliberately and patiently set out to achieve it. Much more often this result has been due either to pure good luck or else to some happy inspiration of the moment.

A wise apologist for our foreign policy would at once concede that it has frequently been characterised by feebleness and indecision, and almost always by a want of clear perception of the end in view; but he could contend with justice that upon the whole, for upwards of a century, it has meant well by other nations, and that accusations of far-sighted duplicity are purely ridiculous.

Our own temptation on the other hand is to visualise a single, gross, overbearing, and opinionated type of the Teuton species. We tend to ignore important differences; and because German public opinion appears to be unanimous in regard to the present War, we are apt to overlook the fact that the love and admiration of the Bavarian and the Saxon for the Prussian are probably some degrees less cordial than those which the men of Kerry and Connemara entertain for the Belfast Covenanters. And we incline also to forget, that though opinion in Germany in favour of war became solid so soon as war was apprehended, and certainly before it was declared, it is exceedingly unlikely, that even in governing circles, there was an equal unanimity as to the procedure which led up to the climax.

If it were really so, the case is unique in history, which shows us at every other crisis of this sort always the same triangle of forces—a War party, a Peace

CHAPTER VII.

International ill-will.

party, and a Wait-and-See party; each of them pulling vigorously in its own direction; each intriguing against, and caballing with, the other two by turns; until at last the group, still struggling, falls back on the side of safety or, as in the recent instance, pitches over the edge of the precipice.

It would be very hard to persuade any student of history that something of this sort was not occurring both in Vienna and Berlin during the months of June and July 1914. While he would admit to more than a suspicion that intelligences had been passing for a considerably longer period—for a year at least[1] —between the War parties in these two capitals, he would be inclined to take the view, that in the last stage of all, the Berlin group went staggering to perdition, dragging after it the Vienna group, which by that time was struggling feebly in the opposite direction.

When we come to consider the German case it is wise to bear in mind the erroneous judgments which foreigners have passed upon ourselves. It is probable that the One-ness of things which we discover in their actions is to some extent an illusion, like that which they have discovered in our own. Indeed it is a fruitless task to hunt for logic and consistency in things which, in their nature, are neither logical nor consistent. For most of us, who have but a limited range of German books, state papers, journalism, and acquaintances to judge from, it would be vain and foolish to pretend that in a chapter, or a volume, we can lay bare the German attitude of

[1] We have recently learned from Signor Giolitti, ex-Premier of Italy, that in August 1913 the Foreign Minister, the late Marquis di San Giuliano, was sounded by Austria-Hungary as to whether he would join in an attack upon Servia.

International ill-will.

mind. The most we can hope to do is to illuminate this complex subject at certain points; and these for the most part are where the edges rub, and where German policy and temperament have happened to come into conflict with our own.

PART II

THE SPIRIT OF GERMAN POLICY

CHRISTIAN: Met you with nothing else in that Valley?

FAITHFUL: Yes, I met with *Shame*. But of all the Men I met with in my Pilgrimage, he I think bears the wrong name: . . . this boldfaced *Shame*, would never have done.

CHRISTIAN: Why, what did he say to you?

FAITHFUL: What! why he objected against Religion itself; he said it was a pitiful low sneaking business for a Man to mind Religion; he said that a tender conscience was an unmanly thing, and that for a Man to watch over his words and ways, so as to tye up himself from that hectoring liberty that the brave spirits of the times accustom themselves unto, would make me the Ridicule of the times.

He objected also, that but few of the Mighty, Rich, or Wise, were ever of my opinion; nor any of them, neither, before they were perswaded to be Fools, and to be of a voluntary fondness to venture the loss of all, *for no body else knows what*.

Yea, he did hold me to it at that rate also about a great many more things than here I relate; as, that it was a *shame*. . . to ask my neighbour forgiveness for petty faults, or to make restitution where I had taken from any. He said also that Religion made a man grow strange to the great because of a few vices (which he called by finer names). . . .

The Pilgrim's Progress.

CHAPTER I

THE BISMARCKIAN EPOCH

CHAPTER I. — The Bismarckian epoch.

ALL nations dream—some more than others; while some are more ready than others to follow their dreams into action. Nor does the prevalence, or even the intensity, of these national dreams seem to bear any fixed relation to the strength of will which seeks to turn them into achievement.

After 1789 there was a great deal of dreaming among the nations of Europe. At the beginning of it all was revolutionary France, who dreamed of offering freedom to all mankind. A few years later, an altogether different France was dreaming furiously of glory for her own arms. In the end it was still France who dreamed; and this time she sought to impose the blessings of peace, order, and uniformity upon the whole world. Her first dream was realised in part, the second wholly; but the third ended in ruin.

Following upon this momentous failure came a short period when the exhausted nations slept much too soundly to dream dreams. During this epoch Europe was parcelled out artificially, like a patchwork quilt, by practical and unimaginative diplomatists, anxious certainly to take securities for a lasting

CHAPTER I.

peace, but still more anxious to bolster up the ancient dynasties.

The Bismarckian epoch.

Against their arbitrary expedients there was soon a strong reaction, and dreaming began once more among the nations, as they turned in their sleep, and tried to stretch their hampered limbs. At the beginning their dreaming was of a mild and somewhat futile type. It called itself 'liberalism'—a name coined upon the continent of Europe. It aimed by methods of peaceful persuasion, at reaching the double goal of nationality as the ideal unit of the state, and popular representation as the ideal system of government. Then the seams of the patchwork, which had been put together with so much labour at Vienna [1] and Aix-la-Chapelle,[2] began to gape. Greece struggled with some success to free herself from the Turk,[3] and Belgium broke away from Holland,[4] as at a much later date Norway severed her union with Sweden.[5] In 1848 there were revolutions all over Europe, the objects of which were the setting up of parliamentary systems. In all directions it seemed as if the dynastic stitches were coming undone. Italy dreamed of union and finally achieved it,[6] expelling the Austrian encroachers—though not by peaceful persuasion—and disordering still further the neatly sewn handiwork of Talleyrand, Metternich, and Castlereagh. Finally, the Balkans began to dream of Slav destinies, unrealisable either under the auspices of the Sublime Porte or in tutelage to the Habsburgs.[7]

But of all the nations which have dreamed since days long before Napoleon, none has dreamed more

[1] 1814. [2] 1818. [3] 1821–1829. [4] 1830. [5] 1905. [6] 1859–1861. [7] 1875–1878.

The Bismarckian epoch.

nobly or more persistently than Germany. For the first half of the nineteenth century it seemed as if the Germans were satisfied to behold a vision without attempting to turn it into a reality. Their aspirations issued in no effective action. They dreamed of union between their many kingdoms, principalities, and duchies, and of building up a firm empire against which all enemies would beat in vain; but until 1864 they had gone but a few steps towards the achievement of this end.

Then within a period of seven years, Prussia, the most powerful of the German states, planned, provoked, and carried to a successful issue three wars of aggression. By a series of swift strokes, the genius of Bismarck snatched Schleswig-Holstein from the Danes, beat down the pretensions of Austria to the leadership of the Teutonic races, and wrested the provinces of Alsace and Lorraine from France. When Denmark was invaded by Germanic armies in February 1864, the vision of unity seemed as remote as ever; by January 1871 it was fully achieved. When at Versailles, in the Hall of Mirrors, in the stately palace of the Bourbons, King William accepted from the hands of his peers—the sovereign rulers of Germany—an imperial crown, the dream of centuries was fulfilled.

Austria, indeed, stood aloof; but both by reason of her geographical situation and the heterogeneous ancestry of her people that was a matter only of small account. Union was, for all practical purposes complete. And what made the achievement all the more marvellous was the fact, that the vision had been realised by methods which had no place in the gentle speculations of those, who had cherished the

CHAPTER I.

The Bismarckian epoch.

hope of unity with the most fervent loyalty. It had been accomplished by the Prussians, who of all races between the Alps and the Baltic, between the mountain barriers of Burgundy and the Polish Marshes, are the least German in blood,[1] and who of all Germans dream the least. It had been carried through, not by peaceful persuasion, nor on any principles of Liberalism, nor in any of the ways foreseen by the philosophers and poets who had beheld visions of the millennium. Union was the triumph of craft and calculation, courage and resolve, 'blood and iron.'

The world in general, whose thoughts at this time were much more congenially occupied with International Exhibitions, and Peace Societies, and the ideals of Manchester statesmanship, was inclined to regard the whole of this series of events as an anachronism—as the belated offspring of 'militarism' and 'feudalism.' These were well known to be both in their dotage; they could not possibly survive for many years. What had happened, therefore, did not startle mankind simply because the nature of it was not understood. The spirit of the age, wholly possessed, as it was, by an opposite set of ideas, was unable to comprehend, to believe in, or even to consider with patience, phenomena which, according to prevailing theories, had no reasonable basis of existence.

In some quarters, indeed, efforts were made to gloss over the proceedings of Prince Bismarck, and to fit them into the fashionable theory of a universe, flowing with the milk of human kindness and the

[1] The admixture of Slavonic and Wendish blood in the Prussian stock is usually calculated by ethnologists at about half and half.

The Bismarckian epoch.

honey of material prosperity. It was urged that the Germans were a people, pure in their morals, industrious in their habits, the pioneers of higher education and domestic economy. For the most part, British and American public opinion was inclined to regard these various occurrences and conquests as a mediaeval masquerade, in rather doubtful taste, but of no particular significance and involving no serious consequences. Even in that enlightened age, however, there were still a few superstitious persons who saw ghosts. To their eyes the shade of Richard Cobden seemed in some danger of being eclipsed in the near future by that of Niccolo Machiavelli; though the former had died in great honour and prestige only a few years earlier, while the latter had been dead, discredited, and disavowed for almost as many centuries.

After 1870 Germany entered upon a period of peaceful prosperity. Forges clanged, workshops throbbed, looms hummed, and within twenty years, the ebb of emigration had entirely ceased. Indeed, not only was there work in the Fatherland for all its sons, but for others besides; so that long before another twenty years had passed away, the tide had turned and immigrants were pouring in.

At first the larger part of German exports was cheap and nasty, with a piratical habit of sailing under false colours, and simulating well-known British and other national trade-marks. But this was a brief interlude. The sagacity, thoroughness, and enterprise of manufacturers and merchants soon guided their steps past this dangerous quicksand, and the label *made in Germany* ceased to be a reproach.

CHAPTER I.

The Bismarckian epoch.

Students and lovers of truth laboured at discovery; and hard upon their heels followed a crowd of practical inventors—the gleaners, scavengers, and rag-pickers of science. Never had the trade of any country thriven with a more wonderful rapidity. Though still of necessity a borrower by very reason of her marvellous expansion, Germany nevertheless began to make her influence felt in the financial sphere. Her own ships carried her products to the ends of the earth, and fetched home raw materials in exchange. And not only this, her merchant fleets began to enter into successful competition for the carrying trade of the world, even with the Mistress of the Seas herself.

For a score of years after the fall of Paris, Germany found but little time for dreaming. Meanwhile, by an astute if somewhat tortuous policy, and under the impenetrable shield of the finest army in Europe, Bismarck kept safe the empire which he had founded. He declined to be drawn into adventures either at home or abroad, either in the new world or the old. He opposed the colonial aspirations of a few visionaries, who began to make some noise towards the end of his long reign, and silenced them with some spacious but easy acquisitions in Africa and the East. He consolidated the Prussian autocracy, and brought its servant, the bureaucracy, to the highest pitch of efficiency. He played with the political parties in the Reichstag as if they had been a box of dominoes, combining them into what patterns he pleased. At the same time he fostered the national well-being with ceaseless vigilance, and kept down popular discontent by the boldness and thoroughness of his social legislation. But for Bismarck himself

The Bismarckian epoch.

the age of adventure was past. It was enough that by the labours of an arduous lifetime, he had made of Germany a puissant state, in which all her children, even the most restless, could find full scope for their soaring ambitions.

CHAPTER II

AFTER BISMARCK

CHAPTER II.

After Bismarck.

WITH the dismissal of Bismarck in 1890, Germany entered upon a new phase. Then once again her people began to dream, and this time furiously. They had conquered in war. They had won great victories in peace. According to their own estimate they were the foremost thinkers of the world. They found themselves impelled by a limitless ambition and a superb self-confidence. But the vision which now presented itself to their eyes was disordered and tumultuous. Indeed it was less dream than nightmare; and in some degree, no doubt, it owed its origin, like other nightmares, to a sudden surfeit—to a glut of material prosperity.[1]

Why did Germany with her larger population still lag behind Britain in commerce and shipping? Surely the reason could only be that Britain, at every turn, sought to cripple the enterprise of her young rival. Why had Britain a great and thriving colonial empire, while Germany had only a few tracts of tropical jungle and light soil, not particularly prosperous or promising? The reason could only be that, out of jealousy, Britain had obstructed Teutonic acquisition. Why was Germany tending

[1] "L'Allemand est né bête; la civilisation l'a rendu méchant."—HEINE.

After Bismarck.

to become more and more isolated and unpopular in Europe? The reason could only be that the crafty and unscrupulous policy of Britain had intrigued, with some success, for her political ostracism.

It is useless to argue with a man in a nightmare. He brushes reason aside and cares not for facts. But to seekers after truth it was obvious, that so far from making any attack upon German commerce, Britain, by adhering to her system of free trade at home and in her dependencies, had conferred a boon immeasurable on this new and eager competitor. So far from hindering Germany's acquisition of colonies, Britain had been careless and indifferent in the matter; perhaps too much so for the security of some of her own possessions. It was Bismarck, much more than Britain, who had put obstacles in the way of German colonial expansion. With a sigh of relief (as we may imagine) this great statesman saw the partition of the vacant territories of the world completed, and his fellow-countrymen thereby estopped from wasting their substance, and dissipating their energies, in costly and embarrassing adventures. So far from holding aloof from Germany or attempting to isolate her among European nations, we had persisted in treating her with friendliness, long after she had ceased to be friendly. One of our leading statesmen had even gone the length of suggesting an alliance, and had been denounced immediately by the whole German press, although it was understood at the time that he had spoken with the august encouragement of the Kaiser and his Chancellor.[1] It was Germany herself, deprived of the guidance of Bismarck, who by blustering at

[1] Mr. Chamberlain at Leicester on November 30, 1899.

CHAPTER II. — After Bismarck.

her various neighbours, and threatening them in turn, had aroused their suspicions and achieved her own isolation.

The grievances against Britain which figured in the phantasmagoria of the German nightmare were obviously tinged with envy. There were other grievances against France, and these were tinged with annoyance. For France, although she had been beaten on to her knees, had nevertheless had the impudence to make a successful recovery. There were also grievances against Russia, and these were tinged with fear. Her vast adjacent territories and teeming population, her social and industrial progress, the reformation of her government, and the rapid recuperation of her military and naval power, constituted in German eyes the gravest menace of all.

Self-confidence and ambition were the original stuff—the warp and the weft—of which the German dream was made; but these admirable and healthy qualities rapidly underwent a morbid deterioration. Ambition degenerated into groundless suspicion, and self-confidence into arrogance. It was a considerable time, however, before Germany was realised to have become a public danger by reason of her mental affliction. Until her prophets and high priests began preaching from the housetops as a divine ordinance, that Germany was now so great, prosperous, and prolific as to need the lands of her neighbours for her expansion, her symptoms were not generally recognised. It was not really pressure of population, but only the oppression of a nightmare which had brought her to this restless and excited condition. In terms of psychology, the disease from which Germany has been suffering of late years is known as megalomania, in the slang of the street-corner as madness of the swollen head.

After Bismarck.

The dreams of a nation may be guided well or ill by statesmen, or they may be left altogether unguided. The dreams of Italy under Cavour, and those of Germany under Bismarck, were skilfully fostered and directed with great shrewdness to certain practical ends. But in considering the case of Germany under William the Second, our feeling is that although popular imaginings have been controlled from above with even greater solicitude than before, the persons who inspired and regulated them have been lacking in the sense of proportion. The governing power would seem to have been the victim of changing moods, conflicting policies, and disordered purposes.

When we piece together the various schemes for the aggrandisement of the Fatherland, which German writers have set forth with increasing boldness and perfect gravity during the past ten years, we are confronted with an immense mosaic—a conception of the most grandiose character. On examination each of these projects is found to be based upon two fundamental assumptions :—The first, that the present boundaries of Germany and her possessions overseas are too narrow to contain the legitimate aspirations of the German race :—The second that it is the immediate interest of Germany, as well as a duty which she owes to posterity, to remedy this deficiency, by taking from her neighbours by force what she requires for her own expansion. There is a third assumption, not however of a political so much as an ethical character, which is stated with

CHAPTER II.

After Bismarck.

equal frankness and conviction—that war on an extensive scale is necessary, from time to time, in order to preserve the vigour of the German people and their noble spirit.

One school of dreamers, with its gaze fixed upon the Atlantic trade-routes, insists upon the absurdity of resting content with a western sea-board of some two hundred miles. The estuaries of the Elbe and the Weser alone are exclusively German; that of the Ems is shared with the Dutch; while the far more valuable harbour-mouths of the Rhine and the Scheldt are in the possession of Holland and Belgium. Put into plain language what this means is, that both Holland and Belgium must be incorporated in the German Empire; if by treaty, so much the better for all parties concerned; but if diplomacy should fail to accomplish the desired absorption, then it must be brought about by war. Nor has it been overlooked, that in order to complete the rectification, and to secure the keys of the Baltic, it would be necessary to 'admit' Denmark also into the privileges of the Germanic Empire.

Another school looks to the south-east and broods upon the day, not far distant, when the Germans of Austria-Hungary—a small but dominating minority of the whole population—will be driven, by reasons of self-defence, to seek a federal inclusion in the Empire of the Hohenzollerns. And it is surmised that for somewhat similar reasons the Magyars of Hungary will at the same time elect to throw in their lot with Teutons rather than with Slavs.

When that day arrives, however, it is not merely the German and Magyar territories of the Habsburg Emperor-King which will need to be incorporated

After Bismarck.

in the Hohenzollern Empire, but the whole congeries of nations which at present submits, more or less reluctantly, to the rule of Vienna and Buda-Pest. There must be no break-up of the empire of Francis Joseph, no sentimental sacrifice to the mumbo-jumbos of nationality. The Italians of Trieste and Fiume, the Bohemians, the Croats, the Serbs, the Roumanians of Transylvania, and the Poles of Galicia must all be kept together in one state, even more firmly than they are to-day. The Germans of Austria will not be cordially welcomed, unless they bring this dowry with them to the altar of imperial union.

But to clear eyes, looking into the future, more even than this appears to be necessary. Austria will be required to bring with her, not merely all her present possessions, but also her reversionary prospects, contingent remainders, and all and sundry her rights of action throughout the whole Balkan peninsula, which sooner or later must either accept the hegemony of the German Empire or submit to annexation at the sword's point. Advantageous as it would be for the Fatherland to obtain great harbours for her commerce at the head of the Adriatic, these acquisitions might easily become valueless in practice if some rival barred the right of entry through the Straits of Otranto. Salonica again, in her snug and sheltered corner of the Aegean, is essential as the natural entrepôt for the trade of Asia Minor and the East; while there can be no hope, until the mouths of the Danube, as well as the Dardanelles and the Bosphorus, are firmly held, of turning the Black Sea into a Germanic lake.

The absorption of the Balkan peninsula, involving

After Bismarck.

as it must the occupation of Constantinople and European Turkey, would carry with it, as a natural consequence, the custody of the Sultan and the control of his Asiatic dominions. These vast territories which extend from Smyrna to the Caucasus, from Syria to the Persian Gulf, from the Black Sea to the Gulf of Aden, contain some of the richest and most fertile tracts upon the surface of the globe. Massacre, misrule, and oppression have indeed converted the greater part of these regions into a state hardly to be distinguished from the barest deserts of Arabia. But a culture which has lapsed through long neglect may be reclaimed by new enterprise. All that is required to this end is such shelter and encouragement as a stable government would afford.

What more suitable instrument for this beneficent recovery than the peculiar genius of the Teuton race? Would not the whole world gain by the substitution of settled order for a murderous anarchy, of tilth and industry for a barren desolation? The waters of Tigris and Euphrates are still sweet. It needs but the energy and art of man to lead them in channelled courses, quenching the longings of a thirsty land, and filling the Mesopotamian waste with the music of a myriad streams. The doom of Babylon is no curse eternal. It awaits but the sword of Siegfried to end the slumbers of two thousand years. Where great cities and an ancient civilisation lie buried under drifted sand, great cities may be raised once more, the habitations of a hardier race, the seminaries of a nobler civilisation.

This vision, more fanciful and poetically inspired than the rest, has already advanced some consider-

After Bismarck.

able way beyond the frontiers of dreamland. When the Turko-Russian War came to an end [1] the influence of Germany at Constantinople was as nearly as possible nil; and so long as Bismarck remained in power, no very serious efforts were made to increase it. But from the date of Bismarck's dismissal [2] down to the present day, it has been the steady aim of German policy to control the destinies of the Turkish Empire. These attempts have been persistent, and in the main successful.

It mattered not what dubious personage or party might happen to be in the ascendant at Stamboul, the friendship of Germany was always forthcoming. It was extended with an equal cordiality to Abdul Hamid; to the Young Turks when they overthrew Abdul Hamid; to the Reactionaries when they overthrew the Young Turks; to the Young Turks again when they compounded matters with the Reactionaries. The largesse of Berlin bankers refreshed the empty treasuries of each despot and camarilla in turn, so soon as proofs could be produced of positive, or even of presumptive predominance. At the same time the makers of armaments, at Essen and elsewhere, looked to it, that a sufficient portion of these generous loans was paid in kind, and that the national gain was not confined to high policy and high finance. The reform of the Turkish army was taken in hand zealously by Prussian soldiers. Imperial courtesies cemented the bricks which usury, commerce, and diplomacy had laid so well. At a time when the late Sultan was ill-regarded by the whole of Europe, on account of his supposed complicity in Armenian massacres, the

[1] March 1878. Treaty of Berlin, July 1878. [2] 1890.

CHAPTER II.

After Bismarck.

magnanimity of the Kaiser took pity on the pariah, and a visit of honour to the Bosphorus formed an incident in the Hohenzollern pilgrimage to the Holy Sepulchre.

The harvest of these endeavours was reaped at a later date in the form of vast concessions for lines of railway running through Asia Minor to the Persian Gulf. It is needless to enter here into a discussion of the famous and still unsettled controversy regarding the Baghdad route, except to say that this project for the benefit, not merely of Turkey, but of the whole human race, was to be realised under German direction and according to German plans and specifications; it was to be administered under German control; but it was to be paid for in the main out of the savings of England and France.

The scheme was no less bold than ingenious. Obligations were imposed upon Turkey which it was clearly impossible for Turkey to discharge. In the event of her failure it was likely to go hard with the original shareholders, and somewhat hard with the Sublime Porte itself; but on the other hand it was not likely to go hard with Germany, or to involve her in anything more irksome than a labour of love—a protectorate over Asia Minor and Arabia.[1]

These are the main dreams which German writers, with a genuine enthusiasm and an engaging frankness, have set out in the pages of books and periodicals—the North Sea dream, the Austrian dream, the Balkan dream, and the Levantine dream. But these dreams by no means exhaust the Teuton fancy.

Wars are contemplated calmly as inevitable

[1] Cf. *The Anglo-German Problem*, by C. Sarolea, p. 247, and following.

After Bismarck.

incidents in the acquisition of world-power—war with France, war with England, war either of army corps or diplomacy with Belgium, Holland, and Denmark. And as victory is also contemplated, just as confidently, various bye-products of considerable value are likely to be secured during the process, and as a result.

The greater part of north-western Africa, which lies along the seaboards of the Mediterranean and the Atlantic, is under the French flag. The greater part of eastern Africa from Alexandria to Capetown is in the hands of the British. The central region of Africa is Belgian. In the north there is Tripoli which is now Italian; and in various quarters patches and scattered islands which are Portuguese. The former might be tolerated as a harmless enclave; the latter might readily be acquired by compulsory purchase. What would then remain of the Dark Continent is already German. So that, as the results of the wars and victories which are considered by German thinkers to be inevitable, the whole of Africa would shortly pass into German hands.

With the destinies of Africa in the keeping of a virile race, accustomed to face great problems in no piecemeal fashion, but as a whole, vast transformations must ensue. Before their indomitable will and scientific thoroughness, the dusky savage will lay aside his ferocity, and toil joyously at the arts of peace. Under an indefatigable and intelligent administration, desert, jungle, forest, and swamp will yield their appropriate harvests. Timber, oil, cotton, rubber, tea, coffee, and every variety of raw material will gradually become available in limitless supplies. Jewels and precious metals will

CHAPTER II.

After Bismarck.

be dug out of the bowels of the earth. Flocks and herds will roam in safety over the rich uplands—no robber bands to drive them off; no wild beasts to tear them limb from limb; no murrain or envenomed fly to strike them down by tens of thousands. For as the armies of the Kaiser are invincible against all human foes, so also are his men of science invincible, in their ceaseless war against disease of man and beast. In the end they also will conquer in their own sphere, no less certainly than the soldier in his; for their courage is as high and their devotion faces death, or worse than death, with equanimity.

The Dark Continent, which in all its history has never known either peace or order, will then at last know both. Even the stiff-necked Africander, jealous of his antique shibboleths of freedom, will not refuse incorporation in an Empire to which the land of his forefathers will already have become bound in federal ties. And the dowry which Holland is expected to bring with her, will be not only the good will of the South African Dutch, but the rich islands of the East, where merchant-adventurers planted her flag, in days when the fleets of Rotterdam disputed, not unsuccessfully, with London herself the primacy of the seas.

Finally, there is the dream of the farthest East. This is of such simple grandeur that it may be stated in a few sentences. When the war between China and Japan came to an end in 1895 Germany, acting in concert with France and Russia, forced the victorious troops of the Mikado to forgo all the fruits of their conquest. When three years later Germany herself seized upon the reversion of Kiao-Chau, she saw a vision of an empire, greater than that which had been secured to her envied rival by the daring of Clive and the forethought of Warren Hastings. If England could hold and rule India, a mightier than England could surely hold and rule China, containing though it does a full quarter of the human race.

CHAPTER II.

After Bismarck.

CHAPTER III

THE GERMAN PROJECT OF EMPIRE

CHAPTER III.

The German project of empire.

THE German project of empire is a gorgeous fabric. The weft of it is thread of gold, but the warp of it has been dipped in the centaur's blood. It is the pride of its possessor; but it is likely to be his undoing. It ravishes his fancy with the symmetry and vastness of the pattern; yet these very two qualities, which so much excite his admiration, have shown themselves in the past singularly unpropitious to high imperial adventures.

No man of action worthy of the name will ever take history for his guide. He would rightly refuse to do so, even were it possible, which it is not, to write history truthfully. But with all their deficiencies, history books have certain sibylline qualities which make them worth consulting upon occasions; and as to symmetry and vastness this oracle, if consulted, would speak clearly enough. Of all false enticements which have lured great princes to their ruin, these two have the biggest tale of victims to their score.

The British Empire, like the Roman, built itself slowly. It was the way of both nations to deal with needs as needs occurred, and not before. Neither of them charted out their projects in advance, there-

The German project of empire.

after working to them, like Lenôtre, when he laid out the gardens of Versailles. On the contrary, a strip was added here, a kingdom there, as time went on, but not in accordance with any plan or system. In certain cases, no doubt, the reason for annexation was a simple desire for possession. But much more often the motive was apprehension of one kind or another. Empire-builders have usually achieved empire as an accident attending their search after security—security against the ambition of a neighbour, against lawless hordes which threaten the frontier, against the fires of revolution and disorder spreading from adjacent territories. Britain, like Rome before her, built up her empire piecemeal; for the most part reluctantly; always reckoning up and dreading the cost, labour, and burden of it; hating the responsibility of expansion, and shouldering it only when there seemed to be no other course open to her in honour or safety. Symmetry did not appeal to either of these nations any more than vastness. Their realms spread out and extended, as chance and circumstances willed they should, like pools of water in the fields when floods are out.

We cannot but distrust the soundness of recent German policy, with its grandiose visions of universal empire, if we consider it in the light of other things which happened when the world was somewhat younger, though possibly no less wise. The great imaginative conquerors, though the fame of their deeds still rings down the ages, do not make so brave a show, when we begin to examine into the permanency of their achievements. The imperial projects of Alexander, of the Habsburgs, the Grand Monarque, and Napoleon—each of whom drew out

The German project of empire.

a vast pattern and worked to it—are not among those things which can be said with any justice to have endured. None of them were ever fully achieved; while some were broken in pieces, even during the lifetimes of their architects.

To treat the whole world as if it were a huge garden, for which one small race of men, who have worked busily in a single corner of it, can aspire to make and carry out an all-comprehending plan, is in reality a proof of littleness and not largeness of mind. Such vaulting ambitions are the symptoms of a dangerous disease, to be noted and distrusted. And none ever noted these tendencies more carefully or distrusted them more heartily than the two greatest statesmen whom Prussia has produced. Frederick the Great rode his own Pegasus-vision on curb and martingale. The Great Bismarck reined back the Pegasus-vision of his fellow-countrymen on to its haunches with an even sterner hand. "One cannot," so he wrote in later years—"one cannot see 'the cards of Providence so closely as to anticipate 'historical development according to one's own 'calculation."

Those very qualities of vastness and symmetry which appear to have such fatal attraction for the pedantocracy repel the practical statesman; and woe to the nation which follows after the former class rather than the latter, when the ways of the two part company! To the foreign observer it seems as if Germany, for a good many years past, has been making this mistake. Perhaps it is her destiny so to do. Possibly the reigns of Frederick and Bismarck were only interludes. For Germany followed the pedantocracy during a century or more,

The German project of empire.

while it preached political inaction and contentment with a shorn and parcelled Fatherland. She was following it still, when Bismarck turned constitutionalism out of doors and went his own stern way to union. And now once again she seems to be marching in a fatal procession after the same Pied Pipers, who this time are engaged, with a surpassing eloquence and fervour, in preaching discontent with the narrow limits of a united empire, and in exhorting their fellow-countrymen to proceed to the Mastery of the World.

Among an imaginative race like the Germans, those who wield the weapons of rhetoric and fancy are only too likely to get the better of those surer guides, who know from hard experience that the world is a diverse and incalculable place, where no man, and no acre of land, are precisely the same as their next-door neighbours, where history never repeats itself, and refuses always—out of malice or disdain—to travel along the way which ingenious Titans have charted for it. But it is not every generation which succeeds in producing a Frederick the Great or a Bismarck, to tame the dreamers and use them as beasts of draught and burden.

The complete mosaic of the German vision is an empire incomparably greater in extent, in riches, and in population, than any which has yet existed since the world first began to keep its records. Visionaries are always in a hurry. This stupendous rearrangement of the Earth's surface is confidently anticipated to occur within the first half of the present century. It is to be accomplished by a race distinguished for its courage, industry, and devotion,—let us admit so much without grudging.

CHAPTER III.

The German project of empire.

But in numbers—even if we count the Teutons of the Habsburg Empire along with those of the Hohenzollern—it amounts upon the highest computation to less than eighty millions. This is the grain of mustard-seed which is confidently believed to have in it 'the property to get up and spread,' until within little more than a generation, it will dominate and control more than seven hundred millions of human souls.

Nor to German eyes, which dwell lovingly, and apparently without misgiving, upon this appalling prospect of symmetry and vastness, are these the sum total of its attractions. The achievement of their vision would bring peace to mankind. For there would then be but two empires remaining, which need give the overlords of the world the smallest concern. Of these Russia, in their opinion, needs a century at least in which to emerge out of primitive barbarism and become a serious danger; while in less than a century, the United States must inevitably crumble to nonentity, through the worship of false gods and the corruption of a decadent democracy. Neither of these two empires could ever hope to challenge the German Mastery of the World.

In South America as in North, there is already a German garrison, possessing great wealth and influence. And in the South, at any rate, it may well become, very speedily, an imperative obligation on the Fatherland to secure, for its exiled children, more settled conditions under which to extend the advantages of German commerce and Kultur. President Monroe has already been dead a hundred years or more. According to the calculations of the pedantocracy, his famous doctrine will need some stronger backing than the moral disapprobation of a hundred millions of materially-minded and unwarlike people, in order to withstand the pressure of German diplomacy, if it should summon war-ships and transports to its aid.

The German project of empire.

So in the end we arrive at an exceedingly strange conclusion. For that very thing, which the philanthropists have all these years been vainly endeavouring to bring about by means of congresses of good men, and resolutions which breathe a unanimity of noble aspirations, may be achieved in a single lifetime by a series of bold strokes with the German sword. Then at last Universal Peace will have been secured.

At this point the Prussian professor and the pacifist apostle, who turned their backs upon one another so angrily at the beginning, and started off, as it seemed, in opposite directions, are confronting one another unexpectedly at the other side of the circle of human endeavour. They ought surely to shake hands; for each, if he be honest, will have to own himself the convert of the other. "You 'admit then after all," cries the triumphant Pacifist, "that Peace is the real end of human endeavour!" "Whether or no," grunts the other in reply, "this 'at any rate was the only road to it."

One wonders—will the Pacifist be content? He has reached his goal sure enough; though by means which he has been accustomed to denounce as the end of all true morality? Will the Professor, on the other hand, be well pleased when he discovers that by the very triumph of his doctrines he has made war for ever impossible,—manliness, therefore, and all true virtue likewise impossible,—thereby damning

CHAPTER III.

The German project of empire.

the souls of posterity to the end of time? "To put 'questions in this quarter with a hammer, and to 'hear perchance that well-known hollow sound 'which tells of blown-out frogs"[1]—this is a joy, no doubt; and it is all we are ever likely to arrive at by the cross-examination of dreamers.

[1] Nietzsche, *The Twilight of Idols.*

CHAPTER IV

THE NEW MORALISTS

CHAPTER IV.

The new moralists.

The dream of German expansion, as year by year it took firmer hold upon the popular imagination, produced, as might have been expected, a desire that it might be realised. From the stage of vague and ardent longing it was but a short way to the next, where a determined will began to put forth efforts towards achievement. But as mankind in the mass, whether in Germany or England, is still to some extent hampered by human nature, by a number of habits, traditions, and instincts, and by various notions of good and evil, justice and injustice—which the subtlest philosophers and most eloquent rhetoricians have not yet succeeded in eradicating—a need was felt for what the text-books in their solemn nomenclature call *an ethical basis.* In plain words, the German people wanted to have right on their side—if possible, old-fashioned, Sunday-school, copy-book Right. Failing that, even such a plea as the wolf maintained against the lamb would be a great deal better than nothing.

This tendency in a nation to look about for justification and a righteous plea, when it is preparing to possess itself of property belonging to its neighbours, is for the most part a subconscious process, not only

CHAPTER IV.

The new moralists.

among the common people, but also among the leaders themselves. It resembles the instinct among hens which produces in them an appetite for lime when the season has come to begin laying. It was through some natural impulse of this sort, and not through mere cynicism, hypocrisy, or cool calculation, that German publicists discovered all the grievances which have been already touched upon. For even if the possession of these grievances did not altogether give the would-be aggressors right up to the point of righteousness, it certainly put their neighbours in the wrong, and branded the French dove and the British lamb with turpitude in the eyes of the German people.

The grievances against France were, that although she had been vanquished in 1870, although her population had actually decreased since that date, and although therefore she had neither the right to nor any need for expansion, she had nevertheless expanded in Africa as well as in the East, to a far greater extent than Germany herself, the victorious power, whose own population had meanwhile been increasing by leaps and bounds.

The grievances against Britain were that she was supposed to have made war upon German trade, to have prevented her young rival from acquiring colonies, and to have intrigued to surround the Teuton peoples with a ring of foes. Britain had helped France to occupy and hold her new territories. Britain had been mainly responsible for the diplomatic defeat of Germany at Algeciras in 1905 and again over Agadir in 1911. Moreover when Germany, during the South African war, had attempted, in the interests of international morality, to combine the nations against us, we had foiled her high-minded

The new moralists.

and unselfish endeavours. When at an earlier date she had sought, by the seizure of Kiao-Chau and by a vigorous concentration, to oust British influence and trade from their position of predominance in China, we had countered her efforts by the occupation of Wei-hai-wei and the Japanese alliance.

As regards command of the sea we had likewise frustrated German ambitions. After a certain amount of vacillation, and a somewhat piteous plea for a general diminution of armaments—backed up by an arrest of our own, which Germany interpreted, perhaps not unnaturally, as a throwing up of the sponge and beginning of the end of our naval supremacy—we had actually had the treachery (for it was nothing less) to upset all her calculations, and turn all her efforts and acceleration to foolishness, by resuming the race for sea-power with redoubled energy. And although to our own eyes, and even possibly to the eyes of impartial observers, none of these doings of ours—in so far as they were truly alleged—could be rightly held to constitute any real grievance, that consideration was irrelevant. For when a man is in search of a grievance he will find it, if he be earnest enough, in the mere fact that his intended adversary stammers, or has a wart upon his nose.

German statesmen were happy in having established these grievances to their own satisfaction; but something more was necessary in order that their morality might rest upon a sure foundation. German policy must be absolutely right, and not merely relatively right by contrast with those neighbours whose power she sought to overthrow, and whose territories she wished to annex. And although this

CHAPTER IV.

The new moralists.

effort to establish German policy on the principle of Right involved a recasting of Christian morality, it was not shirked on that account. On the contrary it was undertaken in a most energetic spirit.

The first great influence in this readjustment of popular conceptions of right and wrong was the historian Heinrich von Treitschke.[1] He boldly differentiated the moral obligations of the private individual from those of a government charged with the destinies of a nation.[2] The duties of a man to his family, neighbours, and society Treitschke left undisturbed. In this sphere of human life the teaching of the Sermon on the Mount not only remained unchallenged, but was upheld and reinforced. Statecraft, however, fell under a different category.

The true principle of private conduct was Love for one's Neighbour, but the true principle of the state was Power. The duty of a virtuous ruler was to seek power, more power, and always more power, on behalf of the nation he was called upon to govern. The internal power of the state over the action of its own subjects was absolute, and it was a duty owed by each generation of rulers to posterity, to see to it that in their own time, the external power of the

[1] Heinrich von Treitschke, son of a Saxon general of Bohemian-Slavonic origin; born at Dresden 1834. Deafness following upon a fever in childhood prevented him from adopting the profession of arms; 1858–1863 lectured on history at Leipzig; 1863–1866 professor at Freiburg; 1866–1874 professor at Heidelberg; 1874 until his death in 1896 professor of history and politics at Berlin.

[2] "Thus it follows from this, that we must distinguish between public 'and private morality. The order of rank of the various duties must 'necessarily be for the State, as it is power, quite other than for individual 'men. A whole series of these duties, which are obligatory on the individual, 'are not to be thought of in any case for the State. To maintain itself 'counts for it always as the highest commandment; that is absolutely 'moral for it. And on that account we must declare that of all political 'sins that of weakness is the most reprehensible and the most contemptible; 'it is in politics the sin against the Holy Ghost. . . ."—*Selections*, p. 32.

The new moralists.

state was increased at the expense of its neighbours.[1] To secure this end wars were inevitable; and despite the sufferings which wars entailed, they were far from regrettable, for the reason that they preserved the vigour, unity, and devotion of the race, while stimulating the virtues of courage and self-sacrifice among private citizens.[2]

Nations, he maintained, cannot safely stand still. They must either increase their power or lose it, expand their territories or be prepared to see them shorn away. No growth of spiritual force or material well-being within the state will preserve it, if it fails to extend its authority and power among its neighbours. Feelings of friendliness, chivalry, and pity are absurd as between nations. To speak even of justice in such a connection is absurd. Need and Might together constitute Right. Nor ought the world to regret the eating-up of weak nations by the strong, of small nations by the great, because—a somewhat bold conclusion—great and powerful nations alone are capable of producing what the world requires in thought, art, action, and virtue. For how can these things flourish nobly in a timid, cowering state, which finds itself driven by force of circumstances to make-believes and fictions, to

[1] "That must not hinder us from declaring joyfully that the gifted 'Florentine, with all the vast consequence of his thinking, was the first 'to set in the centre of all politics the great thought: *The State is power.* 'For that is the truth; and he who is not man enough to look this truth 'in the face ought to keep his hands off politics."—*Ibid.* p. 28.

[2] ". . . to the historian who lives in the world of will it is immediately 'clear that the demand for a perpetual peace is thoroughly reactionary; 'he sees that with war all movement, all growth, must be struck out of 'history. It has always been the tired, unintelligent, and enervated 'periods that have played with the dream of perpetual peace. . . ."—*Selections,* p. 25.

"It is precisely political idealism that demands wars, while materialism 'condemns them. What a perversion of morality to wish to eliminate 'heroism from humanity!"—*Ibid.* p. 24.

CHAPTER IV.

The new moralists.

the meanest supplications and to devices of low cunning, in order to preserve an independence which, as it can only exist on sufferance, is nothing better than a sham ?[1]

As the Hohenzollerns, the noblest and most capable of modern dynasties, had never been content merely to reign, but had always maintained their 'divine right' of ruling and dominating the Prussian Kingdom—as Prussia itself, the most manly and energetic of modern nations, had not been content merely to serve as the figurehead of a loose confederation, but had insisted upon becoming supreme master and imposing its own system, policy, and ideals upon all Germany—so was it the duty and destiny of united Germany, under these happy auspices, having been taught and seasoned by long centuries of stern and painful apprenticeship, to issue forth in the meridian vigour of her age and seize upon the Mastery of the World.

If Treitschke, the eloquent historian, succeeded to his own satisfaction and that of a very large proportion of German statesmen, soldiers, intellectuals, and publicists in taking high policy altogether out of the jurisdiction of Christian morals, Friedrich Wilhelm Nietzsche,[2] the even more eloquent and infinitely more subtle poet-philosopher, made a cleaner and

[1] ". . . if we survey history in the mass, it is clear that all real master- 'pieces of poetry and art arose upon the soil of great nationalities ;" and "The poet and artist must be able to react upon a great nation. When 'did a masterpiece ever arise among a petty little nation ?"—*Ibid.* p. 19.

[2] Friedrich Wilhelm Nietzsche, son of a village pastor of Polish ancestry ; born at Röcken in Saxony 1844 ; served in the German army for a few months in 1867 ; injured in mounting his horse ; 1869–1879 professor of classical philology at Bâle which entailed naturalisation as a Swiss subject ; served in ambulance in war of 1870–1871 ; 1879–1889 in bad health, wrote and travelled ; 1889 became insane and remained so till his death in 1900.

bolder cut, and got rid of Christian morality even in the sphere of private conduct.

The new moralists.

Nietzsche was but little interested or concerned in the practical problems of statecraft which engrossed the patriotic mind of Treitschke. The destinies of the German nation were for him a small matter in comparison with those of the human race. But nevertheless his vigorously expressed contempt for the English, their ways of life and thought, the meanness of their practical aims, and the degradation of their philosophic ideals,[1] was comforting to his fellow-countrymen, who were relieved to find that the nation whom they desired to despoil was so despicable and corrupt. This train of argument was deceptive and somewhat dangerous; for it led his German readers to overlook the fact, that the broad front of his attack aimed at enveloping and crushing the cherished traditions of the Teuton race no less than those of the Anglo-Saxon.[2]

[1] "What is lacking in England, and has always been lacking, that 'half-actor and rhetorician knew well enough, the absurd muddlehead, 'Carlyle, who sought to conceal under passionate grimaces what he knew 'about himself: namely, what was *lacking* in Carlyle, real *power* of intellect, 'real *depth* of intellectual perception, in short, philosophy."—*Beyond Good and Evil*, p. 210.

"The Englishman, more gloomy, sensual, headstrong, and brutal than 'the German—is for that very reason, as the baser of the two, also the 'most pious."—*Ibid.* p. 211.

"The English coarseness and rustic demureness is still more satisfactorily 'disguised by Christian pantomime, and by praying and psalm-singing (or, 'more correctly, it is thereby explained and differently expressed); and 'for the herd of drunkards and rakes who formerly learned moral grunting 'under the influence of Methodism (and more recently as the 'Salvation 'Army'), a penitential fit may really be the relatively highest manifestation 'of 'humanity' to which they can be elevated."—*Ibid.* p. 211.

"The European ignobleness, the plebeianism of modern ideas, is 'England's work and invention."—*Ibid.* p. 213.

[2] "I believe only in French culture, and regard everything else in 'Europe which calls itself 'culture' as a misunderstanding. I do not 'even take the German kind into consideration. . . . The few instances 'of higher culture with which I have met in Germany were all French in 'their origin."—*Ecce Homo*, p. 27.

CHAPTER IV.

The new moralists.

Nietzsche's derision and dislike of the Prussian spirit, of militarism, and of what he conceived to be the spurious principle of nationality, his vague, disinterested cosmopolitanism or Europeanism, are as the poles apart from the aims and ideas of Treitschke and the German patriots.[1] Nietzsche is not concerned to evolve a sovereign and omnipotent state, but a high overmastering type of man, who shall inherit the earth and dominate—not for their good, but for his own—the millions who inhabit it. His ideal is a glorious aristocracy of intellect, beauty, courage, self-control, felicity, and power, scornfully smiling, exuberantly vital. The evolution, ever higher and higher, of this fine oligarchy of super-men is the one absolute end of human endeavour. The super-men will use and direct the force and instincts of 'the herd'—even the capacities of kings, soldiers, law-

---

"Wherever Germany extends her sway, she *ruins* culture."—*Ibid.* p. 38.

"Culture and the state are antagonists: a 'culture-state' is merely a 'modern idea. The one lives upon the other, the one flourishes at the 'expense of the other. All great periods of culture have been periods of 'political decline; that which was great from the standpoint of culture 'was always unpolitical—even anti-political. . . . In the history of Euro-'pean culture the rise of the (German) Empire signifies, above all, a displace-'ment of the centre of gravity. Everywhere people are already aware of 'this: in things that really matter—and these after all constitute culture—'the Germans are no longer worth considering. . . . The fact that there 'is no longer a single German philosopher worth mentioning is an increasing 'wonder."—*The Twilight of the Idols*, p. 54.

"Every great crime against culture for the last four centuries lies on 'their [the German] conscience. . . . It was the Germans who caused 'Europe to lose the fruits, the whole meaning of her last period of greatness—'the period of the Renaissance. . . ."—*Ecce Homo*, p. 124.

"The future of German culture rests with the sons of Prussian officers."—*The Genealogy of Morals*, p. 222.

"If any one wishes to see the 'German soul' demonstrated *ad oculos*, 'let him only look at German taste, at German arts and manners: what 'boorish indifference to 'taste'!"—*The Antichrist*.

[1] "What quagmires and mendacity there must be about if it is possible, 'in the modern European hotchpotch, to raise questions of *race*."

A Nation—"Men who speak one language and read the same newspapers."—*The Genealogy of Morals*, p. 226.

The new moralists.

givers, and administrators—to make the world a fit place for their own development. The millions of slaves are to be considered merely as a means to this end. Concern about them for their own sakes, above all pity for their sufferings, or regard on the part of the super-men for their resentment—except to guard against it—is a mistake. The serenity of the super-man must not allow itself to be disturbed and distracted by any such considerations. It is for him to take what he needs or desires, to impose order on the world, so that it may be a fit environment for the evolution of his own caste, and, so far as he can compass it, to live like the gods.[1]

It is clear that although Nietzsche chaunts a pæan in admiration of "the magnificent blonde brute, 'avidly rampant for spoil and victory,"[2] and although he is constantly found, as it were, humming this refrain, he had no intention of taking the Prussian as his ideal type—still less of personifying Prussia itself as a super-state engaged in a contest for supremacy with a herd of inferior nations. He does not trouble himself in the least about nations, but only about individual men. Yet, like others who have had the gift of memorable speech, he might

[1] "A boldly daring, splendidly overbearing, high-flying, and aloft-up-'dragging class of higher men, who had first to teach their century—and 'it is the century of the *masses*—the conception 'higher man.'"—*Beyond Good and Evil,* p. 219.

"This man of the future, this tocsin of noon and of the great verdict, 'which renders the will again free, who gives back to the world its goal 'and to man his hope, this Antichrist and Antinihilist, this conqueror of 'God and of Nothingness—*he must one day come.*"—*The Genealogy of Morals*, p. 117.

[2] "The blonde beast that lies at the core of all aristocratic races."—*The Genealogy of Morals*, p. 42.

"The profound, icy mistrust which the German provokes, as soon as 'he arrives at power,—even at the present time,—is always still an after-'math of that inextinguishable horror with which for whole centuries 'Europe has regarded the wrath of the blonde Teuton beast."—*Ibid.*

CHAPTER IV.

The new moralists.

well marvel, were he still alive, at the purposes to which his words have been turned by orators and journalists, desirous to grind an edge on their own blunt axes.

General von Bernhardi[1] may be taken as a type of the sincere but unoriginal writer who turns all texts to the support of his own sermon. He is an honest, literal fellow. In spite of all his ecstatic flights of rhetoric he is never at all in the clouds—never any farther from the earth's surface than hopping distance. Notwithstanding, he quietly appropriates any Nietzschean aphorisms the sound and shape of which appear to suit his purpose, and uses them to drive home his very simple and concrete proposition that it is the duty of Germany to conquer the world.

One imagines from his writings that Bernhardi has no quarrel with Christianity, no wish whatsoever to overturn our accepted notions of morality. He is merely a soldier with a fixed idea, and he is very much in earnest. His literary methods remind one somewhat of the starlings in spring-time, perched on the backs of sheep and cattle, picking off the loose hairs to line their nests. This is the highly practical and soldierly use to which he puts philosophers, poets, and men of letters generally—laying them under contribution to garnish his discourse.

It is probably true that the average soldier who fought on the German side at Ypres and elsewhere

[1] Friedrich von Bernhardi: born 1849 at St. Petersburg, where his father Theodor von Bernhardi was a Councillor of the Prussian Legation; entered a Hussar regiment in 1869; military attaché at Berne in 1881; in 1897 he was chief of the General Staff of the 16th Army Corps; in 1908 he was appointed commander of the 7th Army Corps; retired in the following year. He was a distinguished cavalry general, and is probably the most influential German writer on current politico-military problems.

The new moralists.

was hardly more conversant with the writings of Treitschke, Nietzsche, and Bernhardi than the average British soldier opposed to him was with those of Herbert Spencer, Mr. Bernard Shaw, and Mr. Norman Angell. It is very unlikely, however, that the battle of Ypres would ever have been fought had it not been for the ideas which sprang from these and similar sources. The influence of the written and spoken word upon German policy and action is glaringly manifest.[1] It inspired and supported the high bureaucrats at Berlin, and had equally to do, if indirectly, with the marching of the humblest raw recruits shoulder to shoulder to be shot down on the Menin Road. For by a process of percolation through the press and popular literature, the doctrines of these teachers—diluted somewhat, it is true, and a good deal disguised and perverted—had reached a very wide audience. Though the names of these authors were for the most part unknown, though their opinions had never been either understood or accepted by the common people, the effects of their teaching had made themselves felt in every home in Germany.

The German private soldier would not have been shot down unless these eloquent sermons had been preached. None the less, he had never grasped or understood, far less had he adhered to and professed, the cardinal doctrines which they contained. He still believed in the old-fashioned morality, and thought that states as well as individual men were bound to act justly. It was this faith which gave

[1] Probably not less so upon British policy and *in*action. As water i the result of blending oxygen and hydrogen in certain proportions, so i the present war the resultant of German militarism and British anti-militarism in combination.

CHAPTER IV.

The new moralists.

him his strength, and made him die gladly. For he believed that Germany had acted justly, the Allies unjustly, that it was his task, along with other good men and true, to win victory for his Emperor and safety for his Fatherland, and to crush the treacherous and malignant aggressors.

In spite of all this preliminary discoursing which had been going on for many years past, like artillery preparation before an infantry attack—about world-power, will-to-power, and all the rest of it—nothing is more remarkable than the contrast presented, immediately after war broke out, between the blatancy of those writers who had caused the war and the bleating of those (in many cases the same) who sought to justify Germany's part in it to their countrymen and the world.

On the enlightened principles of Treitschke and Bernhardi, Britain would have acted not only wisely, but in the strictest accordance with her duty to her own state, had she indeed contrived and compassed this war, believing circumstances to be favourable for herself and unfavourable for Germany. Not another shred of right or reason was required.[1] But when war actually burst out, all these new-fangled doctrines went by the board. Though the ink was hardly dry upon Bernhardi's latest exhortation—of which several hundred thousand copies had been sold, and in which he urged his fellow-countrymen to watch their time and make war when it suited them, without remorse and no matter on what plea—

[1] "Every State has as sovereign the undoubted right to declare war 'when it chooses, consequently every State is in the position of being able 'to cancel any treaties which have been concluded."—Treitschke, *Selections*, p. 15.

"It is not only the right, but the moral and political duty of the states-'man to bring about a war."—Bernhardi, *Germany and the Next War*, p. 41.

The new moralists.

in spite of this fact, there was a singular lack of Stoicism among 'the brethren' when war was declared against Russia and France. When Britain joined in, and when things began to go less well than had been expected, Stoicism entirely disappeared. Indeed there is something highly ludicrous, at the same time painful—like all spectacles of human abasement—in the chorus of whines and shrill execration, which at once went up to heaven from that very pedantocracy whose leaders, so short a time before, had been preaching that, as between the nations of the earth, Might is Right, and Craft is the trusty servant of Might.[1]

These scolding fakirs were of an infinite credulity, inasmuch as they believed that Sir Edward Grey was the reincarnation of Machiavelli. Yet on their own principles, what was there in this discovery to be in the least shocked at? British statesmen (it is hardly necessary to repeat it) had not walked in the footsteps of the Florentine; had not provoked the war; had not wished for it; had tried with all their might to prevent it; but if they had done the very reverse, would they not merely have been

[1] Towards the end of March 1915 General von Bernhardi published in the *New York Sun* an article the object of which was to explain to the American people how much his previous writings had been misunderstood and perverted by the malice of the enemy. Long before this date, however, there was strong presumptive evidence that the distinguished military author was unfavourably regarded by the Super-men at Berlin. He had been useful before the war for preparing the Teutonic youth for Armageddon; but after hostilities began it was discovered that, so far as neutral opinion was concerned, it would have been better had he been wholly interdicted from authorship under the national motto—*verboten.* As to the tenour of imperial communications to the popular fire-eating publicist during the winter 1914–1915, might we venture to paraphrase them into the vulgar vernacular as follows?—"We've got to thank you and your damned 'books, more than anything else, for the present mess with America. Get 'busy, and explain them all away if you can."—Any one of the labours of Hercules was easier.

CHAPTER IV.

The new moralists.

taking a leaf out of the sacred book of the pedantocracy—out of Bernhardi's book, out of Nietzsche's book, out of Treitschke's book? Why, then, all these unpleasant howlings and ravings?

The answers are not hard to find. The careful plans and theories of the German bureaucrats had been turned topsy-turvy because England had joined in the war when, according to the calculations of the augurs, she should have remained neutral. That mistake must have been sufficiently annoying in itself to disturb the equanimity even of professional philosophers. And further, in spite of all the ingenious, eloquent, and sophistical exhortations of the prophets, the old morality still kept its hold upon the hearts of men. When trouble arose they turned to it instinctively—priesthood as well as people—and the later gospel fell flat like a house of cards. Immediately war came there was an appeal to old-fashioned justice, and the altars of the little, new-fangled, will-to-power gods were deserted by their worshippers.

When statesmen are laying out policies, and moralists are setting up systems, it is worth their while to make certain that they are not, in fact, engaged upon an attempt to make water flow uphill; above all, that their ingenious new aqueducts will actually hold water, which in this instance they certainly did not.

CHAPTER V

THE STATECRAFT OF A PRIESTHOOD

CHAPTER V.

The statecraft of a priesthood.

THE thoroughness and efficiency of the Germans are admitted even by hostile critics. In the practical sphere they have excelled in military preparations, in the encouragement of industry, and in the organisation of finance. But they have achieved an even more remarkable success than any of these; for they have so arranged their educational system that it is drilled hardly less admirably than their army.[1] From the primary schools to the universities everything is ordered, so that the plastic mind of youth is forced into a political mould which suits the purposes of government. Patriotism of the pattern approved by the authorities is inculcated directly or indirectly in every class-room. While thought is left ostentatiously free in regard to private morals and religious foundations, the duties of the citizen to the state, the duties of the state to posterity, the relations of Germany to the outside world, are subjects upon which independent speculation is not tolerated.

[1] "We may declare that the problem of training in arms and turning 'to real account the energies of the nation was first undertaken in thorough 'earnestness by Germany. *We possess in our army a characteristic, necessary 'continuation of the school-system.* For many men there is no better means 'of training; for them drilling, compulsory cleanliness, and severe discipline 'are physically and morally indispensable in a time like ours, which unchains 'all spirits."—Treitschke, *Selections*, pp. 106-107.

CHAPTER V.

The statecraft of a priesthood.

Even schoolmasters and professors have their ambitions; but unless they contribute their quota to the support of imperial ideals, their careers are unlikely to prosper. It is not enough that a lecturer should not run counter to state policy; he must actively promote its ends before he can hope to be transferred to a sphere of greater dignity and influence. Pedagogy is a branch of the Civil Service just as much as the Treasury or the Public Health Department. Teachers from the lowest to the highest grades are the stipendiaries of the bureaucracy. If they render useful services they are promoted. If they fail to render useful services they are passed over. If they indulge in dangerous speculations they are sent adrift. Not merely the army, but the whole German nation, is disciplined, during the period of its impressionable youth, with the object of inclining its mind to support state policy through thick and thin.

The schools feed the universities; the universities feed the press, the learned professions, and the higher grades in industry and finance. Private conversation, as well as what is published in newspapers, magazines, and books, bears the impress of the official mint to a degree unthinkable in England or America, Russia or France. Theories of politics are devised by ingenious sophists, exactly as the machinery at Essen is contrived by engineers—for the express purpose of forwarding Prussian policy. History is twisted and distorted in order to prepare the way for imperial ambitions by justifying them in advance.

It is a signal triumph for the thoroughness of German methods that all the thinkers, dreamers,

CHAPTER V.

The statecraft of a priesthood.

poets, and prophets, with but a few exceptions, should have been commandeered and set to work thinking, dreaming, poetising, and prophesying to the glory of the Kaiser, and his army, and his navy, and his counsellors, and his world policy, and the conquests and expansion which are entailed therein.

It is somewhat startling, however, to find the intellectuals thus mobilised, and all but unanimous, on the official side; for hitherto in history they have rarely agreed among themselves, and the greater part have usually favoured the Opposition rather than the Government. Nor does this close alliance between learning and the bureaucracy seem altogether satisfactory. For thought loses its fine edge when it is set to cut millstones of state. It loses its fine temper in the red heat of political controversy. By turning utilitarian it ceases to be universal; and what is perhaps even worse, it ceases to be free. It tends more and more to become the mere inventor of things which will sell at a profit; less and less the discoverer of high principles which the gods have hidden out of sight. It would hardly be possible to imagine a more complete reversal of attitude than that which has occurred in Germany between the beginning of the nineteenth century and the present time; and though this change may serve admirably the immediate purposes of the state, it does not augur well for the future of German thought.

The similarities and contrasts of history are interesting to contemplate. In the ferment of thought and action which occurred in France during the generation preceding the battle of Valmy, and that other which has been going on in Germany in the

CHAPTER V.

generation preceding the battle of the Marne, there are various likenesses and unlikenesses.

The statecraft of a priesthood.

In France before the Revolution, as in Germany to-day, a bureaucracy, responsible solely to the monarch, directed policy and controlled administration. But in France this bureaucracy was incompetent, unpractical, and corrupt. Its machinery was clogged with dead matter of every kind, with prejudices, traditions, and statutes, many of which had outlived their original purposes. The *Struldbrugs,* discovered by Gulliver during his voyages, were a race of men whose mortal souls were incased in immortal bodies. The French monarchy was of this nature, and the soul of it was long since dead. Inefficiency was everywhere apparent; and, as a natural consequence, the whole system had become a butt, at which each brilliant writer in turn levelled his darts of derision and contempt.

In Germany, although the political mechanism is the same, the conditions are diametrically the opposite. The bureaucracy and the monarchy which it supports, have proved themselves highly efficient and adaptive. The arrangement has worked with a marvellous success. It has cherished the material, if not the spiritual, well-being of the people. The wealth-producing and belly-filling activities of the race have been stimulated to an extent never yet attained by any form of government, either popular or despotic. Administration has been honest, thrifty, and singularly free from the usual dull negatives of officialdom and the pedantries of red tape. In all directions industrial prosperity has increased, under the fostering care of the state, by leaps and bounds. Anything more remote from the bankrupt empire of

The statecraft of a priesthood.

Louis XVI. it would be impossible to conceive. And as a natural consequence, brilliant German writers have for the most part [1] spent their forces of rhetoric and fancy in idealising the grandeur and nobility of an order of things, under which resources, comfort, and luxury have expanded with such amazing strides.

In the case of France the aim of the intellectuals was to pull down existing institutions, in that of Germany it has been to bolster them up, to extend and develop them to their logical conclusions. But the second were no less agents of destruction than the first. Each alike, as a condition of success, required that a new order of moral and political ideas should be set up; each attained a certain measure of success; and the results which followed were those which usually follow, when new wine is poured into old bottles.

The ideas of the French Revolution cast themselves into the mould of republicanism. A picture wholly imaginary and fictitious was drawn of the institutions of Greece and Rome in ancient days. *Liberty*, *Equality*, and *Fraternity* were believed to have been the foundations of these famous states. Patriots on the banks of the Seine conceived themselves to be re-incarnations of Aristides and the Gracchi, of Pericles, of one Brutus or the other—it mattered little which. Political idealism passed rapidly into a kind of religious fervour.

The German masquerade is very different from this, but it is no less a masquerade. What covers the new faith, indeed, is not plumage borrowed from the Greeks and Romans, but habiliments which are supposed to have clad the heroic forms of ancestral Teutons. The student on his way to doctor's degree—the

[1] Nietzsche is one of the rare exceptions.

CHAPTER V.

The state-craft of a priesthood.

intelligent clerk scanning the high-road to fortune from the eminence of office-stool—dream in their pensive leisure to emulate the heroes of Asgard, to merit and enjoy the glories of Valhalla. But the noble shapes and gorgeous colourings in which the modern young German of honest, sober, and industrious character has chosen to see his destiny prefigured, are no less imaginary and fictitious than those others, with which eloquent notaries'-clerks, and emancipated, unfrocked priests, decked themselves out for the admiration of the Paris mob. In Germany as in France political idealism passed into a kind of religious fervour, which inspired men to a mimicry of old-Wardour-Street shams, and led them to neglect the development of their own true natures.

During quiet times that stream of events, which we are wont to call human progress, is occupied incessantly in throwing up dams, of one sort or another, throughout the world. Tree-trunks and logs, which have been swept down by former floods of conquest and invasion, jam at some convenient rocky angle, as the river falls to its normal level. Against these obstacles the drift and silt of habit, custom, law, convention, prejudice, and tradition slowly collect, settle, and consolidate. An embankment is gradually formed, and the waters are held up behind it ever higher and higher. The tribal pool becomes a pond or nation; and this again, if conditions remain favourable—for so long, that is to say, as there are no more raging and destructive floods,—extends into a lake or inland sea of empire. . . . "See," cry the optimists, "see what a fine, smooth, silvery sheet of 'civilisation, culture, wealth, happiness, comfort, and

The statecraft of a priesthood.

'what not besides, where formerly there was but an 'insignificant torrent brawling in the gorge!" . . . But the pessimists, as is their nature, shake their heads, talk anxiously of the weight of waters which are banking up behind, and of the unreliable character of the materials out of which the dam has grown. "Some day," they warn us, "the embankment 'will burst under the heavy pressure; or, more likely 'still, some ignorant, heedless, or malicious person 'will begin to fiddle and tamper with the casual 'structure; and then what may we expect?"

There has been considerable nervousness of late among rulers of nations as to the soundness of their existing barrages. For the most part, however, they have concerned themselves with internal dangers—with watching propagandists of the socialist persuasion—with keeping these under a kind of benevolent police supervision, and in removing ostentatiously from time to time the more glaring of their alleged grievances. This procedure has been quite as noticeable in the case of autocracies, as in countries which enjoy popular institutions.

Treitschke and Bernhardi—even Nietzsche himself—valued themselves far more highly as builders-up than as pullers-down. It is always so with your inspired inaugurators of change. It was so with Rousseau and those other writers, whose thoughts, fermenting for a generation in the minds of Frenchmen, brought about the Revolution. The intellectuals of the eighteenth century, like those of the nineteenth, aimed at getting rid of a great accumulation of insanitary rubbish. But this was only a troublesome preliminary, to be hurried through with as quickly as possible, in order that the much greater

CHAPTER V.

work of construction might proceed upon the cleared site.

The statecraft of a priesthood.

Treitschke made a hole in the German dam when he cut an ancient commonplace in two, and tore out the one half of it. Nietzsche turned the hole into a much vaster cavity by pulling out the other half. Bernhardi and the pedantocracy worked lustily at the business, with the result that a great part of the sticks, stones, and mud of tradition are now dancing, rumbling, and boiling famously in the flood. Whether they have injured our dam as well as their own, we are hardly as yet in a position to judge.

The profounder spirit of Nietzsche realised clearly enough the absurdity of supposing that the conflicting beliefs and aspirations of mankind could all be settled and squared in a few bustling decades—that the contradictions, paradoxes, and antinomies of national existence could be written off with a few bold strokes of the sword, and the world started off on the road to perfection, like a brisk debtor who has purged his insolvency in the Bankruptcy Court. But the enthusiasm of Treitschke and Bernhardi made them blind to these considerations. Had not the formula been discovered, which would overcome every obstacle—that stroke of genius, the famous bisection of the commonplace? For private conduct, the Sermon on the Mount; for high statecraft, Machiavelli's *Prince*! Was ever anything simpler, except perhaps the way of Columbus with the egg?

When we push our examination further, into the means which Germany has been urged by her great thinkers to employ in preparing for this premeditated war, for provoking it when the season should be ripe,

CHAPTER V.

The statecraft of a priesthood.

and for securing victory and spoils, we are struck more than ever by the gulf which separates the ideas of the German pedantocracy from those of the rest of the world. Nor can we fail to be impressed by the matter-of-fact and businesslike way in which the military and civil powers have set to work to translate those notions into practice.

No kind of priesthood has ever yet exercised a great and direct influence upon national policy without producing calamity. And by an ill fate, it has always been the nature of these spiritual guides to clutch at political power whenever it has come within their reach.

Of all classes in the community who are intellectually capable of having ideas upon public affairs, a priesthood—or what is the same thing, a pedantocracy—is undoubtedly the most mischievous, if it succeeds in obtaining power. It matters not a whit whether they thunder forth their edicts and incitements from church pulpits or university chairs, whether they carry their sophistical projects up the back stairs of Catholic King or Lutheran Kaiser, whether, having shaved their heads and assumed vows of celibacy, they dwell in ancient cloisters, or, having taken unto themselves wives and begotten children, they keep house in commonplace villa residences. None of these differences is essential, or much worth considering. The one class is as much a priesthood as the other, and the evils which proceed from the predominance of the one, and the other, are hardly distinguishable.

They stand ostentatiously aloof from the sordid competitions of worldly business. They have forsworn, or at any rate forgone, the ordinary prizes of

CHAPTER V.

The statecraft of a priesthood.

wealth and position. And for these very reasons they are ill equipped for guiding practical affairs. Their abstinences are fatal impediments, and render them apt to leave human nature out of their reckoning. They are wanting in experience of the difficulties which beset ordinary men, and of the motives which influence them. Knowing less of such matters (for all their book learning) than any other class of articulately-speaking men, they find it by so much the easier to lay down rules and regulations for the government of the world.

To a priesthood, whether ecclesiastical or academic, problems of politics and war present themselves for consideration in an engaging simplicity. They evolve theories of how people live, of how they ought to live; and both sets of theories are mainly cobwebs. There is no place in their philosophy for anything which is illogical or untidy. Ideas of compromise and give-and-take, are abominations in priestly eyes—at any rate when they are engaged in contemplation of worldly affairs. And seeing that the priesthood aspires, nevertheless, to govern and direct a world which is illogical and needs humouring, there is nothing wonderful, if when it has achieved power, it should blunder on disaster in the name of principle, and incite men to cruelties in the name of humanity. 'Clericalism,' said a French statesman, and English statesmen have echoed his words—'Clericalism is the enemy.' And this is right, whether the priesthood be that of Rome or John Calvin, of economic professors expounding Adam Smith in the interests of Manchester, or history professors improving upon Treitschke in the interests of the Hohenzollern dynasty.

The statecraft of a priesthood.

Priests and professors when they meddle in politics are always the same. They sit in their studies or cells, inventing fundamental principles; building thereon great edifices of reasoned or sentimental brickwork which splits in the sun and crumbles in the storm. Throughout the ages, as often as they have left their proper sphere, they have been subject to the same angry enthusiasms and savage obstinacies. Their errors of judgment have been comparable only to their arrogance. Acts of cruelty and treachery, meanness and dishonour,[1] which would revolt the ordinary German or Englishman, commend themselves readily, on grounds of sophistry or logic, to these morbid ascetics, so soon as they begin busying themselves with the direction of public affairs.

It would be unfair to judge any country by its political professors. At the same time, if any country is so foolish as to follow such guides, there is a probability of mischief in national—still more in international—affairs. For they are as innocent as the lawyers themselves, of any knowledge of the real insides of things. They differ of course from the lawyers in many ways. They are ever for making changes for the sake of symmetry; while the man of law is for keeping as he is until the last moment; or at any rate until it is clearly his interest to budge. A priesthood has a burning faith in its own handwrought idols; the lawyer on the contrary, does not go readily to the stake, does not catch fire easily, being rather of the nature of asbestos. When lawyers monopolise political power—even when they merely

[1] Cf. Professor Kuno Meyer, *Times*, December 24, 1914, and March 8, 1915.

CHAPTER V.

The statecraft of a priesthood.

preponderate, as of late years they have seemed to do more and more in all democratic countries, whether of the monarchical or republican type—they invariably destroy by insensible gradations that which is most worth preserving in man or state, the soul. But they do not bring on sudden catastrophe as a priesthood does; their method is to strangle slowly like ivy.

In England, nowadays—indeed ever since the 'eighties, when professors of Political Economy became discredited as political guides—there are not many evidences of priestly influence. Certainly there is nothing of an organised kind. What exists is erratic and incalculable. There is much clamour; but it is contradictory, spasmodic, and inconstant, without any serious pretence, either of learning or science, to support it. Each of our prophets is in business for himself. There is no tinge of Erastianism about any of them. For the most part they are the grotesques and *lions comiques* of the world of letters, who prophesy standing on their heads, or grinning through horse-collars, and mistaking always "the twinkling of their own sophisticated minds for wisdom."

Alliance between a priesthood and a bureaucracy tends gradually to produce, as in the case of China, an oppressive uniformity—not unlike that aimed at by the more advanced socialists—where every fresh innovation is a restriction hampering the natural bent. On the other hand an alliance between a priesthood and a military caste—especially when the bureaucracy is ready to act in sympathy—is one of the commonest causes of international convulsions.

CHAPTER V.

The statecraft of a priesthood.

Oddly enough, the soldier, who affects to despise men of words and make-believes, and who on this account has an instinctive dislike and distrust of the lawyer—so violent indeed that it often puts him in the wrong, and leaves him at the mercy of the object of his contempt—is dangerously apt to become the tool of anything which bears a likeness to Peter the Hermit. It is not really the lawyer's confidence in the efficacy of words which revolts the soldier, nearly so much as the kind of words used, the temperament of him who uses them, and the character of the make-believes which it is sought to establish. The unworldliness, simplicity, idealism, and fervour of the priesthood make strong appeals to a military caste, which on the contrary is repelled by what it conceives to be the cynicism, opportunism, and self-seeking of lawyer statecraft.

More especially is it difficult for the military caste to resist the influence of the priesthood when, as in Germany of recent years, they have insisted upon giving the warrior the most important niche in their temple, and on burning incense before him day and night. Working industriously in their studies and laboratories they have found moral justification for every course, however repugnant to established ideas, which may conceivably make it easier to attain victory and conquest. The soldier might have scruples about doing this or that; but when he is assured by inspired intellectuals, that what would best serve his military ends is also the most moral course of action, how can he—being a man of simple mind—presume to doubt it; though he may occasionally shudder as he proceeds to put it into execution?

CHAPTER V.

The statecraft of a priesthood.

German thoroughness is an admirable quality, but even thoroughness may be carried to extremes which are absurd, or something worse.

No nation has a right to complain if another chooses to drill armies, build fleets, accumulate stores of treasure, weapons, and material; nor is it incumbent upon any nation to wear its heart upon its sleeve, or to let the whole world into its secrets, military or political. In so far as Germany has acted upon these principles she was well within her rights. As a result we have suffered heavily; but we must blame ourselves for being ill-prepared; we have no justification for complaining because Germany was well-prepared.

There are some kinds of preparation, however, which it does not seem possible to justify, if the world is to consist as heretofore of a large number of independent states, between whose citizens it is desirable to maintain a certain friendliness and freedom of intercourse. German activities in various directions, for many years before war broke out, make one wonder what state of things was contemplated by German statesmen, as likely to prevail when war should be over. What, for instance, is to be the status of Germans visiting or residing in other countries—seeking to trade with them—to borrow money from them—to interchange with them the civilities of ordinary life, or those more solemn courtesies which are practised by societies of learning and letters? Will the announcement *civis Germanicus sum* be enough henceforth to secure the stranger a warm welcome and respect? Or will such revelation of his origin be more likely to lead to his speedy re-embarkation for the land of his nativity?

The statecraft of a priesthood.

Spying has always been practised since the beginning of time; but it has rarely been conducted in such a manner as to produce general uneasiness, or any sensible restraint upon private relations. Logically, it would be unfair to condemn recent German enterprises in this direction, seeing that she has only extended an accepted nuisance on to a much vaster scale. But here again logic is a misleading guide. There is something in the very scale of German espionage which has changed the nature of this institution. It has grown into a huge organised industry for the debauching of vain, weak, and greedy natures; for turning such men—for the most part without their being aware of it—into German agents. The result of Teutonic thoroughness in this instance is a domestic intrusion which is odious, as well as a national menace which cannot be disregarded. Many of these hostile agencies may surely be termed treacherous, seeing that they have aimed, under the guise of friendly intercourse, at forwarding schemes of invasion and conquest.

We are familiar enough with the vain purse-proud fellow, who on the strength of a few civil speeches from the Kaiser—breathing friendship and the love of peace—has thenceforward flattered himself that his mission in life was to eradicate suspicion of German intentions from the minds of his British fellow-countrymen. This is the unconscious type of agent, useful especially in sophisticated circles, and among our more advanced politicians of anti-militarist sympathies.

Then we have the naturalised, or unnaturalised, magnate of finance or industry, to whom business prosperity is the great reality of life, politics and

CHAPTER V.

The statecraft of a priesthood.

patriotism being by comparison merely things of the illusory sort. It would cause him no very bitter anguish of heart to see England humiliated and her Empire dissolved, providing his own cosmopolitan undertakings continued to thrive undisturbed by horrid war. He, also, has very likely been the recipient of imperial suavities. In addition to this, however, he has been encouraged to imagine that he enjoys in a peculiar degree the confidence of the German Foreign Office. The difficulties which so shrewd a fellow must have in believing in the innocence of German intentions must be considerable at the outset; but they are worn away by the constant erosion of his private interests. Britain must not cross Germany:—that is his creed in a nutshell. This is the semi-conscious type of agent; and he carries great weight in business circles, and even sometimes in circles much higher than those frequented by the money-changers.

We may resent such influences as these, now that we have become more or less sensible of the effect which they have had during recent years in hindering our preparations for defence; but here we cannot fairly charge Germany with any breach of custom and tradition. We must blame ourselves for having given heed to their counsellors. But it is different when we come to such things as the wholesale corruption of the subjects of friendly nations—a network of careful intrigue for the promotion of rebellion—lavish subsidies and incitements for the purpose of fostering Indian unrest, Egyptian discontent, and South African treason—the supply of weapons and munitions of war on the shortest notice, and most favourable terms, to any one and every one who seems inclined to engage in civil war in Ireland or elsewhere.

The statecraft of a priesthood.

The whole of this procedure has been justified in advance and advocated in detail by Bernhardi and the priesthood. Belgium, France, Russia, and Britain are doubtless peculiarly alive to the iniquity of these practices, for the reason that their moral judgment has been sharpened by personal suffering. But they do not denounce the system solely because they themselves have been injured by it, but also because it seems to them to be totally at variance with all recent notions regarding the comity of nations. If we may use such an old-fashioned term, it appears to us to be wrong.

If methods such as these are henceforth to be practised by the world in general, must not all international communion become impossible, as much in time of peace as during a war? Indeed must not human existence itself become almost intolerable? Friendliness, hospitality, courtesies of every sort, between men and women of one country and those of another, must cease absolutely, if the world should become a convert to these German doctrines. Travel must cease; for no one likes to be stripped naked and searched at every frontier. Trade and financial operations must also be restricted, one would imagine, to such an extent that ultimately they will wither and die.

And if the world in general after the war is ended does *not* become a convert to these German doctrines of treacherous preparation, made in friendly territories during time of peace, what then will be its attitude towards Germany and the Germans; for they presumably have no intention of abandoning these practices? It is an unpleasant problem, but it will have to be faced sooner or later.

The statecraft of a priesthood.

For obviously, although every sensible man believes, and many of us know by actual experience, that the instincts of Germans, in all private relations, are as loyal and honourable as those of most other races which inhabit the earth, no nation can afford any longer to have dealings with them on equal terms, if they have decided to allow their instincts to be used and abused, over-ridden and perverted, by a bureaucracy whose ideal is thoroughness, and by a priesthood which has invented a new system of morals to serve a particular set of ends. Not only the allied nations which are at present at war with Germany, but any country whose interests may conceivably, at any future time, come into conflict with those of that far-sighted empire, will be forced in self-defence to take due precautions. It is clear enough that more efficacious means than mere scraps of naturalisation paper will be needed to secure mankind against the abuse of its hospitality by Teutonic theorists.

The whole of this strange system, those methods which, even after somewhat painful experience of their effects, we are still inclined in our less reflective moments to regard as utterly incredible—is it possible to summarise them in a few sentences? What are the accepted maxims, the orthodox formulas of Prussian statecraft?

Power, more power, world-power; these according to German theory, as well as practice, should be the dominant principles of the state.

When a nation desires territories belonging to its neighbours, let it take them, if it is strong enough.

No further justification is needed than mere appetite for possession, and the strength to satisfy it.

The state-craft of a priesthood.

War is in itself a good thing and not a bad. Like a purge, or a course of the waters of Aix, it should be taken, every half-century or so, by all nations which aim at preserving the vigour of their constitutions.

During the intervening periods the chief duty of the state is to prepare for war, so that when it comes, victory, and with it benefits of the material, as well as of the spiritual sort, may be secured.

No means which will help to secure victory are immoral, whether in the years preceding the outbreak of hostilities, or afterwards, when the war is in full course. If the state, aided by its men of science, could find any safe and secret means of sending a plague, as an advance guard, to ravage the enemy, where is the objection? The soul of a Prussian soldier might revolt against this form of warfare, but at what point would it conflict with the teachings of the priesthood? Nor can we imagine, were the thing possible, that the bureaucracy would allow itself to be hampered by any scruples.

As to the declaration of war, let it be made when the state is in a strong position and its prey in a weak one. This is the all-important consideration. The actual pretext is only a secondary matter, though worthy of attention for the effect it may have on the action of neutrals. And as war is a game of chance, it is wise and right to 'correct fortune,' so far as this can be accomplished during years of peace and under the cloak of amity, by the aid of spies, secret agents, accomplices, traitors, rebels, and what not besides.

The state which has evolved this system and laid

CHAPTER V.

The statecraft of a priesthood.

down these rules, without the least attempt at secrecy or concealment, is the most efficient machine of the fighting and administrative kind at present existing in the world—perhaps which has ever existed in the world. But as you increase the size, power, and complexity of a machine there are obvious dangers unless you can also increase the calibre of the men who have to drive and direct it. This is a much more difficult problem than the other; and there is no evidence to show that it has been solved in the case of Germany. The more powerful the machine, the greater is apt to be the disaster if it is mishandled.

In history the blunders of bureaucracy are a byword. They have been great and many, even when, as in Germany to-day, the bureaucracy is in the full vigour of its age, and in the first flower of uprightness; for a bureaucracy, in order to retain its efficiency, must remain incorruptible, and that is one of the hardest things to secure.

As for the priesthoods, if they are to be of any use, their faith must burn brightly. And the faith of a priesthood is very apt to burn itself out—very apt also to set fire to other things during the process; even to the edifice of popular virtue and the imperial purple itself, which things—unlike the Phoenix, the Salamander, and the Saint—are none the better or stronger for being burned.

We are constantly being told by high authorities that the moral objective of the present war is 'to put down militarism,' and 'abolish it' off the face of the earth. There are few of us who do not wish that this aim may be crowned with success; but militarism is a tough weed to kill, and something more than the mere mowing of it down by some outside scythesman will be necessary, one imagines, in order to get rid of it.

The state-craft of a priesthood.

The true moral objective of the war is something much more important than this. A blacker evil than militarism is that violation of private trust and public honour which is known as the Prussian System, and which has recently been 'marching through rapine, to the disintegration,' not of a single nation, or group of nations, but of the whole fabric of human society, including its own. It is an elaborate contrivance of extreme artificiality, a strange perversion of the nature of man. These are its inherent weaknesses; and fortunately, by reason of them, it is more vulnerable to hard blows than militarism which, with all its vices, and extravagancies, is rooted in instincts which are neither depraved nor ignoble.

Militarism might continue to thrive under adversity, and after the heaviest defeat, as it has done in times past; but the life of the Prussian System—that joint invention of the most efficient bureaucracy in the world, and of a priesthood whose industry can only be matched by its sycophancy and conceit—hangs upon the thread of success. Like the South Sea Bubble, or any of those other impostures of the financial sort, which have temporarily beguiled the confidence of mankind, it must collapse utterly under the shock of failure. It depends entirely on credit, and its powers of recuperation are nil. When its assets are disclosed, the characters of its promoters will be understood. The need, therefore, is to bring it at all costs to a complete demonstration of failure.

CHAPTER V.

The statecraft of a priesthood.

We have been urged by our own anti-militarists not to inflict suffering and humiliation on Germany. But this is not a matter of the slightest importance one way or the other. It has but little to do with the issue which it is our business to settle, if we have the good fortune to come out victorious from the present struggle. To set up the suffering and humiliation of Germany as the object of high policy would cover the Allies with contempt; but to shrink from such things, if they should happen to stand between the Allies and the utter moral bankruptcy of the Prussian System, would overwhelm them with a burden far heavier and more shameful than contempt.

CHAPTER VI

THE DEVIL'S ADVOCATE

CHAPTER VI.

The devil's advocate.

A German might fairly contend that British criticism of his moral ideas and political system is tainted throughout by ignorance and prejudice, and that all our talk of autocracy, bureaucracy, pedantocracy, military caste, and sham constitutionalism is merely an attempt to avoid the real issue by calling things, which we happen to dislike, by bad names. Political institutions, he might insist, must be judged by their fruits. If this test were applied, Germany in his opinion would have nothing to fear in any comparison.

"We Germans," writes a correspondent, the Freiherr von Hexenküchen,[1] "are not inferior in in-'telligence or education to any other race. Had 'this been so, we could never have reached, in so 'short a period as four decades, the proud position 'which we now occupy in science, invention, manu-'facture, commerce, finance, and administration.[2]

[1] This letter, which is dated April 1, 1915, arrived at its destination (*via* Christiania and Bergen) about ten days later. It had not the good fortune, however, to escape the attentions of the Censor, the ravages of whose blacking-brush will be noted in the abrupt termination of sundry paragraphs.

[2] "The empires which during the past forty years have made the greatest 'relative material progress are undoubtedly Germany and Japan—neither 'of them a democracy, but both military states."

CHAPTER VI.

The devil's advocate.

'Consequently, if we are well content to live under 'the institutions we possess, this cannot be put down 'either to our want of enterprise or to the dulness 'of our understandings.

"Our people have already shown that they are 'willing to fight and die for these very institutions 'which you Englishmen affect to regard with so much 'contempt. Possibly your people are equally willing 'to fight and die for theirs. I do not deny this; 'but it is not yet proved; it remains to be proved.

"I do not assert that your people are inferior to 'mine in their readiness to fight and die when they 'are actually faced with a great national danger. 'But I do claim that mine are superior to yours in 'the constancy of their devotion to duty. For a 'hundred years past—not only in periods of stress 'and danger, which stirred the national imagination, 'but equally in times of peace and prosperity, which 'always tend to encourage the growth of comfort and 'the love of ease—each succeeding generation has 'been found willing to train itself in the use of arms, 'so as to be prepared, if occasion should arise, to 'defend the Fatherland.

"When the present war broke out was there a 'firmer loyalty or a more patriotic response to the 'call to arms among your people or among mine? 'Will your people fight and suffer more gladly for 'their 'democratic' ideals than mine will for their 'Kaiser and Fatherland? . . . Surely, upon your 'own principles no comparison should be possible 'between the warmth of your devotion and the 'tepidity of ours.

"Is our system really so reactionary and mechani-'cal as you imagine? In an age which has learned

The devil's advocate.

'as its special lesson the advantages, in ordinary 'business affairs of life, of organisation, thoroughness, 'long views, reticence, and combined effort, guided 'by a strong central control, is it reaction, or is it 'progress, to aim at applying the same principles to 'the greatest, most complex, and infinitely most 'important of all businesses—that of government 'itself? Can a nation hope to survive which refuses, 'in the name of freedom, to submit to control in 'these respects, if it should be faced by competition 'with another, which has been wise enough to employ 'quiet experts instead of loquacious amateurs—'any more than a cotton mill could escape bank-'ruptcy were it managed on a system of party 'government?

"Our civil service, which you are pleased to 'describe as a Bureaucracy, is distinguished among 'all others existing at the present time, by the calibre 'of its members, by its efficiency and honesty, by its 'poverty, and not less by the honour in which it is 'held notwithstanding its poverty. You laugh at 'our love for calling men, and also their wives, by 'the titles of their various offices—Herr this and Frau 'that, from the humblest inspector of drains to the 'Imperial Chancellor himself! And no doubt there 'is a ludicrous side to this practice. But it marks 'at least one important thing—that membership 'of our civil service is regarded as conferring honour. 'So far, we have succeeded in maintaining public 'officials of all grades in higher popular respect than 'men who devote their lives to building up private 'fortunes, and also to those others who delight 'and excel in interminable debate.

"You are used to boast, and I daresay rightly,

CHAPTER VI.

The devil's advocate.

'of the personal honesty and pecuniary disinterestedness of your politicians; and you assume as a matter of course that your civil servants, with such high standards and examples ever before their eyes, are likewise incorruptible. We invert this order. With us the honour of our civil servants is the chief thing; we assume that our politicians must follow suit. They are probably as upright as your own, thanks partly to tradition, but also to the vigilance of their superiors, the professionals, who carry on the actual business of government. With you the fame of the showy amateur fills the mouths of the public. We, on the contrary, exalt the expert, the man who has been trained to the job he undertakes. In so doing we may be reactionaries and you may be progressives; but the progress of Germany since 1870—a progress in which we are everywhere either already in front of you, or else treading closely on your heels—does not seem to furnish you with a conclusive argument.

"As for what you call our Pedantocracy, meaning thereby our professors and men of letters, it is true that these exercise a great influence upon public opinion. We have always respected learning and thought. It is in the German nature so to do. I admit that our learned ones are rather too much inclined to imagine, that because they are students of theory, they are therefore qualified to engage in practice. They are apt to offer their advice and service officiously, and occasionally in a ridiculous manner. But, if my recollection of the English newspapers be correct, this is no more so with us than with you. There is apparently something in the professorial nature which impels men of this

The devil's advocate.

'calling to the drafting of manifestoes and the 'signing of round-robins in times of excitement. 'They may be officious and absurd, but they are not 'wholly despicable, since they act thus quite as much 'from earnestness as from vanity. If our academi-'cians on such occasions mislead more people than 'your own it is due to their virtues, to the greater 'zeal and success with which they have won the 'confidence of their former pupils.[1]

"You are fond of sneering at our Military Caste 'and attribute to it the most malign influence upon 'public affairs. But there again, believe me, you 'exaggerate. Our officers are undoubtedly held in 'great respect, even in some awe. And the reason 'is that they are known to be brave, and like those 'you call the bureaucracy, to have preferred com-'parative poverty in the public service to the pursuit 'of riches. To say that they have no influence upon 'policy would of course be absurd. It is inevitable 'that in the present state of the world, soldiers will 'always have great influence in certain departments 'of public affairs. This must be so in any country

[1] It is not quite clear to what incidents the Freiherr is referring. He may be thinking of a certain round-robin which appeared a few days before the war, giving a most handsome academic testimonial of humanity and probity to the German system ; or he may have in mind a later manifestation in February last, when there suddenly flighted into the correspondence columns of the *Nation* a ' gaggle ' of university geese, headed appropriately enough by a Professor of Political Economy, by name Pigou, who may be taken as the type of that peculiarly British product, the unemotional sentimentalist. To this ' gaggle ' of the heavier fowls there succeeded in due course a ' glory ' of poetical and literary finches, twittering the same tune—the obligation on the Allies not to inflict suffering and humiliation on Germany—on Germany, be it remembered, as yet unbeaten, though this was rather slurred over in their spring-song of lovingkindness. The Freiherr, plunged in his heathen darkness, no doubt still believed Germany to be not only unbeaten but victorious, and likely to continue on the same course. He must therefore have been somewhat puzzled by so much tender concern on the part of our professors, etc. for sparing his feelings at the end of the war.

CHAPTER VI.

The devil's advocate.

'which is not plunged in dreams. For it is their 'business to guarantee national security, and to keep 'watch over the growth of military strength among 'the neighbours and rivals of Germany. If the 'general staff foresees dangers, and can give reason- 'able grounds for its anticipations, it is clear that the 'military view must carry weight with the Kaiser 'and his ministers. And surely there can be no 'question that this is right.

"The officers of the German Army are a caste, 'if you like to put it that way. But in every form 'of government under the sun, unless conceivably 'in some tiny oriental despotism, the predominance 'of a certain caste, or the competition between 'different castes, is absolutely essential to the working 'of the machinery.

"It is not regrettable in our opinion if a caste, 'which has considerable weight in public affairs, is 'a manly one, contemptuous of wealth and sophistry, 'ready always to risk its own life for the faith which 'is in it. The influence of a military caste may have 'its drawbacks; but at any rate it has kept the 'peace in Germany for not far short of half a century '—kept it successfully until, as some people have 'thought, the professors acquired too large a share 'of power.

"Is it so certain, moreover, that the lawyer 'caste, the self-advertising caste, and the financial 'caste are not all of them a great deal worse, even a 'great deal more dangerous to peace? Is a country 'any more likely to be safe, happy, and prosperous 'under the regime of a talking caste—of windbags 'resourcefully keeping their bellows full of air, and 'wheedling the most numerous with transparent

The devil's advocate.

'falsehoods — than where civil servants of tried 'wisdom and experience are responsible for carrying 'on affairs of state, aided at their high task by sober 'military opinion ?[1]

"As for our Kaiser, whom you regard as a crafty 'and ambitious tyrant, he appears in our view as 'the incarnation of patriotic duty, burdened though 'not overwhelmed by care—a lover of peace, so long 'as peace may be had with honour and safety; but 'if this may not be, then a stern, though reluctant, 'drawer of the sword. It is true that the Kaiser's 'government is in many important respects a purely 'personal government. His is the ultimate responsi- 'bility for high policy. He fulfils the function in 'our system of that strong central power, without 'which the most ingeniously constructed organisation 'is but impotence.

"The German people are ahead of the English 'and the Americans in self-knowledge; for they 'realise that there are many things appertaining 'to government, which cannot be discussed in the 'newspapers, or on the platform, any more than the 'policy and conduct of a great business can be made 'known in advance to the staff, and to trade com- 'petitors all over the world. And so, believing the 'Kaiser's government to be honest, capable, and 'devoted to the public weal, the German people 'trust it without reservation to decide when action 'shall be taken in a variety of spheres.

"This system of ours which is founded in reason, 'and in experience of modern conditions, and which

[1] Comment has already been made on the difficulty each nation has in understanding the spirit of the institutions of its neighbours. If this is borne in mind these depreciatory references of the Freiherr may be forgiven.

CHAPTER VI.

The devil's advocate.

'is upheld by the unfaltering confidence of a great 'people, you are wont to condemn as tyrannical and 'reactionary. But can democracy stand against it? '—Democracy infirm of purpose, jealous, grudging, 'timid, changeable, unthorough, unready, without 'foresight, obscure in its aims, blundering along in 'an age of lucidity guided only by a faltering and 'confused instinct! Given anything like an equal 'contest, is it conceivable that such an undis- 'ciplined chaos can prevail against the Hohenzollern 'Empire?

"Of late your newspapers have been busily 'complaining of what they call 'German lies,' 'boast- 'fulness,' and 'vulgar abuse.' They have taunted 'our government with not daring to trust the people. 'Our Headquarters bulletins have been vigorously 'taken to task by the Allies on these and other 'grounds.

"But all nations will acclaim their victories louder 'than they will trumpet their defeats. This is in 'human nature. No official communiqué will ever 'be a perfect mirror of truth. It will never give the 'whole picture, but only a part; and by giving only 'a part it will often mislead. Were we to believe 'literally what the various governments have hitherto 'given out as regards their respective advances, the 'Germans by this time might perhaps have been at 'Moscow in the East and somewhere about the 'Azores in the West. But by the same token the 'Russians should have been on the Rhine and the 'French and English Allies at Berlin.

"I read your newspapers, and I read our own. 'I do not think our journalists, though they do their 'best, can fairly claim to excel yours in the contest

CHAPTER VI.

The devil's advocate.

'of boastfulness and vulgar abuse. And as regards 'the utterances of responsible public men in our 'two countries, can you really contend that we 'Germans are more open to the reproach of vain-'glorious and undignified speech than the British? 'Our Kaiser denies having used the words, so often 'attributed to him in your press, about 'General 'French's contemptible little army,' and in Germany 'we believe his denial. But even if he did in fact 'utter this expression, is it not quite as seemly and 'restrained as references to 'digging rats out of 'a hole'—as applied to our gallant navy—or to that 'later announcement from the same quarter which 'was recently addressed to the Mayor of Scarborough 'about 'baby-killers'? Such expressions are re-'grettable, no doubt, but not of the first importance. 'They are a matter of temperament. An ill-balanced, 'or even a very highly-strung nature, will be betrayed 'into blunders of this sort more readily than the 'phlegmatic person, or one whose upbringing has 'been in circles where self-control is the rule of 'manners.

"But what puzzles us Germans perhaps more than 'any of your other charges against us is, when you 'say that our rulers do not trust the people as the 'British Government does.

"You accuse our War Office of publishing accounts 'of imaginary victories to revive our drooping con-'fidence, and of concealing actual disasters lest our 'country should fall into a panic of despondency. 'There was surely nothing imaginary about the fall 'of Liège, Namur, Maubeuge, Laon, or La Fere. 'The engagements before Metz, at Mons, Charleroi, 'and Amiens, the battles of Lodz and Lyck, were

CHAPTER VI.

The devil's advocate.

'not inconsiderable successes for German arms, 'or at the very least for German generalship. 'The victory of Tannenberg was among the greatest 'in history, reckoning in numbers alone. Our 'government made no secret of the German retire- 'ment—retreat if you prefer the term—from the 'Marne to the Aisne, or of that other falling back 'after the first attempt on Warsaw. Naturally they 'laid less emphasis on reverses than on conquests, 'but what government has ever acted otherwise? 'Certainly not the French, or the Russian, or your 'own. And what actual disasters have we concealed? 'In what respect, as regards the conduct of this war, 'have we, the German people, been trusted less than 'yours?

"I am especially interested, I confess, as a student 'of British politics, in this matter of 'trusting the 'people.' All your great writers have led me to 'believe that here lies the essential difference between 'your system and ours, and that the great superiority 'of yours to ours is demonstrated in the confidence 'which your statesmen never hesitate to place in 'the wisdom, fortitude, and patriotism of the people. 'Frankly, I do not understand it. Trust must surely 'have some esoteric meaning when applied to your 'populace which foreigners are unable to apprehend. 'I can discover no other sense in your phrase about ''trusting the people,' than that they are trusted 'not to find out their politicians. It certainly 'cannot be believed that you trust your people to 'hear the truth; for if so why has your government 'practised so rigorous an economy of this virtue, 'doling it out very much as we have lately been doing 'with our wheat and potatoes?

CHAPTER VI.

The devil's advocate.

"Has your government not concealed actual 'disaster—concealed it from their own people, though 'from no one else; for all the world was on the broad 'grin? Everybody knew of your misfortune save 'a certain large portion of the British public. The 'motive of your government could not have been 'to hide it away from the Germans, or the Austrians, 'or from neutrals, for the illustrated papers all 'over the globe, even in your own colonies, contained 'pictures reproduced from photographs of the occur-'rence. It was only possible to muzzle the press and 'blindfold the people of the United Kingdom, and 'these things your government did; acting no doubt 'very wisely.

"Again after the great German victory over the 'Russians at Tannenberg in September last, an 'official bulletin of simple and conspicuous candour 'was published at Petrograd which confirmed in most 'of the . . . .

'. . . . .

'. . . . .

'. . . . .

'. . . . .

'. . . . .

'. . . . .

'. . . . .

'. . . . .

"Why did your Press Bureau during the heavy 'fighting from the middle of October to the middle of 'November persist in maintaining that 'the British 'are still gaining ground.' The British resistance 'from the beginning to the end of the four weeks' battle 'round Ypres is not likely to be forgotten by our 'German soldiers, still less to be belittled by them.

CHAPTER VI.

The devil's advocate.

'It was surely a great enough feat of arms to bear the 'light of truth. But . . . .
'. . . . .
'. . . . .

"But is the same true of the British people? 'Can they be trusted to bear the light of truth?

"You cannot wonder if we Germans, and for that 'matter the whole world, have drawn certain con-'clusions from these and other incidents. We do 'not doubt that your ministers have acted wisely 'in suppressing bad tidings; but why should they 'have taken all those pains and endured the derision, 'while incurring the distrust, of foreign countries—'a material injury, mind you, and not merely a 'sentimental one—unless they had known, only too 'well, that publication of this or that piece of news 'would have too painfully affected the nerves of your 'people? Concealment of checks, reverses, and 'disasters which had not already become known 'to the Austrians and ourselves might have served a 'useful military purpose; but what purpose except 'that of a sedative for British public opinion could 'be served by the concealment of such matters when 'we, your enemies, knew them already? Have you 'ever thought of asking your American friends in 'what order they would place the candour of the 'official communications which emanate from Berlin, 'Petrograd, Paris, and London?

"Shortly before Christmas one of your legal 'ministers, who, I understand, is specially responsible 'for looking after the Press Bureau, explained to the 'House of Commons the principles by which he had 'been guided in the suppression of news and comment. 'He should refuse, he said, to publish any criticism

CHAPTER VI.

The devil's advocate.

'which might tend to disturb popular confidence in 'the Government, or which might cause the people 'of England to think that their affairs were in a 'really serious state. On practical grounds there is no 'doubt something to be said for such a policy; but '(will you tell me?) has any autocratic government 'ever laid down a more drastic rule for blindfolding 'the people in order to preserve its own existence?[1]

"Pondering upon these things, I scratch my 'head and marvel what you can possibly have had 'in yours, when you used to assure us that the 'surpassing merit of the English political system was 'that it trusted the people, the inherent weakness of 'ours, the Austrian, and the Russian that they did not.

"Your Prime Minister, speaking in the early 'autumn, thus adjured the men of Wales:—'Be 'worthy of those who went before you, and leave to 'your children the richest of all inheritances, the 'memory of fathers who, in a great cause, put self-'sacrifice before ease, and honour above life itself.' 'These are noble words, of Periclean grandeur. 'But have they met with a general response? Are 'these sentiments prevalent outside government 'circles, among those—the bulk of your people—'who do not come under the direct influence of minis-'terial inspiration and example? If so, why then

[1] I have had considerable difficulty in discovering the basis of this extraordinary charge. It seems to consist of the following passage from a speech by Sir Stanley Buckmaster, the Solicitor-General and Chairman of the Press Bureau on November 12, 1914. It is distressing to see how far national prejudice is apt to mislead a hostile critic like the Freiherr von Hexenküchen: "Criticism of the Government, or of members of the 'Government, is not that which I have ever stopped, except when such 'criticism is of such a character that it might destroy public confidence 'in the Government, which at this moment is charged with the conduct of 'the war, or might in any way weaken the confidence of the people in the 'administration of affairs, or otherwise cause distress or disturbance amongst 'people in thinking their affairs were in a really serious state."

CHAPTER VI.

The devil's advocate.

'have your rulers not screwed up their courage 'to call for national service? Why do they still 'continue to depend for their recruits upon sensa'tional advertisements, newspaper puffs, oratorical 'entreaties, and private influence of a singularly 'irregular sort?

"Is not this the reason?—Your government is 'afraid—even in this great struggle, where (as they 'put it) your future existence as a nation is at stake—'that the English people—or at any rate so large a 'proportion of them, as if rendered uncomfortable 'could create a political disturbance—is not even yet 'prepared to make the necessary sacrifices. And 'so, to the amazement of us Germans, you let the 'older men, with families dependent on them, go 'forth to the war, urged on by a high sense of duty, 'while hundreds of thousands of young unmarried 'men are still allowed to stay at home.

"You are still, it would appear, enamoured of 'your voluntary system. You have not yet abandoned 'your belief that it is the duty of the man, who 'possesses a sense of duty, to protect the skin, family, 'and property of the man who does not. To us 'this seems a topsy-turvy creed, and not more 'topsy-turvy than contemptible. In Germany and 'France—where for generations past the doctrine of 'private sacrifice for the public weal is ingrained, 'and has been approved in principle and applied in 'practice with unfaltering devotion—a 'voluntary' 'system might conceivably have some chance of pro'viding such an army as you are in search of. But 'to the United Kingdom surely it is singularly in'applicable? Let me illustrate my meaning by a 'comparison.

"Our Kaiser in his New Year's message—which 'in Germany we all read with enthusiasm, and con-'sidered very noble and appropriate—summed up the '*military* situation by saying that after five months' 'hard and hot fighting the war was still being 'waged almost everywhere off German soil, and on 'the enemies' territories. And he summed up the '*domestic* situation by saying (and this, believe me, 'is true) that our nation stands in unexampled 'harmony, prepared to sacrifice its heart's blood for 'the defence of the Fatherland. Another three 'months have passed away, and these statements 'still hold good.

CHAPTER VI.

The devil's advocate.

"The point to which I chiefly wish to call your 'attention is one of numbers, and I will take my 'estimates of numbers from your own most famous 'newspaper experts.

"Your claim, as I understand it, is that on New 'Year's Day 1915 you had—exclusive of Indian troops 'and Dominion contingents—between 2,000,000 and '2,500,000 men training and in the field.

"Germany alone (here again I quote your English 'experts), without reckoning Austria, has actually 'put into the field during the past five months '5,000,000 men. Of these it is stated by your news-'papers that she has lost in round figures 1,500,000, 'who have either been killed, or taken prisoners, 'or are too severely wounded to return as yet to 'the fighting line. But in spite of this depletion, 'your military statisticians tell us that Germany 'and her ally, at New Year's Day, still outnumbered 'the Allies on both the Eastern and the Western 'frontier.

"The same high authorities tell us further, that

CHAPTER VI.

The devil's advocate.

'during this period of five months, the German 'Government has called upon the civil population, 'has appealed to able-bodied men who had previously 'been exempt from military service, and that by 'this means it has obtained, and has been engaged in 'training, arming, and equipping another 4,000,000 'or 4,500,000 who, it is anticipated, will become 'available for war purposes in new formations, during 'the spring and summer of the present year.

"Our Government, therefore, according to your 'own account, has not been afraid to ask the civil 'population to serve, and this is the response. Does 'it look as if the national spirit had been quenched 'under our autocratic system?

"Out of our whole population of sixty-five millions 'we have apparently raised for military service on 'land and naval service at sea, between 9,000,000 and '11,000,000 men since this war began. Out of your 'whole population of forty-five millions you have 'succeeded in raising for these same purposes only 'something between 2,000,000 and 2,500,000 men. 'And in your case, be it observed, in order to attract 'recruits, you have offered good wages and munificent 'separation allowances; while in our case men serve 'without pay.

"This numerical comparison is worth carrying a 'stage further. Germany and her ally have between 'them a total population of 115,000,000. The United 'Kingdom (including the people of European stock 'who inhabit the various Dominions), France, Russia, 'Belgium, Servia, and Montenegro number in round 'figures about 280,000,000. Roughly speaking, these 'are odds of seven to three against us. And I am 'leaving out of account all the non-European races—

The devil's advocate.

'the Turks on the one side, the Japanese and the 'Indians on the other. If these were included the 'odds would be much heavier.

"And yet our Kaiser spoke but the simple 'truth, when he told us on New Year's Day that, 'after five months of war, the German armies were 'almost everywhere on the territories of their enemies. 'We are not only keeping you back and defying 'all your efforts to invade us; but like the infant 'Hercules, we have gripped you by your throats, and 'were holding you out at arm's length!

"I do not of course pretend to look at this matter 'except from the German standpoint; but is there 'any flaw in my reasoning, is there anything at all 'unfair, if I thus sum up my conclusions?—By 'Midsummer next—after stupendous efforts of the 'oratorical and journalistic kind—after an enormous 'amount of shouting, music-hall singing, cinema films, 'and showy advertising of every description—after 'making great play with the name and features of a 'popular field-marshal, in a manner which must have 'shocked both his natural modesty and soldierly 'pride—after all this you expect, or say you expect, 'that you will possess between two and two-and-a-half 'millions of men trained, armed, equipped, and ready 'to take the field.

"As against this, during the same period, and 'out of the less military half of our male population, 'without any shouting or advertising to speak of, 'we shall have provided approximately double that 'number. We have raised these new forces quietly, 'without any fuss, and without a word of protest 'from any of our people. We are training them 'without any serious difficulty. We are arming

CHAPTER VI.

The devil's advocate.

'them, equipping them, clothing them, and housing 'them without any difficulty at all.

"To conclude this interesting contrast, may I 'ask you—is it true, as the French newspapers allege, 'that you are about to invite, or have already invited, 'your Japanese Allies to send some portion of their 'Army to European battlefields? With what face 'can you make this appeal when you have not yet 'called upon your own people to do, what every other 'people engaged in the present struggle, has already 'done?

"After you have pondered upon this strange and 'startling contrast, will you still hold to the opinion 'that the German system—which you have affected 'to despise, on the ground that it does not rest upon 'what you are pleased to term 'a popular basis'—is 'at any point inferior to your own in its hold upon 'the hearts of the people?

What is meant by the phrase—'a popular 'basis'? Is it something different from the support 'of the people, the will of the people, the devotion 'of the people? And if it is different, is it better—'judging, that is, by its results in times of trouble—'or is it worse?"

So the cultured Freiherr, watching democracy at work in Britain, its ancient home, concludes with this question—"Is this timid, jealous, and distracted 'thing possessed of any real faith in itself; and if so, 'will it fight for its faith to the bitter end? Is the 'British system one which even the utmost faith in it 'can succeed in propping up? Does it possess any 'inherent strength; or is it merely a thing of paste-'board and make-believe, fore-ordained to perish?"

CHAPTER VII

THE CONFLICT OF SYSTEMS AND IDEAS

CHAPTER VII.

The conflict of systems and ideas.

THE Freiherr's discourse raises a large number of questions, some of them unarguable. Others again are too much so; for if once started upon, argument with regard to them need never end. Some of his contentions have already been dealt with in previous chapters; some on the other hand, such as the British methods of recruiting, will be considered later on. It must, however, be admitted that his taunts and criticisms do not all rebound with blunted points from our shield of self-complacency; some, if only a few, get home and rankle.

We are challenged to contrast our faith in our own political institutions with that of the Germans in theirs; also to measure the intrinsic strength of that form of political organisation called 'democracy' against that other form which is known as 'autocracy.'

The German state is the most highly developed and efficient type of personal monarchy at present known to the world. Its triumphs in certain directions have been apparent from the beginning. It would be sheer waste of time to dispute the fact that Germany was incomparably better prepared, organised, and educated for this war—the purpose of which was the spoliation of her neighbours—

CHAPTER VII.

than any of her neighbours were for offering resistance.

The conflict of systems and ideas.

But what the Freiherr does not touch upon at all is the conflict between certain underlying ideas of right and wrong—old ideas, which are held by Russia, France, and ourselves, and which now find themselves confronted by new and strange ideas which have been exceedingly prevalent among the governing classes in Germany for many years past. He does not raise *this* issue, any more than his fellow-countrymen now raise it either in America or at home. It is true that there was a flamboyant outburst from a few faithful Treitschkians and Nietzschians, both in prose and poetry, during those weeks of August and September which teemed with German successes; but their voices soon sank below audibility—possibly by order *verboten*—in a swiftly dying fall. We, however, cannot agree to let this aspect of the matter drop, merely because patriotic Germans happen to have concluded that the present time is inopportune for the discussion of it.

There are two clear and separate issues. From the point of view of posterity the more important of these, perhaps, may prove to be this conflict in the region of moral ideas. From the point of view of the present generation, however, the chief matter of practical interest is the result of a struggle for the preservation of our own institutions, against the aggression of a race which has not yet learned the last and hardest lesson of civilisation—how to live and let live.

The present war may result in the bankruptcy of the Habsburg and Hohenzollern dynasties. It is very desirable, however, to make clear the fact

The conflict of systems and ideas.

that the alternative is the bankruptcy of 'democracy.' Our institutions are now being subjected to a severer strain than they have ever yet experienced. Popular government is standing its trial. It will be judged by the result; and no one can say that this is an unfair test to apply to human institutions.

No nation, unless it be utterly mad, will retain a form of government which from some inherent defect is unable to protect itself against external attack. Is democratic government capable of looking ahead, making adequate and timely preparation, calling for and obtaining from its people the sacrifices which are necessary in order to preserve their own existence? Can it recover ground which has been lost, and maintain a long, costly, and arduous struggle, until, by victory, it has placed national security beyond the reach of danger?

Defeat in the present war would shake popular institutions to their foundations in England as well as France; possibly also in regions which are more remote than either of these. But something far short of defeat—anything indeed in the nature of a drawn game or stalemate—would assuredly bring the credit of democracy so low that it would be driven to make some composition with its creditors.

Words, like other currencies, have a way of changing their values as the world grows older. Until comparatively recent times 'democracy' was a term of contempt, as 'demagogue' still is to-day.

The founders of American Union abhorred 'Democracy,'[1] and took every precaution which occurred to them in order to ward it off. Their aim was

[1] Washington, Hamilton, Madison, Jay.

CHAPTER VII.

The conflict of systems and ideas.

'Popular,' or 'Representative Government'—a thing which they conceived to lie almost at the opposite pole. Their ideal was a state, the citizens of which chose their leaders at stated intervals, and trusted them. Democracy, as it appeared in their eyes, was a political chaos where the people chose its servants, and expected from them only servility. There was an ever-present danger, calling for stringent safeguards, that the first, which they esteemed the best of all constitutional arrangements, would degenerate into the second, which they judged to be the worst.

Until times not so very remote it was only the enemies of Representative Government, or its most cringing flatterers, who spoke of it by the title of Democracy. Gradually, however, in the looseness of popular discussions, the sharpness of the original distinction wore off, so that the ideal system and its opposite—the good and the evil—are now confounded together under one name. There is no use fighting against current terminology; but it is well to bear in mind that terminology has no power to alter facts, and that the difference between the two principles still remains as wide as it was at the beginning.

When a people becomes so self-complacent that it mistakes its own ignorance for omniscience—so jealous of authority and impatient of contradiction that it refuses to invest with more than a mere shadow of power those whose business it is to govern—when the stock of leadership gives out, or remains hidden and undiscovered under a litter of showy refuse—when those who succeed in pushing themselves to the front are chiefly concerned not to lead, but merely to act the parts of leaders 'in silver slippers and amid applause'—when the chiefs of parties are so fearful of unpopularity that they will not assert their own opinions, or utter timely warnings, or proclaim what they know to be the truth—when such things as these come to pass the nation has reached that state which was dreaded by the framers of the American Constitution, and which—intending to warn mankind against it—they branded as 'Democracy.'

The conflict of systems and ideas.

Self-criticism makes for health in a people; but it may be overdone. If it purges the national spirit it is good; but if it should lead to pessimism, or to some impatient breach with tradition, it is one of the worst evils. One is conscious of a somewhat dangerous tendency in certain quarters at the present time to assume the worst with regard to the working of our own institutions.

Critics of this school have pointed out (what is undoubtedly true) that Germany has been far ahead of us in her preparations. Every month since war began has furnished fresh evidence of the far-sightedness, resourcefulness, thoroughness, and efficiency of all her military arrangements. Her commercial and financial resources have also been husbanded, and organised in a manner which excites our unwilling admiration. And what perhaps has been the rudest shock of all, is the apparent unity and devotion of the whole German people, in support of a war which, without exaggeration, may be said to have cast the shadow of death on every German home.

These critics further insist that our own nation has not shown itself more loyal, and that it did not rouse itself to the emergency with anything approaching the same swiftness. Timidity and a wilful self-

The conflict of systems and ideas.

deception, they say, have marked our policy for years before this war broke out. They marked it again when the crisis came upon us. Have they not marked it ever since war began? And who can have confidence that they will not continue to mark it until the end, whatever the end may be?

The conclusion therefore at which our more despondent spirits have arrived, is that the representative system has already failed us—that it has suffered that very degradation which liberal minds of the eighteenth century feared so much. How can democracy in the bad sense—democracy which has become decadent—which is concerned mainly with its rights instead of with its duties—with its comforts more than with the sacrifices which are essential to its own preservation—how can such a system make head against an efficient monarchy sustained by the enthusiastic devotion of a vigorous and intelligent people?

It does not seem altogether wise to despair of one's own institutions at the first check. Even democracy, in the best sense, is not a flawless thing. Of all forms of government it is the most delicate, more dependent than any other upon the supply of leaders. There are times of dearth when the crop of leadership is a short one. Nor are popular institutions, any more than our own vile bodies, exempt from disease. Disease, however, is not necessarily fatal. The patient may recover, and in the bracing air of a national crisis, such as the present, conditions are favourable for a cure.

And, after all, we may remind these critics that in 1792 democracy did in fact make head pretty successfully against monarchy. Though it was miserably unprovided, untrained, inferior to its enemies in every-

The conflict of systems and ideas.

thing save spirit and leadership, the states of Europe nevertheless—all but England—went down before it, in the years which followed, like a row of ninepins. Then as now, England, guarded by seas and sea-power, had a breathing-space allowed her, in which to adjust the spirit of her people to the new conditions.

That Germany will not conquer us with her arms we may well feel confident. But unless we conquer her with *our arms*—and this is a much longer step—there is a considerable danger that she may yet conquer us with *her ideas*. In that case the world will be thrown back several hundred years; and the blame for this disaster, should it occur, will be laid—and laid rightly—at the door of Democracy, because it vaunted a system which it had neither the fortitude nor the strength to uphold.

When we pass from the conflict between systems of government, and come to the other conflict of ideas as to right and wrong, we find ourselves faced with an antagonism which is wholly incapable of accommodation. In this war the stakes are something more than any of the material interests involved. It is a conflict where one faith is pitted against another. No casuistry will reconcile the ideal which inspires English policy with the ideal which inspires German policy. There is no sense—nothing indeed but danger—in arguing round the circle to prove that the rulers of these two nations are victims of some frightful misunderstanding, and that really at the bottom of their hearts they believe the same things. This is entirely untrue: they believe quite different things; things indeed which are as nearly as possible opposites.

CHAPTER VII.

The conflict of systems and ideas.

Our own belief is old, ingrained, and universal. It is accepted equally by the people and their rulers. We have held it so long that the articles of our creed have become somewhat blurred in outline—overgrown, like a memorial tablet, by moss and lichen.

In the case of our enemy the tablet is new and the inscription sharp. He who runs may read it in bold clear-cut lettering. But the belief of the German people in the doctrine which has been carved upon the stone is not yet universal, or anything like universal. It is not even general. It is fully understood and accepted only in certain strata of society; but it is responsible, without a doubt, for the making in cold blood of the policy which has led to this war. When the hour struck which the German rulers deemed favourable for conquest, war, according to their creed, became the duty as well as the interest of the Fatherland.

But so soon as war had been declared, the German people were allowed and even encouraged to believe that the making of war from motives of self-interest was a crime against humanity—the Sin against the Holy Ghost. They were allowed and encouraged to believe that the Allies were guilty of this crime and sin. And not only this, but war itself, which had been hymned in so many professorial rhapsodies, as a noble and splendid restorer of vigour and virtue, was now execrated with wailing and gnashing of teeth, as the most hideous of all human calamities.

It is clear from all this that the greater part of the German people regarded war in exactly the same light as the whole of the English people did. In itself it was a curse; and the man who deliberately contrived it for his own ends, or even for those of his

The conflict of systems and ideas.

country, was a criminal. The German people applied the same tests as we did, and it is not possible to doubt that in so doing they were perfectly sincere. They acted upon instinct. They had not learned the later doctrines of the pedantocracy, or how to steer by a new magnetic pole. They still held by the old Christian rules as to duties which exist between neighbours. To their simple old-fashioned loyalty what their Kaiser said must be the truth. And what their Kaiser said was that the Fatherland was attacked by treacherous foes. That was enough to banish all doubts. For the common people that was the reality and the only reality. Phrases about world-power and will-to-power—supposing they had ever heard or noticed them—were only mouthfuls of strange words, such as preachers of all kinds love to chew in the intervals of their discourses.

When the priests and prophets found themselves at last confronted by those very horrors which they had so often invoked, did their new-found faith desert them, or was it only that their tongues, for some reason, refused to speak the old jargon? Judging by their high-flown indignation against the Allies it would rather seem as if, in the day of wrath, they had hastily abandoned sophistication for the pious memories of their unlettered childhood. Their apostasy was too well done to have been hypocrisy.

With the rulers it was different. They knew clearly enough what they had done, what they were doing, and what they meant to do. When they remained sympathetically silent, amid the popular babble about the horrors of war and iniquity of peace-breakers, their tongues were not paralysed by remorse—they were merely in their cheeks. Their

CHAPTER VII.

sole concern was to humour public opinion, the results of whose disapproval they feared, quite as much as they despised its judgment.

The conflict of systems and ideas.

That war draws out and gives scope to some of the noblest human qualities, which in peace-time are apt to be hidden out of sight, no one will deny. That it is a great getter-rid of words and phrases, which have no real meaning behind them—that it is a great winnower of true men from shams, of staunch men from boasters and blowers of their own trumpets—that it is a great binder-together of classes, a great purifier of the hearts of nations, there is no need to dispute. Occasionally, though very rarely, it has proved itself to be a great destroyer of misunderstanding between the combatants themselves.

But although the whole of this is true, it does not lighten the guilt of the deliberate peace-breaker. Many of the same benefits, though in a lesser degree, arise out of a pestilence, a famine, or any other great national calamity; and it is the acknowledged duty of man to strive to the uttermost against these and to ward them off with all his strength. It is the same with war. To argue, as German intellectuals have done of late, that in order to expand their territories they were justified in scattering infection and deliberately inviting this plague, that the plague itself was a thing greatly for the advantage of the moral sanitation of the world—all this is merely the casuistry of a priesthood whom the vanity of rubbing elbows with men of action has beguiled of their salvation.

Somewhere in one of his essays Emerson introduces an interlocutor whom he salutes as 'little Sir.' One feels tempted to personify the whole corporation of German pedants under the same title. When they

The conflict of systems and ideas.

talk so vehemently and pompously about the duty of deliberate war-making for the expansion of the Fatherland, for the fulfilment of the theory of evolution, even for the glory of God on high, our minds are filled with wonder and a kind of pity.

Have they ever seen war except in their dreams, or a countryside in devastation? Have they ever looked with their own eyes on shattered limbs, or faces defaced, of which cases, and the like, there are already some hundreds of thousands in the hospitals of Europe, and may be some millions before this war is ended? Have they ever reckoned—except in columns of numerals without human meaning—how many more hundreds of thousands, in the flower of their age, have died and will die, or—more to be pitied—will linger on maimed and impotent when the war is ended? Have they realised any of these things, except in diagrams, and curves, and statistical tables, dealing with the matter—as they would say themselves, in their own dull and dry fashion—'under its broader aspects'—in terms, that is, of population, food-supply, and economic output?

Death, and suffering of many sorts occur in all wars—even in the most humane war. And this is not a humane war which the pedants have let loose upon us. Indeed, they have taught with some emphasis that humanity, under such conditions, is altogether a mistake.

"Sentimentality!" cries the 'little Sir' impatiently, "sickly sentimentality! In a world of 'men such things must be. God has ordained war."

Possibly. But what one feels is that the making of war is the Lord's own business and not the 'little Sir's.' It is the Lord's, as vengeance is, and earth-

CHAPTER VII.

quakes, floods, and droughts; not an office to be undertaken by mortals.

The conflict of systems and ideas.

The 'little Sir,' however, has devised a new order for the world, and apparently he will never rest satisfied until Heaven itself conforms to his initiative. He is audacious, for like the Titans he has challenged Zeus. But at times we are inclined to wonder—is he not perhaps trying too much? Is he not in fact engaged in an attempt to outflank Providence, whose pivot is infinity? And for this he is relying solely upon the resources of his own active little finite mind. He presses his attack most gallantly against human nature — back and forwards, up and down — but opposing all his efforts is there not a screen of adamantine crystal which cannot be pierced, of interminable superficies which cannot be circumvented? Is he not in some ways like a wasp, which beats itself angrily against a pane of glass?

PART III

THE SPIRIT OF BRITISH POLICY

I saw then in my Dream that he went on *thus*, even until he came at a bottom, where he saw, a little out of the way, three Men fast asleep with Fetters upon their heels.

The name of the one was *Simple*, another *Sloth*, and the third *Presumption*.

Christian then seeing them lie in this case, went to them, if peradventure he might awake them. And cried, You are like them that sleep on the top of a Mast, for the dead Sea is under you, a Gulf that hath no bottom. Awake therefore and come away; be willing also, and I will help you off with your Irons. He also told them, If he that goeth about like a *roaring Lion* comes by, you will certainly become a prey to his teeth.

With that they lookt upon him, and began to reply in this sort: *Simple* said, *I see no danger*; *Sloth* said, *Yet a little more sleep*; and *Presumption* said, *Every Vat must stand upon his own bottom*. And so they lay down to sleep again, and *Christian* went on his way.

The Pilgrim's Progress.

CHAPTER I

A REVOLUTIONARY PERIOD

(*January* 1901–*July* 1914)

CHAPTER I. — A revolutionary period.

It is not true to say that this is a war between the rival principles of democracy and autocracy. A too great absorption in our own particular sector of the situation has led certain writers to put forward, as a general explanation, this formula which is not only inadequate, but misleading. The real issue is something wider and deeper than a struggle between forms of government. It is concerned with the groundwork of human beliefs.

And yet it is unquestionably true to say, that by reason of Germany's procedure, this war is being waged against democracy—not perhaps by intention, but certainly in effect. For if the Allies should be defeated, or even if they should fail to conquer their present enemies, the result must necessarily be wounding to the credit of popular institutions all the world over, fatal to their existence in Europe at any rate, fatal conceivably at no long distance of time to their existence elsewhere than in Europe. For mankind, we may be sure, is not going to put up with any kind of government merely because it is ideally beautiful. No system will be tolerated

CHAPTER I.

A revolutionary period.

indefinitely which does not enable the people who live under it to protect themselves from their enemies. The instinct of self-preservation will drive them to seek for some other political arrangement which is competent, in the present imperfect condition of the world, to provide the first essential of a state, which is Security.

But although the whole fabric of democracy is threatened by this war, the principle of autocracy is not challenged by it either directly or indirectly. France and England are not fighting against personal monarchy any more than Russia is fighting against popular government. So far as the forms of constitutions are concerned each of the Allies would be well content to live and let live. They are none of them spurred on by propagandist illusions like the armies of the First Republic. Among Russians, devotion to their own institutions, and attachment to the person of their Emperor are inspired not merely by dictates of political expediency and patriotism, but also by their sense of religious duty.[1] It is inconceivable that the national spirit of Russia could ever have been roused to universal enthusiasm merely in order to fight the battles of democracy. And yet Russia is now ranged side by side with the French Republic and the British Commonwealth in perfect unison. What has induced her to submit to sacrifices —less indeed than those of Belgium, but equal to those of France, and much greater so far than our own—unless some issue was at stake wider and deeper even than the future of popular government?

The instincts of a people are vague and obscure. The reasons which are put forward, the motives

[1] Cf. 'Russia and her Ideals,' *Round Table*, December 1914.

A revolutionary period.

which appear upon the surface, the provocations which lead to action, the immediate ends which are sought after and pursued, rarely explain the true causes or proportions of any great national struggle. But for all that, the main issue, as a rule, is realised by the masses who are engaged, although it is not realised through the medium of coherent argument or articulate speech.

The present war is a fight, not between democracy and autocracy, but between the modern spirit of Germany and the unchanging spirit of civilisation. And it is well to bear in mind that the second of these is not invincible. It has suffered defeat before now, at various epochs in the world's history, when attacked by the same forces which assail it to-day. Barbarism is not any the less barbarism because it employs weapons of precision, because it avails itself of the discoveries of science and the mechanism of finance, or because it thinks it worth while to hire bands of learned men to shriek pæans in its praise and invectives against its victims. Barbarism is not any the less barbarism because its methods are up to date. It is known for what it is by the ends which it pursues and the spirit in which it pursues them.

The modern spirit of Germany is materialism in its crudest form—the undistracted pursuit of wealth, and of power as a means to wealth. It is materialism, rampant and self-confident, fostered by the state — subsidised, regulated, and, where thought advisable, controlled by the state—supported everywhere by the diplomatic resources of the state—backed in the last resort by the fleets and armies of the state. It is the most highly organised machine,

CHAPTER I.

A revolutionary period.

the most deliberate and thorough-going system, for arriving at material ends which has ever yet been devised by man. It is far more efficient, but not a whit less material, than 'Manchesterism' of the Victorian era, which placed its hopes in 'free' competition, and also than that later development of trusts and syndicates—hailing from America—which aims at levying tribute on society by means of 'voluntary' co-operation. And just as the English professors, who fell prostrate in adoration before the prosperity of cotton-spinners, found no difficulty in placing self-interest upon the loftiest pedestal of morality, so German professors have succeeded in erecting for the joint worship of the Golden Calf and the War-god Wotun, high twin altars which look down with pity and contempt upon the humbler shrines of the Christian faith.

The morality made in Manchester has long ago lost its reputation. That which has been made in Germany more recently must in the end follow suit; for, like its predecessor, it is founded upon a false conception of human nature and cannot endure. But in the interval, if it be allowed to triumph, it may work evil, in comparison with which that done by our own devil-take-the-hindmost philosophers sinks into insignificance.

Looking at the present war from the standpoint of the Allies, the object of it is to repel the encroachments of materialism, working its way through the ruin of ideas, which have been cherished always, save in the dark ages when civilisation was overwhelmed by barbarism. Looking at the matter from our own particular standpoint, it is also incidentally a struggle for the existence of democracy. The chief question

A revolutionary period.

we have to ask ourselves is whether our people will fight for their faith and traditions with the same skill and courage as the Germans for their material ends? Will they endure sacrifices with the same fortitude as France and Russia? Will they face the inevitable eagerly and promptly, or will they play the laggard and by delay ruin all—themselves most of all? . . . This war is not going to be won for us by other people, or by some miraculous intervention of Providence, or by the Germans running short of copper, or by revolutions in Berlin, nor even by the break-up of the Austrian Empire. In order to win it we shall have to put out our full strength, to organise our resources in men and material as we have never done before during the whole of our history. We have not accomplished these things as yet, although we have expressed our determination, and are indeed willing to attempt them. We were taken by surprise, and the immediate result has been a great confusion, very hard to disentangle.

Considering how little, before war began, our people had been taken into the confidence of successive governments, as to the relations of the British Empire with the outside world; how little education of opinion there had been, as to risks, and dangers, and means of defence; how little leading and clear guidance, both before and since, as to duties—considering all these omissions one can only marvel that the popular response has been what it is, and that the confusion was not many times worse.

What was the mood of the British race when this war broke upon them so unexpectedly? To what extent were they provided against it in a material sense? And still more important, how far were

CHAPTER I.

A revolutionary period.

their minds and hearts prepared to encounter it? It is important to understand those things, but in order to do this it is necessary to look back over a few years.

By a coincidence which may prove convenient to historians, the end of the nineteenth century marked the beginning of a new epoch [1]—an interlude, of brief duration as it proved—upon which the curtain was rung down shortly before midnight on the 4th of August 1914.

Between these two dates, in a space of something over thirteen years, events had happened in a quick succession, both within the empire and abroad, which disturbed or dissolved many ancient understandings. The spirit of change had been busy with mankind, and needs unknown to a former generation had grown clamorous. Objects of hope had presented themselves, driving old ideas to the wall, and unforeseen dangers had produced fresh groupings, compacts, and associations between states, and parties, and individual men.

In Europe during this period the manifest determination of Germany to challenge the naval supremacy of Britain, by the creation of a fleet designed and projected as the counterpart of her overwhelming army, had threatened the security of the whole continent, and had put France, Russia, and England upon terms not far removed from those of an alliance. The gravity of this emergency had induced our politicians to exclude, for the time being, this department of public affairs from the bitterness of their party struggles; and it had also drawn

[1] Queen Victoria died on January 22, 1901.

CHAPTER I.

the governments of the United Kingdom and the Dominions into relations closer than ever before, for the purpose of mutual defence.[1]

A revolutionary period.

In the meanwhile there had been developments even more startling in the hitherto unchanging East. Japan, as the result of a great war,[2] had become a first-class power, redoubtable both by sea and land. China, the most populous, the most ancient, and the most conservative of despotisms, had suddenly sought her salvation under the milder institutions of a republic.[3]

The South African war, ended by the Peace of Pretoria, had paved the way for South African Union.[4] The achievement of this endeavour had been applauded by men of all parties; some finding in it a welcome confirmation of their theories with regard to liberty and self-government; others again drawing from it encouragement to a still bolder undertaking. For if South Africa had made a precedent, the existing state of the world had supplied a motive, for the closer union of the empire.

Within the narrower limits of the United Kingdom changes had also occurred within this period which, from another point of view, were equally momentous. In 1903 Mr. Chamberlain had poured new wine into old bottles, and in so doing had hastened the inevitable end of Unionist predominance by changing on a sudden the direction of party policy. In the unparalleled defeat which ensued two and a half years later the Labour party appeared for the first time, formidable both in numbers and ideas.

A revolution had likewise been proceeding in

[1] Imperial Conference on Defence, summer of 1909.
[2] 1904–1905. [3] 1911. [4] May 1902.

CHAPTER I.

A revolutionary period.

our institutions as well as in the minds of our people. The balance of the state had been shifted by a curtailment of the powers of the House of Lords [1]—the first change which had been made by statute in the fundamental principle of the Constitution since the passing of the Act of Settlement.[2] In July 1914 further changes of a similar character, hardly less important under a practical aspect, were upon the point of receiving the Royal Assent.[3]

Both these sets of changes—that which had been already accomplished and the other which was about to pass into law—had this in common, that even upon the admissions of their own authors they were incomplete. Neither in the Parliament Act nor in the Home Rule Act was there finality. The composition of the Second Chamber had been set down for early consideration, whilst a revision of the constitutional relations between England, Scotland, and Wales was promised so soon as the case of Ireland had been dealt with.

It seemed as if the modern spirit had at last, in earnest, opened an inquisition upon the adequacy of our ancient unwritten compact, which upon the whole, had served its purpose well for upwards of two hundred years. It seemed as if that compact were in the near future to be tested thoroughly, and examined in respect of its fitness for dealing with the needs of the time—with the complexities and the vastness of the British Empire—with the evils which prey upon us from within, and with the dangers which threaten us from without.

Questioners were not drawn from one party alone.

[1] Parliament Act became law August 1911.

[2] 1689.

[3] Home Rule Bill became law August 1914.

A revolutionary period.

They were pressing forwards from all sides. It was not merely the case of Ireland, or the powers of the Second Chamber, or its composition, or the general congestion of business, or the efficiency of the House of Commons: it was the whole machinery of government which seemed to need overhauling and reconsideration in the light of new conditions. Most important of all these constitutional issues was that which concerned the closer union of the Empire.

It was little more than eighty years since the Iron Duke had described the British Constitution as an incomparably devised perfection which none but a madman would seek to change. That was not now the creed of any political party or indeed of any thinking man. No one was satisfied with things as they were. Many of the most respectable old phrases had become known for empty husks, out of which long since had dropped whatever seed they may originally have contained. Many of the old traditions were dead or sickly, and their former adherents were now wandering at large, like soldiers in the middle ages, when armies were disbanded in foreign parts, seeking a new allegiance, and constituting in the meanwhile a danger to security and the public peace.

And also, within this brief period, the highest offices had become vacant, and many great figures had passed from the scene. Two sovereigns had died full of honour. Two Prime Ministers had also died, having first put off the burden of office, each at the zenith of his popularity. Of the two famous men upon the Unionist side who remained when Lord Salisbury tendered his resignation, the one since 1906 had been wholly withdrawn from public life,

CHAPTER I.

while the other, four years later, had passed the leadership into younger hands.[1]

A revolutionary period.

There is room for an almost infinite variety of estimate as to the influence which is exercised by pre-eminent characters upon public affairs and national ideals. The verdict of the day after is always different from that of a year after. The verdict of the next generation, while differing from both, is apt to be markedly different from that of the generation which follows it. The admiration or censure of the moment is followed by a reaction no less surely than the reaction itself is followed by a counter-reaction. Gradually the oscillations become shorter, as matters pass out of the hands of journalists and politicians into those of the historian. Possibly later judgments are more true. We have more knowledge, of a kind. Seals are broken one by one, and we learn how this man really thought and how the other acted, in both cases differently from what had been supposed. We have new facts submitted to us, and possibly come nearer the truth. But while we gain so much, we also lose in other directions. We lose the sharp savour of the air. The keen glance and alert curiosity of contemporary vigilance are lacking. Conditions and circumstances are no longer clear, and as generation after generation passes away they become more dim. The narratives of the great historians and novelists are to a large extent either faded or false. We do not trust the most vivid presentments written by the man of genius in his study a century after the event, while we know well that even the shrewdest of contemporaneous observers is certain to omit many

[1] Mr. Chamberlain died July 2, 1914; Mr. Balfour resigned the leadership of the Unionist party on November 8, 1911.

A revolutionary period.

of the essentials. If Macaulay is inadequate in one direction, Pepys is equally inadequate in another. And if the chronicler at the moment, and the historian in the future are not to be wholly believed, the writer who comments after a decade or less upon things which are fresh in his memory is liable to another form of error; for either he is swept away by the full current of the reaction, or else his judgments are embittered by a sense of the hopelessness of swimming against it.

This much, however, may be said safely—that the withdrawal of any pre-eminent character from the scene, whether it be Queen Victoria or King Edward, Lord Salisbury or Mr. Chamberlain, produces in a greater or less degree that same loosening of allegiance and disturbance of ideas, which are so much dreaded by the conservative temperament from the removal of an ancient institution. For a pre-eminent character is of the same nature as an institution. The beliefs, loyalties, and ideals of millions were attached to the personality of the Queen. The whole of that prestige which Queen Victoria drew from the awe, reverence, affection, and prayers of her people could not be passed along with the crown to King Edward. The office of sovereign was for the moment stripped and impoverished of some part of its strength, and was only gradually replenished as the new monarch created a new, and to some extent a different, loyalty of his own. So much is a truism. But, when there is already a ferment in men's minds, the disappearance in rapid succession of the pre-eminent characters of the age helps on revolution by putting an end to a multitude of customary attachments, and by setting sentiments adrift to wander in search of new heroes.

CHAPTER I.

A revolutionary period.

A change of some importance had also come over the character of the House of Commons. The old idea that it was a kind of grand jury of plain men, capable in times of crisis of breaking with their parties, had at last finally disappeared. In politics there was no longer any place for plain men. The need was for professionals, and professionals of this sort, like experts in other walks of life, were worthy of their hire.

The decision to pay members of Parliament came as no surprise. The marvel was rather that it had not been taken at an earlier date, seeing that for considerably more than a century this item had figured in the programmes of all advanced reformers. The change, nevertheless, when it came, was no trivial occurrence, but one which was bound fundamentally to affect the character of the popular assembly; whether for better or worse was a matter of dispute.

Immense, however, as were the possibilities contained in the conversion of unpaid amateurs into professional and stipendiary politicians, what excited even more notice at the time than the thing itself, were the means by which it was accomplished. No attempt was made to place this great constitutional reform definitely and securely upon the statute book. To have followed this course would have meant submitting a bill, and a bill would have invited discussion at all its various stages. Moreover, the measure might have been challenged by the House of Lords, in which case delay would have ensued; and a subject, peculiarly susceptible to malicious misrepresentation, would have been kept—possibly for so long as three years—under the critical eyes of public opinion.

A revolutionary period.

Apparently this beneficent proposal was one of those instances, so rare in modern political life, where neither publicity nor advertisement was sought. On the contrary, the object seemed to be to do good by stealth; and for this purpose a simple financial resolution was all that the law required. The Lords had recently been warned off and forbidden to interfere with money matters, their judgment being under suspicion, owing to its supposed liability to be affected by motives of self-interest. The House of Commons was therefore sole custodian of the public purse; and in this capacity its members were invited to vote themselves four hundred pounds a year all round, as the shortest and least ostentatious way of raising the character and improving the quality of the people's representatives.

Even by July 1914 the effect of this constitutional amendment upon our old political traditions had become noticeable in various directions. But the means by which it was accomplished are no less worthy of note than the reform itself, when we are endeavouring to estimate the changes which have come over Parliament during this short but revolutionary epoch. The method adopted seemed to indicate a novel attitude on the part of members of the House of Commons towards the Imperial Exchequer, on the part of the Government towards members of the House of Commons, and on the part of both towards the people whom they trusted. It was adroit, expeditious, and businesslike; and to this extent seemed to promise well for years to come, when the professionals should have finally got rid of the amateurs, and taken things wholly into their own hands. Hostile critics, it is true, denounced the

CHAPTER I.

A revolutionary period.

reform bluntly as corruption, and the method of its achievement as furtive and cynical; but for this class of persons no slander is ever too gross—*They have said. Quhat say they? Let them be saying.*

The party leaders were probably neither worse men nor better than they had been in the past; but they were certainly smaller; while on the other hand the issues with which they found themselves confronted were bigger.

Great characters are like tent-pegs. One of their uses is to prevent the political camp from being blown to ribbons. Where they are too short or too frail, we may look for such disorders as have repeated themselves at intervals during the past few years. A blast of anger or ill-temper has blown, or a gust of sentiment, or even a gentle zephyr of sentimentality, and the whole scene has at once become a confusion of flapping canvas, tangled cordage, and shouting, struggling humanity. Such unstable conditions are fatal to equanimity; they disturb the fortitude of the most stalwart follower, and cause doubt and distrust on every hand.

Since the Liberal Government came into power in the autumn of 1905, neither of the great parties had succeeded in earning the respect of the other; and as the nature of man is not subject to violent fluctuations, it may safely be concluded that this misfortune had been due either to some defect or inadequacy of leadership, or else to conditions of an altogether extraordinary character.

During these ten sessions the bulk of the statute book had greatly increased, and much of this increase was no doubt healthy tissue. This period, notwith-

A revolutionary period.

standing, will ever dwell in the memory as a squalid episode. Especially is this the case when we contrast the high hopes and promises, not of one party alone, with the results which were actually achieved.

Democracy, if the best, is also the most delicate form of human government. None suffers so swiftly or so sorely from any shortage in the crop of character. None is so dependent upon men, and so little capable of being supported by the machine alone. When the leading of parties is in the hands of those who lack vision and firmness, the first effect which manifests itself is that parties begin to slip their principles. Some secondary object calls for and obtains the sacrifice of an ideal. So the Unionists in 1909 threw over the order and tradition of the state, the very ark of their political covenant, when they procured the rejection of the Budget by the House of Lords. So the Liberal Government in 1910, having solemnly undertaken to reform the constitution—a work not unworthy of the most earnest endeavour—went back upon their word, and abandoned their original purpose. For one thing they grew afraid of the clamour of their partisans. For another they were tempted by the opportunity of advantages which—as they fondly imagined—could be easily and safely secured during the interval while all legislative powers were temporarily vested in the Commons. Nor were these the only instances where traditional policy had been diverted, and where ideals had been bargained away, in the hope that thereby objects of a more material sort might be had at once in exchange.

The business of leadership is to prevent the abandonment of the long aim for the sake of the short. The rank and file of every army is at all times most

CHAPTER I.

A revolutionary period.

dangerously inclined to this fatal temptation, not necessarily dishonestly, but from a lack of foresight and sense of proportion.

Some dim perception of cause and effect had begun to dawn during the years 1912 and 1913 upon the country, and even upon the more sober section of the politicians. An apprehension had been growing rapidly, and defied concealment, that the country was faced by a very formidable something, to which men hesitated to give a name, but which was clearly not to be got rid of by the customary methods of holding high debates about it, and thereafter marching into division lobbies. While in public, each party was concerned to attribute the appearance of this unwelcome monster solely to the misdeeds of their opponents, each party knew well enough in their hearts that the danger was due at least in some measure to their own abandonment of pledges, principles, and traditions.

At Midsummer 1914 most people would probably have said that the immediate peril was Ireland and civil war. A few months earlier many imagined that trouble of a more general character was brewing between the civil and military powers, and that an issue which they described as that of 'the Army *versus* the People' would have to be faced. A few years earlier there was a widespread fear that the country might be confronted by some organised stoppage of industry, and that this would lead to revolution. Throughout the whole of this period of fourteen years the menace of war with Germany had been appearing, and disappearing, and reappearing, very much as a whale shows his back, dives, rises at some different spot, and dives again. For the moment, however, this particular anxiety did not weigh heavily on the public mind. The man in the street had been assured of late by the greater part of the press and politicians—even by ministers themselves—that our relations with this formidable neighbour were friendlier and more satisfactory than they had been for some considerable time.

A revolutionary period.

At Midsummer 1914, that is to say about six weeks before war broke out, the pre-eminent character in British politics was the Prime Minister. No other on either side of the House approached him in prestige, and so much was freely admitted by foes as well as friends.

When we are able to arrive at a fair estimate of the man who is regarded as the chief figure of his age, we have an important clue to the aspirations and modes of thought of the period in which he lived. A people may be known to some extent by the leaders whom it has chosen to follow.

Mr. Asquith entered Parliament in 1886, and before many months had passed his reputation was secure. Mr. Gladstone, ever watchful for youthful talent, promoted him at a bound to be Home Secretary, when the Cabinet of 1892 came into precarious existence. No member of this government justified his selection more admirably. But the period of office was brief. Three years later, the Liberal party found itself once again in the wilderness, where it continued to wander, rent by dissensions both as to persons and principles, for rather more than a decade.

When Sir Henry Campbell-Bannerman returned to office in the autumn of 1905, Mr. Asquith became

CHAPTER I.

A revolutionary period.

Chancellor of the Exchequer, and was speedily accepted as the minister next in succession to his chief. He was then just turned fifty, so that, despite the delays which had occurred, it could not be said that fortune had behaved altogether unkindly. Two and a half years later, in April 1908, he succeeded to the premiership without a rival, and without a dissentient voice.

The ambition, however, which brought him so successfully to the highest post appeared to have exhausted a great part of its force in attainment, and to have left its possessor without sufficient energy for exercising those functions which the post itself required. The career of Mr. Asquith in the highest office reminds one a little of the fable of the Hare and the Tortoise. In the race which we all run with slow-footed fate, he had a signal advantage in the speed of his intellect, in his capacity for overtaking arrears of work which would have appalled any other minister, and for finding, on the spur of the moment, means for extricating his administration from the most threatening positions. But of late, like the Hare, he had come to believe himself invincible, and had yielded more and more to a drowsy inclination. He had seemed to fall asleep for long periods, apparently in serene confidence that, before the Tortoise could pass the winning-post, somebody or something—in all probability the Unionist party with the clamour of a premature jubilation—would awaken him in time to save the race.

So far as Parliament was concerned, his confidence in his own qualities was not misplaced. Again and again, the unleadered energies or ungoaded indolence of his colleagues landed the Government

A revolutionary period.

in a mess. But as often as this happened Mr. Asquith always advanced upon the scene and rescued his party, by putting the worst blunder in the best light. He obligingly picked his stumbling lieutenants out of the bogs into which—largely, it must be admitted, for want of proper guidance from their chief—they had had the misfortune to fall. Having done this in the most chivalrous manner imaginable, he earned their gratitude and devotion. In this way he maintained a firm hold upon the leadership; if indeed it can properly be termed leadership to be the best acrobat of the troupe, and to step forward and do the feats after your companions have failed, and the audience has begun to 'boo.'

Some years ago Mr. Asquith propounded a maxim —*wait-and-see*—which greatly scandalised and annoyed the other side. This formula was the perfectly natural expression of his character and policy. In the peculiar circumstances of the case it proved itself to be a successful parliamentary expedient. Again and again it wrought confusion among his simple-minded opponents, who—not being held together by any firm authority—followed their own noses, now in one direction, now in another, upon the impulse of the moment. It is probable that against a powerful leader, who had his party well in hand, this policy of makeshift and delay would have brought its author to grief. But Unionists were neither disciplined nor united, and they had lacked leadership ever since they entered upon opposition.

For all its excellency, Mr. Asquith's oratory never touched the heart. And very rarely indeed did it succeed in convincing the cool judgment of people who had experience at first hand of the matters

CHAPTER I.

A revolutionary period.

under discussion. There was lacking anything in the nature of a personal note, which might have related the ego of the speaker to the sentiments which he announced so admirably. Also there was something which suggested that his knowledge had not been gained by looking at the facts face to face; but rather by the rapid digestion of minutes and memoranda, which had been prepared for him by clerks and secretaries, and which purported to provide, in convenient tabloids, all that it was necessary for a parliamentarian to know.

The style of speaking which is popular nowadays, and of which Mr. Asquith is by far the greatest master, would not have been listened to with an equal favour in the days of our grandfathers. In the Parliaments which assembled at Westminster in the period between the passing of the Reform Bill and the founding of the Eighty Club,[1] the country-gentlemen and the men-of-business—two classes of humanity who are constantly in touch with, and drawing strength from, our mother earth of hard fact [2] —met and fought out their differences during two generations. In that golden age it was all but unthinkable that a practising barrister should ever have become Prime Minister. The legal profession at this time had but little influence in counsel; still less in Parliament and on the platform. The middle classes were every whit as jealous and distrustful

[1] 1832–1880.

[2] They had an excellent sense of reality as regards their own affairs, and there between them covered a fairly wide area; but they were singularly lacking either in sympathy or imagination with regard to the affairs of other nations and classes. Their interest in the poor was confined for the most part to criticism of *one another* with regard to conditions of labour. The millowners thought that the oppression of the peasantry was a scandal; while the landowners considered that the state of things prevailing in factories was much worse than slavery. Cf. Disraeli's *Sybil.*

A revolutionary period.

of the intervention of the lawyer-advocate in public affairs as the landed gentry themselves. But in the stage of democratic evolution, which we entered on the morrow of the Mid-Lothian campaigns, and in which we still remain, the popular, and even the parliamentary, audience has gradually ceased to consist mainly of country-gentlemen interested in the land, and of the middle-classes who are engaged in trade. It has grown to be at once less discriminating as to the substance of speeches, and more exacting as to their form.

A representative assembly which entirely lacked lawyers would be impoverished; but one in which they are the predominant, or even a very important element, is usually in its decline. It is strange that an order of men, who in their private and professional capacities are so admirable, should nevertheless produce baleful effects when they come to play too great a part in public affairs. Trusty friends, delightful companions, stricter perhaps than any other civil profession in all rules of honour, they are none the less, without seeking to be so, the worst enemies of representative institutions. The peculiar danger of personal monarchy is that it so easily submits to draw its inspiration from an adulatory priesthood, and the peculiar danger of that modern form of constitutional government which we call democracy, is that lawyers, with the most patriotic intentions, are so apt to undo it.

Lawyers see too much of life in one way, too little in another, to make them safe guides in practical matters. Their experience of human affairs is made up of an infinite number of scraps cut out of other people's lives. They learn and do hardly anything

CHAPTER I.

A revolutionary period.

except through intermediaries. Their clients are introduced, not in person, but in the first instance, on paper—through the medium of solicitors' 'instructions.' Litigants appear at consultations in their counsel's chambers under the chaperonage of their attorneys; their case is considered; they receive advice. Then perhaps, if the issue comes into court, they appear once again, in the witness-box, and are there examined, cross-examined, and re-examined under that admirable system for the discovery of truth which is ordained in Anglo-Saxon countries, and which consists in turning, for the time being, nine people in every ten out of their true natures into hypnotised rabbits. Then the whole thing is ended, and the client disappears into the void from whence he came. What happens to him afterwards seldom reaches the ears of his former counsel. Whether the advice given to him in consultation has proved right or wrong in practice, rarely becomes known to the great man who gave it.

Plausibility, an alert eye for the technical trip or fall—the great qualities of an advocate—do not necessarily imply judgment of the most valuable sort outside courts of law. The farmer who manures, ploughs, harrows, sows, and rolls in his crop is punished in his income, if he has done any one of these things wrongly, or at the wrong season. The shopkeeper who blunders in his buying or his selling, or the manufacturer who makes things as they should not be made, suffers painful consequences to a certainty. His error pounds him relentlessly on the head. Not so the lawyer. His errors for the most part are visited on others. His own success or non-success is largely a matter of words and pose. If he is confident and adroit, the dulness of the jury or the senility of the bench can be made to appear, in the eyes of the worsted client, as the true causes of his defeat. And the misfortune is that in politics, which under its modern aspect is a trade very much akin to advocacy, there is a temptation, with all but the most patriotic lawyers, to turn to account at Westminster the skill which they have so laboriously acquired in the Temple.

A revolutionary period.

Of course there have been, and will ever be, exceptions. Alexander Hamilton was a lawyer, though he was a soldier in the first instance. Abraham Lincoln was a lawyer. But we should have to go back to the 'glorious revolution' of 1688 before we could find a parallel to either of these two in our own history. Until the last two decades England has never looked favourably on lawyer leaders. This was regarded by some as a national peculiarity; by others as a safeguard of our institutions. But by the beginning of the twentieth century it was clear that lawyers had succeeded in establishing their predominance in the higher walks of English politics, as thoroughly as they had already done wherever parliamentary government exists throughout the world.

During this epoch, when everything was sacrificed to perspicuity and the avoidance of boredom, Mr. Asquith's utterances led the fashion. His ministry was composed to a large extent of politicians bred in the same profession and proficient in the same arts as himself; but he towered above them all, the supreme type of the lawyer-statesman.

His method was supremely skilful. In its own way it had the charm of perfect artistry, even though

CHAPTER I.

A revolutionary period.

the product of the art was hardly more permanent than that of the *cordon bleu* who confections ices in fancy patterns. And not only was the method well suited to the taste of popular audiences, but equally so to the modern House of Commons. That body, also, was now much better educated in matters which can be learned out of newspapers and books; far more capable of expressing its meanings in well-chosen phrases arranged in a logical sequence; far more critical of words—if somewhat less observant of things—than it was during the greater part of the reign of Queen Victoria.

To a large extent the House of Commons consisted of persons with whom public utterance was a trade. There were lawyers in vast numbers, journalists, political organisers, and professional lecturers on a large variety of subjects. And even among the labour party, where we might have expected to find a corrective, the same tendency was at work, perhaps as strongly as in any other quarter. For although few types of mankind have a shrewder judgment between reality and dialectic than a thoroughly competent 'workman,' labour leaders were not chosen because they were first-class workmen, but because they happened to be effective speakers on the platform or at the committee table.

To a critic, looking on at the play from outside, Mr. Asquith's oratory appeared to lack heart and the instinct for reality; his leadership, the qualities of vigilance, steadfastness, and authority. He did not prevail by personal force, but by adroit confutation. His debating, as distinguished from his political, courage would have been admitted with few reservations even by an opponent.

A revolutionary period.

Few were so ready to meet their enemies in the gate of discussion. Few, if any, were so capable of retrieving the fortunes of their party—even when things looked blackest—if it were at all possible to accomplish this by the weapons of debate. But the medium must be debate—not action or counsel—if Mr. Asquith's pre-eminence was to assert itself. In debate he had all the confidence and valour of the *maître d'armes*, who knows himself to be the superior in skill of any fencer in his own school.

Next to Lord Rosebery he was the figure of most authority among the Liberal Imperialists, and yet this did not sustain his resolution when the Cabinet of 1905 proceeded to pare down the naval estimates. He was the champion of equal justice, as regards the status of Trades Unions, repelling the idea of exceptional and favouring legislation with an eloquent scorn. Yet he continued to hold his place when his principles were thrown overboard by his colleagues in 1906. Again when he met Parliament in February 1910 he announced his programme with an air of heroic firmness.[1] It is unnecessary to recall the particulars of this episode, and how he was upheld in his command only upon condition that he would alter his course to suit the wishes of mutineers. And in regard to the question of Home Rule, his treatment of it from first to last had been characterised by the virtues of patience and humility, rather than by those of prescience or courage.

A 'stellar and undiminishable' something, around which the qualities and capacities of a man revolve obediently, and under harmonious restraint—like

[1] *I.e.* curtailment of the powers of the House of Lords *and* its reform. Only the first was proceeded with.

A revolutionary period.

the planetary bodies—is perhaps as near as we can get to a definition of human greatness. But in the case of Mr. Asquith, for some years prior to July 1914, the central force of his nature had seemed inadequate for imposing the law of its will upon those brilliant satellites his talents. As a result, the solar system of his character had fallen into confusion, and especially since the opening of that year had appeared to be swinging lop-sided across the political firmament hastening to inevitable disaster.

CHAPTER II

THREE GOVERNING IDEAS

CHAPTER II.

Three governing ideas.

At the death of Queen Victoria the development of the British Commonwealth entered upon a new phase. The epoch which followed has no precedent in our own previous experience as a nation, nor can we discover in the records of other empires anything which offers more than a superficial and misleading resemblance to it. The issues of this period presented themselves to different minds in a variety of different lights; but to all it was clear that we had reached one of the great turning-points in our history.

The passengers on a great ocean liner are apt to imagine, because their stomachs are now so little troubled by the perturbation of the waves, that it no longer profits them to offer up the familiar prayer 'for those in peril on the sea.' It is difficult for them to believe in danger where everything appears so steady and well-ordered, and where they can enjoy most of the distractions of urban life, from a cinematograph theatre to a skittle-alley, merely by descending a gilded staircase or crossing a brightly panelled corridor. But this agreeable sense of safety is perhaps due in a greater degree to fancy, than to the changes which have taken place in the essential facts. As dangers have been diminished in one direction

Three governing ideas.

risks have been incurred in another. A blunder to-day is more irreparable than formerly, and the havoc which ensues upon a blunder is vastly more appalling. An error of observation or of judgment—the wrong lever pulled or the wrong button pressed—an order which miscarries or is overlooked — and twenty thousand tons travelling at twenty knots an hour goes to the bottom, with its freight of humanity, merchandise, and treasure, more easily, and with greater speed and certainty, than in the days of the old galleons—than in the days when Drake, in the *Golden Hind* of a hundred tons burden, beat up against head winds in the Straits of Magellan, and ran before the following gale off the Cape of Storms.

Comfort, whether in ships of travel or of state, is not the same thing as security. It never has been, and it never will be.

The position after Queen Victoria's death also differed from all previous times in another way. After more than three centuries of turmoil and expansion, the British race had entered into possession of an estate so vast, so rich in all natural resources, that a sane mind could not hope for, or even dream of, any further aggrandisement. Whatever may be the diseases from which the British race suffered during the short epoch between January 1901 and July 1914, megalomania was certainly not one of them.

The period of acquisition being now acknowledged at an end, popular imagination became much occupied with other things. It assumed, too lightly and readily perhaps, that nothing was likely to interfere with our continuing to hold what we had got. If there was not precisely a law of nature, which precluded the possessions of the British Empire from ever being

Three governing ideas.

taken away, at any rate there was the law of nations. The public opinion of the world would surely revolt against so heinous a form of sacrilege. Having assumed so much, placidly and contentedly, and without even a tremor either as to the good-will or the potency of the famous Concert of Europe, the larger part of public opinion tended to become more and more engrossed in other problems. It began to concern itself earnestly with *the improvement of the condition of the people*, and with *the reform and consolidation of institutions*. Incidentally, and as a part of each of these endeavours, the development of an estate which had come, mainly by inheritance, into the trusteeship of the British people, began seriously to occupy their thoughts.

These were problems of great worth and dignity, but nevertheless there was one condition of their successful solution, which ought to have been kept in mind, but which possibly was somewhat overlooked. If we allowed ourselves to be so much absorbed by these two problems that we gave insufficient heed to our defences, it was as certain as any human forecast could be, that the solution of a great deal, which was perplexing us in the management of our internal affairs, would be summarily taken out of the hands of Britain and her Dominions and solved according to the ideas of strangers.

If we were to bring our policy of social and constitutional improvement and the development of our estate to a successful issue, we must be safe from interruption from outside. We must secure ourselves against foreign aggression; for we needed time. Our various problems could not be solved in a day or even in a generation. The most urgent

CHAPTER II.

of all matters was *security*, for it was the prime condition of all the rest.

Three governing ideas.

We desired, not merely to hold what we had got, but to enjoy it, and make it fructify and prosper, in our own way, and under our own institutions. For this we needed peace within our own sphere; and therefore it was necessary that we should be strong enough to enforce peace.

During the post-Victorian period—this short epoch of transition—there were therefore three separate sets of problems which between them absorbed the energies of public men and occupied the thoughts of all private persons, at home and in the Dominions, to whom the present and future well-being of their country was a matter of concern.

The first of these problems was *Defence*: How might the British Commonwealth, which held so vast a portion of the habitable globe, and which was responsible for the government of a full quarter of all the people who dwelt thereon—how might it best secure itself against the dangers which threatened it from without?

The second was the problem of *the Constitution*: How could we best develop, to what extent must we remake or remould, our ancient institutions, so as to fit them for those duties and responsibilities which new conditions required that they should be able to perform? Under this head we were faced with projects, not merely of local self-government, of 'Home Rule,' and of 'Federalism'; not merely with the working of the Parliament Act, with the composition, functions, and powers of the Second Chamber, with the Referendum, the Franchise, and

Three governing ideas.

such like; but also with that vast and even more perplexing question — what were to be the future relations between the Mother Country and the self-governing Dominions on the one hand, and between these five democratic nations and the Indian Empire and the Dependencies upon the other?

For the third set of problems no concise title has yet been found. *Social Reform* does not cover it, though perhaps it comes nearer doing so than any other. The matters involved here were so multifarious and, apparently at least, so detached one from another —they presented themselves to different minds at so many different angles and under such different aspects —that no single word or phrase was altogether satisfactory. But briefly, what all men were engaged in searching after—the Labour party, no more and no less than the Radicals and the Tories—was how we could raise the character and material conditions of our people; how by better organisation we could root out needless misery of mind and body; how we could improve the health and the intelligence, stimulate the sense of duty and fellowship, the efficiency and the patriotism of the whole community.

Of these three sets of problems with which the British race has recently been occupying itself, this, the third, is intrinsically by far the most important.

It is the most important because it is an end in itself whereas the other two are only the means for achieving this end. Security against foreign attack is a desirable and worthy object only in order to enable us to approach this goal. A strong and flexible constitution is an advantage only because we believe it will enable us to achieve our objects, better and more quickly, than if we are compelled to go on working

CHAPTER II.

Three governing ideas.

under a system which has become at once rigid and rickety. But while we were bound to realise the superior nature of the third set of problems, we should have been careful at the same time to distinguish between two things which are very apt to be confused in political discussions—*ultimate importance* and *immediate urgency*.

We ought to have taken into our reckoning both the present state of the world and the permanent nature of man—all the stuff that dreams and wars are made on. We desired peace. We needed peace. Peace was a matter of life and death to all our hopes. If defeat should once break into the ring of our commonwealth—scattered as it is all over the world, kept together only by the finest and most delicate attachments—it must be broken irreparably. Our most immediate interest was therefore to keep defeat, and if possible, war, from bursting into our sphere—as Dutchmen by centuries of laborious vigilance have kept back the sea with dikes.

The numbers of our people in themselves were no security; nor our riches; nor even the fact that we entertained no aggressive designs. For as it was said long ago, 'it never troubles a wolf how many the sheep be.' They find no salvation in their heavy fleeces and their fat haunches; nor even in the meekness of their hearts, and in their innocence of all evil intentions.

The characteristic of this period may be summed up in one short sentence; the vast majority of the British people were bent and determined—as they had never been bent and determined before—upon leaving their country better than they had found it.

CHAPTER II.

Three governing ideas.

To some this statement will seem a paradox. "Was there ever a time," they may ask, "when 'there had been so many evidences of popular unrest, 'discontent, bitterness and anger; or when there had 'ever appeared to be so great an inclination, on the 'one hand to apathy and cynicism, on the other 'hand to despair?"

Were all this true, it would still be no paradox; but only a natural consequence. Things are very liable to slip into this state, when men who are in earnest—knowing the facts as they exist in their respective spheres; knowing the evils at first hand; believing (very often with reason) that they understand the true remedies—find themselves baulked, and foiled, and headed off at every turn, their objects misconceived and their motives misconstrued, and the current of their wasted efforts burying itself hopelessly in the sand. Under such conditions as these, public bodies and political parties alike—confused by the multitude and congestion of issues—are apt to bestow their dangerous attentions, now on one matter which happens to dart into the limelight, now upon another; but in the general hubbub and perplexity they lose all sense, both of true proportion and natural priority. Everything is talked about; much is attempted in a piecemeal, slap-dash, impulsive fashion; inconsiderably little is brought to any conclusion whatsoever; while nothing, or next to nothing, is considered on its merits, and carried through thoughtfully to a clean and abiding settlement. . . . The word 'thorough' seemed to have dropped out of the political vocabulary. In an age of specialism politics alone was abandoned to the Jack-of-all-trades.

CHAPTER II.

Three governing ideas.

This phenomenon—the depreciated currency of public character—was not peculiar to one party more than another. It was not even peculiar to this particular time. It has shown itself at various epochs—much in the same way as the small-pox and the plague—when favoured by insanitary conditions. The sedate Scots philosopher, Adam Smith, writing during the gloomy period which fell upon England after the glory of the great Chatham had departed, could not repress his bitterness against "that insidious 'and crafty animal, vulgarly called a statesman 'or politician, whose councils are directed by the 'momentary fluctuations of affairs." It would seem as if the body politic is not unlike the human, and becomes more readily a prey to vermin, when it has sunk into a morbid condition.

Popular judgment may be trusted as a rule, and in the long run, to decide a clear issue between truth and falsehood, and to decide it in favour of the former. But it becomes perplexed, when it is called upon to discriminate between the assurances of two rival sets of showmen, whose eagerness to outbid each other in the public favour leaves truthfulness out of account. In the absence of gold, one brazen counterfeit rings very much like another. People may be suspicious of both coins; but on the whole their fancy is more readily caught by the optimist effigy than the pessimist. They may not place entire trust in the 'ever-cheerful man of sin,' with his flattery, his abounding sympathy, his flowery promises, and his undefeated hopefulness; but they prefer him at any rate to 'the melancholy Jaques,' booming maledictions with a mournful constancy, like some bittern in the desolation of the marshes.

Three governing ideas.

So far as principles were concerned most of the trouble was unnecessary. Among the would-be reformers—among those who sincerely desired to bring about efficiency within their own spheres—there was surprisingly little that can truly be called antagonism. But competition of an important kind—competition for public attention and priority of treatment—had produced many of the unfortunate results of antagonism. It was inevitable that this lamentable state of things must continue, until it had been realised that one small body of men, elected upon a variety of cross issues, could not safely be left in charge of the defence of the Empire, the domestic welfare of the United Kingdom, and the local government of its several units.

It was not merely that the various aims were not opposed to one another; they were actually helpful to one another. Often, indeed, they were essential to the permanent success of one another. The man who desired to improve the conditions of the poor was not, therefore, the natural enemy of him who wanted to place the national defences on a secure footing. And neither of these was the natural enemy of others who wished to bring about a settlement of the Irish question, or of the Constitutional question, or of the Imperial question. But owing partly to the inadequacy of the machinery for giving a free course to these various aspirations—partly to the fact that the machinery itself was antiquated, in bad repair, and had become clogged with a variety of obstructions—there was an unfortunate tendency on the part of every one who had any particular object very much at heart, to regard every one else who was equally concerned about any other object as an impediment in his path.

Three governing ideas.

The need of the time, of course, was leadership—a great man—or better still two great men, one on each side—like the blades of a pair of scissors—to cut a way out of the confusion by bringing their keen edges into contact. But obviously, the greater the confusion the harder it is for leadership to assert itself. We may be sure enough that there were men of character and capacity equal to the task if only they could have been discovered. But they were not discovered.

There were other things besides the confusion of aims and ideas which made it hard for leaders to emerge. The loose coherency of parties which prevailed during the greater part of the nineteenth century had given place to a set of highly organised machines, which employed without remorse the oriental method of strangulation, against everything in the nature of independent effort and judgment. The politician class had increased greatly in numbers and influence. The eminent and ornamental people who were returned to Westminster filled the public eye, but they were only a small proportion of the whole; nor is it certain that they exercised the largest share of authority. When in the autumn of 1913 Sir John Brunner determined to prevent Mr. Churchill from obtaining the provisions for the Navy which were judged necessary for the safety of the Empire, the method adopted was to raise the National Liberal Federation against the First Lord of the Admiralty, and through the agency of that powerful organisation to bring pressure to bear upon the country, members of Parliament, and the Cabinet itself.

Three governing ideas.

It is unpopular to say that the House of Commons has deteriorated in character, but it is true. An assembly, the members of which cannot call their souls their own, will never tend in an upward direction. The machines which are managed with so much energy and skill by the external parasites of politics, have long ago taken over full responsibility for the souls of their nominees. According to 'Gresham's law,' bad money, if admitted into currency, will always end by driving out good. A similar principle has been at work for some time past in British public life, by virtue of which the baser kind of politicians, having got a footing, are driving out their betters at a rapid pace. Few members of Parliament will admit this fact; but they are not impartial judges, for every one is naturally averse from disparaging an institution to which he belongs.

During the nineteenth century, except at the very beginning, and again at the very end of it, very few people ever thought of going into Parliament, or even into politics, in order that they might thrive thereby, or find a field for improving their private fortunes. This cannot be said with truth of the epoch which has just ended. There has been a change both in tone and outlook during the last thirty years. Things have been done and approved by the House of Commons, elected in December 1910, which it is quite inconceivable that the House of Commons, returned in 1880, would ever have entertained. The Gladstonian era had its faults, but among them laxity in matters of finance did not figure. Indeed private members, as well as statesmen, not infrequently

Three governing ideas.

crossed the border-line which separates purism from pedantry; occasionally they carried strictness to the verge of absurdity; but this was a fault in the right direction—a great safeguard to the public interest, a peculiarly valuable tendency from the standpoint of democracy.

A twelvemonth ago a number of very foolish persons were anxious to persuade us that the predominant issue was the Army *versus* the People. But even the crispness of the phrase was powerless to convince public opinion of so staggering an untruth. The predominant issue at that particular moment was only what it had been for a good many years before—the People *versus* the Party System.

What is apt to be ignored is, that with the increase of wealth on the one hand, and the extension of the franchise on the other, the Party System has gradually become a vested interest upon an enormous scale, —like the liquor trade of which we hear so much, or the *haute finance* of which perhaps we hear too little. Rich men are required in politics, for the reason that it is necessary to feed and clothe the steadily increasing swarms of mechanics who drive, and keep in repair, and add to, that elaborate machinery by means of which the Sovereign People is cajoled into the belief that its Will prevails. From the point of view of the orthodox political economist these workers are as unproductive as actors, bookmakers, or golf professionals; but they have to be paid, otherwise they would starve, and the machines would stop. So long as there are plenty of rich men who desire to become even richer, or to decorate their names with titles, or to move in shining circles, this is not at all likely to occur, unless the Party System suddenly collapsed, in which case there would be acute distress.

Three governing ideas.

There are various grades of these artisans or mechanicians of politics, from the professional organiser or agent who, upon the whole, is no more open to criticism than any other class of mankind which works honestly for its living—down to the committee-man who has no use for a candidate unless he keeps a table from which large crumbs fall in profusion. The man who supplements his income by means of politics is a greater danger than the other who openly makes politics his vocation. The jobbing printer, enthusiastically pacifist or protectionist, well paid for his hand-bills, and aspiring to more substantial contracts; the smart, ingratiating organiser, or hustling, bustling journalist, who receives a complimentary cheque, or a bundle of scrip, or a seat on a board of directors from the patron whom he has helped to win an election—very much as at ill-regulated shooting parties the head-keeper receives exorbitant tips from wealthy sportsmen whom he has placed to their satisfaction—all these are deeply interested in the preservation of the Party System. Innocent folk are often heard wondering why candidates with such strange names—even stranger appearance—accents and manner of speech which are strangest of all—are brought forward so frequently to woo the suffrages of urban constituencies. Clearly they are not chosen on account of their political knowledge; for they have none. There are other aspirants to political honours who, in comeliness and charm of manner, greatly excel them; whose speech is more eloquent, or at any rate less unintelligible. Yet London caucuses in particular have

CHAPTER II. — Three governing ideas.

a great tenderness for these bejewelled patriots, and presumably there must be reasons for the preference which they receive. One imagines that in some inscrutable way they are essential props of the Party System in its modern phase.

The drawing together of the world by steam and electricity has brought conspicuous benefits to the British Empire. The five self-governing nations of which it is composed come closer together year by year. Statesmen and politicians broaden the horizons of their minds by swift and easy travel. But there are drawbacks as well as the reverse under these new conditions. To some extent the personnel of democracy has tended to become interchangeable, like the parts of a bicycle; and public characters are able to transfer their activities from one state to another, and even from one hemisphere to another, without a great deal of difficulty. This has certain advantages, but possibly more from the point of view of the individual than from that of the Commonwealth. After failure in one sphere there is still hope in another. Mr. Micawber, or even Jeremy Diddler, may go the round, using up public confidence at one resting-place after another. For the Party System is a ready employer, and providing a man has a glib tongue, a forehead of brass, or an open purse, a position will be found for him without too much enquiry made into his previous references.

In a world filled with confusion and illusion the Party System has fought at great advantage. Indeed it is generally believed to be so firmly entrenched that nothing can ever dislodge it. There are dangers, however, in arguing too confidently from use and wont. Conspicuous failure or disaster might bring

Three governing ideas.

ruin on this revered institution, as it has often done in history upon others no less venerable. The Party System has its weak side. Its wares are mainly make-believes, and if a hurricane happens to burst suddenly, the caucus may be left in no better plight than Alnaschar with his overturned basket. The Party System is not invulnerable against a great man or a great idea. But of recent years it has been left at peace to go its own way, for the reason that no such man or idea has emerged, around which the English people have felt that they could cluster confidently. There has been no core on which human crystals could precipitate and attach themselves, following the bent of their nature towards a firm and clear belief—or towards the prowess of a man—or towards a Man possessed by a Belief. The typical party leader during this epoch has neither been a man in the heroic sense, nor has he had any belief that could be called firm or clear. For the most part he has been merely a Whig or Tory tradesman, dealing in opportunism ; and for the predominance of the Party System this set of conditions was almost ideal. It was inconceivable that a policy of *wait-and-see* could ever resolve a situation of this sort. To fall back on lawyerism was perhaps inevitable in the circumstances; but to think that it was possible to substitute lawyerism for leadership was absurd.

And yet amid this confusion we were aware—even at the time—and can see much more clearly now the interlude is ended—that there were three great ideas running through it all, struggling to emerge, to make themselves understood, and to get themselves realised. But unfortunately what were realities to ordinary men were only counters according

CHAPTER II.

Three governing ideas.

to the reckoning of the party mechanicians. The *first* aim and the *second*—the improvement of the organisation of society and the conditions of the poor—the freeing of local aspirations and the knitting together of the empire—were held in common by the great mass of the British people, although they were viewed by one section and another from different angles of vision. The *third* aim, however—the adequate defence of the empire—was not regarded warmly, or even with much active interest, by any organised section. The people who considered it most earnestly were not engaged in party politics. The manipulators of the machines looked upon the *first* and the *second* as means whereby power might be gained or retained, but they looked askance upon the *third* as a perilous problem which it was wiser and safer to leave alone. The great principles with which the names—among others—of Mr. Chamberlain, Lord Roberts, and Mr. Lloyd George are associated, were at no point opposed one to another. Each indeed was dependent upon the other two for its full realisation. And yet, under the artificial entanglements of the Party System, the vigorous pursuit of any one of the three seemed to imperil the success of both its competitors.

CHAPTER III

POLICY AND ARMAMENTS

CHAPTER III.

Policy and armaments.

In the post-Victorian epoch, which we have been engaged in considering, the aim of British foreign policy may be summed up in one word—Security. It was not aggression; it was not revenge; it was not conquest, or even expansion of territories; it was simply Security.

It would be absurd, of course, to imagine that security is wholly, or even mainly, a question of military preparations. "All this is but a sheep 'in a lion's skin, where the people are of weak 'courage;" or where for any reason, the people are divided among themselves or disaffected towards their government.

The defences of every nation are of two kinds, the organised and the unorganised; the disciplined strength of the Navy and the Army on the one hand, the vigour and spirit of the people upon the other.

The *vigour* of the people will depend largely upon the conditions under which they live, upon sufficiency of food, the healthiness or otherwise of their employments and homes, the proper nourishment and upbringing of their children. It is not enough that rates of wages should be good, if those who earn them

CHAPTER III.

Policy and armaments.

have not the knowledge how to use them to the best advantage. It is not always where incomes are lowest that the conditions of life are worst. Measured by infant mortality, and by the health and general happiness of the community, the crofters of Scotland, who are very poor, seem to have learned the lesson *how to live* better than the highly paid workers in many of our great manufacturing towns.

Education—by which is meant not merely board-school instruction, but the influence of the home and the surrounding society—is not a less necessary condition of vigour than wages, sanitary regulations, and such like. The spiritual as well as the physical training of children, the nature of their amusements, the bent of their interests, the character of their aims and ideals, at that critical period when the boy or girl is growing into manhood or womanhood—all these are things which conduce directly, as well as indirectly, to the vigour of the race. They are every bit as much a part of our system of national defence as the manœuvring of army corps and the gun-practice of dreadnoughts.

The *spirit* of the people, on the other hand, will depend for its strength upon their attachment to their own country; upon their affection for its customs, laws, and institutions; upon a belief in the general fairness and justice of its social arrangements; upon the good relations of the various classes of which society is composed. The spirit of national unity is indispensable even in the case of the most powerful autocracy. It is the very foundation of democracy. Lacking it, popular government is but a house of cards, which the first serious challenge from without, or the first strong outburst of dis-

CHAPTER III.

Policy and armaments.

content from within will bring tumbling to the ground. Such a feeling of unity can only spring from the prevalence of an opinion among every class of the community, that their own system, with all its faults, is better suited to their needs, habits, and traditions than any other, and that it is worth preserving, even at the cost of the greatest sacrifices, from foreign conquest and interference.

While a people sapped by starvation and disease will be wanting in the *vigour* necessary for offering a prolonged and strenuous resistance, so will a people, seething with class hatred and a sense of tyranny and injustice, be wanting in the *spirit*. The problem, however, of these unorganised defences, fundamental though it is, stands outside the scope of the present chapter, which is concerned solely with those defences which are organised.

The beginning of wisdom with respect to all problems of defence is the recognition of the two-headed principle that *Policy depends on Armaments just as certainly as Armaments depend on Policy.*

The duty of the Admiralty and the War Office is to keep their armaments abreast of the national endeavour. It is folly to do more: it is madness to do less. The duty of the Foreign Minister is to restrain and hold back his policy, and to prevent it from ambitiously outrunning the capacity of the armaments which are at his disposal. If he does otherwise the end is likely to be humiliation and disaster.

When any nation is unable or unwilling to provide the armaments necessary for supporting the policy which it has been accustomed to pursue and would

CHAPTER III.

Policy and armaments.

like to maintain, it should have the sense to abandon that policy for something of a humbler sort before the bluff is discovered by the world.[1]

It may possibly appear absurd to dwell with so much insistence upon a pair of propositions which, when they are set down in black and white, will at once be accepted as self-evident by ninety-nine men out of a hundred. But plain and obvious as they are, none in the whole region of politics have been more frequently ignored. These two principles have been constantly presenting themselves to the eyes of statesmen in a variety of different shapes ever since history began.

It may very easily happen that the particular policy which the desire for security requires, is one which the strength of the national armaments at a given moment will not warrant the country in pursuing. Faced with this unpleasant quandary, what is Government to do, if it be convinced of the futility of trying to persuade the people to incur the sacrifices necessary for realising the national aspirations? Is it to give up the traditional policy, and face the various consequences which it is reasonable to anticipate? Or is it to persevere in the policy, and continue acting as if the forces at its disposal were sufficient for its purpose, when in fact they are nothing of the kind? To follow the former course

[1] American writers have urged criticism of this sort against the armaments of the U.S.A., which they allege are inadequate to uphold the policy of the 'Monroe Doctrine.' The German view of the matter has been stated by the Chancellor (April 7, 1913) when introducing the Army Bill:—"History knows of no people which came to disaster because it had exhausted itself in the making of its defences; but history knows of many 'peoples which have perished, because, living in prosperity and luxury, 'they neglected their defences. A people which thinks that it is not rich 'enough to maintain its armaments shows merely that it has played its 'part."

Policy and armaments.

calls for a surrender which the spirit of the people will not easily endure, and which may even be fatal to the independent existence of the state. But to enter upon the latter is conduct worthy of a fraudulent bankrupt, since it trades upon an imposture, which, when it is found out by rival nations, will probably be visited by still severer penalties.

But surely Government has only to make it clear to the people that, unless they are willing to bring their armaments abreast of their policy, national aspirations must be baulked and even national safety itself may be endangered. When men are made to understand these things, will they not certainly agree to do what is necessary, though they may give their consent with reluctance ? [1]

It is very certain, however, that this outside view of the case enormously underrates the difficulties which stare the politician out of countenance. In matters of this sort it is not so easy a thing to arrive at the truth ; much less to state it with such force and clearness that mankind will at once recognise it for truth, and what is said to the contrary for falsehood. The intentions of foreign governments, and the dangers arising out of that quarter, are subjects which it is singularly difficult to discuss frankly, without incurring the very evils which every government seeks to avoid. And if these things are not easy to discuss, it is exceedingly easy for faction or fanatics to misrepresent them.[2] Moreover, the lamentations of the Hebrew prophets bear witness to the

[1] So the argument runs, and the course of our naval policy since Mr. Stead's famous press campaign in 1884 will be cited as an encouragement.

[2] *E.g.* in the winter of 1908 and spring of 1909, when an influential section of the supporters of the present Cabinet chose to believe the false assurances of the German Admiralty, and freely accused their own Government of mendacity.

CHAPTER III.

Policy and armaments.

deafness and blindness of generations into whom actual experience of the evils foretold had not already burnt the lesson which it was desired to teach. Evils which have never been suffered are hard things to clothe with reality until it is too late, and words, even the most eloquent and persuasive, are but a poor implement for the task.

The policy of a nation is determined upon, so as to accord with what it conceives to be its honour, safety, and material interests. In the natural course of events this policy may check, or be checked by, the policy of some other nation. The efforts of diplomacy may be successful in clearing away these obstructions. If so, well and good; but if not, there is nothing left to decide the issue between the two nations but the stern arbitrament of war.

Moreover, diplomacy itself is dependent upon armaments in somewhat the same sense as the prosperity of a merchant is dependent upon his credit with his bankers. The news system of the world has undergone a revolution since the days before steam and telegraphs. It is not merely more rapid, but much ampler. The various governments are kept far more fully informed of one another's affairs, and as a consequence the great issues between nations have become clear and sharp. The most crafty and smooth-tongued ambassador can rarely wheedle his opponents into concessions which are contrary to their interests, unless he has something more to rely upon than his own guile and plausibility. Army corps and battle fleets looming in the distance are better persuaders than the subtlest arguments and the deftest flattery.

What, then, is the position of a statesman who

Policy and armaments.

finds himself confronted by a clash of policies, if, when the diplomatic deadlock occurs, he realises that his armaments are insufficient to support his aim? In such an event he is faced with the alternative of letting judgment go by default, or of adding almost certain military disaster to the loss of those political stakes for which his nation is contending with its rival. Such a position must be ignominious in the extreme; it might even be ruinous; and yet it would be the inevitable fate of any country whose ministers had neglected the maxim that policy in the last resort is dependent upon armaments.

If we are in search of an example we shall find it ready to our hand. The Empire of China is comparable to our own at least in numbers; for each of them contains, as nearly as may be, one quarter of the whole human race. And as China has hitherto failed utterly to make her armaments sufficient, under the stress of modern conditions, to support even that meek and passive policy of possession which she has endeavoured to pursue, so she has been compelled to watch in helplessness while her policy has been disregarded by every adventurer. She has been pressed by all the nations of the world and obliged to yield to their demands. Humiliating concessions have been wrung from her; favours even more onerous, in the shape of loans, have been forced upon her. The resources with which nature has endowed her have been exploited by foreigners against her will. Her lands have been shorn from her and parcelled out among those who were strong, and who hungered after them. This conquest and robbery has proceeded both by wholesale and retail.

CHAPTER III.

Policy and armaments.

Because she yielded this to one claimant, another, to keep the balance even, has insisted upon that. Safe and convenient harbours, fortified places, islands, vast stretches of territory, have been demanded and taken from her almost without a struggle; and all this time she has abstained with a timid caution from anything which can justly be termed provocation. For more than half a century, none the less, China has not been mistress in her own house.

The reason of this is plain enough—China had possessions which other nations coveted, and she failed to provide herself with the armaments which were necessary to maintain them.

The British people likewise had possessions which other nations coveted—lands to take their settlers, markets to buy their goods, plantations to yield them raw materials. If it were our set determination to hold what our forefathers won, two things were necessary: the first, that our policy should conform to this aim; the second, that our armaments should be sufficient to support our policy.

A nation which desired to extend its possessions, to round off its territories, to obtain access to the sea, would probably regard conquest, or at all events absorption, as its highest immediate interest. This would be the constant aim of its policy, and if its armaments did not conform to this policy, the aim would not be realised. Examples both of failure and success are to be found in the history of Russia from the time of Peter the Great, and in that of Prussia from the days of the Great Elector.

A nation—like England or Holland in the sixteenth, seventeenth, and eighteenth centuries—which was seeking to secure against its commercial rivals, if necessary by force of arms, new markets among civilised but unmilitary races, would require a policy and armaments to correspond.

Policy and armaments.

The British Empire in the stage of development which it had reached at the end of the Victorian era did not aim at acquisition of fresh territories or new markets, save such as might be won peacefully by the skill and enterprise of its merchants. It sought only to hold what it already possessed, to develop its internal resources, and to retain equal rights with its commercial rivals in neutral spheres. But in order that those unaggressive objects might be realised, there was need of a policy, different indeed from that of Elizabeth, of Cromwell, or of Chatham, but none the less clear and definite with regard to its own ends. And to support this policy there was need of armaments, suitable in scale and character.

It was frequently pointed out between the years 1901 and 1914 (and it lay at the very root of the matter), that while *we* were perfectly satisfied with things as they stood, and should have been more than content—regarding the subject from the standpoint of our own interests—to have left the map of the world for ever, as it then was drawn, another nation was by no means so well pleased with existing arrangements. To this envious rival it appeared that we had taken more than our fair share—as people are apt to do who come early. We had wider territories than we could yet fill with our own people; while our neighbour foresaw an early date at which his race would be overflowing its boundaries. We had limitless resources in the Dominions and Dependencies

Policy and armaments.

overseas, which when developed would provide a united empire with markets of inestimable value. In these respects Germany was in a less favourable position. Indeed, with the exceptions of Russia and the United States, no other great Power was so fortunately placed as ourselves; and even these two nations, although they had an advantage over the British Empire by reason of their huge compact and coterminous territories, still did not equal it in the vastness and variety of their undeveloped resources.

Clearly, therefore, the policy which the needs of our Commonwealth required at this great turning-point in its history, was not only something different from that of any other great Power, but also something different from that which had served our own purposes in times gone by. Like China, our aim was peaceful possession. Unlike China, we ought to have kept in mind the conditions under which alone this aim was likely to be achieved. It might be irksome and contrary to our peaceful inclinations to maintain great armaments when we no longer dreamed of making conquests; but in the existing state of the world, armaments were unfortunately quite as necessary for the purpose of enabling us to hold what we possessed, as they ever were when our forefathers set out to win the Empire.

In 1904, with the object of promoting harmony between the policy and armaments of the British Empire, Mr. Balfour created the Committee of Imperial Defence. This was undoubtedly a step of great importance. His purpose was to introduce a system, by means of which ministers and high officials responsible for the Navy and Army would

Policy and armaments.

be kept in close touch with the trend of national policy, in so far as it might affect the relations of the Commonwealth with foreign Powers. In like manner those other ministers and high officials, whose business it was to conduct our diplomacy, maintain an understanding with the Dominions, administer our Dependencies, and govern India, would be made thoroughly conversant with the limitations to our naval and military strength. Having this knowledge, they would not severally embark on irreconcilable or impracticable projects or drift unknowingly into dangerous complications. The conception of the Committee of Imperial Defence, therefore, was due to a somewhat tardy recognition of the two-headed principle, that armaments are mere waste of money unless they conform to policy, and that policy in the last resort must depend on armaments.

The Committee was maintained by Mr. Balfour's successors, and was not allowed (as too often happens when there is a change of government) to fall into discredit and disuse.[1] But in order that this body of statesmen and experts might achieve the ends in view, it was essential for them to have realised clearly, not only the general object of British policy—which indeed was contained in the single word 'Security' —but also the special dangers which loomed in the near future. They had then to consider what reciprocal obligations had already been contracted with other nations, whose interests were to some extent the same as our own, and what further undertakings of a similar character it might be desirable to enter

[1] Innovations of this particular sort have possibly a better chance of preserving their existence than some others. 'Boards are screens,' wrote John Stuart Mill, or some other profound thinker; and in politics screens are always useful.

CHAPTER III.

Policy and armaments.

into. Finally, there were the consequences which these obligations and undertakings would entail in certain contingencies. It was not enough merely to mumble the word 'Security' and leave it at that. What security implied in the then existing state of the world was a matter which required to be investigated in a concrete, practical, and business-like way.

Unfortunately, the greater part of these essential preliminaries was omitted, and as a consequence, the original idea of the Committee of Imperial Defence was never realised. Harmonious, flexible, and of considerable utility in certain directions, it did not work satisfactorily as a whole. The trend of policy was, no doubt, grasped in a general way; but, as subsequent events have proved, the conditions on which alone that line could be maintained, and the consequences which it involved, were not at any time clearly understood and boldly faced by this august body in its corporate capacity.

The general direction may have been settled; but certainly the course was not marked out; the rocks and shoals remained for the most part uncharted. The committee, no doubt, had agreed upon a certain number of vague propositions, as, for example, that France must not be crushed by Germany, or the neutrality of Belgium violated by any one. They knew that we were committed to certain obligations—or, as some people called them, 'entanglements'—and that these again, in certain circumstances, might commit us to others. But what the whole amounted to was not realised in barest outline, by the country, or by Parliament, or by the Government, or even, we may safely conjecture, by the Committee itself.

Policy and armaments.

We have the right to say this, because, if British policy had been realised as a whole by the Committee of Imperial Defence, it would obviously have been communicated to the Cabinet, and in its broader aspects to the people; and this was never done. It is inconceivable that any Prime Minister, who believed, as Mr. Asquith does, in democratic principles, would have left the country uneducated, and his own colleagues unenlightened, on a matter of so great importance, had his own mind been clearly made up.

When the crisis occurred in July 1914, when Germany proceeded to action, when events took place which for years past had been foretold and discussed very fully on both sides of the North Sea, it was as if a bolt had fallen from the blue. Uncertainty was apparent in all quarters. The very thing which had been so often talked of had happened. Germany was collecting her armies and preparing to crush France. The neutrality of Belgium was threatened. Yet up to, and on, Sunday, August 2, there was doubt and hesitation in the Cabinet, and until some days later, also in Parliament and the country.[1]

When, finally, it was decided to declare war, the course of action which that step required still appears to have remained obscure to our rulers. Until the Thursday following it was not decided to send the Expeditionary Force abroad. Then, out of timidity, only two-thirds of it were sent.[2] Transport arrangements which were all ready for moving the whole force had to be hastily readjusted. The delay was

[1] This is obvious from the White Paper without seeking further evidence in the ministerial press or elsewhere.

[2] Of the six infantry divisions included in the Expeditionary Force only four were sent in the first instance; a fifth arrived about August 24; a sixth about mid-September.

CHAPTER III.

not less injurious than the parsimony; and the combination of the two nearly proved fatal.

Policy and armaments.

If the minds of the people and their leaders were not prepared for what happened, if in the moral sense there was unreadiness; still more inadequate were all preparations of the material kind—not only the actual numbers of our Army, but also the whole system for providing expansion, training, equipment, and munitions. It is asking too much of us to believe that events could have happened as they did in England during the fortnight which followed the presentation of the Austrian Ultimatum to Servia, had the Committee of Imperial Defence and its distinguished president taken pains beforehand to envisage clearly the conditions and consequences involved in their policy of 'Security.'

As regards naval preparations, things were better indeed than might have been expected, considering the vagueness of ideas in the matter of policy. We were safeguarded here by tradition, and the general idea of direction had been nearly sufficient. There was always trouble, but not as a rule serious trouble, in establishing the case for increases necessary to keep ahead of German efforts. There had been pinchings and parings—especially in the matter of fast cruisers, for lack of which, when war broke out, we suffered heavy losses—but except in one instance—the abandonment of the Cawdor programme—these had not touched our security at any vital point.

Thanks largely to Mr. Stead, but also to statesmen of both parties, and to a succession of Naval Lords who did not hesitate, when occasion required it, to risk their careers (as faithful servants ever will) rather than certify safety where they saw danger—

Policy and armaments.

thanks, perhaps, most of all to a popular instinct, deeply implanted in the British mind, which had grasped the need for supremacy at sea—our naval preparations, upon the whole, had kept abreast of our policy for nearly thirty years.

As regards the Army, however, it was entirely different. There had been no intelligent effort to keep our military strength abreast of our policy; and as, in many instances, it would have been too bitter a humiliation to keep our policy within the limits of our military strength, the course actually pursued can only be described fitly as a game of bluff.

There had never been anything approaching agreement with regard to the functions which the Army was expected to perform. Not only did political parties differ one from another upon this primary and fundamental question, but hardly two succeeding War Ministers had viewed it in the same light. There had been schemes of a bewildering variety; but as the final purpose for which soldiers existed had never yet been frankly laid down and accepted, each of these plans in turn had been discredited by attacks, which called in question the very basis of the proposed reformation.

While naval policy had been framed and carried out in accordance with certain acknowledged necessities of national existence, military policy had been alternately expanded and deflated in order to assuage the anxieties, while conforming to the prejudices—real or supposed—of the British public. In the case of the fleet, we had very fortunately arrived, more than a generation ago, at the point where it was a question of what the country needed; as regards the

Policy and armaments.

Army, it was still a question of what the country would stand. But how could even a politician know what the country would stand until the full case had been laid before the country? How was it that while Ministers of both parties had the courage to put the issue more or less nakedly in the matter of ships, they grew timid as soon as the discussion turned on army corps? If the needs of the Commonwealth were to be the touchstone in the one case, why not also in the other? The country will stand a great deal more than the politicians think; and it will stand almost anything better than vacillation, evasion, and untruth. In army matters, unfortunately, it has had experience of little else since the battle of Waterloo.

Mathematicians, metaphysicians, and economists have a fondness for what is termed 'an assumption.' They take for granted something which it would be inconvenient or impossible to prove, and thereupon proceed to build upon it a fabric which compels admiration in a less or greater degree, by reason of its logical consistency. There is no great harm in this method so long as the conclusions, which are drawn from the airy calculations of the study, are confined to the peaceful region of their birth; but so soon as they begin to sally forth into the harsh world of men and affairs, they are apt to break at once into shivers. When the statesman makes an assumption he does so at his peril; or, perhaps, to speak more correctly, at the peril of his country. For if it be a false assumption the facts will speedily find it out, and disasters will inevitably ensue.

Our Governments, Tory and Radical alike, have

Policy and armaments.

acted in recent times as if the British Army were what their policy required it to be—something, that is, entirely different from what it really was. Judging by its procedure, the Foreign Office would appear to have made the singularly bold assumption that, in a military comparison with other nations, Britain was still in much the same relative position as in the days of Napoleon. Sustained by this tenacious but fantastic tradition, Ministers have not infrequently engaged in policies which wiser men would have avoided. They have uttered protests, warnings, threats which have gone unheeded. They have presumed to say what would and would not be tolerated in certain spheres; but having nothing better behind their despatches than a mere assumption which did not correspond with the facts, they have been compelled to endure rebuffs and humiliations. As they had not the prudence to cut their coat according to their cloth, it was only natural that occasionally they should have had to appear before the world in a somewhat ridiculous guise.

British statesmen for nearly half a century had persisted in acting upon two most dangerous assumptions. They had assumed that one branch of the national armaments conformed to their policy, when in fact it did not. And they had assumed also, which is equally fatal, that policy, if only it be virtuous and unaggressive, is in some mysterious way self-supporting, and does not need to depend on armaments at all.

The military preparations of Britain were inadequate to maintain the policy of Security, which British Governments had nevertheless been engaged in pursuing for many years prior to the outbreak of

CHAPTER III.

Policy and armaments.

the present war.[1] On the other hand, the abandonment of this policy was incompatible with the continuance of the Empire. We could not hope to hold our scattered Dependencies and to keep our Dominions safe against encroachments unless we were prepared to incur the necessary sacrifices.

[1] "Our Army, as a belligerent factor in European politics, is almost a 'negligible quantity. This Empire is at all times practically defenceless 'beyond its first line. Such an Empire invites war. Its assumed security 'amid the armaments of Europe, and now of Asia, is insolent and provoca-'tive" (Lord Roberts, October 22, 1912). Nothing indeed is more insolent and provocative, or more likely to lead to a breach of the peace, than undefended riches among armed men.

CHAPTER IV

THE BALANCE OF POWER

CHAPTER IV.

The balance of power.

DURING the whole period of rather more than thirteen years—which has been referred to in previous pages as the post-Victorian epoch, and which extended roughly from January 1901, when Queen Victoria died, to July 1914, when war was declared—the British Army remained inadequate for the purpose of upholding that policy which British statesmen of both parties, and the British people, both at home and in the Dominions, were engaged in pursuing—whether they knew it or not—and were bound to pursue, unless they were prepared to sacrifice their independence.

The aim of that policy was the security of the whole empire. This much at any rate was readily conceded on all hands. It was not enough, however, that we approved the general aim of British policy. A broad but clear conception of the means by which our Government hoped to maintain this policy, and the sacrifices which the country would have to make in order to support this policy, was no less necessary. So soon, however, as we began to ask for further particulars, we found ourselves in the region of acute controversy. 'Security' was a convenient political formula, which could be accepted as readily by the

CHAPTER IV.

man who placed his trust in international law, as by his neighbour who believed in battle fleets and army corps.

The balance of power.

In considering this question of security we could not disregard Europe, for Europe was still the storm-centre of the world. We could not afford to turn a blind eye towards the ambitions and anxieties of the great continental Powers. We were bound to take into account not only their visions but their nightmares. We could not remain indifferent to their groupings and alliances, or to the strength and dispositions of their armaments.

That the United Kingdom was a pair of islands lying on the western edge of Europe, and that the rest of the British Empire was remote, and unwilling to be interested in the rivalries of the Teuton, Slav, and Latin races, did not affect the matter in the least. Nowadays no habitable corner of the earth is really remote; and as for willingness or unwillingness to be interested, that had nothing at all to do with the question. For it was clear that any Power, which succeeded in possessing itself of the suzerainty of Europe, could redraw the map of the world at its pleasure, and blow the Monroe Doctrine, no less than the British Empire, sky-high.

Looking across thousands of leagues of ocean, it was difficult for the Dominions and the United States to understand how their fortunes, and the ultimate fate of their cherished institutions, could possibly be affected by the turmoil and jealousies of —what appeared in their eyes to be—a number of reactionary despotisms and chauvinistic democracies. Even the hundred and twenty leagues which separate Hull from Emden, or the seven which divide Dover from Calais, were enough to convince many people

CHAPTER IV.

The balance of power.

in the United Kingdom that we could safely allow Europe to 'stew in her own juice.' But unfortunately for this theory, unless a great continental struggle ended like the battle of the Kilkenny cats, the outside world was likely to find itself in an awkward predicament, when the conqueror chose to speak with it in the gates, at a time of his own choosing.

British policy since 1901 had tended, with ever increasing self-consciousness, towards the definite aim of preventing Germany from acquiring the suzerainty of Western Europe. It was obvious that German predominance, if secured, must ultimately force the other continental nations, either into a German alliance, or into a neutrality favourable to German interests. German policy would then inevitably be directed towards encroachments upon British possessions. Germany had already boldly proclaimed her ambitions overseas. Moreover, she would find it pleasanter to compensate, and soothe the susceptibilities of those nations whom she had overcome in diplomacy or war, and to reward their subsequent services as allies and friendly neutrals, by paying them out of our property rather than out of her own. For this reason, if for no other, we were deeply concerned that Germany should not dominate Europe if we could help it.

During this period, on the other hand, Germany appeared to be setting herself more and more seriously to acquire this domination. Each succeeding year her writers expressed themselves in terms of greater candour and confidence. Her armaments were following her policy. The rapid creation of a fleet—the counterpart of the greatest army in Europe—and the recent additions to the striking power of her

CHAPTER IV.

The balance of power.

already enormous army could have no other object. Certainly from 1909 onwards, it was impossible to regard German preparations as anything else than a challenge, direct or indirect, to the security of the British Empire.

Consequently the direction of British policy returned, gradually, unavowedly, but with certainty, to its old lines, and became once more concerned with the maintenance of the *Balance of Power* as the prime necessity. The means adopted were the Triple Entente between Britain, France, and Russia. The object of this understanding was to resist the anticipated aggressions of the Triple Alliance, wherein Germany was the predominant partner.

The tendency of phrases, as they grow old, is to turn into totems, for and against which political parties, and even great nations, fight unreasoningly. But before we either yield our allegiance to any of these venerable formulas, or decide to throw it out on the scrap-heap, there are advantages in looking to see whether or not there is some underlying meaning which may be worth attending to. It occasionally happens that circumstances have changed so much since the original idea was first crystallised in words, that the old saying contains no value or reality whatsoever for the present generation. More often, however, there is something of permanent importance behind, if only we can succeed in tearing off the husk of prejudice in which it has become encased. So, according to Disraeli, "the *divine right* of Kings 'may have been a plea for feeble tyrants, but the 'divine right of government is the keystone of human 'progress." For many years the phrase *British interests*, which used to figure so largely in speeches

The balance of power.

and leading articles, has dropped out of use, because it had come to be associated unfavourably with bondholders' dividends. The fact that it also implied national honour and prestige, the performance of duties and the burden of responsibilities was forgotten. Even the doctrine of *laissez faire*, which politicians of all parties have lately agreed to abjure and contemn, has, as regards industrial affairs, a large kernel of practical wisdom and sound policy hidden away in it. But of all these derelict maxims, that which until quite recently, appeared to be suffering from the greatest neglect, was the need for maintaining the *Balance of Power* in Europe. For close on two generations it had played no overt part in public controversy, except when some Tory matador produced it defiantly as a red rag to infuriate the Radical bull.

If this policy of the maintenance of the *Balance of Power* has been little heard of since Waterloo, the reason is that since then, until quite recently, the *Balance of Power* has never appeared to be seriously threatened.[1] And because the policy of maintaining this balance was in abeyance, many people have come to believe that it was discredited. Because it was not visibly and actively in use it was supposed to have become entirely useless.

This policy can never become useless. It must inevitably come into play, so soon as any Power appears to be aiming at the mastery of the continent. It will ever remain a matter of life or death, to the United Kingdom and to the British Empire, that no continental state shall be allowed to obtain

[1] It can hardly be overlooked, however, that this principle, rightly or wrongly interpreted, had something to do with the Crimean War (1854–56) and with the British attitude at the Congress of Berlin (1878)

command, directly or indirectly, of the resources, diplomacy, and armaments of Europe.

The balance of power.

In the sixteenth century we fought Philip of Spain to prevent him from acquiring European predominance. In the seventeenth, eighteenth, and nineteenth centuries we fought Louis XIV., Louis XV., and Napoleon for the same reason. In order to preserve the balance of power, and with it our own security, it was our interest under Elizabeth to prevent the Netherlands from being crushed by Spain. Under later monarchs it was our interest to prevent the Netherlands, the lesser German States, Prussia, Austria, and finally the whole of Europe from being crushed by France. And we can as ill afford to-day to allow France to be crushed by Germany, or Holland and Belgium to fall into her power. The wheel has come round full circle, but the essential British interest remains constant.

The wheel is always turning, sometimes slowly, sometimes with startling swiftness. Years hence the present alliances will probably be discarded. It may be that some day the danger of a European predominance will appear from a different quarter—from one of our present allies, or from some upstart state which may rise to power with an even greater rapidity than the Electorate of Brandenburg. Or it may be that before long the New World, in fact as well as phrase, may have come in to redress the balance of the Old. We cannot say, because we cannot foresee what the future holds in store. But from the opening of the present century, the immediate danger came from Germany, who hardly troubled to conceal the fact that she was aiming at predominance by mastery of the Low Countries and by crushing France.

That this danger was from time to time regarded seriously by a section of the British Cabinet, we know from their own statements both before war broke out and subsequently. It was no chimera confined to the imaginations of irresponsible and panic-stricken writers. In sober truth the balance of power in Europe was in as much danger, and the maintenance of it had become as supreme a British interest, under a Liberal government at the beginning of the twentieth century, as it ever was under a Whig government at the close of the seventeenth and opening of the eighteenth.

The balance of power.

The stealthy return of this doctrine into the region of practical politics was not due to the prejudices of the party which happened to be in power. Quite the contrary. Most Liberals distrusted the phrase. The whole mass of the Radicals abhorred it. The idea which lay under and behind the phrase was nevertheless irresistible, because it arose out of the facts. Had a Socialist Government held office, this policy must equally have imposed itself and been accepted with a good or ill grace, for the simple reason that, unless the balance of power is maintained in Europe, there can be no security for British freedom, under which we mean, with God's help, to work out our own problems in our own way.

English statesmen had adopted this policy in fact, if unavowedly—perhaps even to some extent unconsciously—when they first entered into, and afterwards confirmed, the Triple Entente. And having once entered into the Triple Entente it was obvious that, without risking still graver consequences, we could never resume the detached position which we occupied before we took that step. It is difficult to

CHAPTER IV.

The balance of power.

believe—seeing how the danger of German predominance threatened France and Russia as well as ourselves—that we should not have excited the ill-will of those two countries had we refused to make common cause by joining the Triple Entente. It was obvious, however, to every one that we could not afterwards retire from this association without incurring their hostility. If we had withdrawn we should have been left, not merely without a friend in Europe, but with all the chief Powers in Europe our enemies—ready upon the first favourable occasion to combine against us.

There is only one precedent in our history for so perilous a situation—when Napoleon forced Europe into a combination against us in 1806. And this precedent, though it then threatened our Empire with grave dangers, did not threaten it with dangers comparable in gravity with those which menaced us a century later.

The consequences of breaking away from the Triple Entente were sufficiently plain. "We may 'build ships against one nation, or even against a 'combination of nations. But we cannot build ships 'against half Europe. If Western Europe, with all 'its ports, its harbours, its arsenals, and its resources, 'was to fall under the domination of a single will, no 'effort of ours would be sufficient to retain the 'command of the sea. It is a balance of power 'on the continent, which alone makes it possible 'for us to retain it. Thus the maintenance of the 'balance of power is vital to our superiority at sea, 'which again is vital to the security of the British 'Empire." [1]

[1] Viscount Milner in the *United Service Magazine*, January 1912.

The balance of power.

Security in the widest sense was the ultimate end of our policy—security of mind, security from periodic panic, as well as actual military security. Looked at more closely, the immediate end was defence—the defence of the British Empire and of the United Kingdom.

In the existing condition of the world a policy of 'splendid isolation' was no longer possible. Conditions with which we are familiar in commercial affairs, had presented themselves in the political sphere, and co-operation on a large scale had become necessary in order to avoid bankruptcy. England had entered into the Triple Entente because her statesmen realised, clearly or vaguely, that by doing so we should be better able to defend our existence, and for no other reason.

After 1911 it must have been obvious to most people who considered the matter carefully that in certain events the Triple Entente would become an alliance. It is the interest as well as the duty of allies to stand by one another from first to last, and act together in the manner most likely to result in victory for the alliance. What then was the manner of co-operation most likely to result in victory for that alliance which lay dormant under the Triple Entente?

But first of all, to clear away one obscurity—*Invasion* was not our problem; *Defence* was our problem; for the greater included the less.

The word 'defence' is apt to carry different meanings to different minds. The best defence of England and British interests, at any given time, may or may not consist in keeping our main army in the United Kingdom and waiting to be attacked here. It all depends upon the special circumstances

CHAPTER IV.

The balance of power.

of each case. The final decision must be governed by one consideration, and one only—how to strike the speediest, heaviest, and most disabling blow at the aggressor. If by keeping our army in England and endeavouring to lure the enemy into our toils, that end is most likely to be accomplished, then it is obviously best to keep our army here. If by sending it into the north of France to combine with the French the supreme military object has a superior chance of being achieved, then it is best to send it into the north of France.

A defensive war cannot be defined and circumscribed as a war to drive out invaders, or even to prevent the landing of invaders. The best way to defend your castle may be to man the walls, to fall upon the enemy at the ford, to harry his lands, or even to attack him in his castle. There is no fixed rule. The circumstances in each case make the rule.

A war is not less a defensive war if you strike at your enemy in his own territory, or if you come to the aid of your ally, whose territory has been invaded or is threatened. In the circumstances which prevailed for a considerable number of years prior to the outbreak of the present war, it gradually became more and more obvious, that our soundest defence would be joint action with France upon her north-eastern frontier. For there, beyond any doubt, would Germany's supreme effort be made against the Triple Entente. If the attack failed at that point, it would be the heaviest and most disabling blow which our enemy could suffer. If, on the other hand, it succeeded, France and England would have to continue the struggle on terms immensely less favourable.

The balance of power.

This opinion was not by any means unanimously or clearly held; but during the summer of 1911 and subsequently, it was undoubtedly the hypothesis upon which those members of our Government relied, who were chiefly responsible for the conduct of foreign affairs. Unfortunately Parliament and the country had never accepted either the policy or its consequences; they had never been asked to accept either the one or the other; nor had they been educated with a view to their acceptance.

At that time the error was exceedingly prevalent, that it is a more comfortable business fighting in your own country than in somebody else's. From this it followed that it would be folly to engage in what were termed disapprovingly 'foreign adventures,' and that we should be wise to await attack behind our own shores. Recent events have wrought such a complete and rapid conversion from this heresy, that it is no longer worth while wasting words in exposing it. It is necessary, however, to recall how influential this view of the matter was, not only up to the declaration of war, but even for some time afterwards.

As to the precise form of co-operation between the members of the Triple Entente in case of war, there could be no great mystery. It was obvious to any one who paid attention to what happened during the summer and autumn of 1911, that in the event of Germany attacking France over the Agadir dispute, we had let it be understood and expected, that we should send our Expeditionary Force across the Channel to co-operate with the French army on the north-eastern frontier.

CHAPTER V

THE MILITARY SITUATION

(*August* 1911)

CHAPTER V.

The military situation.

THE full gravity of the Agadir incident, though apparent to other nations, was never realised by the people of this country. The crisis arose suddenly in July 1911. Six weeks later it had subsided; but it was not until well on in the autumn that its meanings were grasped, even by that comparatively small section of the public who interest themselves in problems of defence and foreign affairs. From October onwards, however, an increasing number began to awake to the fact, that war had only been avoided by inches, and to consider seriously—many of them for the first time in their lives—what would have happened if England had become involved in a European conflict.

From various official statements, and from discussions which from time to time had taken place in Parliament, it was understood that our 'Expeditionary Force' consisted of six infantry divisions, a cavalry division, and army troops;[1] also that the national resources permitted of this force being kept up to full strength for a period of at least six months, after making all reasonable deductions for the wastage of

[1] In all about 160,000 men, of whom some 25,000 were non-combatants.

The military situation.

war. Was this enough? Enough for what? . . . To uphold British policy; to preserve Imperial security; to enable the Triple Entente to maintain the balance of power in Europe. These were vague phrases; what did they actually amount to? . . . The adequacy or inadequacy of such an army as this for doing what was required of it—for securing speedy victory in event of war—or still better for preserving peace by the menace which it opposed to German schemes of aggression—can only be tested by considering the broad facts with regard to numbers, efficiency, and readiness of all the armies which would be engaged directly, or indirectly, in a European struggle.

War, however, had been avoided in 1911, and not a few people were therefore convinced that the menace of the available British army, together with the other consequences to be apprehended from the participation of this country, had been sufficient to deter Germany from pursuing her schemes of aggression, if indeed she had actually harboured any notions of the kind. But others, not altogether satisfied with this explanation and conclusion, were inclined to press their enquiries somewhat further. Supposing war had actually been declared, would the British force have been sufficient—acting in conjunction with the French army—to repel a German invasion of France and Belgium, to hurl back the aggressors and overwhelm them in defeat? Would it have been sufficient to accomplish the more modest aim of holding the enemy at his own frontiers, or even—supposing that by a swift surprise he had been able to overrun Belgium—at any rate to keep him out of France?

CHAPTER V.

The military situation.

When people proceeded to seek for answers to these questions, as many did during the year 1912, they speedily discovered that, in considerations of this sort, the governing factor is numbers—the numbers of the opposing forces available at the outbreak of war and in the period immediately following. The tremendous power of national spirit must needs be left out of such calculations as a thing immeasurable, imponderable, and uncertain. It was also unsafe to assume that the courage, intelligence, efficiency, armament, transport, equipment, supplies, and leadership of the German and Austrian armies would be in any degree inferior to those of the Triple Entente. Certain things had to be allowed for in a rough and ready way;[1] but the main enquiry was forced to concern itself with numerical strength.

There was not room for much disagreement upon the broad facts of the military situation, among soldiers and civilians who, from 1911 onwards, gave themselves to the study of this subject at the available sources of information; and their estimates have been confirmed, in the main, by what has happened since war began. The Intelligence departments of London, Paris, and Petrograd—with much ampler means of knowledge at their disposal—can have arrived at no other conclusions. What the English War Office knew, the Committee of Imperial Defence likewise knew; and the leading members of the Cabinet, if not the whole Government, must be presumed to have been equally well informed.

It was assumed in these calculations, that in case of tension between the Triple Entente and the Triple

[1] Such, for instance, as the fact that the time-table of German mobilisation appeared to be somewhat more rapid than that of the French, and much more so than that of the Russians.

The military situation.

Alliance, the latter would not be able—in the first instance at all events—to bring its full strength into the struggle. For unless Germany and Austria managed their diplomacy before the outbreak of hostilities with incomparable skill, it seemed improbable that the Italian people would consent to engage in a costly, and perhaps ruinous, war—a war against France, with whom they had no quarrel; against England, towards whom they had long cherished feelings of friendship; on behalf of the Habsburg Empire, which they still regarded—and not altogether unreasonably — with suspicion and enmity.

But although the neutrality of Italy might be regarded as a likelihood at the opening of the war, it could not be reckoned on with any certainty as a permanent condition. For as no one can forecast the course of a campaign, so no one can feel secure that the unexpected may not happen at any moment. The consequences of a defeat in this quarter or in that, may offer too great temptations to the cupidity of onlookers; while diplomacy, though it may have bungled in the beginning, is sure to have many opportunities of recovering its influence as the situation develops. Consequently, unless and until Italy actually joined in the struggle on the side of the Triple Entente, a considerable section of the French army would, in common prudence, have to be left on guard upon the Savoy frontier.

In a war brought on by the aggressive designs of Germany, the only nations whose participation could be reckoned on with certainty—and this only supposing that Britain stood firmly by the policy upon which her Government had embarked—were Russia,

CHAPTER V.

France, and ourselves on the one side, Germany and Austria-Hungary on the other.

The military situation.

It would certainly be necessary for Germany, as well as Austria, to provide troops for coast defences, and also for the frontiers of neutral countries, which might have the temptation, in certain circumstances, to deneutralise themselves at an inconvenient moment, if they were left unwatched. On the north and west were Denmark, Holland, and Belgium, each of which had a small field army, besides garrison and fortress troops which might be turned to more active account upon an emergency. On the south and east were Montenegro, Servia, and Roumania, whose military resources were on a considerable scale, and whose neutrality was not a thing altogether to be counted on, even before the Balkan war[1] had lowered the prestige of Turkey. In addition there was Italy, who although a pledged ally in a defensive war was not likely, for that reason, to consider herself bound to neutrality, benevolent or otherwise, if in her judgment, the particular contingencies which called for her support had not arisen at the outset.

After taking such precautions as seemed prudent under these heads, Germany would then be obliged to detach for service, in co-operation with the Austrians in Poland, and along the whole eastern border, a sufficient number of army corps to secure substantial superiority over the maximum forces which Russia, hampered by an inadequate railway system and various military considerations,[2] could

[1] The first Balkan war broke out in the autumn of 1912.

[2] Russia had anxieties of her own with regard to the intentions of Roumania, of Turkey in Persia and the Caucasus, and of China and Japan in the Far East.

be expected to bring into the field and maintain there during the first few months of the war.

The military situation.

It was reckoned[1] after taking all these things into account, that Germany would have available, for the invasion of France, an army consisting of some ninety divisions—roughly, rather more than a million and three-quarters of men—and that she could maintain this force at its full strength—repairing the wastage of war out of her ample reserves—for a period of at least six months. It was assumed that the Kaiser, relying upon the much slower mobilisation of Russia, would undoubtedly decide to use the whole of this huge force in the west, in the hope that before pressure could begin to make itself felt in the east, France would either have been crushed, as she was in 1870, or so much mangled that it would be possible to send reinforcements of an overwhelming character to make victory secure in Poland.

Against this German force of 1,800,000, France, according to the best information available, could put into the field and maintain at full strength for a similar period of six months about 1,300,000 men. But this was the utmost that could be expected of the French, and the initial discrepancy of 500,000 men was very serious. It precluded all reasonable hope on their part of being able to take the offensive, to which form of warfare the genius of the people was most adapted. It would compel them to remain on the defensive, for which it was believed at that

[1] These calculations were worked out in various ways, but the net results arrived at were always substantially the same. In view of the fact that the main conclusions have been amply proved by the results of the present war, it does not seem worth while to weary the reader with more sums in arithmetic than are absolutely necessary.

CHAPTER V.

time—though wrongly, as events have proved—that they were ill suited by temperament as well as tradition.

The military situation.

If England joined in the war by land as well as sea the numerical deficiency would be reduced to 340,000 on the arrival of our Expeditionary Force. In this connection, as well as for other reasons, the attitude of Holland and Belgium, and that of Germany with respect to these two countries, were clearly matters of high importance.

Holland had a field army of four divisions, and her interests could be summed up in the words, 'preservation of independence.' She would naturally wish to avoid being actively embroiled in the war on one side or the other; and, fortunately for her, she had every reason to believe that her neutrality would not be disturbed or questioned. Her territories lay to one side of the probable campaign area, and moreover, whatever might be the ulterior designs of Germany with regard to western expansion, it was obvious that her immediate interests must necessarily lie in Dutch neutrality, which would be infinitely more useful to her than a Dutch alliance. For Holland holds the mouths of the Scheldt and Rhine, and so long as she remained neutral, it was anticipated that imports and exports would readily find their way into and out of Germany. This advantage would cease were Britain to establish a blockade of these inlets, as she would certainly do if they belonged to a hostile Power.

In certain respects Belgium was in the same case as Holland. She likewise had a field army of four divisions, and her interests could be summed up in the words, 'preservation of independence.' But here all resemblance between the two countries ended.

CHAPTER V.

The military situation.

Belgium was not merely the southern portion (Holland being the northern) of that Naboth's vineyard, the possession of which German visionaries had proclaimed to be essential to Teutonic world-power. Belgium was more even than this. If the permanent possession of Belgian territory was a political object in the future, temporary occupation was no less a military necessity of the present. For in order that Germany might benefit in full measure by her numerical superiority, Belgian roads and railways were required, along which to transport her troops, and Belgian hills and plains on which to deploy them. If Germany were confined to the use of her own frontiers she would not only lose in swiftness of attack, but her legions would be piled up, one behind another, like a crowd coming out of a theatre. She needed space on which to spread out her superior numbers in order that her superior numbers might make certain of victory.

There was an idea at this time (1911 – 12) that Germany would be satisfied to keep to the south-east of the fortified line of the Meuse—moving through Luxemburg and the mountains of the Ardennes—and that if Belgium saw fit to yield, under protest, to *force majeure*, the northern region, containing the great plain of Flanders and all cities of importance, would be left inviolate. This theory was probably erroneous, for the reason that—as the event has shown—Germany required a greater space and more favourable ground, than would have been provided under this arrangement, in order to bring her great superiority to bear.

CHAPTER V.

The military situation.

With the French on the other hand there was no similar advantage to be gained by the violation of Belgian neutrality. From their point of view the shorter the battle front could be kept the better. If Belgium chose to range herself by the side of France as a willing ally it would undoubtedly be a great gain; but if she chose to remain neutral the French could have no object in invading or occupying her territories.

It was assumed, and no doubt rightly, that, like Holland, Belgium would prefer to remain neutral—leaving the question of future absorption to take care of itself—provided she could do this without enduring the humiliation of allowing foreign armies to violate her soil. For she knew that, in the event of a French victory, her independence would remain assured; whereas, if the Germans were successful, she would have avoided awakening their hostility and giving them an excuse for annexation. But even if Belgium, under gross provocation, were forced to take sides against Germany, the deficit in numbers on the side of the Triple Entente would only be reduced by some eighty or a hundred thousand men. The deficit would still stand, roughly, at a quarter of a million men.

In view of the foregoing considerations it was clearly absurd to think that our own small force was at all adequate, in a military sense, to deter Germany from engaging in a war of aggression. Had we been able, during the years 1912 to 1914, to see into the minds of the German General Staff we should probably have realised that this inadequacy was even greater than it appeared. We should then have

The military situation.

known that the numbers of the Kaiser's striking force had been carefully understated; and that the amount of preparations in the way of material had been hidden away with an equal industry. We should also have learned, that the sending of our army abroad was viewed with scepticism in German military circles, as an event hardly likely to occur. But even if our Expeditionary Force did go, it was altogether inadequate to redress the adverse balance; still more inadequate to bring an immediate victory within the range of practical possibility. It was inadequate to hold back the premeditated invasion, either at the German frontier, or even at the French frontier. It was inadequate to make Belgian resistance effective, even if that nation should determine to throw in its lot with the Triple Entente.

As a matter of the very simplest arithmetic our land forces were inadequate for any of these purposes. They were unequal to the task of maintaining the balance of power by giving a numerical superiority to the armies of the Triple Entente. Our armaments therefore did not correspond with our policy. It was clear that they would not be able to uphold that policy if it were put to the supreme test of war. It was impossible to abandon our policy. It was not impossible, and it was not even in 1912 too late, to have set about strengthening our armaments. Nothing of the kind, however, was undertaken by the Government, whose spokesmen, official and unofficial, employed themselves more congenially in deriding and rebuking Lord Roberts for calling attention to the danger.

Of course if it had been possible to place reliance upon the statement of the English War Minister,

CHAPTER V.

The military situation.

made little more than a year before war broke out,[1] that every soldier under the voluntary system is worth ten conscripts, we and our Allies would have been in a position of complete security. In that case our force of 160,000 would have been the equivalent of 1,600,000 Germans, and we should from the first have been in a superiority of more than a million over our enemies.

Even if we could have credited the more modest assumption of the Attorney-General — made nearly four months after war broke out—that one volunteer was worth three 'pressed' men, the opposing forces would have been somewhere about an equality.[2]

Unfortunately both these methods of ready-reckoning were at fault, except for their immediate purpose of soothing, or deluding the particular audiences to which they were addressed. The words were meaningless and absurd in a military sense; though conceivably they possessed some occult political virtue, and might help, for a time at least, to avert the retribution which is due to unfaithful stewards.

Both these distinguished statesmen, as well as

[1] Colonel Seely at Heanor, April 26, 1913.

[2] Sir John Simon (Attorney-General and a Cabinet Minister), at Ashton-under-Lyne, November 21, 1914. . . . This speech is instructive reading. It is also comforting for the assurance it contains, that if the speaker approved of our taking part in this war (as he vowed he did) his audience might rest satisfied that it was indeed a righteous war; seeing that war was a thing which, on principle, he (Sir John Simon) very much reprehended. And yet we are *not* wholly convinced and reassured. There is a touch of over-emphasis—as if perhaps, after all, the orator needed the support of his own vehemence to keep him reminded of the righteousness. The pacifist in war-paint is apt to overact the unfamiliar part. One wonders from what sort of British officer at the front the Attorney-General had derived the impression that 'one' of our own voluntary soldiers—gallant fellows though they are—is the equal of 'three' of the Germans who face him, or of the Frenchmen who fight by his side. . . . This speech puts us not a little in mind of *Evangelist's* warning to *Christian,* with regard to *Mr. Legality's* fluent promises to relieve him of his burden—"There is nothing in all this noise save a design to 'beguile thee of thy salvation."

The military situation.

many of their colleagues and followers, were beset by the error of false opposites. A soldier who has enlisted voluntarily, and another who is a conscript or 'pressed' man, have equally to fight their country's enemies when they are ordered to do so. In both cases the particular war may be against their consciences and judgments; and their participation in it may therefore be involuntary.

Of two men—equal in age, strength, training, and courage—one of whom believes his cause to be just, while the other does not, there can be no doubt that the former will fight better than the latter—even though the latter was enlisted under the voluntary system while the former was a conscript or 'pressed' man. In this sense the superiority of the 'voluntary' principle is incontestable. But is there any evidence to show, that either the original soldiers, or the new levies, of the German army are risking their lives in this war any less willingly than our own countrymen, who went out with the Expeditionary Force, or those others who have since responded to Lord Kitchener's appeal? Is there any reason to suppose that they are fighting any less bravely and intelligently? [1]

Another matter of importance in these calculations with regard to the military strength of the Triple Entente and the Triple Alliance was the time limit.

There are three periods in war. There is the *onset* of war, where swiftness of action is what tells most; there is the *grip* of war, where numbers of

[1] Sir John Simon clinched his arithmetical calculation of 'three' to 'one,' by stating that 'the Kaiser already knew it'; and this reassuring statement was received with 'laughter and cheers.' The laughter we can understand.

CHAPTER V.

trained men are what tell most; and there is the *drag* of war, when what tells most is the purse.

The military situation.

Speaking by the book, it is of course numbers which tell all the way through. At the beginning—in the *onset*—the aim is to hurl superior numbers at a vital point—taking the enemy by surprise, and thereby disordering his whole plan of campaign—very much as you knock a limpet off a rock, with a sharp unexpected blow.

If this effort fails to settle matters, then we are in the *grip*. Here it is a case of sheer heavy slogging of all the available trained troops. The weaker side is driven to the defensive. It is found making use of every artificial and natural advantage to counteract the superiority which threatens it, and which must speedily prevail, if only it be superior enough.

Finally, after a longer or shorter period of indecisive deadlock, the time comes when trained troops and material of war accumulated in advance begin to run short—when new levies, raised since the war broke out, begin to take the field, well or ill equipped, well or ill armed, as the case may be. When this stage is reached we are in the *drag* of war; and the side which can best afford to feed, clothe, and arm its fresh reinforcements stands at an enormous advantage.

In 1870 war was announced on July 15th, and formally declared on the 19th. Three weeks later, on August 6th, the important battles of Woerth and Spicheren were won by the Germans. On September 2nd, the issue of the war was decided, when the Emperor of the French, with his main army, surrendered at Sedan. Metz fell in the last days of October, and Paris on the first day of March in the

The military situation.

following year. In that war the *onset* settled everything. There was no real *grip* of the opposing forces. The German attack had been so swift, vigorous, and successful that France was knocked out in the first round.

The speed with which great armies can be mobilised and hurled against one another has not diminished in the forty odd years which have elapsed since the *débâcle.* On the contrary, the art of war has been largely concerned in the interval with the vital question, how to get in the first deadly blow.

The military view was, that probably not earlier than the fifteenth day—certainly not later than the twenty-first—a battle would take place which must be of the highest importance, and which might quite well be decisive. It might make ultimate German victory only a matter of time; or it might only determine whether the ensuing campaign was to be waged on French or German soil—whether there was to be a German invasion of France or a Franco-British invasion of Germany. Consequently, if our Expeditionary Force was to render assistance at the critical time, it must reach its position on the frontier within a fortnight of the outbreak of war.

As to the *drag* of war, the Triple Entente had the advantage, if that stage were ever reached. For the purses of England, France, and Russia were much longer than those of Germany and Austria. It was important, however, to remember that there would be no hope for us in the *drag* of war, if Germany could deliver a heavy enough blow at the beginning, as she did in 1870.

These were the considerations as to time, which presented themselves to students of the military

CHAPTER V.

The military situation.

situation during the breathing space which followed upon the Agadir crisis. The substantial accuracy of this forecast was confirmed by what happened during August and September of last year. In 1914 war was declared by Germany on August 1st. For several days before she had been engaged actively in mobilisation. Three weeks later three important battles—on the road to Metz, at Charleroi, and at Mons [1]—were won by the Germans. If it had not been for the unexpected obstacle of Liége the last two engagements would in all probability have been fought at an even earlier date, and in circumstances much more unfavourable to the Franco-British forces. But in the early days of September, instead of the crushing defeat of Sedan, there was the victory of the Marne, and the Germans were forced to retreat to entrenched positions north of the Aisne.[2]

The *onset* period was ended; but the issue had not been settled as in 1870. France and England had not been knocked out in the first round. To this extent the supreme German endeavour had miscarried. Nevertheless a great advantage had been secured by our enemies, inasmuch as it was now apparent that the ensuing campaign—the *grip* of war—would be contested, not on German soil, but in France and Belgium.

The value of the assistance which the British Navy would be able to render to the cause of the Triple Entente was a consideration of the highest importance. But while the fleet, if the national confidence in it were justified, would render invaluable assistance to military operations, it was necessary

[1] The battle in Northern Alsace was fought on August 21 and 22. A French army was driven back at Charleroi on the 22nd, and the British at Mons on the 23rd.

[2] September 6-12.

The military situation.

to bear in mind—what Englishmen in recent times have been very apt to forget—that no success at sea, whether it consisted in the wholesale destruction of hostile ships, or in an absolute blockade of the enemy's coast, could by itself determine the main issue of a European contest of this character. Disaster in a land battle could not be compensated for, nor could the balance of power be maintained, by any naval victory. War would not be brought to an end favourable to the Triple Entente, even by a victory as complete as that of Trafalgar. It is also well to remember that peace came, not after Trafalgar, but after Waterloo, nearly ten years later.

The strange idea that the security of the British Empire can be maintained by the Navy alone, seems to be derived by a false process of reasoning, from the undeniable truth, that the supremacy of our Navy is essential to our security. But though it is essential—and the first essential—it is not the only essential of security.

An insular Power, largely dependent on sea-borne food supplies and raw materials for its industries—a Power which governs an empire in the East, which has dependencies scattered in every sea, which is politically united with immense but sparsely peopled dominions in the four quarters of the globe—must keep command of the sea. If that supremacy were once lost the British Empire, as an empire, would come to an end. Its early dissolution would be inevitable. Therefore it is true enough to say that if the German Alliance—or any other alliance—were to win a decisive naval victory against Britain, it would end the war completely and effectively so far as we were concerned.

CHAPTER V.

The military situation.

But the converse is not the case, and for obvious reasons. In a contest with a continental enemy who conquers on land, while we win victory after victory at sea, the result will not be a settlement in our favour, but a drawn issue. And the draw will be to his advantage, not our own. For having overthrown the balance of power by reason of his successful campaign and invasions, he will then be free to concentrate his whole energies upon wresting away naval supremacy from the British Empire. In time the Sea Power which is only a Sea Power will be overborne with numbers, and finally worsted by the victorious Land Power. For how is it possible to fight with one hand against an enemy with two hands? The fleets of Europe which at last must be combined against us, if we allow any rival to obtain a European predominance, are too heavy odds. German preparations alone were already causing us grave anxiety nearly three years before the Agadir crisis occurred. How then could we hope to build against the whole of Europe? Or even against half of Europe, if the other half remained coldly neutral?

CHAPTER VI

THE MILITARY SITUATION

(*August* 1914)

Chapter VI.

The military situation.

SUCH was the position of affairs at July 1911, as it appeared to the eyes of people who—during the ensuing period—endeavoured to arrive at an understanding of the problem without regard to the exigencies of party politics. Between that date and July 1914, when war broke out, various changes took place in the situation. The general effect of these changes was adverse to Britain and her allies.

In 1911 the German estimates provided for considerable increases, especially in artillery and machine-guns. The peace strength of the Army was raised.

In the following year, 1912, further additions were made to the peace strength, and two new army corps were formed out of existing units—one for the Polish, the other for the French frontier. Artillery and machine-guns were very greatly increased in the ordinary estimates of that year, and again in those of 1913. In addition, Germany at the same time added a squadron to her fleet in the North Sea, by arranging to keep more ships permanently in commission.

CHAPTER VI.

The military situation.

But early in 1913 it became known, that the German Government was about to introduce an Army Bill, providing for immense and sensational additions. The sum of £50,000,000 was to be raised by loan for initial expenditure. The increased cost of upkeep on the proposed new establishment would amount to £9,500,000 per annum. Sixty-three thousand more recruits were to be taken each year. The total peace strength of the Army was to be raised by approximately 200,000 men. Nearly four millions sterling was to be spent on aircraft, and ten and a half on fortifications; while the war-chest was to be raised from six to eighteen millions. Twenty-seven thousand additional horses were to be purchased.

These proposals were timed to take effect the same autumn; so that by the following Midsummer (1914), the military strength of Germany would have reaped the main benefit which was anticipated from the enormous additions.

It was not in the power of France to increase the actual total of her numbers, because for many years past she had already taken every man who was physically fit for military service. About eighty per cent of the young Frenchmen who came each year before the revision boards had been enlisted; whereas in Germany—up to the passing of the new Army Law—considerably less than fifty per cent had been required to serve. The German Army as a consequence was composed of picked men, while the French Army contained a considerable proportion who were inferior both in character and physique.

But in the face of the new German menace France had to do the best she could. She had to do it alone, for the reason that the British Government entertained conscientious and insuperable objections to bearing its due share of the burden.

The military situation.

Already, prior to the sensational expansion of Germany in 1913, France had endeavoured to counteract the current yearly increases in the military estimates of her neighbour, by various reorganisations and regroupings of active units, and by improvements calculated to improve the efficiency of the reserves. But when information was forthcoming [1] as to the nature and extent of the developments proposed under the German Army Bill of 1913, it was at once realised that more drastic measures were essential to national safety.

Before the German projects were officially announced, the French Government took the bold step of asking the legislature to sanction a lengthening of the period of active military service from two years to three, and an extension of the age limit of the reserves from forty-seven to forty-nine. Power was also taken to summon, in case of emergency, the annual contingent of recruits a year before their due time. Increases in artillery, engineers, railways, barrack accommodation, and subsidiary services were asked for and obtained. The cost of these, when the whole sum came to be calculated, was found to amount to £32,000,000.

Apart, therefore, from material preparations of one kind and another, Germany was taking steps to add 200,000 men to her striking force, and the intentions of France were approximately the same. In the

[1] Germany took time by the forelock, and began to carry through the contemplated programme before disclosing the terms of the Army Bill to the legislature. Consequently her intentions were known in a general way to every Intelligence department in Europe, long before they were actually announced.

CHAPTER VI.

The military situation.

case of Germany, however, the increases of strength would be operative by Midsummer 1914, while with France they would not take effect until two years later.[1]

Germany, moreover, was arranging to take 63,000 more recruits annually. France was unable to obtain any more recruits, as she already took all that were fit to bear arms. The increase in her striking force was made mainly at the expense of her reserves. Year by year, therefore, the numerical inferiority of France must become more marked.

Russia meanwhile was proceeding with her programme of military extension and reorganisation which had been decided on after the Japanese war. A great part of her expenditure was being devoted to the improvement of her exceedingly defective system of railways and communications, and to the fortification of the Gulf of Finland.

Austria did not remain stationary in military preparations any more than her neighbours. Her intake of recruits was 181,000 in 1912. It was decided to raise it to 206,000 in 1913, and again to 216,000 in 1914.

In the British Army, during this critical period, there had of course been no increases, but the reverse.

[1] In going through the memoranda upon which this chapter is based, I came across a paper written at the end of July 1913 by a retired soldier friend, in answer to a request on my part for certain technical information as to French and German preparations. On the margin of the document, which gives a very full and able analysis, he had added the following post-script as an expression of his personal opinion. "*N.B.—Most Important:* 'The German Bill takes immediate effect. The French only takes effect 'in 1916 because (1) the French are not going to retain the class which 'finishes its service this year with the colours; (2) comparatively few are fit 'for enrolment at twenty; (3) there has been great delay in Parliament . . . '*A year from now will be the critical time.* Germany will have had the full 'benefit from her Bill, whereas France will have a mass of young recruits 'still under instruction. The strain on officers will be tremendous in order 'to knock this mass of raw men into shape." It is rarely that a prophecy is fulfilled practically to a day.

The military situation.

The Regular Forces, which had been reduced in 1906 by nine battalions,[1] were in 1914 some eight thousand men under their nominal strength. The Territorials, which had never yet reached the figure postulated by their originator, were at this date about 47,000 short. The Army Reserve was doomed in the near future to an automatic shrinkage on a considerable scale, owing to the reductions which had been effected in the Regular Forces, from which the reservists were drawn at the expiry of their terms of service.

Actually, therefore, the weakness of our own military position had become more marked since 1911. Relatively it had undergone an even greater change for the worse, owing to the stupendous German programme, to the fact that we had lagged behind in the matter of aircraft, and that our naval preponderance was not so great as it had been three years earlier.

The events which occurred in the Turkish peninsula between October 1912, when the first Balkan war broke out, and August 1913, when the second was ended by the Treaty of Bucharest, were not without their bearing upon the general balance of power in Europe. Turkey had collapsed before the onset of

[1] Mr. Haldane, the Secretary of State for War, in justifying this reduction explained that 'his infantry was in excess, the artillery was deficient.' He would rather not have cut off these nine battalions, "but he could not use 'them. He had four more than he could mobilise" (Auchterarder, December 29, 1906). In his view "the first step to doing anything for developing the 'national basis of the Army was to cut something off the Regular Forces" (Newcastle, September 15, 1906). "He did not think Compulsory Training 'would be adopted in this country until after England had been invaded 'once or twice" (London, December 1, 1911). The British, however, had the best reasons for feeling secure: they "were always a nation of splendid 'fighters. They were never ready, but they fought the better the less 'ready they were . . ." (Glasgow, January 6, 1912).

CHAPTER VI.

The military situation.

the allied states of Montenegro, Servia, Bulgaria, and Greece, and this was a serious injury to German interests. The Ottoman Empire had been warmly suitored, over a long period of years, by the diplomacy of Berlin, with a view to co-operation in certain contingencies. On the other hand, the result of the second war—fomented by the intrigues of Vienna—in which Bulgaria was finally overpowered by the other three states, destroyed for the time being Slav solidarity, and thereby considerably relieved the apprehensions of Austria with regard to her southern frontier and recently annexed provinces of Bosnia and Herzegovina. . . . Profit-and-loss accounts of this sort are impossible to work out upon an arithmetical basis, and perhaps the chief importance of such occurrences as these lies in the effect which they produce upon the nerves of the onlookers. On the whole—judging by the tone of diplomacy at the time—the Balkan series of events appeared to have raised greater anxieties in the Chancelleries of Germany and Austria than in any other quarter; though why this should have been so, it is difficult to understand.

Looking back at the Balkan struggle in the light of subsequent events, it appears to us now a great deal less remarkable for what it actually produced than for what it failed to produce. It failed to set Europe in a blaze, and yet it afforded far better opportunities for doing this than the Serajevo murders in June 1914.

The full inner history of the negotiations between the Great Powers, for six months prior to the Treaty of Bucharest, will be interesting reading, if it ever sees the light. If even one of them had chosen to work for war during this period, nothing could have

The military situation.

kept the peace. If one or two of them had been apathetic, war must inevitably have come of itself. But even France—who at that time was showing signs of superficial excitement, and on that account was credited, not only in the German press, but in a section of our own, with chauvinistic designs—worked hard for peace. It is certain that Germany desired peace; many well-informed people indeed believed that at this time she desired peace more ardently than any other state. It is true that a few days before the Treaty of Bucharest was signed, Italy had been secretly sounded by Austria as to whether she would join with her two allies in making an attack on Servia; but the Italian reply being of a kind that took away all hope of securing the military assistance of that country in the proposed adventure, the Concert of Europe continued to perform the pacific symphony apparently in perfect accord.

The policy of Germany, in 1912 and 1913, to preserve peace, and her efforts—equally successful—in the following year to provoke war, were probably due to one and the same cause. Two dates from Germany's point of view were of supreme importance—*the summer of 1914*, when her new military preparations would be complete, and when the Kiel Canal—having been widened and deepened[1]—would

[1] On June 23, 1914, the Emperor William opened the new lock at the North Sea end of the Kiel Canal. On the following day he performed the same function at the Baltic end. The *Times* correspondent remarks that the Emperor's passage through the Canal on this occasion was of symbolical rather than practical significance, as on the one hand German Dreadnoughts had already used the widened passage experimentally, while on the other hand it would be a long time before the whole work was finished. He continues: "The extension works, which were begun in 1907, are, however, of vast importance, especially to the Navy. The Canal has been 'made two metres deeper, and has been doubled in breadth. The places 'at which large ships can pass one another have been increased in number, 'and at four of them Dreadnoughts can be turned. There are now four

CHAPTER VI.

The military situation.

be available for the passage of Dreadnoughts; *the summer of 1916*, by which date the French Army increases were due to take effect, and the Russian scheme of military reorganisation would have been carried through. From the point of view of Berlin and Vienna war could be waged to greatest advantage so soon as the first of these two dates had been reached. If, however, Italy, always a doubtful participator, could have been tempted by self-interest to make common cause with her allies in the summer of 1913, the certainty of her adherence would have turned the scales in favour of the earlier date. For Italy could put an army of 700,000 men into the field; and this no doubt would have more than compensated for the benefits which might have been lost by anticipating the ideal moment by a year.

' instead of two, at each end, which means a great saving of time in getting ' a fleet through. Above all, the distance between Kiel and Wilhelmshaven ' for battleship purposes is reduced from more than 500 to only 80 nautical ' miles. The new locks at Brunsbüttel and Holtenau are the largest in the ' world."—The *Times*, June 25, 1914.

CHAPTER VII

A TRAGEDY OF ERRORS

CHAPTER VII.

A tragedy of errors.

It may be said—up to the very outbreak of war it was said very frequently—that the mere power and opportunity to make an outrageous attack are nothing without the will to do so. And this is true enough. Every barber who holds his client by the nose could cut his throat as easily as shave his chin. Every horse could kick the groom, who rubs him down, into the next world if he chose to do so. What sense, then, could there be in allowing our minds to be disturbed by base suspicions of our enterprising and cultured neighbour? What iota of proof was there that Germany nourished evil thoughts, or was brooding on visions of conquest and rapine?

So ran the argument of almost the whole Liberal press; and a considerable portion of the Unionist press echoed it. Warnings were not heeded. They came only from unofficial quarters, and therefore lacked authority. Only the Government could have spoken with authority; and the main concern of members of the Government, when addressing parliamentary or popular audiences, appeared to be to prove that there was no need for anxiety. They went further in many instances, and denounced

CHAPTER VII.

those persons who ventured to express a different opinion from this, as either madmen or malefactors.

A tragedy of errors.

Nevertheless a good deal of proof had already been published to the world—a good deal more was known privately to the British Government—all of which went to show that Germany had both the will and intention to provoke war, if a favourable opportunity for doing so should present itself.

For many years past—in a multitude of books, pamphlets, leading articles, speeches, and university lectures—the Germans had been scolding us, and threatening us with attack at their own chosen moment. When Mr. Churchill stated bluntly, in 1912, that the German fleet was intended as a challenge to the British Empire, he was only repeating, in shorter form and more sober language, the boasts which had been uttered with yearly increasing emphasis and fury, by hundreds of German patriots and professors.

With an engaging candour and in every fount of type, unofficial Germany had made it abundantly clear how she intended to carry her designs into execution—how, first of all, France was to be crushed by a swift and overwhelming attack—how Russia was then to be punished at leisure—how after that, some of the nations of Europe were to be forced into an alliance against the British Empire, and the rest into a neutrality favourable to Germany—how finally the great war, which aimed at making an end of our existence, was to begin. And though, from time to time, there were bland official utterances which disavowed or ignored these outpourings, the outpourings continued all the same. And each year they became more copious, and achieved a readier sale.

CHAPTER VII.

A tragedy of errors.

Those, however, who were responsible for British policy appear to have given more credit to the assurances of German diplomacy than to this mass of popular incitement. The British nation has always chosen to plume itself upon the fact that the hearts of British statesmen are stronger than their heads; and possibly their amiable credulity, in the present instance, might have been forgiven, had their means of ascertaining truth been confined to the statements of incontinent publicists and responsible statesmen. But there were other proofs available besides words of either sort.

The Liberal Government came into office in the autumn of 1905. Ministers can hardly have had time to master the contents of their various portfolios, before German aggression burst rudely in upon them. Conceivably the too carefully calculating diplomatists of Berlin had concluded, that the principles of the new Cabinet would tend to keep England neutral under any provocation, and that a heaven-sent opportunity had therefore arrived for proceeding with the first item in their programme by crushing France. It is a highly significant fact that early in 1906, only a few months after Sir Henry Campbell-Bannerman's advent to power, he found himself faced with the prospect of a European war, which was only averted when our Foreign Minister made it clear to Germany, that in such an event this country would range herself upon the side of France.[1]

[1] The Editor of the *Westminster Gazette* should be an unimpeachable witness: "The (German) Emperor's visit to Tangier (March 1905) was 'followed by a highly perilous passage of diplomacy, in which the German 'Government appeared to be taking risks out of all proportion to any 'interest they could have had in Morocco. The French sacrificed their

CHAPTER VII.

This was the *first* warning.

A tragedy of errors.

The British answer to it was to utter renewed protestations of friendly confidence. As an earnest of our good intentions, the shipbuilding programme [1] of the previous Government was immediately reduced. The burden of armaments became the burden of innumerable speeches. In well-chosen words Germany was coaxed and cajoled to acquiesce in our continued command of the sea; but finding in our action or inaction an opportunity for challenging it, she turned a polite ear—but a deaf one—and pushed forward her preparations with redoubled speed. In vain did we on our part slow down work at our new naval base in the Firth of Forth. In vain did we reduce our slender army to even smaller dimensions.[2] In vain did we plead disinterestedly with Germany, for a reduction in the pace of competition in naval armaments, on the terms that we should be allowed to possess a fleet nearly twice as strong as her own. For the most part, during this period, official Germany remained discreetly silent, for the reason that silence served her purpose best; but when the persistency of our entreaties made some sort of

---

'Foreign Minister (M. Delcassé) in order to keep the peace, but the Germans 'were not appeased, and the pressure continued. It was the general belief 'at this time, that nothing but the support which the British government 'gave to the French averted a catastrophe in the early part of 1906, or 'induced the Germans to accept the Algeciras conference as the way out 'of a dangerous situation."—*The Foundations of British Policy* (p. 15), by J. A. Spender.

[1] The Cawdor Programme.

[2] Mr. Haldane reduced the Army by nine battalions (*i.e.* 9000 men) in 1906. He stated that he had no use for them. This meant a great deal more, when the reserve-making power is taken into consideration. . . . "The Regular Army . . . has been reduced by over 30,000 men; not only 'a present, but a serious prospective loss."—Lord Roberts in the House of Lords, April 3, 1913.

A tragedy of errors.

answer necessary, we were given to understand by unofficial Germany—rather roughly and gruffly—that a certain class of requests was inadmissible as between gentlemen.

Then suddenly, having up to that time lulled ourselves into the belief that our fine words had actually succeeded in buttering parsnips, we awoke—in the late autumn of 1908—to the truth, and fell immediately into a fit of panic. Panic increased during the winter and following spring, and culminated during the summer, in an Imperial Defence Conference with the Dominions.

We had curtailed our shipbuilding programme and slowed down our preparations. Thereby we had hoped to induce Germany to follow suit. But the effect had been precisely the opposite: she had increased her programme and speeded up her preparations. At last our Government became alive to what was going on, and in tones of reverberant anxiety informed an astonished nation that the naval estimates called for large additions.

Ministers, indeed, were between the devil and the deep sea. The supremacy of the British Fleet was menaced; the conscience of the Radical party was shocked—shocked not so much at the existence of the menace as at official recognition of it, and at the cost of insuring against it. It was so much shocked, indeed, that it took refuge in incredulity; and—upon the strength of assurances which were of course abundantly forthcoming from the German Admiralty, who averred upon their honour that there had been neither addition nor acceleration—roundly accused its own anointed ministers of bearing false witness against an innocent neighbour.

CHAPTER VII.

A tragedy of errors.

None the less, large sums were voted, and the Dominions came forward with generous contributions. Sir Wilfrid Laurier, indeed, who had been nourished and brought up on a diet of dried phrases, was sceptical. To this far-sighted statesman there appeared to be no German menace either then or subsequently. The whole thing was a mere nightmare, disturbing the innocent sleep of Liberalism and democracy.[1]

This was the *second* warning.

The *third* warning came in the form of subterranean rumblings, inaudible to the general public, but clearly heard by ministerial ears.

In July 1909, while the Imperial Conference on Defence was in session, Herr von Bethmann-Hollweg succeeded Prince Bülow as German Chancellor. Up to that time there had been the menace of the mailed fist, the rattling sabre, and the shining armour. Henceforward there was the additional menace of a diplomacy playing for time, with a careless and unconcealed contempt for the intelligence, the courage, and the honour of the British people and their statesmen.[2] The German Government had clearly formed the opinion that our ministers were growing more and more afraid of

[1] Even four years later we find Sir Wilfrid Laurier wedded to the belief that the German Emperor was one of the great men of the present age; wonderfully endowed by intellect, character, and moral fibre; his potent influence was always directed towards peace. — Canadian *House of Commons Debates*, February 27, 1913, 4364. The whole of this speech (4357-4364) in opposition to Mr. Borden's Naval Forces Bill is interesting reading, as is also a later speech, April 7, 1913, on the same theme (7398-7411).

[2] *How Britain Strove for Peace*, by Sir Edward Cook: especially pp. 18-35; also *Why Britain is at War*, by the same author. These two pamphlets are understood to be a semi-official statement authorised by the British Government.

A tragedy of errors.

asking their party to support increased naval estimates, and that it was only necessary to go on, alternately dangling and withdrawing illusory proposals for a naval understanding and a general agreement, in order to steal ahead of us in the race. Here, as in many other instances, the Germans had observed not altogether incorrectly; but they had drawn the wrong inference from the facts.

During the summer and autumn of 1910 was held the famous but futile Constitutional Conference, the primary object of which was to settle the quarrel between the two Houses of Parliament. With steadily increasing clumsiness, German diplomacy, through all this anxious time, was engaged in holding out its hand and withdrawing it again; until even men whose minds were worried with more immediate cares, could no longer ignore the gravity of the situation.

The Conference adjourned for the holiday season, but resumed its sessions in October. The public assurances of those who took part in it on both sides agree in this, that nothing except the special subject for which it had been called into existence was ever discussed at its meetings. But many other things were certainly discussed outside its meetings—on the doorstep and the staircase, and in the anterooms. Among these topics the dangers of the international situation, and the peril of imperial security were the chief.

In October and November 1910 there was a great secret of *Polichinelle*. Conceivably we may learn from some future historian even more about it than we knew at the time. All that need be said here with reference to the matter is, that many persons on

CHAPTER VII.

A tragedy of errors.

both sides found themselves faced with a position of affairs, where the security of the country plainly required measures for its defence, of a character and upon a scale, which neither political party could hope to carry through Parliament and commend to the country, unless it were supported by the more responsible section of its opponents.

Neither party, however, was willing to pay the price necessary for the support of the other, and as a consequence imperial interests suffered. It is not necessary, however, to conclude from this lamentable failure that a sordid spirit of faction was the explanation. In the constitutional sphere certain principles were in conflict, which the parties concerned had the honesty to hold by, but lacked the sympathy, and possibly the intelligence, to adjust. The acrimony of an immediate controversy distorted the vision of those engaged in it; so that the proportions of domestic and foreign dangers were misjudged.

The failure of this constitutional conference was welcomed at the time by exultant shoutings among many, perhaps the majority, of the rank and file of politicians upon both sides. It was not so regarded, however, by the country, which in a remarkable degree refused to respond to the incitements of violence and hatred with which it was plied during the ensuing election. There was at this time, for no very definite reason, a widespread popular uneasiness, and something approaching a general disgust with politicians.

Among more considerate men on both sides, the breakdown was frankly spoken of as one of the great calamities in our political history. It was more than that. It was in reality one of the greatest which have ever befallen Europe.

A tragedy of errors.

During the following July (1911), while in this country we were deeply engaged in the bitter climax of the constitutional struggle, there sounded a *fourth* strident warning from the gong of the German Chancellery.

The Agadir incident is one of the strangest which have occurred in British history during recent years. Its full gravity was not realised outside a very narrow circle at the time of its occurrence; and when subsequently it became more widely understood there was a curious conspiracy to hush it up—or, perhaps, not so much a conspiracy, as a general instinct of concealment—a spontaneous gesture of modesty—as if the British nation had been surprised bathing.

At the beginning of July the German cruiser *Panther* appeared at Agadir in Morocco. This visit was intended and understood as a direct challenge to France. Diplomacy was immediately in a stir.

Three weeks later Mr. Lloyd George spoke at the Mansion House, making it clear that England would not tolerate this encroachment. Even amid the anger and excitement which attended the last stages of the Parliament Bill, this statement created a deep impression throughout the country, and a still deeper impression in other countries.

Then the crisis appeared to fade away. Germany was supposed to have become amenable. We returned to our internecine avocations. The holiday season claimed its votaries, and a great railway strike upset many of their best-laid plans. The inhabitants of the United Kingdom are accustomed to think

A tragedy of errors.

only on certain topics during August and September, and it is hard to break them of their habits. To reconsider a crisis which had arisen and passed away some two and a half months earlier, was more than could be expected of us when we returned to work in the autumn.

But Mr. Lloyd George's speech was capable of only one interpretation,—if Germany had persisted in her encroachment, this country would have gone to war in August or September 1911 in support of France. His words had no other meaning, and every highly placed soldier and sailor was fully aware of this fact, and made such preparations in his own sphere as the case required. But from what has transpired subsequently, it does not seem at all clear that more than two or three of the Cabinet in the least realised what was happening. Parliament did not understand the situation any more than the country did.

Later on, when people had time to concentrate their minds on such matters, there was a thrill of post-dated anxiety—a perturbation and disapproval; criticism upon various points; a transference of Mr. McKenna from the Admiralty to the Home Office, and of Mr. Churchill from the Home Office to the Admiralty. Indignant anti-militarists, supporters for the most part of the Government, allowed themselves to be mysteriously reduced to silence. Business men, who had been shocked when they learned the truth, suffered themselves to be persuaded that even the truth must be taken with a pinch of salt. There was, in fact, a sort of general agreement that it was better to leave the summer embers undisturbed, lest a greater conflagra-

A tragedy of errors.

tion might ensue. The attitude of the orthodox politician was that of a nervous person who, hearing, as he imagines, a burglar in his bedroom, feels happier and safer when he shuts his eyes and pulls the blankets over his head.

A few months later, at the beginning of the following year (1912), the *fifth* warning of the series was delivered.

It differed from its predecessors inasmuch as it was addressed to the ears of the British Government alone. Neither the Opposition nor the country heard anything of it until more than two years later—until the battles of Alsace, of Charleroi, and of Mons had been lost—until the battle of the Marne had been won—until the British Army was moving north to take up a position in Flanders. Then we learned that, when Lord Haldane had visited Berlin in the month of February 1912, he had done so at the special request of the Kaiser, in order to consider how Anglo-German misunderstandings might be removed.

Lord Haldane would have acted more wisely had he stopped his journey *en route*, and never entered Berlin at all. For, two days before the date appointed for his visit, proposals for large increases of the German Army and Navy were laid before the Reichstag. His mission was to abate competition in armaments, and here was an encouraging beginning! Was it contempt, or insolence, or a design to overawe the supposed timidity of the emissary; or was it merely a blundering effort to steal a march in the negotiations by facing the ambassador on his arrival with a *fait accompli*? Possibly it was a combination of all these; but at any rate it was exceedingly clumsy, and no less significant than clumsy.

A tragedy of errors.

As to the mission—Germany was willing in a vague way to 'retard'—whatever that may mean—though not to abandon, or reduce, her naval programme, providing the British Government would agree to remain neutral in any war which Germany might choose to wage. France might be crushed and Belgium annexed; but in either event England must stand aside and wait her turn. On no other terms would the Kaiser consent to a *rapprochement* with this country, or allow the blessed words 'retardation of the naval programme' to be uttered by official lips.

An undertaking of this tenor went beyond those assurances of non-aggressive intent which Lord Haldane, on behalf of his own Government, was fully prepared to give. We would not be a party to any unprovoked attack on Germany—was not that sufficient? It was plainly insufficient. It was made clear that Germany desired a free hand to establish herself in a position of supremacy astride of Europe. So Lord Haldane returned profitless from his wayfaring, and the British Government was at its wits' end how to placate the implacable.

The way they chose was well-doing, in which they wearied themselves perhaps overmuch, especially during the Balkan negotiations. For Germany did not want war at that time, for the reasons which have been given already. And so, rather surlily, and with the air of one who was humouring a crank—a pusillanimous people whose fixed idea was pacifism—she consented that we should put ourselves to vast trouble to keep the peace for her benefit. If

A tragedy of errors.

war had to come in the end, it had much better have come then—so far as we were concerned—seeing that the combined balance of naval and military power was less unfavourable to the Triple Entente at the beginning of 1913 than it was some fifteen months later. . . . This was all the notice we took of the fifth warning. We earned no gratitude by our activities, nor added in any way thereby to our own safety.

The Haldane mission is a puzzle from first to last. The Kaiser had asked that he should be sent. . . . For what purpose? . . . Apparently in order to discuss the foreign policy of England and Germany. But surely the Kaiser should have been told that we kept an Ambassador at Berlin for this very purpose; an able man, habituated to stand in the strong sunlight of the imperial presence without losing his head; but, above all, qualified to converse on such matters (seeing that they lay within his own province) far better than the most profound jurist in Christendom. Or if our Ambassador at Berlin could not say what was required, the German Ambassador in London might easily have paid a visit to Downing Street; or the Foreign Ministers of the two countries might have arranged a meeting; or even the British Premier and the German Chancellor might have contrived to come together. Any of these ways would have been more natural, more proper, more likely (one would think) to lead to business, than the way which was followed.

One guesses that the desire of the Kaiser that Lord Haldane should be sent, was met half-way by the desire of Lord Haldane to go forth; that there was some temperamental affinity between these

CHAPTER VII.

two pre-eminent characters—some attraction of opposites, like that of the python and the rabbit.

A tragedy of errors.

Whatever the reasons may have been for this visit, the results of it were bad, and indeed disastrous. To have accepted the invitation was to fall into a German trap; a trap which had been so often set that one might have supposed it was familiar to every Foreign Office in Europe! Berlin has long delighted in these extra-official enterprises, undertaken behind the backs of accredited representatives. Confidences are exchanged; explanations are offered 'in the frankest spirit'; sometimes understandings of a kind are arrived at. But so far as Germany is concerned, nothing of all this is binding, unless her subsequent interests make it desirable that it should be. The names of the irregular emissaries, German, British, and cosmopolitan, whom the Kaiser has sent to London and received at Berlin—unbeknown to his own Foreign Office—since the beginning of his reign, would fill a large and very interesting visitors' book. One would have imagined that even so early as February 1912 this favourite device had been found out and discredited even in Downing Street.

Lord Haldane was perhaps even less well fitted for such an embassy by temperament and habit of mind, than he was by position and experience. Lawyer-statesmanship, of the modern democratic sort, is of all forms of human agency the one least likely to achieve anything at Potsdam. The British emissary was tireless, industrious, and equable. His colleagues, on the other hand, were overworked, indolent, or flustered. Ready on the shortest notice to mind everybody else's business, he was allowed to mind far too much of it; and he appears to have minded most of it rather ill than well. He was no more suited to act for the Foreign Office than King Alfred was to watch the housewife's cakes.

A tragedy of errors.

The man whose heart swells with pride in his own ingenuity usually walks all his life in blinkers. It is not surprising that Lord Haldane's visit to the Kaiser was a failure, that it awoke distrust at the time, or that it opened the way to endless misrepresentation in the future. What surprises is his stoicism; that he should subsequently have shown so few signs of disappointment, distress, or mortification; that he should have continued up to the present moment to hold himself out as an expert on German psychology;[1] that he should be still upheld by his journalistic admirers, to such an extent that they even write pamphlets setting out to his credit 'what he did to thwart Germany.'[2]

We have been told by Mr. Asquith,[3] what was thought by the British Government of the outcome of Lord Haldane's embassy. We have also been informed by Germany, what was thought of it by high officials at Berlin; what inferences they drew from these conversations; what hopes they founded upon them. We do not know, however, what was thought of the incident by the other two members of the Entente; how it impressed the statesmen of Paris and Petrograd; for they must have known of the occurrence—the English representative not being one whose comings and goings would easily

[1] Lord Haldane has explained German conduct in the present war by a sudden change of spirit, such as once befell a collie dog which owned him as master, and which after a blameless early career, was possessed by a fit of depravity in middle life and took to worrying sheep. Thus in a single metaphor he extenuates the German offence and excuses his own blindness!

[2] "Lord Haldane: What he did to thwart Germany." Pamphlet published by the *Daily Chronicle.*

[3] At Cardiff, October 2, 1914.

CHAPTER VII.

A tragedy of errors.

escape notice. The British people were told nothing; they knew nothing; and therefore, naturally enough, they thought nothing about the matter.

The British Cabinet—if Mr. Asquith's memory is to be relied on—saw through the devilish designs of Germany so soon as Lord Haldane, upon his return, unbosomed himself to the conclave in quaking whispers. We know from the Prime Minister, that when he heard how the Kaiser demanded a free hand for European conquests, as the price of a friendly understanding with England, the scales dropped from his eyes, and he realised at once that this merely meant the eating of us up later. But one cannot help wondering, since Mr. Asquith was apparently so clear-sighted about the whole matter, that he made no preparations whatsoever—military, financial, industrial, or even naval (beyond the ordinary routine)—against an explosion which—the mood and intentions of Germany being what they were now recognised to be—might occur at any moment.

As to what Germany thought of the incident we know of course only what the high personages at Berlin have been pleased to tell the world about their 'sincere impressions.' They have been very busy doing this—hand upon heart as their wont is—in America and elsewhere. According to their own account they gathered from Lord Haldane's mission that the British Government and people were very much averse from being drawn into European conflicts; that we now regretted having gone quite so far as we had done in the past, in the way of entanglements and understandings; that while we could not stand by, if any other country was being threatened directly on account of arrangements it had come to with England, England certainly was by no means disposed to seek officiously for opportunities of knight-errantry. In simple words the cases of Tangier and Agadir were coloured by a special obligation, and were to be distinguished clearly from anything in the nature of a general obligation or alliance with France and Russia.

CHAPTER VII.

A tragedy of errors.

It is quite incredible that Lord Haldane ever said anything of this kind; for he would have been four times over a traitor if he had—to France; to Belgium; to his own country; also to Germany whom he would thus have misled. It is also all but incredible that a single high official at Berlin ever understood him to have spoken in this sense. But this is what the high officials have assured their own countrymen and the whole of the neutral world that they did understand; and they have called piteously on mankind to witness, how false the British Government was to an honourable understanding, so soon as trouble arose in July last with regard to Servia. Such are some of the penalties we have paid for the luxury of indulging in amateur diplomacy.

The German bureaucracy, however, always presses things too far. It is not a little like Fag in *The Rivals*—"whenever it draws on its invention for a 'good current lie, it always forges the endorsements 'as well as the bill." As a proof that the relations of the two countries from this time forward were of the best, inferences have been drawn industriously by the high officials at Berlin as to the meaning and extent of Anglo-German co-operation during the Balkan wars; as to agreements with regard to Africa already signed, but not published, in which Downing

CHAPTER VII.

A tragedy of errors.

Street had shown itself 'surprisingly accommodating'; as to other agreements with regard to the Baghdad Railway, the Mesopotamian oil-fields, the navigation of the Tigris, and access through Basra to the Persian Gulf. These agreements, the earnest of a new *entente* between the Teuton nations—the United States subsequently to be welcomed in—are alleged to have been already concluded, signed and awaiting publication when war broke out.[1] Then trouble arises in Servia; a mere police business—nothing more—which might have been settled in a few days or at any rate weeks, if perfidious Albion had not seized the opportunity to work upon Muscovite suspicions, in order to provoke a world-war for which she had been scheming all the time!

The *sixth* warning was the enormous German Army Bill and the accompanying war loan of 1913. By comparison, the five previous warnings were but ambiguous whispers. And yet this last reverberation had apparently no more effect upon the British Government than any of the rest.

With all these numerous premonitions the puzzle is, how any government could have remained in doubt as to the will of Germany to wage war when-

[1] If this were really so, it is remarkable that Germany has not published these opiate documents, which lulled her vigilance and were the cause of her undoing. In the *New York Evening Post* (February 15, 1915) there is a letter signed 'Historicus' in which the German version of the *facts* is not seriously questioned, although a wholly different *inference* is drawn: "This extremely conciliatory attitude of England is another proof of the 'pacific character of her foreign policy. But, unfortunately, German 'political thought regards force as the sole controlling factor in international 'relations, and cannot conceive of concessions voluntarily made in answer 'to claims of a more or less equitable nature. To the German mind such 'actions are infallible indications of weakness and decadence. Apparently 'Grey's attitude towards German claims in Turkey and Africa was so 'interpreted, and the conclusion was rashly reached that England could 'be ignored in the impending world-war."

ever her power seemed adequate and the opportunity favourable for winning it. The favourite plea that the hearts of Mr. Asquith and his colleagues were stronger than their heads does not earn much respect. Knowing what we do of them in domestic politics, this excuse would seem to put the quality of their heads unduly low. The true explanation of their omissions must be sought elsewhere than in their intellects and affections.

A tragedy of errors.

It is important to remember that none of the considerations which have been set out in this chapter can possibly have been hidden from the Foreign Office, the War Office, the Admiralty, the Prime Minister, the Committee of Imperial Defence, or the inner or outer circles of the Cabinet. Important papers upon matters of this kind go the round of the chief ministers. Unless British public offices have lately fallen into a state of more than Turkish indolence, of more than German miscalculation, it is inconceivable that the true features of the situation were not laid before ministers, dinned into ministers, proved and expounded to ministers, by faithful officials, alive to the dangers which were growing steadily but rapidly with each succeeding year. And although we may only surmise the vigilant activity of these subordinates, we do actually know, that Mr. Asquith's Government was warned of them, time and again, by other persons unconcerned in party politics and well qualified to speak.

But supposing that no one had told them, they had their own wits and senses, and these were surely enough. A body of men whose first duty is the

CHAPTER VII.

A tragedy of errors.

preservation of national security—who are trusted to attend to that task, paid for performing it, honoured under the belief that they do attend to it and perform it—cannot plead, in excuse for their failure, that no one had jogged their elbows, roused them from their slumbers or their diversions, and reminded them of their duty.

Mr. Asquith and his chief colleagues must have realised the interdependence of policy and armaments; and they must have known, from the year 1906 onwards, that on the military side our armaments were utterly inadequate to maintain our policy. They must have known that each year, force of circumstances was tending more and more to consolidate the Triple Entente into an alliance, as the only means of maintaining the balance of power, which was a condition both of the freedom of Europe and of British security. They knew—there can be no doubt on this point—what an immense numerical superiority of armed forces Germany and Austria together could bring, first against France at the *onset* of war, and subsequently, at their leisure, against Russia during the *grip* of war. They knew that a British Expeditionary Army of 160,000 men would not make good the difference—would come nowhere near making good the difference. They must have known that from the point of view of France and Belgium, the special danger of modern warfare was the crushing rapidity of its opening phase. They must have been kept fully informed of all the changes which were taking place in the military situation upon the continent to the detriment of the Triple Entente. They had watched the Balkan war and measured its effects. They knew

A tragedy of errors.

the meanings of the critical dates—1914–1916—better, we may be sure, than any section of their fellow-countrymen. And even although they might choose to disregard, as mere jingoism, all the boasts and denunciations of German journalists and professors, they must surely have remembered the events which preceded the conference at Algeciras, and those others which led up to the Defence Conference of 1909. They can hardly have forgotten the anxieties which had burdened their hearts during the autumn of 1910. Agadir cannot have been forgotten; the memory of Lord Haldane's rebuff was still green; and the spectre of the latest German Army Bill must have haunted them in their dreams.

There is here no question of being wise after the event. The meaning of each of these things in turn was brought home to the Prime Minister and his chief colleagues as it occurred—firstly, we may be sure, by their own intelligence—secondly, we may be equally sure, by the reports of their responsible subordinates—thirdly, by persons of knowledge and experience, who had no axe to grind or interest to serve.

It is therefore absurd to suppose that ministers could have failed to realise the extent of the danger, or of our unpreparedness to meet it, unless they had purposely buried their heads in the sand. They knew that they had not a big enough army, and that this fact might ruin their whole policy. Why did they never say so? Why, when Lord Roberts said so, did they treat him with contumely, and make every effort to discredit him? Why was nothing done by them during their whole period of office to increase the Army and thereby diminish the

CHAPTER VII.

A tragedy of errors.

numerical superiority of their adversaries. On the contrary, they actually reduced the Army, assuring the country that they had no use for so many trained soldiers. Moreover, the timidity or secretiveness of the Government prevented England from having, what is worth several army corps, and what proved the salvation of France—a National Policy, fully agreed and appealing to the hearts and consciences of the whole people.

The answers to these questions must be sought in another sphere. The political situation was one of great perplexity at home as well as abroad, and its inherent difficulties were immeasurably increased by the character and temperament of Mr. Asquith, by the nature no less of his talents than of his defects. The policy of wait-and-see is not necessarily despicable. There are periods in which it has been the surest wisdom and the truest courage; but this was not one of those periods, nor was there safety in dealing either with Ireland or with Germany upon this principle. When a country is fully prepared it can afford to wait and see if there will be a war; but not otherwise.

Sir Edward Grey is a statesman whose integrity and disinterestedness have never been impugned by friend or foe; but from the very beginning of his tenure of office he has appeared to lack that supreme quality of belief in himself which stamps the greatest foreign ministers. He has seemed at times to hesitate, as if in doubt whether the dangers which he foresaw with his mind's eye were realities, or only nightmares produced by his own over-anxiety. We have a feeling also that in the conduct of his office he had

A tragedy of errors.

played too lonely a part, and that such advice and sympathy as he had received were for the most part of the wrong sort. What he needed in the way of counsel and companionship was simplicity and resolution. What he had to rely on was the very reverse of this.

Lord Haldane, as we have learned recently, shared largely in the work of the Foreign Office; a man of prodigious industry, but over-ingenious, and of a self-complacency which too readily beguiled him into the belief that there was no opponent who could not be satisfied, no obstacle which could not be made to vanish—by argument.

Moreover, Sir Edward Grey had to contend against enemies within his own household. In the Liberal party there was a tradition, which has never been entirely shaken off, that all increase of armaments is provocative, and that all foreign engagements are contrary to the public interest. After the Agadir crisis he was made the object of a special attack by a large and influential section of his own party and press, and was roundly declared to be no longer possible as Foreign Minister.[1] There can be no doubt that the attempt to force Sir Edward Grey's resignation in the winter 1911–1912 was fomented by German misrepresentation and intrigue, skilfully acting upon the peculiar susceptibilities of radical fanaticism. Nor is there any doubt that the attacks which were made upon the policy of Mr. Churchill, from the autumn of 1912 onwards, were fostered by

[1] "The time has now come to state with a clearness which cannot be 'mistaken that Sir Edward Grey as Foreign Secretary is impossible."—*Daily News*, January 10, 1912. The *Daily News* was not a lonely voice speaking in the wilderness. Similar threats have been levelled against Mr. Churchill.

CHAPTER VII.

the same agency, using the same tools, and aiming at the same objects.

A tragedy of errors.

The orthodoxy of Mr. Churchill was suspect on account of his Tory ancestry and recent conversion; that of Sir Edward Grey on the ground that he was a country gentleman, bred in aristocratic traditions, trained in Foreign Affairs under the dangerous influences of Lord Rosebery, and therefore incapable of understanding the democratic dogma that loving-kindness will conquer everything, including Prussian ambitions.

Surely no very vivid imagination is needed to penetrate the mystery of Cabinet discussions on defence for several years before war broke out. Behind the Cabinet, as the Cabinet well knew, was a party, one half of which was honestly oblivious of all danger, while the other half feared the danger much less than it hated the only remedy. Clearly the bulk of the Cabinet was in cordial sympathy either with one or other of these two sections of their party. Sir Edward Grey accordingly had to defend his policy against an immense preponderance of settled convictions, political prejudices, and personal interests. And at the same time he seems to have been haunted by the doubt lest, after all, his fears were only nightmares. Mr. Churchill, there is no difficulty in seeing, must have fought very gallantly; but always, for the reason already given, with one hand tied behind his back. He had all his work cut out to maintain the Navy, which was under his charge, in a state of efficiency; and this upon the whole he succeeded in doing pretty efficiently.[1]

[1] It has been stated on good authority, that Mr. McKenna upheld the national interests with equal firmness, and against equal, if not greater opposition, while he was at the Admiralty.

A tragedy of errors.

If we may argue back from public utterances to Cabinet discussions, it would appear that the only assistance—if indeed it deserved such a name—which was forthcoming to these two, proceeded from Mr. Asquith and Lord Haldane. The former was by temperament opposed to clear decisions and vigorous action. The latter—to whom the mind of Germany was as an open book—bemused himself, and seems to have succeeded in bemusing his colleagues to almost as great an extent.

In fancy, we can conjure up a scene which must have been enacted, and re-enacted, very often at Number 10 Downing Street in recent years. We can hear the warnings of the Foreign Minister, the urgent pleas of the First Lord of the Admiralty, the scepticism, indifference, or hostility expressed by the preponderant, though leaderless, majority in the Cabinet. *Simple* said, *I see no danger*; *Sloth* said, *Yet a little more sleep*; and *Presumption* said, *Every Vat must stand upon his own bottom*. . . . We can almost distinguish the tones of their Right Honourable voices.

The situation was governed by an excessive timidity—by fear of colleagues, of the caucus, of the party, and of public opinion—by fear also of Germany. Mr. Asquith, and the Cabinet of which he was the head, refused to look their policy between the eyes, and realise what it was, and what were its inevitable consequences. They would not admit that the *Balance of Power* was an English interest, or that they were in any way concerned in maintaining it. They would not admit that our Entente with France and Russia was in fact an alliance. They thought they could send British officers to arrange plans of

CHAPTER VII.

A tragedy of errors.

campaign with the French General Staff—could learn from this source all the secret hopes and anxieties of France—could also withdraw the greater part of their fleet from the Mediterranean, under arrangement for naval co-operation with our present ally [1]—all without committing this country to any form of understanding! They boasted that they had no engagements with France, which puzzled the French and the Russians, and convinced nobody; save possibly themselves, and a section of their own followers. They had in fact bound the country to a course of action—in certain events which were not at all improbable—just as surely by drifting into a committal, as if they had signed and sealed a parchment. Yet they would not face the imperative condition. They would not place their armaments on a footing to correspond with their policy.

Much of this is now admitted more or less frankly, but justification is pleaded, in that it was essential to lead the country cautiously, and that the Government could do nothing unless it had the people behind it. In these sayings there is a measure of truth. But as a matter of fact the country was not led at all. It was trapped. Never was there the slightest effort made by any member of the Government to educate the people with regard to the national dangers,

[1] A large section of the Liberal party watched with jealous anxiety our growing intimacy with France. In 1913, however, they discovered in it certain consolations in the withdrawal of our ships of war from the Mediterranean; and they founded upon this a demand for the curtailing of our own naval estimates. France according to this arrangement was to look after British interests in the Mediterranean, Britain presumably was to defend French interests in the Bay of Biscay and the Channel. When, however, the war-cloud was banking up in July 1914, these very people who had been most pleased with our withdrawal from the Mediterranean, were those who urged most strongly that we should now repudiate our liabilities under the arrangement.

A tragedy of errors.

responsibilities, and duties. When the crisis occurred the hand of the whole British Empire was forced. There was no other way; but it was a bad way. And what was infinitely worse, was the fact that, when war was declared—that war which had been discussed at so many Cabinet meetings since 1906—military preparations were found to be utterly inadequate in numbers; and in many things other than numbers. The politician is right in thinking that, as a rule, it is to his advantage if the people are behind him; but there are times when we can imagine him praying that they may not be too close.

We have been given to understand that it was impossible for the Government to acknowledge their policy frankly, to face the consequences, and to insist upon the necessary preparations in men and material being granted. It was impossible, because to have done so would have broken the Liberal party—that great instrument for good—in twain. The Cabinet would have fallen in ruin. The careers of its most distinguished members would have been cut short. Consider what sacrifices would have been contained in this catalogue of disasters.

That is really what we are now beginning to consider, and are likely to consider more and more as time goes on.

A great act of self-sacrifice—a man's, or a party's—may sometimes make heedless people realise the presence of danger when nothing else will. Suppose Mr. Asquith had said, "I will only continue to hold 'office on one condition," and had named the condition—'that armaments should correspond to policy' —the only means of safety. He might thereupon have disappeared into the chasm; but like Curtius he

CHAPTER VII.

A tragedy of errors.

might have saved the City. It would have made a great impression, Mr. Asquith falling from office for his principles. Those passages of Periclean grandeur, spoken after war broke out, about the crime of Germany against humanity—about sacrificing our own ease—about duty, honour, freedom, and the like—were wonderfully moving. Would there, however, have been occasion for them, if in the orator's own case, the sacrifice had been made before the event instead of after it, or if he had faithfully performed the simplest and chief of all the duties attaching to his great position ?

The present war, as many of us thought, and still think, was not inevitable. None have maintained this opinion in the past with greater vehemence than the Liberal party. But the conditions on which it could have been avoided were, that England should have been prepared, which she was not ; and that she should have spoken her intentions clearly, which she did not.

When the war is ended, or when the tide of it has turned and begun to sweep eastward, there will be much coming and going of the older people, and of women, both young and old, between England and France. They have waited, and what is it that they will then be setting forth to see ? . . . From Mons to the Marne, and back again to Ypres, heaps of earth, big and little, shapeless, nameless, numberless—the graves of men who did not hesitate to sacrifice either their careers or their lives when duty called them. Desolation is the heaviest sacrifice of all ; and those who will, by and by, go on this pilgrimage have suffered it, ungrudgingly and with pride, because their country needed it. If this war was

CHAPTER VII.

A tragedy of errors.

indeed inevitable there is no more to be said. But what if it was not inevitable? What if there would have been no war at all—or a less lingering and murderous war—supposing that those, who from the trust reposed in them by their fellow-countrymen should have been the first to sacrifice their careers to duty, had not chosen instead to sacrifice duty to their careers? It was no doubt a service to humanity to save the careers of politicians from extinction, to keep ministers in office from year to year, to preserve the Liberal party—that great instrument for good—unfractured. These benefits were worth a great price; but were they worth quite so great a price as has been paid?

PART IV

DEMOCRACY AND NATIONAL SERVICE

Now I saw still in my Dream, that they went on until they were come to the place that *Simple* and *Sloth* and *Presumption* lay and slept in, when *Christian* went by on Pilgrimage. And behold they were hanged up in irons, a little way off on the other side.

Then said *Mercy* to him that was their Guide and Conductor, What are those three men ? and for what are they hanged there ?

GREAT-HEART : These three men were men of very bad qualities, they had no mind to be Pilgrims themselves, and whosoever they could they hindered. They were for sloth and folly themselves, and whoever they could persuade with, they made so too, and withal taught them to presume that they should do well at last. They were asleep when *Christian* went by, and now you go by they are hanged.

MERCY : But could they persuade any to be of their opinion ?

GREAT-HEART : Yes, they turned several out of the way. There was *Slow-pace*, that they persuaded to do as they. They also prevailed with one *Short-wind*, with one *No-heart*, with one *Linger-after-Lust*, and with one *Sleepy-head*, and with a young woman her name was *Dull*, to turn out of the way and become as they. Besides they brought up an ill report of your Lord, persuading others that he was a Task-master. They also brought up an evil report of the good Land saying 'twas not half so good as some pretend it was. They also began to vilify his Servants, and to count the very best of them meddlesome troublesome busy-bodies.

The Pilgrim's Progress.

CHAPTER I

THE BRITISH ARMY AND THE PEACE OF EUROPE

CHAPTER I.

The British Army and the peace of Europe.

MANY people who were not in the habit of concerning themselves with party politics endeavoured, during the autumn of 1911, and from that time forward, to straighten out their ideas on the twin problems of Foreign Policy and Defence. They were moved thereto mainly by the Agadir incident. Moreover, a year later, the Balkan war provided an object lesson in the success of sudden onset against an unprepared enemy. Gradually also, more and more attention was focussed upon the large annual increases in preparation of the warlike sort, which successive budgets, presented to the Reichstag, had been unable to hide away. In addition to these, came, early in 1913, the sensational expansion of the German military establishment and the French reply to it, which have already been considered.

Private enquirers of course knew nothing of Lord Haldane's rebuff at Berlin in 1912, for that was a Government secret. Nor had they any means of understanding more than a portion of what was actually afoot on the Continent of Europe in the matter of armaments and military preparations. Their sole sources of information were official papers and public discussions. Many additional facts beyond

CHAPTER I.

The British Army and the peace of Europe.

these are brought to the notice of governments through their secret intelligence departments. All continental powers are more or less uncandid, both as regards the direction and the amount of their expenditure on armaments. In the case of Germany concealment is practised on a greater scale and more methodically than with any other. Ministers obviously knew a great deal more than the British public; but what was known to the man-in-the-street was sufficiently disquieting, when he set himself to puzzle out its meanings.

At this time (during 1912, and in the first half of 1913, until anxiety with regard to Ireland began to absorb public attention) there was a very widely-spread and rapidly-growing concern as to the security of the country. For nearly seven years Lord Roberts, with quiet constancy, had been addressing thin and, for the most part, inanimate gatherings on the subject of National Service. Suddenly he found himself being listened to with attention and respect by crowded audiences.

Lord Roberts had ceased to be Commander-in-Chief in 1904. After his retirement, and in the same year, he revisited the South African battle-fields. During this trip, very reluctantly—for he was no lover of change—he came to the conclusion that in existing circumstances 'national service' was a necessity. On his return to England he endeavoured to persuade Mr. Balfour's Government to accept his views and give effect to them. Failing in this, he resigned his seat upon the Committee of Imperial Defence in 1905, in order that he might be able to advocate his opinion freely. He was then in his seventy-fourth year. It was not, however, until seven years later[1] that his words can be said to have arrested general attention.

The British Army and the peace of Europe.

The truth was that the nation was beginning to be dissatisfied with what it had been told by party speakers and newspapers, on the one side and the other, regarding the state of the national defences. It had not even the consolation of feeling that what the one said might be set against the other, and truth arrived at by striking a balance between them. This method of the party system, which was supposed to have served fairly well in other matters, failed to reassure the nation with regard to its military preparations. The whole of this subject was highly complicated, lent itself readily to political mystery, and produced in existing circumstances the same apprehensions among ordinary men as those of a nervous pedestrian, lost in a fog by the wharf side, who finds himself beset by officious and quarrelsome touts, each claiming permission to set him on his way.

The nation was disquieted because it knew that it had not been told the whole truth by either set of politicians. It suspected the reason of this to be that neither set had ever taken pains to understand where the truth lay. It had a notion, moreover, that the few who really knew, were afraid—for party reasons—to speak out, to state their conclusions, and to propose the proper remedies, lest such a course might drive them from office, or prevent them from ever holding it. Beyond any doubt it was true that at this time many people were seriously disturbed by the unsatisfactory character of recent Parliamentary discussions, and earnestly desired to know

[1] October 1912.

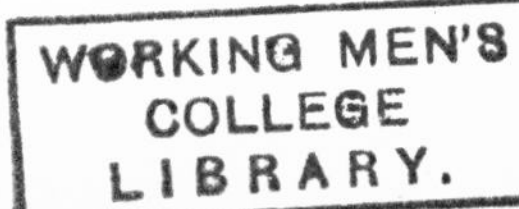

the real nature of the dangers to be apprehended, and the adequacy of our preparations for meeting them.

The British Army and the peace of Europe.

There had always been a difficulty in keeping the Army question from being used as a weapon in party warfare. As to this—looking back over a long period of years—there was not much to choose between the Radicals, Liberals, or Whigs upon the one hand, and the Unionists, Conservatives, or Tories on the other. Military affairs are complicated and technical; and the very fact that the line of country is so puzzling to the ordinary man had preserved it as the happy hunting-ground of the politician. When an opportunity presented itself of attacking the Government on its army policy, the opposition—whether in the reign of Queen Victoria or in that of Queen Anne—rarely flinched out of any regard for the national interest. And when Parliamentary considerations and ingrained prejudices made it seem a risky matter to undertake reforms which were important, or even essential, the Government of the day just as rarely showed any disposition to discharge this unpopular duty.

While at times naval policy, and even foreign policy, had for years together been removed out of the region of purely party criticism, army policy had ever remained embarrassed by an evil tradition. From the time of John Churchill, Duke of Marlborough, to the time of Field-Marshal Sir John French—from a date, that is, only a few years after our modern Parliamentary system was inaugurated by the 'Glorious Revolution,' down to the present day—the characteristic of almost every opposition with regard to this matter, had been factiousness, and that of

The British Army and the peace of Europe.

almost every Government evasion. Neither the one side nor the other had ever seemed able to approach this ill-fated topic with courage or sincerity, or to view it with steady constancy from the standpoint of the national interest.

For several years past the country had been watching a conspicuous example of this ingrained habit of manœuvring round the Army in order to obtain party advantage. From 1912 onwards, until more interesting perplexities provided a distraction, a great part of the Liberal press and party had been actively engaged in the attempt to fix the Unionist party with responsibility for the proposals of the National Service League. The Opposition, it is hardly necessary to record, were innocent of this charge—criminally innocent; but it was nevertheless regarded as good party business to load them with the odium of 'conscription.' The 'blood-taxes,' as it was pointed out by one particularly zealous journal, would be no less useful than the 'food-taxes' as an 'election cry,' which at this time—more than ever before—appeared to have become the be-all and end-all of party activities.

It was obvious to the meanest capacity that these industrious politicians were not nearly so much concerned with the demerits, real or supposed, of National Service, as with making their opponents as unpopular as possible. In such an atmosphere of prejudice it would have required great courage and determination in a statesman to seek out and proclaim the true way to security, were it national service or anything else which entailed a sacrifice.

Was it wonderful that when people examined the signs of the times in the early part of 1913,

CHAPTER I.

The British Army and the peace of Europe.

they should have found themselves oppressed by feelings of doubt and insecurity? A huge German military increase; a desperate French effort in reply; war loans (for they were nothing else) on a vast scale in both countries—what was the meaning of it all? To what extent was British safety jeopardised thereby?

To these questions there was no answer which carried authority; the official oracles were dumb. We are a democratic country, and yet none of our rulers had ever yet spoken plainly to us. None of the Secretaries for War, none of the Prime Ministers since the beginning of the century, had ever stated the issue with uncompromising simplicity, as the case required. None of them had ever taken the country into his confidence, either as to the extent of the danger or as to the nature of the remedy. It is necessary to assume—in the light of subsequent events—that these statesmen had in fact realised the danger, and were not ignorant of the preparations which were required to forestall it. Certainly it is hard to believe otherwise; but at times, remembering their speeches and their acts, one is inclined to give them the benefit, if it be a benefit, of the doubt.

The question at issue was in reality a graver matter than the security of the United Kingdom or the British Empire. The outlook was wider even than this. The best guarantee for the preservation of the peace of Europe, and of the World, would have been a British army proportionate to our population and resources. There could be no doubt of this. For half a century or more we had, half unconsciously, bluffed Europe into the belief that we did in fact possess such an army; but gradually it had become

The British Army and the peace of Europe.

plain that this was not the case. Since the Agadir incident the real situation was apparent even to the man in the street—in Paris, Berlin, Brussels, the Hague, Vienna, Rome, and Petrograd—in every capital, indeed, save perhaps in London alone.

If England had possessed such an army as would have enabled her to intervene with effect in European affairs, she would almost certainly never have been called upon to intervene.[1] Peace in that case would have preserved itself. For Europe knew—not from our professions, but from the obvious facts, which are a much better assurance—that our army would never be used except for one purpose only, *to maintain the balance of Power*. She knew this to be our only serious concern; and, except for the single nation which, at any given time, might be aiming at predominance, it was also the most serious concern of the whole of Europe. She knew us to be disinterested, in the diplomatic sense, with regard to all other European matters. She knew that there was nothing in Europe which we wished to acquire, and nothing—save in the extreme south-west, a rock called Gibraltar, and in the Mediterranean an island called Malta—which we held and were determined to maintain. In the chancelleries of Europe all this was clearly recognised. And more and more it was

[1] This view was held by no one more strongly than by Lord Roberts. During the last five-and-twenty years the writer has probably seen as much of soldiers as falls to the lot of most civilians, but nowhere, during that period, from the late senior Field-Marshal downwards, has he ever encountered that figment of the pacifist imagination of which we read so much during 1912–1914—"a military clique which desires to create a 'conscript army on the European model for purposes of aggression on the 'continent of Europe." The one thought of all soldiers was adequate defence. Their one concern was *how to prevent war*. . . . M. Clemenceau once urged that Lord Roberts should receive the Nobel Peace Prize for his advocacy of 'conscription' in England. This proposal was made quite seriously.

CHAPTER I.

coming to be recognised also by the organs of public opinion on the Continent.

The British Army and the peace of Europe.

The population of France is roughly forty millions; that of Germany, sixty-five millions; that of the United Kingdom, forty-five millions. As regards numbers of men trained to bear arms, France by 1911 had already come to the end of her resources; Germany had still considerable means of expansion; Britain alone had not yet seriously attempted to put forth her strength. Had we done so in time the effect must have been final and decisive; there would then have been full security against disturbance of the peace of Europe by a deliberately calculated war.

Europe's greatest need therefore was that Britain should possess an army formidable not only in valour, but also in numbers: her greatest peril lay in the fact that, as to the second of these requirements, Britain was deficient. No power from the Atlantic seaboard to the Ural Mountains, save that one alone which contemplated the conquest and spoliation of its neighbours, would have been disquieted—or indeed anything else but reassured—had the British people decided to create such an army. For by reason of England's peculiar interests—or rather perhaps from her lack of all direct personal interests in European affairs, other than in peace and the balance of power—she was marked out as the natural mediator in Continental disputes. In these high perplexities, however, it is not the justice of the mediator which restrains aggression, so much as the fear inspired by his fleets and the strength of his battalions.

CHAPTER II

THE COMPOSITION OF THE BRITISH ARMY

CHAPTER II.

The composition of the British Army.

THE doubt and anxiety of public opinion in 1912 were not allayed when the strength and composition of the British Army came to be considered.

Leaving out of account those troops which were recruited and maintained in India, the Dominions, and the Dependencies, the actual number of British regulars employed in garrison duty abroad was in round figures 125,000 men. The number in the United Kingdom was approximately the same; but by no means the whole of these were fit to take the field. The total strength of the *Regular Army* in 1912–1913 might therefore be taken at somewhere between 250,000 and 254,000 men,[1] of whom half were permanently out of this country, while from 25,000 to 50,000 could not be reckoned on as available in case of war, for the reason that they were either recent recruits or 'immatures.'[2]

[1] These rough totals were approximately the same in the autumn of 1912, and at the outbreak of war in July 1914.

[2] The exact number of men who could remain in the units when mobilised was difficult to assess, for the reason that it varied considerably according to the trooping season, which begins in August and ends in February. February was therefore the most unfavourable month for comparison, and it is probably not far from the truth to say that at that date 50,000 men out of our nominal home army were unavailable in case of war. Under the extreme stress of circumstances, it had recently been decided that boys of nineteen might serve in Europe in the event of war, so that a good many

CHAPTER II.

The composition of the British Army.

The reserves and additional troops which would be called out in the event of a serious war were so different in character that it was impossible simply to throw them into a single total, and draw conclusions therefrom according to the rules of arithmetic. For when people spoke of the *Army Reserve*, the *Special Reserve*, and the *Territorial Army*, they were talking of three things, the values of which were not at all comparable. The first were fully trained fighting soldiers; the second were lads with a mere smattering of their trade; while the third were little more than an organised schedule of human material—mainly excellent—which would become available for training only at the outbreak of war, and whose liability for service was limited to home defence. The sum-total of these reserves and additional troops was roughly 450,000 men; but this row of figures was entirely meaningless, or else misleading, until the significance of its various factors was grasped.[1]

The first of these categories, the *Army Reserve*, was the only one which could justly claim to rank as a true reserve—that is, as a fighting force, from the outbreak of war equal in calibre to the Continental

---

'immatures' were now nominally 'mature.' Only nominally, however, for even a war minister could not alter the course of nature by a stroke of the pen.

[1] Without wearying the reader too much with figures the German strength may be briefly indicated. That country has a population roughly half as large again as our own (65 millions against 45). The total of fully trained men whom the German Government could mobilise at the declaration of war was something over 4,500,000. Of these some 2,400,000 composed the 'striking force'; the remaining 2,100,000 or thereabouts, the reserve for making good wastage of war. But in addition, Germany had scheduled and inscribed in her *Ersatz*, or recruiting reserve, and in the *Landsturm*, fully 5,000,000 untrained and partially trained men, *with ample equipment and military instructors for them all.* A large proportion of these would be enrolled on mobilisation, and would undertake garrison and other duties, for which they would be fitted after a short period of service, thus freeing all fully trained men for service in the field.

troops against which it would be called upon to take the field.

The composition of the British Army.

The *Army Reserve* consisted of men who had served their full time in the *Regular Army*. They were therefore thoroughly trained and disciplined, needing only a few days—or at most weeks—to rub the rust off them.[1] Nominally their numbers were 137,000 [2] men; but as over 8000 of these were living out of the United Kingdom the net remainder had to be taken at something under 130,000. Moreover, as the *Army Reserve* depended automatically upon the strength of the *Regular Army*, and as the strength of this had recently been reduced, it seemed necessarily to follow that ultimately there would be a considerable diminution.

The second category to which the name of a reserve was given was the *Special Reserve*. This, however, was no true reserve like the first, for it was wholly unfit to take the field upon the outbreak of hostilities. It was the modern substitute for the Militia, and was under obligation to serve abroad in time of war. The term of enlistment was six years, and the training nominally consisted of six months in the first year, and one month in camp in each of the succeeding years. But in practice these conditions had been greatly relaxed. It was believed that, upon the average, the term of training amounted to even less than the proposals of the National Service

[1] For purposes of immediate mobilisation, however, Continental reservists are superior to our own, because in the British Army they lose touch with their regiments, and in case of war will in many cases be serving with officers and comrades whom they know nothing about; whereas in Germany (for example) they come up for periods of training with the regiments to which they belong. Also, at the outset, the proportion of reservists to serving soldiers will be much greater in our case.

[2] This was in 1912. Their numbers appear to have increased somewhat. In July 1914 they were something over 146,000.

CHAPTER II.

The composition of the British Army.

League,[1] which had been criticised from the official standpoint—severely and not altogether unjustly—on the ground that they would not provide soldiers fit to be drafted immediately into the fighting line.

Notwithstanding the inadequacy of its military education, this *Special Reserve* was relied upon in some measure for making up the numbers of our Expeditionary Force [2] at the commencement of war, and individuals from it, and even in some cases units, would therefore have been sent out to meet the conscript armies of the Continent, to which they were inferior, not only in length and thoroughness of training, but also in age. It was important also to bear in mind that they would be led by comparatively inexperienced and untrained officers. The strength of the *Special Reserve* was approximately 58,000 [3] men, or lads. Under the most favourable view it was a corps of apprentices whose previous service had been of a very meagre and desultory character.

The third category was the *Territorial Army*, whose term of service was four years and whose military training, even nominally, only consisted of fifteen days in camp each year, twenty drills the first year, and ten drills each year after that. In reality this training had, on the average, consisted of very much less. This force was not liable for service abroad, but only for home defence.

The minimum strength of the *Territorial Army*

[1] Viz. four months for infantry and six for cavalry.

[2] Twenty-seven battalions of the *Special Reserve* were scheduled to go out as complete units for duty on lines of communication, etc. The report on recruiting for 1912 says that the great majority of recruits for the Special Reserve join between the ages of seventeen and nineteen. It is hardly necessary to point out the folly of putting boys of this age in a situation where they will be peculiarly liable to disease. Continental nations employ their oldest classes of reserves for these duties.

[3] In July 1914 about 61,000.

was estimated beforehand by Lord Haldane at 316,000 men; but these numbers had never been reached. The approximate strength was only 260,000 men, of whom only about half had qualified, both by doing fifteen days in camp, and by passing an elementary test in musketry.[1] These numbers had recently shown a tendency to shrink rather than swell.[2]

CHAPTER II.

The composition of the British Army.

The value of the *Territorial Army*, therefore, was that of excellent, though in certain cases immature, material, available for training upon the outbreak of war. But in spite of its high and patriotic spirit it was wholly unfit to take the field against trained troops until it had undergone the necessary training.

In the event of war we could not safely reckon upon being able to withdraw our garrisons from abroad.[3] Consequently, in the first instance, and until the *Special Reserve* and the *Territorial Army* had been made efficient, all we could reasonably depend upon for serious military operations, either at home or abroad, were that part of the *Regular Army* which was in the United Kingdom, and the *Army Reserve*.

In round figures therefore our soldiers immediately available for a European war (*i.e.* that portion of the *Regular Army* which was stationed at home and the *Army Reserve*) amounted on mobilisation to something much under 250,000 men. Our apprentice troops (the *Special Reserve*), who were really considerably less than *half*-made, numbered something

[1] *I.e.* in the autumn of 1912. They were, therefore, 56,000 short of Lord Haldane's estimate.

[2] Latterly there was a slight improvement in recruiting. In July 1914 the numbers (including permanent staff) were a little over 268,000—48,000 short of Lord Haldane's estimate.

[3] The fact that in certain cases we did so withdraw our garrisons in 1914–1915 without disaster does not invalidate this calculation.

CHAPTER II.

The composition of the British Army.

under 60,000 men. Our *un*made raw material (the *Territorial Army*), excellent in quality and immediately available for training, might be taken at 260,000 men.

The main consideration arising out of this analysis was of course the inadequacy of the British Army to make good the numerical deficiency of the Triple Entente in the Western theatre during the *onset* and the *grip* of war. Supposing England to be involved in a European war, which ran its course and was brought to a conclusion with the same swiftness which had characterised every other European war within the last half century, how were our *half*-made and our *un*made troops to be rendered efficient in time to effect the result in any way whatsoever?

There was yet another consideration of great gravity. If our full Expeditionary Force were sent abroad we should have to strain our resources to the utmost to bring it up to its full nominal strength and keep it there. The wastage of war would necessarily be very severe in the case of so small a force; especially heavy in the matter of officers. Consequently, from the moment when this force set sail, there would be a dearth of officers in the United Kingdom competent to train the *Special Reserve*, the *Territorial Army*, and the raw recruits. Every regular and reserve officer in the country would be required in order to mobilise the Expeditionary Force, and keep it up to its full strength during the first six months. As things then stood there was a certainty—in case of war—of a very serious shortage of officers of suitable experience and age to undertake the duties, which were required under our recently devised military system.[1]

CHAPTER II.

The composition of the British Army.

Half-made soldiers and raw material alike would therefore be left to the instruction of amateur or hastily improvised officers—zealous and intelligent men without a doubt; but unqualified, owing to their own lack of experience, for training raw troops, so as to place them rapidly on an equality with the armies to which they would find themselves opposed. What the British system contemplated, was as if you were to send away the headmaster, and the assistant-masters, and the under-masters, leaving the school in charge of pupil-teachers.

In no profession is the direct personal influence of teaching and command more essential than in the soldier's. In none are good teachers and leaders more able to shorten and make smooth the road to confidence and efficiency. Seeing that we had chosen to depend so largely upon training our army after war began, it might have been supposed, that at least we should have taken care to provide ourselves with a sufficient number of officers and non-commissioned officers, under whose guidance the course of education would be made as thorough and as short as possible. This was not the case. Indeed the reverse was the case. Instead of possessing a large number of officers and non-commissioned officers, beyond those actually required at the outbreak of war for the purpose of

[1] The experience of the past few months makes this criticism appear absurd—in its *under*statement. But of course what was contemplated in 1912–13 was not anything upon the gigantic scale of our present 'New Army'; but only (*a*) the *Special Reserve*, (*b*) the *Territorial Army*, possibly doubled in numbers during the first six months, and (*c*) fresh recruits for the *Regular Army* upon a very considerably enhanced scale. But even for these purposes which were foreseen, the provision of officers was quite inadequate; so inadequate indeed as to appear from the soldier's point of view in the light of a parliamentary farce.

CHAPTER II.

The composition of the British Army.

starting with, and repairing the wastage in the Expeditionary Force, we were actually faced, as things then stood, with a serious initial shortage of the officers required for this one purpose alone.

Lord Haldane in framing the army system which is associated with his name chose to place his trust in a small, highly-trained expeditionary force for immediate purposes, to be supplemented at a later date—if war were obliging enough to continue for so long—by a new army of which the *Territorials* formed the nucleus, and which would not begin its real training until after the outbreak of hostilities. Under the most favourable view this plan was a great gamble; for it assumed that in the war which was contemplated, the *onset* and the *grip* periods would be passed through without crushing disaster, and that England would, in due course, have an opportunity of making her great strength felt in the *drag*. It will be said that Lord Haldane's assumption has been justified by recent events, and in a sense this is true; but by what merest hair-breadth escape, by what sacrifices on the part of our Allies, at what cost in British lives, with what reproach to our national good name, we have not yet had time fully to realise.

But crediting Lord Haldane's system, if we may, with an assumption which has been proved correct, we have reason to complain that he did not act boldly on this assumption and make his scheme, such as it was, complete and effective. For remember, it was contemplated that the great new army, which was to defend the existence of the British Empire in the final round of war, should be raised and trained upon the voluntary principle—upon a wave of patriotic enthusiasm—after war broke out. This new army

The composition of the British Army.

would have to be organised, clothed, equipped, armed, and supplied with ammunition. The 'voluntary principle' did not apply to matters of this kind. It might therefore have been expected that stores would be accumulated, and plans worked out upon the strictest business principles, with philosophic thoroughness, and in readiness for an emergency which might occur at any moment.

Moral considerations which precluded 'conscription' did not, and could not, apply to inanimate material of war, or to plans and schedules of army corps and camps, or to a body of officers enlisted of their own free will. It may have been true that to impose compulsory training would have offended the consciences of free-born Britons; but it was manifestly absurd to pretend that the accumulation of adequate stores of artillery and small arms, of shells and cartridges, of clothing and equipment, could offend the most tender conscience—could offend anything indeed except the desire of the tax-payer to pay as few taxes as possible.

If the British nation chose to bank on the assumption, that it would have the opportunity given it of 'making good' during the *drag* of war, it should have been made to understand what this entailed in the matter of supplies; and most of all in reserve of officers. All existing forces should at least have been armed with the most modern weapons. There should have been arms and equipment ready for the recruits who would be required, and who were relied upon to respond to a national emergency. There should have been ample stores of every kind, including artillery, and artillery ammunition, for that Expeditionary Force upon which, during the first

CHAPTER II.

six months we had decided to risk our national safety.

The composition of the British Army.

But, in fact, we were provided fully in none of these respects. And least of all were we provided in the matter of officers. There was no case of conscience at stake; but only the question of a vote in the House of Commons. We could have increased our establishment of officers by a vote; we could have laid in stores of ammunition, of clothing, of equipment by a vote. But the vote was not asked for—it might have been unpopular—and therefore Lord Haldane's scheme—in its inception a gamble of the most hazardous character—was reduced to a mere make-believe, for the reason that its originator lacked confidence to back his own 'fancy.'

Looking back at the Agadir incident, it seemed plain enough, from a soldier's point of view, that the British Expeditionary Force was inadequate, in a purely military sense, to redress the adverse balance against the French, and beat back a German invasion. The moral effect, however, of our assistance would undoubtedly have been very great, in encouraging France and Belgium by our comradeship in arms, and in discouraging Germany, by making clear to her the firmness of the Triple Entente.

But by the summer of 1914—three years later—this position had undergone a serious change. In a purely military sense, the value of such aid as it had been in our power to send three years earlier, was greatly diminished. The increase in the German striking force over that of France, which had taken effect since 1911, was considerably greater than the total numbers of the army which we held prepared

The composition of the British Army.

for foreign service. This was fully understood abroad; and the knowledge of it would obviously diminish the moral as well as the material effect of our co-operation.

In order that the combined forces of France and England might have a reasonable chance of holding their own [1] against Germany, until Russian pressure began to tell, the smallest army which we ought to have been able to put in the field, and maintain there for six months, was not less than twice that of the existing Expeditionary Force. From a soldier's point of view 320,000 men instead of 160,000 was the very minimum with which there might be a hope of withstanding the German onset; and for the purpose of bringing victory within sight it would have been necessary to double the larger of these figures. In order to reach the end in view, Britain ought to have possessed a striking force at least half as large as that of France, in round figures between 600,000 and 750,000 men.

This was how the matter appeared in 1912, viewed from the standpoint of a soldier who found himself asked to provide a force sufficient, not for conquest—not for the purpose of changing the map of Europe to the advantage of the Triple Entente—but merely in order to safeguard the independence of Belgium and Holland, to prevent France from being crushed by Germany,[2] and to preserve the security of the British Empire.

[1] *I.e.* of holding the Germans at the French frontier and keeping them out of Belgium should they attempt to invade that country.

[2] At the time these totals were worked out the results appeared very startling to the lay mind. Recent experience, however, has proved that the soldiers who worked them out were right when they described them as 'modest estimates.'

CHAPTER II.

The composition of the British Army.

The political question which presented itself to the minds of enquirers was this—If the British nation were told frankly the whole truth about the Army, would it not conceivably decide that complete insurance was a better bargain than half measures? What force ought we to be prepared to send to France during the first fortnight of war in order to make it a moral certainty that Germany would under no circumstances venture to attack France?

To questions of this sort it is obviously impossible to give certain and dogmatic answers. There are occasions when national feeling runs away with policy and overbears considerations of military prudence. The effects of sudden panic, of a sense of bitter injustice, of blind pride or overweening confidence, are incalculable upon any mathematical basis. But regarding the matter from the point of view of the Kaiser's general staff, whose opinion is usually assumed to be a determining factor in German enterprises, a British Expeditionary Force, amounting to something over 600,000 men, would have been sufficient to prevent the occurrence of a coolly calculated war. And in the event of war arising out of some uncontrollable popular impulse, a British Army of this size would have been enough, used with promptitude and under good leadership, to secure the defeat of the aggressor.

An Expeditionary Force of 320,000 men would mean fully trained reserves of something over 210,000 in order to make good the wastage of war during a campaign of six months. Similarly an Expeditionary Force of 600,000 would mean reserves of 400,000. In the former case a total of 530,000 trained soldiers, and in the latter a total of 1,000,000, would therefore have been required.[1]

The composition of the British Army.

Even the smaller of these proposed increases in the Expeditionary Force would have meant doubling the number of trained soldiers in the British Army; the larger would have meant multiplying it by four. Under what system would it be possible to achieve these results if public opinion should decide that either of them was necessary to national security? The answer was as easy to give as the thing itself seemed hard to carry out.

It had become clear a good deal earlier than the year 1914 that the limit of voluntary enlistment, under existing conditions, had already been reached for the *Regular* as well as the *Territorial* Army. If, therefore, greater numbers were required they could only be provided by some form of compulsory service. There was no getting away from this hard fact which lay at the very basis of the situation.

If security were the object of British policy, the Expeditionary Force must be fully trained before war broke out. It would not serve the purpose for which it was intended, if any part of it, or of its reserves, needed to be taught their trade after war began. Thoroughness of training—which must under ordinary circumstances[2] be measured by length of

[1] In this calculation the wastage of war during the first six months has been taken at two-thirds. With the smaller force of 160,000 men, practically the whole army would be in the fighting line all the time, and the wastage consequently would be heavier. It could not wisely be assumed at less than three-fourths for the same period.

[2] Obviously the better and more experienced the officers, the higher the quality of the recruits, and the keener their spirit, the more quickly the desired result will be achieved. The last two have been very potent factors in the rapid education of our present 'New Army.' In a time of abnormal patriotic impulse, the length of time required will be much shortened. Since August 1914 the lack of experienced officers has been the great difficulty.

CHAPTER II.

The composition of the British Army.

training—appeared to be a factor of vital importance. Given anything like equality in equipment, generalship, and position, men who had undergone a full two years' course—like the conscript armies of the Continent—ought to have no difficulty in defeating a much larger force which had less discipline and experience.

The lessons of the South African War were in many ways very useful; but the praise lavishly, and justly, given to volunteer battalions by Lord Roberts and other distinguished commanders, needed to be studied in the light of the circumstances, and these were of a peculiar character. For one thing our antagonists, the Boers, were not trained troops, and moreover, their policy to a large extent was to weary us out, by declining decisive action and engaging us in tedious pursuits. Our volunteers, for the most part, were picked men. Although only half-trained—perhaps in the majority of cases wholly untrained—circumstances in this case permitted of their being given the time necessary for gaining experience in the field before being required to fight. This was an entirely different state of affairs from what might be looked for in a European war, in a densely peopled country, covered with a close network of roads and railways—a war in which great masses of highly disciplined soldiers would be hurled against one another systematically, upon a settled plan, until at last superiority at one point or another should succeed in breaking down resistance. The South African war and a European war were two things not in the least comparable.

Before the nation could be expected to come to a final decision with regard to the insurance premium

The composition of the British Army.

which it was prepared to pay, it would require to be fully informed upon a variety of subordinate points of much importance. Cost was a matter which could not be put lightly on one side; our peculiar obligations in regard to foreign garrisons was another; the nature of our industrial system was a third; and there were many besides. But the main and governing consideration, if we wished to retain our independence as a nation, was—what provisions were adequate to security? The people wanted to know, and had a right to know, the facts. And in the end, with all due regard for our governors, and for the self-importance of political parties, it was not either for ministers or partisans to decide this question on behalf of the people; it was for the people, on full and honest information, to decide it for themselves.

CHAPTER III

LORD ROBERTS'S WARNINGS

CHAPTER III. — Lord Roberts's warnings.

LORD ROBERTS addressed many meetings in favour of National Service during the years which followed his return from South Africa in 1905; but the first of his speeches to arrest widespread popular attention was delivered in the Free Trade Hall at Manchester, on October 22, 1912. A popular audience filled the building to overflowing, listened with respect, and appeared to accept his conclusions with enthusiasm. His words carried far beyond the walls of the meeting-place, and caused something approaching a sensation, or, as some thought, a scandal, in political circles.

Of the commentators upon this speech the greater part were Liberals, and these condemned his utterances with unanimity in somewhat violent language. Official Unionism was dubious, uncomfortable, and disapproving: it remained for the most part dumb. A few voices were raised from this quarter in open reprobation; a few others proclaimed their independence of party discipline and hastened to approve his sentiments.

There was no doubt of one thing—Lord Roberts's speech had at last aroused public interest. For the first time during the National Service agitation

Lord Roberts's warnings.

blood had been drawn. This was mainly due to the object-lesson in the consequences of military unpreparedness, which the first Balkan War was just then unfolding before the astonished eyes of Europe. In addition, those people, who for a year past had been puzzling their heads over the true meaning of the Agadir crisis, had become impressed with the urgent need for arriving at a clear decision with regard to the adequacy of our national defences.

The speech was a lucid and forcible statement of the need for compulsory military training. It was interesting reading at the time it was delivered, and in some respects it is even more interesting to-day. It was compactly put together, not a thing of patches. A man who read any part of it would read it all. Yet in accordance with custom, controversy raged around three isolated passages.

The *first* of these runs as follows: "In the year '1912, our German friends, I am well aware, do 'not—at least in sensible circles—assert dogmatically 'that a war with Great Britain will take place this 'year or next; but in their heart of hearts they 'know, every man of them, that—just as in 1866 'and just as in 1870—war will take place the instant 'the German forces by land and sea are, by their 'superiority at every point, as certain of victory as 'anything in human calculation can be made certain. '*Germany strikes when Germany's hour has struck.* 'That is the time-honoured policy of her Foreign 'Office. That was the policy relentlessly pursued 'by Bismarck and Moltke in 1866 and 1870. It 'has been her policy decade by decade since that 'date. It is her policy at the present hour."

CHAPTER III.

Lord Roberts's warnings.

The *second* passage followed upon the first: "It is an excellent policy. It is or should be the 'policy of every nation prepared to play a great 'part in history. Under that policy Germany has, 'within the last ten years, sprung, as at a bound, 'from one of the weakest of naval powers to the 'greatest naval power, save one, upon this globe."

The *third* passage came later: "Such, gentlemen, 'is the origin, and such the considerations which 'have fostered in me the growth of this conviction— 'the conviction that in some form of National Service 'is the only salvation of this Nation and this Empire. 'The Territorial Force is now an acknowledged 'failure—a failure in discipline, a failure in numbers, 'a failure in equipment, a failure in energy." [1]

The accuracy of the *first* and *third* of these statements now stands beyond need of proof. It was not truer that Germany would strike so soon as her rulers were of opinion that the propitious hour had struck, than it was that, when the British Government came to take stock of their resources at the outbreak of war, they would find the Territorial Army to be lacking in the numbers, equipment, training, and discipline, which alone could have fitted it for its appointed task—the defence of our shores against invasion. Slowly, and under great difficulties, and amid the gravest anxieties these defects had subsequently to be made good, hampering the while our military operations in the critical sphere.

The *second* statement was of a different character, and taken by itself, without reference to the context, lent itself readily to misconception as well as mis-

[1] Manchester, October 22, 1912. Quoted from *Lord Roberts's Message, to the Nation* (Murray), pp. 4-6 and p. 12. The date, however, is there given wrongly as October 25.

Lord Roberts's warnings.

construction. A certain number of critics, no doubt, actually believed, a still larger number affected to believe, that Lord Roberts was here advocating the creation of a British army, for the purpose of attacking Germany, without a shred of justification, and at the first favourable moment.

The whole tenor of this speech, however, from the first line to the last, made it abundantly clear that in Lord Roberts's opinion Britain could have neither motive nor object for attacking Germany; that the sole concern of England and of the British Empire with regard to Germany was, how we might defend our possessions and secure ourselves against her schemes of aggression.

Lord Roberts, however, had in fact pronounced the intentions which he attributed to Germany to be 'an excellent policy,' and had thereby seemed to approve, and recommend for imitation, a system which was revolting to the conscience of a Christian community.

The idea that Lord Roberts could have had any such thoughts in his mind seemed merely absurd to any one who knew him; nay, it must also have seemed inconceivable to any one who had taken the trouble to read the speech itself in an unprejudiced mood. To an ordinary man of sense it did not need Lord Roberts's subsequent letter of explanation [1] to set his opinions in their true light. It was clear that his object, in this 'peccant passage,' had merely been to avoid a pharisaical condemnation of German methods and ambitions, and to treat that country as a worthy, as well as a formidable, antagonist. Being a soldier, however,—

[1] *Manchester Guardian*, November 5, 1912.

CHAPTER III.

Lord Roberts's warnings.

not a practised platform orator alive to the dangers of too-generous concession—he went too far. The words were unfortunately chosen, seeing that so many critics were on the watch, not to discover the true meaning of the speech, but to pounce on any slip which might be turned to the disadvantage of the speaker.

At first there was an attempt on the part of certain London [1] Liberal journals to boycott this speech. Very speedily, however, it seemed to dawn upon them that they had greater advantages to gain by denouncing it. A few days later, accordingly, the torrent of condemnation was running free. The ablest attack appeared in the *Nation*,[2] and as this pronouncement by the leading Radical weekly was quoted with approval by the greater part of the ministerial press throughout the country, it may fairly be taken as representing the general view of the party.

The article was headed *A Diabolical Speech*, and its contents fulfilled the promise of the title. "There ought," said the writer, "to be some means 'of bringing to book a soldier, in the receipt of 'money from the State, who speaks of a friendly 'Power as Lord Roberts spoke of Germany." He was accused roundly of predicting and encouraging a vast and 'hideous conflict' between the two countries. Lord Roberts was a 'successful' [3]

[1] This was not so, however, with the Liberal newspaper of greatest influence in the United Kingdom—the *Manchester Guardian*—which gave a full and prominent report of Lord Roberts's meeting. This journal is honourably free from any suspicion of using the suppression of news as a political weapon.

[2] October 26, 1912. Like the *Manchester Guardian*, the *Nation* made no attempt to boycott the speech.

[3] 'Successful,' not 'distinguished' or 'able' is the word. The amiable stress would appear to be on luck rather than merit.

Lord Roberts's warnings.

soldier; but 'without training in statesmanship.' He 'had never shown any gift for it.' His was 'an average Tory intellect.' He was a 'complete contrast' to Wellington, who possessed two great qualities; for "he set a high value on peace, and 'he knew how to estimate and bow to the governing 'forces of national policy. . . . Lord Roberts pos- 'sesses neither of these attributes. He is a mere 'jingo in opinion and character, and he interprets 'the life and interests of this nation and this Empire 'by the crude lusts and fears which haunt the un- 'imaginative soldier's brain."

We may pause at this breathing-place to take note of the healing influences of time. Radical journalists of 1832, and thereabouts, were wont to say very much the same hard things of the Duke of Wellington, as those of 1912 saw fit to apply to Earl Roberts. . . . We may also remark in passing, upon the errors to which even the most brilliant of contemporary judgments are liable. There has never been a man in our time who set a higher value on peace than Lord Roberts did. He realised, however, not only the intrinsic value of peace, but its market cost. His real crime, in the eyes of pacifists, was that he stated publicly, as often as he had the chance, what price we must be prepared to pay, if we wanted peace and not war. It was in this sense, no doubt, that he did not know 'how to estimate and 'bow to the governing forces of national policy.' His blunt warnings broke in rudely and crudely upon the comfortable discourse of the three counsellors—*Simple, Sloth,* and *Presumption,* who, better than any others, were skilled in estimating the 'governing forces,' and the advantages to be gained by bowing to them.

CHAPTER III.

Lord Roberts's warnings.

The writer in the *Nation* then proceeded to riddle Lord Roberts's theories of defence. "He desires 'us to remain a 'free nation' in the same breath 'that he invites us to come under the yoke of con-'scription"—intolerable, indeed, that the citizens of a free nation should be ordered to fit themselves for defending their common freedom—"conscription, 'if you please, for the unheard-of purpose of overseas 'service in India and elsewhere. . . ." This invitation does not seem to be contained in this, or any other of Lord Roberts's speeches; but supposing it to have been given, it was not altogether 'unheard-of,' seeing that, under the law of conscription prevalent (for example) in Germany, conscript soldiers can be sent to Palestine, or tropical Africa as lawfully as into Luxemburg, Poland, or France. According to the *Nation*, the true theory of defence was Sea Power; but this, it appeared, could not be relied on for all time. . . . "While our naval monopoly—like our 'commercial monopoly—cannot exist for ever, our 'sea power and our national security depend on our 'ability to crush an enemy's fleet. . . . We were never 'so amply insured—so over-insured—against naval 'disaster as we are to-day."

"Lord Roberts's proposition, therefore," the writer continued, "is merely foolish; it is his way of 'commending it, which is merely wicked. He speaks 'of war as certain to take place 'the instant' the 'German forces are assured of 'superiority at every 'point,' and he discovers that the motto of German 'foreign policy is that *Germany strikes when Germany's 'hour has struck.* Germany does not happen to 'have struck anybody since 1870, and she struck 'then to secure national unity, and to put an end to

Lord Roberts's warnings.

'the standing menace of French imperialism. Since 'then she has remained the most peaceful and the 'most self-contained, though doubtless not the most 'sympathetic, member of the European family. . . . 'Germany, the target of every cheap dealer in historic 'slapdash, is in substance the Germany of 1870" (*i.e.* in extent of territory), "with a great industrial 'dominion superadded by the force of science and 'commercial enterprise. That is the story across 'which Lord Roberts scrawls his ignorant libel. . . . 'By direct implication he invites us to do to Germany 'what he falsely asserts she is preparing to do to 'us. These are the morals, fitter for a wolf-pack 'than for a society of Christian men, commended 'as 'excellent policy' to the British nation in the 'presence of a Bishop of the Anglican Church."

This was very vigorous writing; nor was there the slightest reason to suspect its sincerity. In the nature of man there is a craving to believe; and if a man happens to have his dwelling-place in a world of illusion and unreality, it is not wonderful that he should believe in phantoms. The credulity of the *Nation* might appear to many people to amount to fanaticism; but its views were fully shared, though less tersely stated, by the whole Liberal party, by the greater proportion of the British people, and not inconceivably by the bulk of the Unionist opposition as well. The Government alone, who had learned the true facts from Lord Haldane eight months earlier, knew how near Lord Roberts's warnings came to the mark.

This article set the tone of criticism. The *Manchester Guardian* protested against the "insinuation 'that the German Government's views of international

CHAPTER III.

Lord Roberts's warnings.

'policy are less scrupulous and more cynical than 'those of other Governments." Germany has never been accused with justice "of breaking her word, 'of disloyalty to her engagements, or of insincerity. 'Prussia's character among nations is, in fact, not 'very different from the character which Lancashire 'men give to themselves as compared with other 'Englishmen. It is blunt, straightforward, and 'unsentimental. . . ." How foolish, moreover, are our fears of Germany when we come to analyse them. "We have no territory that she could take, except, 'in tropical Africa, which no sane man would go to 'war about. Our self-governing colonies could not 'in any case be held by force; and Canada is pro-'tected in addition by the Monroe doctrine. Egypt 'is not ours to cede. Malta could not be had 'without war with Italy nor India without war with 'Russia." [1]

This was a proud statement of the basis of British security, and one which must have warmed the hearts, and made the blood of Cromwell and Chatham tingle in the shades. Egypt, which we had rescued from a chaos of civil war, bankruptcy, and corruption, which during more than thirty years we had administered as just stewards for the benefit of her people, which we had saved from conquest and absorption by savage hordes—Egypt was not ours to cede. For the rest our dependencies were not worth taking from us, while our 'colonies' could defend themselves. By the grace of Italy's protection we should be secured in the possession of Malta. India would be preserved to us by the goodwill of Russia, and Canada by the strong arm of the United States. . . .

[1] *Manchester Guardian*, October 28, 1912.

Such at that time were the views of the Liberal journal foremost in character and ability.

Lord Roberts's warnings.

Somewhat later the *Daily News* took the field, making up for lost time by an exuberance of misconstruction. . . . "The whole movement as represented by the National Service League is definitely 'unmasked as an attempt to get up, not defence, but 'an invasion of German territory. This discovery, 'which for years has been suspected, is most valuable 'as showing up the real object of the League, with its 'glib talk about military calisthenics. Lord Roberts 'may have been indiscreet, but at least he has 'made it clear that what the League wants is war."[1]

On the same day, in order that the Liberals might not have a monopoly of reprobation, the *Evening Standard*, in an article entitled *A Word with Lord Roberts*, rated him soundly for having "made an attack upon Germany and an attack 'upon the Territorial Force. . . ." "It is mere 'wanton mischief-making for a man with Lord 'Roberts's unequalled prestige to use words which 'must drive every German who reads them to 'exasperation." And yet no signs whatsoever were forthcoming that so much as a single Teuton had been rendered desperate, or had taken the words as in the least degree uncomplimentary. Up to the day of his death—and indeed after his death[2]—Lord Roberts was almost the only Englishman of his time of whom Germans spoke with consistent respect. . . . "Do not," continues this lofty and sapient mentor, "Do not let us talk as if the Kaiser 'could play the part of a Genghis Khan or an Attila, 'ravening round the world at the head of armed

[1] *Daily News*, October 30, 1912. [2] See Preface.

CHAPTER III.

Lord Roberts's warnings.

'hordes to devour empires and kingdoms."[1] And yet how otherwise has the whole British Press been talking ever since the middle of August 1914? If during this period of nine months, the *Evening Standard* has kept all reference to Attila and his Huns out of its columns, its continence is unique.

It would serve no useful purpose to set out further items of criticism and abuse from the leader and correspondence columns of newspapers, or from the speeches of shocked politicians. The *Nation*, the *Manchester Guardian*, and the *Daily News* are entitled, between them, to speak for the Liberal party; and if it cannot be said that the *Evening Standard* is quite similarly qualified in respect of the Unionists, there is still no doubt that the views which it expressed with so much vigour, prescience, and felicity were held by many orthodox members of its party.

Colonel Bromley-Davenport, for example, who had been Financial Secretary to the War Office in the late Unionist Government, spoke out strongly against Lord Roberts's comments upon the efficiency of the Territorial Force. 'Compulsory service,' in his opinion, 'was not necessary. . . .' And then, with a burst of illuminating candour—"Which of the 'great parties in the state would take up compulsory 'service and fight a general election upon it? The 'answer was that neither of the parties would; 'and to ask for compulsory military service was 'like crying for the moon."[2] The power of any proposal for winning elections was to be the touchstone of its truth. It would be impossible to state more concisely the attitude of the orthodox politician.

[1] *Evening Standard*, October 30, 1912.
[2] *Morning Post*, October 30, 1912.

CHAPTER III.

Lord Roberts's warnings.

Which party, indeed, we may well ask, would have fought a general election on anything, however needful, unless it hoped to win on it?

The attitude of Ministers, however, with regard to Lord Roberts's speech is much more worthy of remark than that of independent journalists and members of Parliament. For the Government knew several very important things which, at that time, were still hidden from the eyes of ordinary men.

It was eight months since Lord Haldane had returned from Germany, concealing, under a smiling countenance and insouciant manner, a great burden of care at his heart. If on his return he spoke cheerily on public platforms about the kindness of his entertainment at Berlin, and of the greatness and goodness of those with whom he had there walked and talked, this was merely in order that his fellow-countrymen might not be plunged in panic or despondency. He had learned the mind of Germany, and it was no light lesson. He had imparted his dreadful secret to his colleagues, and we have learned lately from Mr. Asquith himself what that secret was. . . . The rulers of Germany, 'to put it quite plainly,' had asked us for a free hand to overbear and dominate the European world, whenever they deemed the opportunity favourable. They had demanded this of the astounded British emissary, "at a time when 'Germany was enormously increasing both her 'aggressive and defensive resources, and especially 'upon the sea." To such a demand but one answer was possible, and that answer the British Government had promptly given—so we are led to infer—in clear and ringing tones of scorn.[1]

[1] Mr. Asquith at Cardiff, October 2, 1914.

CHAPTER III.

Lord Roberts's warnings.

The Government knew for certain what nobody else did. They knew what the aims of Germany were, and consequently they knew that Lord Roberts had spoken nothing but the truth.

And yet, strange to relate, within a few days we find Mr. Runciman, a member of the Cabinet, administering a severe castigation to Lord Roberts. The Manchester speech was "not only deplorable and 'pernicious,' but likewise 'dangerous.' If it was resented in Germany, Mr. Runciman 'would like 'Germany to know that it is resented no less in 'England. . . ." Lord Roberts had been a great organiser of the National Service League, the object of which was 'practically conscription'; but "he 'knows little of England, and certainly little of the 'North of England, if he imagines we are ever likely 'to submit to conscription"—not even apparently (for there are no reservations) as an alternative to conquest; or as a security against murder, arson, and rape. . . . "War is only inevitable when states-'men cannot find a way round, or through, difficulties 'that may arise; or are so wicked that they prefer 'the hellish method of war to any other method of 'solution; or are so weak as to allow soldiers, arma-'ment makers, or scaremongers to direct their 'policy."[1] Lord Roberts was not, of course, an armament maker, but he was a scaremonger and a soldier, and as such had no right to state his views as to how peace might be kept.

When Sir Edward Grey was asked if any representation had been addressed by Germany to the

[1] Mr. Runciman at Elland, *Manchester Guardian*, October 26, 1912. Sir Walter Runciman, the father of this speaker, appears to be made of sterner stuff. After the Scarborough raid he denounced the Germans as "heinous polecats."

Lord Roberts's warnings.

Foreign Office with reference to Lord Roberts's utterances, he deprecated, with frigid discretion, the idea that either Government should make official representation to the other about 'unwise or pro-'vocative speeches.' [1] When Sir William Byles plied the Secretary of State for War, Colonel Seely, with questions as to the revocability of Lord Roberts's pension, the answer was solemn and oracular, but no rebuke was administered to the interrogator.[2]

But perhaps the most puzzling thing of all, is the persistency with which Mr. Acland (Sir Edward Grey's Under-Secretary) pursued Lord Roberts for some three weeks after the rest were finished with him. It might have been expected that Mr. Acland's chief, who knew 'the dreadful secret,' would have curbed his subordinate's excess of zeal.

Mr. Acland distorted the Manchester speech into an appeal to the British people to put themselves "in a position to strike at the Germans, and to 'smash them in a time of profound peace, and without 'cause." And this fanciful gloss he rightly denounces, in accents which remind us not a little of the Reverend Robert Spalding, as 'nothing less than a wicked 'proposal.' [3] . . . For England to adopt compulsory military service would be "an utterly criminal and 'provocative proceeding against other countries of the 'world. . . ." Here, indeed, is much food for wonder. What single country of the world would have regarded the adoption of national service by England as 'provocative'? What single country, except Germany, would even have objected to it? And what more right would Germany have had to object

[1] *Times*, Parliamentary Report, October 30, 1912.
[2] *Ibid.* November 1, 1912.
[3] Mr. Acland at Taunton, the *Times*, November 5, 1912.

CHAPTER III.

Lord Roberts's warnings.

to our possessing a formidable army, than we had right to object to her possessing a formidable navy?

When some days later Mr. Acland is reproached with having misrepresented Lord Roberts's original statement, he replies loftily that he "was justified 'at the time in supposing that this was his real 'meaning."[1] One wonders why. Lord Roberts had said nothing which any careful reader of his whole speech—an Under-Secretary for Foreign Affairs, for example, quoting and speaking with a due sense of his great responsibilities—could conceivably have understood to bear this interpretation.

A fortnight later Mr. Acland returns to the charge once more. "Lord Roberts," he says courteously, "has since explained that he did not mean what 'his words seemed so plainly to mean"—that is, the smashing of Germany in time of profound peace and without any cause. . . . Danger to peace, the representative of the Foreign Office assures his audience, "does not come from any action of His 'Majesty's Government. It arises, if at all, from 'irresponsible utterances such as those which we 'heard from Lord Roberts. I very much regret 'that harm must have been done between the two 'countries by Lord Roberts's speech."[2]

Although an under-secretary does not always enjoy the full confidence of his official superior, he would presumably obey orders—even an order to hold his tongue—if any were given. Consequently, although Lord Haldane's dreadful secret may have been kept from Mr. Acland, as unfit for his innocent

[1] Letter in the *Times*, November 11, 1912.
[2] Mr. Acland at Rochdale, the *Times*, November 25, 1912.

Lord Roberts's warnings.

and youthful ears, it is surprising that he was never warned of the dangers of the path in which he was so boldly treading. The discourtesies of youth to age are not easily forgiven, especially where they are founded upon misrepresentation, and when, as in this case, the older man was right and the younger wrong as to the facts.

It will be said—it has indeed been already said—by way of excuse for the reticence of the Government with regard to the intentions, which German statesmen revealed to Lord Haldane, at Berlin, in February 1912—that by keeping back from the country the knowledge which members of the Cabinet possessed, they thereby prevented an outbreak of passion and panic which might have precipitated war. This may be true or untrue; it can neither be proved nor controverted; but at any rate it was not in accordance with the principle of trusting the people; nor would it have prevented the Government and their supporters—when war broke out—from making amends to Lord Roberts and others whom, on grounds of high policy, they had felt themselves obliged, in the past to rebuke unjustly and to discredit without warrant in the facts. This course was not impossible. Peel, a very proud man, made amends to Cobden, and his memory does not stand any the lower for it.

With regard to those journalists and private politicians whose mistakes were not altogether their own fault—being due in part at least, to the concealment of the true facts which the Government had practised—it would not have been in the least wounding to their honour to express regret, that they had been unwittingly the means of misleading the people, and traducing those who were endeavouring to lead

CHAPTER III.

Lord Roberts's warnings.

it right. In their patriotic indignation some of these same journalists and politicians had overstepped the limits of what is justifiable in party polemics. They had attacked the teaching at the Military Colleges, because it sought to face the European situation frankly, and to work out in the lecture-room the strategical and tactical consequences which, in case of war, might be forced upon us by our relations with France and Russia. It would have done these high-minded journalists no harm in the eyes of their fellow-countrymen, had they acknowledged frankly that when in former days they had denounced the words of Lord Roberts as 'wicked' and his interpretation of the situation as inspired by "the crude lusts and fears which haunt the 'unimaginative soldier's brain"—when they had publicly denounced as 'a Staff College Cabal' teachers who were only doing their duty—they had unwittingly been guilty of a cruel misjudgment.

It is not a little remarkable that in 1912—indeed from 1905 to 1914—Lord Roberts, who, according to the *Nation*, possessed but 'an average Tory intellect,' should have trusted the people, while a democratic Government could not bring itself to do so. The Cabinet, which knew the full measure of the danger, concealed it out of a mistaken notion of policy. Their henchmen on the platform and in the press did not know the full measure of the danger. They acted either from natural prejudice, or official inspiration—possibly from a mixture of both—when they made light of the danger and held up to scorn any one who called attention to it. The whole body of respectable, word-worshipping, well-to-do Liberals and Conservatives, whom nothing could stir out of their indifference and scepticism, disapproved most strongly of having the word 'danger' so much as mentioned in their presence. The country would to-day forgive all of these their past errors more easily if, when the crisis came, they had acted a manly part and had expressed regret. But never a word of the sort from any of these great public characters!

Lord Roberts's warnings.

CHAPTER IV

LORD KITCHENER'S TASK

CHAPTER IV.

Lord Kitchener's task.

LORD ROBERTS had been seeking for seven years to persuade the nation to realise that it was threatened by a great danger; that it was unprepared to encounter the danger; that by reason of this unpreparedness, the danger was brought much nearer. Until October 1912, however, he had failed signally in capturing the public ear. The people would not give him their attention either from favour or indignation. The cause of which he was the advocate appeared to have been caught in an academic backwater.

But from that time forward, Lord Roberts had no reason to complain of popular neglect. Overcoming his natural disinclination to platform oratory and political agitation, sacrificing his leisure, putting a dangerous strain upon his physical strength, he continued his propaganda at a series of great meetings in the industrial centres. Everywhere he was listened to with respect, and apparently with a great measure of agreement. Only on one occasion was he treated with discourtesy, and that was by a civic dignitary and not by the audience. But he had now become an important figure in the political conflict, and he had to take the consequences, in a stream of abuse and misrepresentation from the party which dis-

Lord Kitchener's task.

approved of his principles; while he received but little comfort from the other party, which lived in constant terror lest it might be thought to approve of them. Lord Roberts's advocacy of national service continued up to the autumn of 1913, when the gravity of the situation in Ireland made it impossible to focus public interest on any other subject.

After the present war had run its course for a month or two, the minds of many people reverted to what Lord Roberts had been urging upon his fellow-countrymen for nine years past. His warnings had come true; that at any rate was beyond doubt. The intentions which he had attributed to Germany were clearly demonstrated, and likewise the vastness and efficiency of her military organisation. The inadequacy of British preparations was made plain. They were inadequate in the sense that they had failed to deter the aggressor from a breach of the peace, and they had been equally inadequate for withstanding his *onset*. The deficiencies of the Territorial Army in numbers, discipline, training, and equipment had made it impossible to entrust it with the responsibility of Home Defence immediately upon the outbreak of war. As a consequence of this, the whole of the Regular Army could not be released for foreign service, although Sir John French's need of reinforcements was desperate. Notwithstanding, however, that Lord Roberts's warnings had come true, many people professed to discover in what had happened a full justification—some even went so far as to call it a 'triumph'—for the voluntary system.

Even after the first battle of Ypres, those who held such views had no difficulty in finding evidences

CHAPTER IV.

Lord Kitchener's task.

of their truth on all hands. They found them in the conduct of our army in France, and in the courage and devotion with which it had upheld the honour of England against overwhelming odds. They found it in the response to Lord Kitchener's call for volunteers, and in the eagerness and spirit of the New Army. They found it in our command of the sea, in the spirit of the nation, and in what they read in their newspapers about the approval and admiration of the world.

In the short dark days of December and January we were cheered by many bold bills and headlines announcing what purported to be victories; and we were comforted through a sad Christmastide by panegyrics on British instinct, pluck, good-temper, energy, and genius for muddling through. Philosophic commentators pointed out that, just as Germany was becoming tired out and short of ammunition, just as she was bringing up troops of worse and worse quality, we should be at our very best, wallowing in our resources of men and material of war. Six months, a year, eighteen months hence—for the estimates varied—Britain would be invincible. Economic commentators on the other hand impressed upon us how much better it was to pay through the nose now, than to have been bleeding ourselves white as the Germans, the French, and the Russians were supposed (though without much justification) to have been doing for a century.

To clinch the triumph of the voluntary system—when the Hour came the Man came with it.

Many of these things were truly alleged. Lord Kitchener at any rate was no mirage. The gallantry of our Army was no illusion; indeed, its heroism

CHAPTER IV.

Lord Kitchener's task.

was actually underrated, for the reason that the extent of its peril had never been fully grasped. Although British commerce had suffered severely from the efforts of a few bold raiders, the achievements of our Navy were such that they could quite fairly be described, as having secured command of the sea.[1] The German fleet was held pretty closely within its harbours. We had been able to move our troops and munitions of war wherever we pleased, and so far, without the loss of a ship, or even of a man. Submarine piracy—a policy of desperation—had not then begun. The quality of the New Army, the rapidity with which its recruits were being turned into soldiers, not only impressed the public, but took by complete surprise the severest of military critics.

This is not the place for discussing how Lord Kitchener came to be appointed Secretary of State for War, or to attempt an estimate of his character and career.[2] He was no politician, but a soldier

[1] Partly by good fortune, but mainly owing to the admirable promptitude and skill with which our naval resources were handled, the bulk of the German fleet was imprisoned from the outset. We did not experience anything like the full effect of our unpreparedness. If Mr. Churchill had not taken his decision on the day following the delivery of the Austrian ultimatum to Servia (July 24) by postponing the demobilisation of the Fleet—to the great scandal of his own party, when the facts first became known—there would have been a very different tale to tell as regards the fate of the British merchant service on the high seas.

[2] Critics of the present Government, such as the editor of the *National Review*, have maintained that Lord Kitchener was forced upon an unwilling Cabinet by the pressure of public opinion; that although he was in England throughout the crisis he was allowed to make all his preparations for returning to Egypt, and was only fetched back as he was on the point of stepping aboard the packet; that the well-known form of Lord Haldane had been seen at the War Office, and that if the Lord Chancellor had, as was intended, relinquished his legal position in order to become Secretary of State for War, we should probably not have sent abroad our Expeditionary Force. It is undeniable that during Sunday, Monday, and Tuesday (August 2, 3, and 4) London was buzzing with a strange rumour (which was fathered altogether falsely upon the French Ambassador) that France did not ask for or require our assistance on land; but only at sea. If this were so the absurdity of

CHAPTER IV.

Lord Kitchener's task.

and an administrator. He was in his sixty-fifth year, and since he had left the Royal Military Academy in 1871, by far the greater part of his work had been done abroad—in the Levant, Egypt, South Africa, and India.[1] In no case had he ever failed at anything he had undertaken. The greater part of his work had been completely successful; much of it had been brilliantly successful. He believed in himself; the country believed in him; foreign nations believed in him. No appointment could have produced a better effect upon the hearts of the British people and upon those of their Allies. The nation felt—if we may use so homely an image in this connection—that Lord Kitchener was holding its hand confidently and reassuringly in one of his, while with the other he had the whole race of politicians firmly by the scruff, and would see to it that there was no nonsense or trouble in that quarter.

It is no exaggeration to say that from that time to this,[2] Lord Kitchener's presence in the Cabinet

---

sending our Expeditionary Force would have been obvious. It is noteworthy that a usually well-inspired section of the Ministerial Press—even after they had reluctantly accepted war as inevitable—were still maintaining stoutly, even so late as Tuesday and Wednesday (4th and 5th), that the Expeditionary Force should not be allowed to cross the channel. Lord Kitchener was appointed on the Thursday, and the Expeditionary Force began to go abroad the following week. The chapter of English political history which begins with the presentation of the Austrian ultimatum to Servia on the 23rd of July, and ends with the appointment of Lord Kitchener on the 6th of August, will no doubt prove to be one of the most interesting in our annals. Whether it will prove to be one of the most glorious or one of the most humiliating exhibitions of British statesmanship we cannot say until we possess fuller knowledge than we do at present of the attitude of ministers at the Cabinets of Friday, Saturday, and Sunday (July 31, August 1 and 2).

[1] Palestine, 1874–1878; Cyprus, 1878–1882; Egypt, 1882–1899; South Africa, 1899–1902; India, 1902–1909; Egypt, 1911–1914. Only during the years 1871–1874 and 1909–1911 does Lord Kitchener appear to have been freed from foreign service, and during a part of the latter interval he was travelling in China and Japan.

[2] End of May 1915.

Lord Kitchener's task.

has counted for more with the country, than that of any other minister, or indeed than all other ministers put together. That in itself proves his possession of very remarkable qualities; for nine such months of public anxiety and private sorrow, as England has lately known, will disturb any reputation which is not firmly founded upon merit. During this time we have seen other reputations come and go; popularities made, and unmade, and remade. We have seen great figures all but vanish into the mist of neglect. But confidence in Lord Kitchener has remained constant through it all. Things may have gone wrong; the Government may have made mistakes; even the War Office itself may have made mistakes; yet the faith of the British people in the man of their choice has never been shaken for an instant.

The highest of all Lord Kitchener's merits is, that being suddenly pitchforked into office by an emergency, he nevertheless grasped at once the two or three main features of the situation, and turned the whole force of his character to dealing with them, letting the smaller matters meanwhile fall into line as best they might. He grasped the dominating factor—that it was essential to subordinate every military and political consideration to supporting France, whose fight for her own existence was equally a fight for the existence of the British Empire. He grasped the urgent need for the enrolment of many hundreds of thousands of men fit for making into soldiers, if we were to win this fight and not lose it. He grasped the need for turning these recruits into soldiers at a pace which hardly a single military expert believed to be possible. He may, or may

CHAPTER IV.

Lord Kitchener's task.

not, have fully grasped at the beginning, the difficulties —mainly owing to dearth of officers—with which he was faced; but when he did grasp them, by some means or another, he succeeded in overcoming them.

It is dangerous to speak of current events in confident superlatives; but one is tempted to do so with regard to the training of the New Army. Even the most friendly among expert critics believed that what Lord Kitchener had undertaken was a thing quite impossible to do in the prescribed time. Yet he has done it. And not only the friendly, but also the severest critics, have admitted that the New Army is already fit to face any continental army, and that, moreover, to all appearance, it is one of the finest armies in history. The sternest proof is yet to come; but it is clear that something not far short of a miracle has been accomplished.

If we search for an explanation of the miracle, we find it quite as much in Lord Kitchener's character as in his methods. Fortunately what was so painfully lacking in the political sphere was present in the military—Leadership.

Despite the support which Lord Kitchener derived from the public confidence he laboured under several very serious disadvantages. A man cannot spend almost the whole of his working life out of England, and then return to it at the age of sixty-four, understanding all the conditions as clearly as if he had never left it. Lord Kitchener was ignorant not only of English political conditions, but also of English industrial conditions, which in a struggle like the present are certainly quite as important as the other. He may well have consoled himself, however, with the reflection that, although he himself was lacking in knowledge, his colleagues were experts in both of these spheres.

CHAPTER IV.

Lord Kitchener's task.

It was inevitable that Lord Kitchener must submit to the guidance of Ministers in the political sphere, providing they agreed with his main objects—the unflinching support of France, and the creation of the New Army.

In the industrial sphere, on the other hand, it was the business of Ministers, not merely to keep themselves in touch with Lord Kitchener's present and future needs, and to offer their advice and help for satisfying them, but also to insist upon his listening to reason, if in his urgent need and unfamiliarity with the business world, he was seen to be running upon danger in any direction.

It is impossible to resist the impression that, while his colleagues held Lord Kitchener very close by the head as to politics, and explained to him very clearly what they conceived the people would stand and would not stand, they did not show anything like the same vigilance or determination in keeping him well advised as to the means of procuring the material of war.

CHAPTER V

MATERIAL OF WAR

CHAPTER V.

Material of war.

As regards the business world the position at this time [1] was a singularly difficult one. Within a few days of the outbreak of war, orders from all parts of the globe were forthcoming, on so vast a scale that the ordinary means of coping with them were wholly inadequate. It was not possible to walk out of the War Office and buy what was wanted in the shops. In a very brief period the whole industrial system of the United Kingdom was congested with orders.

In Lord Kitchener's former experience of military and civil administration the difficulty had usually been to get the money he needed, in order to carry out his reforms and undertakings. But here was a case where he could have all the money he chose to ask for; it was the commodities themselves which could not be had either for money or love.

When war broke out the industries of France and Belgium were paralysed—the former temporarily, the latter permanently. We could buy nothing in France; France, on the other hand, was buying eagerly in England. And so was Russia, not herself as yet a great industrial producer. And so were Belgium,

[1] I am specially referring to August-December 1914.

Material of war.

Servia, Italy, Roumania, Greece, Japan—indeed the whole world, more or less—belligerents and neutrals alike—except the two Powers with which we were at war. All these competitors were in the field against the War Office, running up prices, and making the fortunes of enterprising middlemen, who flocked to the feast, like vultures from all corners of the sky. The industrial situation, therefore, needed the sternest regulation, and needed it at once. For it was essential to secure our own requirements, and to make certain that our Allies secured theirs, at a fair price and in advance of all other purchasers.

Moreover, it was obviously necessary to look an immense way ahead, especially as regards munitions of war; to aid with loans, and encourage with orders, firms able and willing to make what was required. It was essential that makers of arms and supplies should be stimulated to undertake vast increases of their staff and plant. Before the battle of the Marne was ended it was known, only too well, that every nation in Europe—with the single exception of Germany—had grossly underestimated the expenditure of artillery ammunition under conditions of modern warfare. It was of the most immediate urgency to concert with our Allies, and with our manufacturers, in order to set this trouble right. It was as necessary for the Allies to organise their resources as it was for them to organise their armies. The second, indeed, was impossible without the first, as Germany well knew, and in her own case had already practised.

Finally, there was the problem—half industrial, half political—of labour; its hours, conditions, and remuneration. Without the utmost vigilance and

Material of war.

sympathy, without a constant inspiration of duty, without political leadership which appealed to the imagination and heart of the people, there were bound to be endless troubles and confusion; there were bound to be disputes, quarrels, stoppages, and strikes.

The prices of certain munitions and materials were almost anything the makers liked to name. Money was flying about, and everybody was aware of it. Human nature was sorely tempted. The future was anxious and uncertain. People dependent for a living on their own exertions, were beset with a dangerous inclination to hold out their pitchers, in the hopes of catching some portion of the golden shower while it lasted. The idea that workmen were, on the average, any greedier than their masters is only held by persons who have little knowledge of the facts. Cost of living had risen rapidly; this might have been foreseen from the beginning, as well as the dangers which it contained.

In such circumstances as these the baser appetites of mankind are always apt to break loose and gain the upper hand, unless there is a firm leadership of the nation. That is where the statesman should come in, exercising a sagacious control upon the whole organisation of industry; impressing on masters the need for patience and sympathy; on their men the need for moderation; on all the need for sacrifices.

During the months of February, March, and April 1915 there was a loud outcry, led by a member of the Government, deploring the lack of munitions of war, and attributing the deficiency to a want of industry and energy on the part of a

Material of war.

section of the working classes. Their frequent abstentions were condemned, and drunkenness was alleged to have been, in many cases, a contributory cause.

Then Mr. Asquith came forward and astonished the world by denying stoutly that there was, or ever had been, any deficiency in munitions of war.[1] He assured the country that so long ago as September he had "appointed a committee . . . to survey the 'situation."[2] He said nothing about irregularity of work, or about drunkenness as a cause of it. On the contrary, he produced the impression that the Army was as well provided as it could be, and that the behaviour of the whole world of industry had

[1] "I saw a statement the other day *that the operations not only of our 'Army but of our Allies were being crippled, or at any rate hampered, by our 'failure to provide the necessary ammunition. There is not a word of truth 'in that statement.* I say there is not a word of truth in that statement 'which is the more mischievous because if it were believed, it is calculated 'to dishearten our troops, to discourage our Allies, and to stimulate the 'hopes and activities of our enemies. Nor is there any more truth in the 'suggestion that the Government, of which I am the head, have only recently 'become alive to the importance and the urgency of these matters. On the 'contrary, in the earliest days of the war, when some of our would-be 'instructors were thinking of quite other things, they were already receiving 'our anxious attention, and as far back, I think, as the month of September 'I appointed a Committee of the Cabinet, presided over by Lord Kitchener, 'to survey the situation from this point of view—a Committee whose 'labours and inquiries resulted in a very substantial enlargement both on 'the field and of machinery of supply. . . .

"No, the urgency of the situation—and, as I shall show, the urgency 'is great—can be explained without any resort to recrimination or to blame. 'It is due, in the main, to two very obvious causes. It is due, first of all, 'to the unprecedented scale upon which ammunition on both sides has been, 'and is being, expended. *It not only goes far beyond all previous experience, 'but it is greatly in advance of the forecasts of the best experts.*"—Mr. Asquith at Newcastle, April 20, 1915.

[2] There has certainly been no lack of appointments either of committees or individuals. So lately as the 7th of April the newspapers announced a War Office Committee "to secure that the supply of munitions of war shall 'be sufficient to meet all requirements." About a week later came the announcement of a still more august committee—'The Output Committee' —with Mr. Lloyd-George as Chairman and Mr. Balfour as a member of it. If war could be won by appointing committees and creating posts, victory ought long ago to have been secured.

CHAPTER V.

been as impeccable as the foresight and energy of the Government.

Material of war.

The country found it difficult to reconcile these various statements one with another. It found it still more difficult to reconcile Mr. Asquith's assurances with what it had heard, not only from other Ministers, but from generals in their published communications. Private letters from the front for months past had told a very different story from that which was told, in soothing tones, to the Newcastle audience. These had laid stress upon the heavy price paid in casualties, and the heavy handicap imposed on military operations, owing to shortage of artillery ammunition. The appointment of the Committee alone was wholly credited; the rest of these assurances were disbelieved.

Indeed it was impossible to doubt that there had been miscalculation and want of foresight in various directions; and it would have been better to admit it frankly. The blame, however, did not rest upon Lord Kitchener's shoulders, but upon those of his colleagues. They understood the industrial conditions of the United Kingdom; he did not and could not; and they must have been well aware of this fact. It was not Lord Kitchener's business, nor had he the time, to make himself familiar with those matters which are so well understood by the Board of Trade, the Local Government Board, and the Treasury. His business was to help France, to get recruits as best he could, to train them as soon as he could, and to send them out to beat the Germans. It was the business of the Government—expert in British political and industrial conditions—to put him in the way of getting his recruits, and the equipment,

Material of war.

supplies, and munitions of war which were necessary for making them effective.[1]

[1] Since this chapter was printed (May 1915) public opinion has been somewhat distracted by a sensational wrangle as to whether or not the *right kind* of ammunition had been supplied. These are technical matters upon which the ordinary man is no judge. The main point is that—certainly until quite recently—*enough* ammunition was not supplied; nor anything like enough; and this was due to the failure to look far enough ahead in the early days of the war; and to organise our industrial system to meet the inevitable requirements.

CHAPTER VI

METHODS OF RECRUITING

CHAPTER VI.

Methods of recruiting.

IF Lord Kitchener is not to be held primarily responsible for the delay in providing war material, just as little is he to be blamed for the methods of recruiting. For he had to take what the politicians told him. He had to accept their sagacious views of what the people would stand; of 'what they would never stand'; of what 'from the House of Commons' standpoint' was practicable or impracticable.

Lord Kitchener wanted men. During August and September he wanted them at once—without a moment's delay. Obviously the right plan was to ask in a loud voice who would volunteer; to take as many of these as it was possible to house, clothe, feed, and train; then to sit down quietly and consider how many more were likely to be wanted, at what dates, and how best they could be got. But as regards the first quarter of a million or so, which there were means for training at once, there was only one way—to call loudly for volunteers. The case was one of desperate urgency, and as things then stood, it would have been the merest pedantry to delay matters until a system, for which not even a scheme or skeleton existed before the emergency arose, had been devised. The rough and ready

Methods of recruiting.

method of calling out loudly was open to many objections on the score both of justice and efficiency, but the all-important thing was to save time.

Presumably, by and by, when the first rush was over, the Cabinet did sit down round a table to talk things over. We may surmise the character of the conversation which was then poured into Lord Kitchener's ears—how England would never stand this or that; how no freeborn Englishman—especially north of the Humber and the Trent,[1] whence the Liberal party drew its chief support—would tolerate being tapped on the shoulder and told to his face by Government what his duty was; how much less would he stand being coerced by Government into doing it; how he must be tapped on the shoulder and told by other people; how he must be coerced by other people; how pressure must be put on by private persons—employers by threats of dismissal—young females of good, bad, and indifferent character by blandishments and disdain. The fear of starvation for the freeborn Englishman and his family—at that time a real and present danger with many minds—or the shame of receiving a white feather, were the forces by which England and the Empire were to be saved at this time of trial. Moreover, would it not lead to every kind of evil if, at this juncture, the country were to become annoyed with the Government? Better surely that it should become annoyed with any one rather than the Government, whose patriotic duty, therefore, was to avoid unpopularity with more devoted vigilance than heretofore, if such a thing were possible.

One can imagine Lord Kitchener—somewhat weary

[1] Cf. Mr. Runciman, *ante*, p. 344.

CHAPTER VI.

Methods of recruiting.

of discussions in this airy region, and sorely perplexed by all these cobwebs of the party system—insisting doggedly that his business was to make a New Army, and to come to the assistance of France, without a day's unnecessary delay. He must have the men; how was he to get the men?

And one can imagine the response. "Put your 'trust in us, and we will get you the men. We 'will go on shouting. We will shout louder and 'louder. We will paste up larger and larger pictures 'on the hoardings. We will fill whole pages of 'the newspapers with advertisements drawn up 'by the 'livest publicity artists' of the day. We 'will enlist the sympathies and support of the 'press—for this is not an Oriental despotism, but 'a free country, where the power of the press is 'absolute. And if the sympathies of the press are 'cool, or their support hangs back, we will threaten 'them with the Press Bureau. We will tell the 'country-gentlemen, and the men-of-business, that 'it is *their* duty to put on the screw; and most of 'these, being easily hypnotised by the word 'duty,' 'will never dream of refusing. If their action is 'resented, and they become disliked it will be 'very regrettable; but taking a broad view, this 'will not be injurious to the Liberal party in the 'long run.

"Leave this little matter, Lord Kitchener, to 'experts. Lend your great name. Allow us to 'show your effigies to the people. Consider what a 'personal triumph for yourself if, at the end of this 'great war, we can say on platforms that you and we 'together have won it on the Voluntary System. 'Trust in us and our methods. We will boom your

Methods of recruiting.

'New Army, and we will see to it at the same time 'that the Government does not become unpopular, 'and also, if possible, that the Empire is saved."

So they boomed the Voluntary System and the New Army in Periclean passages; touched with awe the solemn chords; shouted as if it had been Jericho.

Two specimens, out of a large number of a similar sort—the joint handiwork apparently of the 'publicity artists,' bettering the moving appeals of the late Mr. Barnum, and of the party managers, inspired by the traditions of that incomparable ex-whip, Lord Murray of Elibank—are given below.[1] It is of course impossible to do justice here to the splendour of headlines and leaded capitals; but the nature of the appeal will be gathered clearly enough. Briefly, the motive of it was to avoid direct compulsion by Government—which would have fallen equally and fairly upon all—and to substitute for this, indirect compulsion and pressure by private individuals—which must of necessity operate unequally, unfairly, and invidiously. To say that this sort of thing is not compulsion, is to say what is untrue. If, as appears to be the case, the voluntary system has broken down, and we are to have compulsion, most honest men and women will prefer that the compulsion should be fair rather than unfair, direct rather than indirect, and that it should be exercised by those responsible for the government of the country, rather than by private persons who cannot compel, but can only penalise.

[1] (A) Four questions to the women of England.

1. You have read what the Germans have done in Belgium. Have you thought what they would do if they invaded England?

2. Do you realise that the safety of your Home and Children depends on our getting more men *now*?

CHAPTER VI.

Methods of recruiting.

By these means, during the past six months, a great army has been got together—an army great in numbers,[1] still greater in spirit; probably one of the noblest armies ever recruited in any cause. And Lord Kitchener has done his part by training this army with incomparable energy, and by infusing into officers and men alike his own indomitable resolution.

The high quality of the New Army is due to the fact that the bulk of it consists of two kinds of men, who of all others are the best material for soldiers. It consists of men who love fighting for its own sake—a small class. It also consists of men who hate fighting, but whose sense of duty is their guiding principle—fortunately a very large class. It consists of many others as well, driven on by divers motives. But the spirit of the New Army—according to the

---

3. Do you realise that the one word "Go" from *you* may send another man to fight for our King and Country?

4. When the War is over and your husband or your son is asked 'What did you do in the great War?'—is he to hang his head because *you* would not let him go?

Women of England do your duty! Send your men *to-day* to join our glorious Army.

GOD SAVE THE KING.

(B) Five questions to those who employ male servants.

1. Have you a butler, groom, chauffeur, gardener, or gamekeeper serving *you* who, at this moment should be serving your King and Country?

2. Have you a man serving at your table who should be serving a gun?

3. Have you a man digging your garden who should be digging trenches?

4. Have you a man driving your car who should be driving a transport wagon?

5. Have you a man preserving your game who should be helping to preserve your Country?

A great responsibility rests on you. Will you sacrifice your personal convenience for your Country's need?

Ask your men to enlist *to-day*.

The address of the nearest Recruiting Office can be obtained at any Post Office.

GOD SAVE THE KING.

[1] How many we have not been told; but that the numbers whatever they may be do not yet reach nearly what is still required we know from the frantic character of the most recent advertisements.

Methods of recruiting.

accounts of those who are in the best position to judge—is the spirit of the first two classes—of the fighters and the sense-of-duty men. It is these who have leavened it throughout.

This magnificent result—for it is magnificent, whatever may be thought of the methods which achieved it—has been claimed in many quarters—Liberal, Unionist, and non-party—as a triumph for the voluntary system. But if we proceed to question it, how voluntary was it really? Also how just? Did the New Army include all, or anything like all, those whose clear duty it was to join? And did it not include many people who ought never to have been asked to join, or even allowed to join, until others—whose ages, occupations, and responsibilities marked them out for the first levies—had all been called up?

There is also a further question—did the country, reading these various advertisements and placards—heroic, melodramatic, pathetic, and facetious—did the country form a true conception of the gravity of the position? Was it not in many cases confused and perplexed by the nature of the appeal? Did not many people conclude, that things could not really be so very serious, if those in authority resorted to such flamboyant and sensational methods—methods so conspicuously lacking in dignity, so inconsistent with all previous ideas of the majesty of Government in times of national peril?

The method itself, no doubt, was only unfamiliar in so far as it used the King's name. It was familiar and common enough in other connections. But a method which might have been unexceptionable for calling attention to the virtues of a shop, a soap, a

CHAPTER VI.

Methods of recruiting.

circus, or a pill, seemed inappropriate in the case of a great nation struggling at the crisis of its fate.[1]

Each of us must judge from his own experience of the effect produced. The writer has heard harsher things said of these appeals by the poor, than by the well-to-do. The simplest and least sophisticated minds are often the severest critics in matters of taste as well as morals. And this was a matter of both. Among townspeople as well as countryfolk there were many who—whether they believed or disbelieved in the urgent need, whether they responded to the appeal or did not respond to it—regarded the whole of this 'publicity' campaign with distrust and dislike, as a thing which demoralised the country, which was revolting to its honour and conscience, and in which the King's name ought never to have been used.[2]

[1] With apologies for the dialect, in which I am not an expert, I venture to set out the gist of a reply given to a friend who set himself to find out why recruiting was going badly in a Devonshire village. . . . "We do-ant 'think nought, Zur, o' them advertaizements and noospaper talk about 'going soldgering. When Guv'ment needs soldgers really sore, Guv'ment 'll 'say so clear enough, like it does when it wants taxes—'*Come 'long, 'Frank Halls, you're wanted.*' . . . And when Guv'ment taps Frank Halls 'on showlder, and sez this, I'll go right enough; but I'll not stir foot till 'Guv'ment does; nor'll any man of sense this zide Exeter."

[2] The following letter which appeared in the *Westminster Gazette* (January 20, 1915), states the case so admirably that I have taken the liberty of quoting it in full:

"DEAR SIR—Every day you tell your readers that we are collecting 'troops by means of voluntary enlistment, yet it is self-evident that our 'recruiting campaign from the first has been a very noisy and a very vulgar 'compulsion, which in a time of immense crisis has lowered the dignity of 'our country and provoked much anxiety among our Allies. Our national 'habit of doing the right thing in the wrong way has never been exercised 'in a more slovenly and unjust manner. It is a crime against morals not 'to use the equitable principles of national service when our country is 'fighting for her life; and this obvious truth should be recognised as a 'matter of course by every true democrat. A genuinely democratic people, 'proud of their past history, and determined to hold their own against 'Germany's blood-lust, would have divided her male population into classes, 'and would have summoned each class to the colours at a given date. 'Those who were essential to the leading trades of the country would have 'been exempted from war service in the field, as they are in Germany;

Methods of recruiting.

On the part of the working-classes there were other objections to the methods employed. They resented the hints and instructions which were so obligingly given by the 'publicity artists' and the 'party managers' to the well-to-do classes—to employers of all sorts—as to how they should bring pressure to bear upon their dependents. And they resented—especially the older men and those with family responsibilities—the manner in which they were invited by means of circulars to signify their willingness to serve—as they imagined in the last dire necessity—and when they had agreed patriotically to do so, found themselves shortly afterwards called upon to fulfil their contract. For they knew that in the neighbouring village—or in the very next house—there were men much more eligible for military

'the younger classes would have been called up first, and no class would 'have been withdrawn from its civil work until the military authorities 'were ready to train it. Instead of this quiet and dignified justice, this 'admirable and quiet unity of a free people inspired by a fine patriotism, 'we have dazed ourselves with shrieking posters and a journalistic clamour 'against 'shirkers,' and loud abuse of professional footballers; and now 'an advertisement in the newspapers assures the women of England that '*they* must do what the State declines to achieve, that they must send their 'men and boys into the field since their country is fighting for her life. What 'cowardice! Why impose this voluntary duty on women when the State 'is too ignoble to look upon her own duty in this matter as a moral obligation?

"The one virtue of voluntary enlistment is that it should be voluntary—'a free choice between a soldier's life and a civilian's life. To use moral 'pressure, with the outcries of public indignation, in order to drive civilians 'from their work into the army—what is this but a most undignified com-'pulsion? And it is also a compulsion that presses unequally upon the 'people, for its methods are without system. Many families send their 'all into the fighting line; many decline to be patriotic. A woman said 'to me yesterday: 'My husband has gone, and I am left with his business. 'Why should he go? Other women in my neighbourhood have their 'husbands still, and it's rubbish to say that the country is in danger when 'the Government allows and encourages this injustice in recruiting. If 'the country is in danger all the men should fight—if their trade work is 'unnecessary to the armies.'

"This point of view is right; the wrong one is advocated by you and by 'other Radicals who dislike the justice of democratic equality.—Yours 'truly, WALTER SHAW SPARROW."

CHAPTER VI.

Methods of recruiting.

service in point of age and freedom from family responsibilities, who, not having either volunteered, or filled up the circular, were accordingly left undisturbed to go about their daily business.[1]

The attitude of the country generally at the outbreak of war was admirable. It was what it should have been—as on a ship after a collision, where crew and passengers, all under self-command, and without panic, await orders patiently. So the country waited—waited for clear orders—waited to be told, in tones free from all ambiguity and hesitation, what they were to do as classes and as individuals. There was very little fuss or confusion. People were somewhat dazed for a short while by the financial crisis; but the worst of that was soon over. They then said to themselves, "Let us get on with our ordinary 'work as hard as usual (or even harder), until we 'receive orders from those responsible for the ship's 'safety, telling us what we are to do."

There was a certain amount of sparring, then and subsequently, between high-minded journalists, who

[1] There have been bitter complaints of this artful way of getting recruits, as a boy 'sniggles' trout. The following letter to the *Times* (April 21, 1915) voices a very widely spread sense of injustice:

"SIR—Will you give me the opportunity to ask a question, which I 'think you will agree is important? When the Circular to Householders 'was issued, many heads of families gave in their names on the assumption 'that they would be called up on the last resort, and under circumstances 'in which no patriotic man could refuse his help. Married men with large 'families are now being called up apparently without the slightest regard 'to their home circumstances. Many of the best of them are surprised and 'uneasy at leaving their families, but feel bound in honour to keep their 'word, some even thinking they have no choice. The separation allowances 'for these families will be an immense burden on the State, and, if the 'breadwinner falls, a permanent burden. Is the need for men still so 'serious and urgent as to justify this? If it is, then I for one, who have 'up to now hoped that the war might be put through without compulsion, 'feel that the time has come to 'fetch' the unmarried shirkers, and I 'believe there is a wide-spread and growing feeling to that effect.—I am, 'Sir, etc., CHARLES G. E. WELBY."

Methods of recruiting,

were engaged in carrying on their own *business as usual*, and hard-headed traders and manufacturers who desired to do likewise. The former were perhaps a trifle too self-righteous, while the latter took more credit than they deserved for patriotism, seeing that their chief merit was common sense. To have stopped the business of the country would have done nobody but the Germans any good, and would have added greatly to our national embarrassment.

At times of national crisis, there will always be a tendency, among most men and women, to misgivings, lest they may not be doing the full measure of their duty. Their consciences become morbidly active; it is inevitable that they should; indeed it would be regrettable if they did not. People are uncomfortable, unless they are doing something they have never done before, which they dislike doing, and which they do less well than their ordinary work. In many cases what they are inspired to do is less useful than would have been their ordinary work, well and thoughtfully done. At such times as these the *Society for Setting Everybody Right* always increases its activities, and enrols a large number of new members. But very soon, if there is leadership of the nation, things fall into their proper places and proportions. Neither business nor pleasure can be carried on as usual, and everybody knows it. There must be great changes; but not merely for the sake of change. There must be great sacrifices in many cases; and those who are doing well must give a helping hand to those others who are doing ill. But all—whether they are doing well or ill from the standpoint of their own private interests—must be prepared to do what the leader of the nation orders them to do.

CHAPTER VI.

Methods of recruiting.

This was fully recognised in August, September, October, and November last. The country expected orders—clear and unmistakable orders—and it was prepared to obey whatever orders it received.

But no orders came. Instead of orders there were appeals, warnings, suggestions, assurances. The panic-monger was let loose with his paint-box of horrors. The diffident parliamentarian fell to his usual methods of soothing, and coaxing, and shaming people into doing a very vague and much-qualified thing, which he termed their duty. But there was no clearness, no firmness. An ordinary man will realise his duty so soon as he receives a definite command, and not before. He received no such command; he was lauded, lectured, and exhorted; and then was left to decide upon his course of action by the light of his own reason and conscience.[1]

He was not even given a plain statement of the

[1] An example of the apparent inability of the Government to do anything thoroughly or courageously is found in a circular letter to shopkeepers and wholesale firms, which was lately sent out by the Home Secretary and the President of the Board of Trade. The object of this enquiry—undertaken at leisure, nine months after the outbreak of war—is to obtain information as to the number of men of military age, who are still employed in these particular trades, and as to the willingness of their employers to spare them if required, and to reinstate them at the end of the war, etc., etc.

The timid futility of this attempt at organising the resources of the country is shown *first* by the fact that it left to the option of each employer whether he will reply or not. Businesses which do not wish to have their employees taken away need not give an answer. It is compulsory for individuals to disclose all particulars of their income; why, therefore, need Government shrink from making it compulsory upon firms to disclose all particulars of their staffs? . . . The *second* vice of this application is that the information asked for is quite inadequate for the object. Even if the enquiry were answered faithfully by every employer and householder in the country, it would not give the Government what they require for the purposes of organising industry or recruiting the army. . . . In the *third* place, a certain group of trades is singled out at haphazard. If it is desired to organise the resources of the country what is needed is a general census of all males between 16 and 60.

One does not know whether to marvel most at the belated timorousness of this enquiry, or at the slatternly way in which it has been framed.

Methods of recruiting.

true facts of the situation, and then left at peace to determine what he would do. He was disturbed in his meditations by shouting—more shouting—ever louder and louder shouting—through some thousands of megaphones. The nature of the appeal was emotional, confusing, frenzied, and at times degrading. Naturally the results were in many directions most unsatisfactory, unbusinesslike, and disorderly. The drain of recruiting affected industries and individuals not only unequally and unfairly, but in a way contrary to the public interest. If Government will not exercise guidance and control in unprecedented circumstances, it is inevitable that the country must suffer.

To judge from the placards and the posters, the pictures and the language, a casual stranger would not have judged that the British Empire stood at the crisis of its fate; but rather that some World's Fair was arriving shortly, and that these were the preliminary flourishes. Lord Kitchener cannot have enjoyed the pre-eminence which was allotted to him in our mural decorations, and which suggested that he was some kind of co-equal with the famous Barnum or Lord George Sanger. Probably no one alive hated the whole of this orgie of vulgar sensationalism, which the timidity of the politicians had forced upon the country, more than he did.[1]

[1] One who is no longer alive—Queen Victoria—would possibly have hated it even more. Imagine her late Majesty's feelings on seeing the walls of Windsor plastered with the legend—'*Be a sport: Join to-day*'—and with other appeals of the same elevating character! . . . But perhaps the poster which is more remarkable than any other—considering the source from which it springs—is one showing a garish but recognisable portrait of Lord Roberts, with the motto, '*He did his duty. Will you do yours?*' If the timidity of politicians is apparent in certain directions, their courage is no less noteworthy in others. The courage of a Government (containing as it does Mr. Asquith, Lord Haldane, Mr. Runciman, Sir John Simon,

CHAPTER VI.

Methods of recruiting.

Having stirred up good and true men to join the New Army, whether it was rightly their turn or not; having got at others in whom the voluntary spirit burned less brightly, by urging their employers to dismiss them and their sweethearts to throw them over if they refused the call of duty, the 'publicity artists' and the 'party managers' between them undoubtedly collected for Lord Kitchener a very fine army, possibly the finest raw material for an army which has ever been got together. And Lord Kitchener, thereupon, set to work, and trained this army as no one but Lord Kitchener could have trained it.

These results were a source of great pride and self-congratulation among the politicians. The voluntary principle—you see how it works! What a triumph! What other nation could have done the same?

Other nations certainly could not have done the same, for the reason that there are some things which one cannot do twice over, some things which one cannot give a second time—one's life for example, or the flower of the manhood of a nation to be made into soldiers.

Other nations could not have done what we were doing, because they had done it already. They had their men prepared when the need arose—which we had not. Other nations were engaged in holding the common enemy at enormous sacrifices until we made ourselves ready; until we — triumphing in our

---

Mr. Harcourt, and Mr. Acland—not to mention others) which can issue such a poster must be of a very high order indeed. One wonders, however, if this placard would not be more convincing, and its effect even greater, were the motto amplified, so as to tell the whole story: "*He did his duty; 'we denounced him for doing it. We failed to do ours; will you, however, 'do yours?*"

Methods of recruiting.

voluntary system, covering ourselves in self-praise, and declaring to the world, through the mouths of Sir John Simon and other statesmen, that each of our men was worth at least three of their 'pressed men' or conscripts—until we came up leisurely with reinforcements—six, nine, or twelve months hence—supposing that by such time, there was anything still left to come up for. If the Germans were then in Paris, Bordeaux, Brest, and Marseilles, there would be—temporarily at least—a great saving of mortality among the British race. If, on the other hand, the Allies had already arrived at Berlin without us, what greater triumph for the voluntary principle could possibly be imagined?

Putting these views and considerations—which have so much impressed us all in our own recent discussions—before a French officer, I found him obstinate in viewing the matter at a different angle. He was inclined to lay stress on the case of Northern France, and even more on that of Belgium, whose resistance to the German invasion we had wished for and encouraged, and who was engaged in fighting our battles quite as much as her own. The voluntary principle, in spite of its triumphs at home—which he was not concerned to dispute—had not, he thought, as yet been remarkably triumphant abroad; and nine months had gone by since war began.

He insisted, moreover, that for years before war was declared, our great British statesmen could not have been ignorant of the European situation, either in its political or its military aspects. Such ignorance was inconceivable. They must have suspected the intentions of Germany, and they must have known the numbers of her army. England had common

CHAPTER VI.

Methods of recruiting.

interests with France. Common interests, if there be a loyal understanding, involve equal sacrifices—equality of sacrifice not merely when the push comes, but in advance of the crisis, in preparation for it—a much more difficult matter. Why then had not our Government told the British people long ago what sacrifice its safety, no less than its honour, required of it to give?

I felt, after talking to my friend for some time, that although he rated our nation in some ways very highly indeed, although he was grateful for our assistance, hopeful of the future, confident that in Lord Kitchener we had found our man, nothing—nothing—not even selections from Mr. Spender's articles in the *Westminster Gazette*, or from Sir John Simon's speeches, or Sir John Brunner's assurances about the protection afforded by international law—could induce him to share our own enthusiasm for the voluntary system. . . . *The triumph of the voluntary system*, he cried bitterly, *is a German triumph: it is the ruin of Belgium and the devastation of France.*

And looking at the matter from a Frenchman's point of view, there is something to be said for his contention.

Apart from any objections which may exist to British methods of recruiting since war broke out—to their injustice, want of dignity, and generally to their demoralising effect on public opinion—there are several still more urgent questions to be considered. Have those methods been adequate? And if so, are they going to continue adequate to the end? Is there, in short, any practical need for conscription?

Methods of recruiting.

We do not answer these questions by insisting that, if there had been conscription in the past, we should have been in a much stronger position when war broke out; or by proving to our own satisfaction, that if we had possessed a national army, war would never have occurred. Such considerations as these are by no means done with; they are indeed still very important; but they lie rather aside from the immediate question with which we are now faced, and which, for lack of any clear guidance from those in authority, many of us have been endeavouring of late to solve by the light of our own judgment.

The answer which the facts supply does not seem to be in any doubt. We need conscription to bring this war to a victorious conclusion. We need conscription no less in order that we may impose terms of lasting peace. Conscription is essential to the proper organisation not only of our manhood, but also of our national resources.[1] Judging by the increasing size, frequency, and shrillness of recent recruiting advertisements, conscription would seem to be equally essential in order to secure the number of recruits necessary for making good the wastage of war, even in the present preliminary stage of the war. And morally, conscription is essential in order that the whole nation may realise, before it is too late, the life-or-death nature of the present struggle; in order also that other nations—our Allies as well as our enemies—may understand—what they certainly do not understand at present—that our spirit is as firm and self-sacrificing as their own.

The voluntary system has broken down long ago.

[1] This aspect is very cogently stated in Mr. Shaw Sparrow's letter to the *Westminster Gazette* quoted on pp. 370-371.

CHAPTER VI.

Methods of recruiting.

It broke down on the day when the King of England declared war upon the Emperor of Germany. From that moment it was obvious that, in a prolonged war, the voluntary system could not be relied upon to give us, in an orderly and businesslike way, the numbers which we should certainly require. It was also obvious that it was just as inadequate for the purpose of introducing speed, order, and efficiency into the industrial world, as strength into our military affairs.

So far, however, most of the accredited oracles of Government have either denounced national military service as un-English, and a sin against freedom; or else they have evaded the issue, consoling their various audiences with the reflection, that it will be time enough to talk of compulsion, when it is clearly demonstrated that the voluntary system can no longer give us what we need. It seems improvident to wait until the need has been proved by the painful process of failure. The curses of many dead nations lie upon the procrastination of statesmen, who waited for breakdown to prove the necessity of sacrifice. Compulsion, like other great changes, cannot be systematised and put through in a day. It needs preparation. If the shoe begins to pinch severely in August, and we only then determine to adopt conscription, what relief can we hope to experience before the following midsummer? And in what condition of lameness may the British Empire be by then?

"But what," it may be asked, "of all the official 'and semi-official statements which have been uttered 'in a contrary sense? Surely the nation is bound 'to trust its own Government, even although no ‘facts and figures are offered in support of their ‘assurances.’’

CHAPTER VI.

Methods of recruiting.

Unfortunately it is impossible to place an implicit faith in official and semi-official statements, unless we have certain knowledge that they are confirmed by the facts. There has been an abundance of such statements in recent years—with regard to the innocence of Germany's intentions — with regard to the adequacy of our own preparations — while only a few weeks ago Mr. Asquith himself was assuring us that neither the operations of our own army, nor those of our Allies' armies, had ever been crippled, or even hampered, by any want of munitions.

When, therefore, assurances flow from the same source—assurances that there is no need for compulsory military service—that the voluntary system has given, is giving, and will continue to give us all we require—we may be forgiven for expressing our incredulity. Such official and semi-official statements are not supported by any clear proofs. They are contradicted by much that we have heard from persons who are both honest, and in a position to know. They are discredited by our own eyes when we read the recruiting advertisements and posters. It seems safer, therefore, to dismiss these official and semi-official assurances, and trust for once to our instinct and the evidence of our own senses. It seems safer also not to wait for complete breakdown in war, or mortifying failure in negotiations for peace, in order to have the need for national service established beyond a doubt.

CHAPTER VII

PERVERSITIES OF THE ANTI-MILITARIST SPIRIT

CHAPTER VII.

Perversities of the anti-militarist spirit.

IF 'National Service,' or 'Conscription,' has actually become necessary already, or may conceivably become so before long, it seems worth while to glance at some of the considerations which have been urged in favour of this system in the past, and also to examine some of the causes and conditions which have hitherto led public opinion in the United Kingdom, as well as in several of the Dominions, to regard the principle of compulsion with hostility and distrust. The true nature of what we call the 'Voluntary System,' and the reasons which have induced a large section of our fellow-countrymen to regard it as one of our most sacred institutions, are worth looking into, now that circumstances may force us to abandon it in the near future.

Beyond the question, whether the system of recruiting, which has been employed during the present war, can correctly be described as 'voluntary,' there is the further question, whether the system, which is in use at ordinary times, and which produces some 35,000 men per annum, can be so described. Lord Roberts always maintained that it could not, and that its true title was 'the Conscription of Hunger.'

Perversities of the anti-militarist spirit.

Any one who has watched the recruiting-sergeant at work, on a raw cold day of winter or early spring, will be inclined to agree with Lord Roberts. A fine, good-humoured, well-fed, well-set-up fellow, in a handsome uniform, with rows of medals which light up the mean and dingy street, lays himself alongside some half-starved poor devil, down in his luck, with not a rag to his back that the north wind doesn't blow through. The appetites and vanities of the latter are all of them morbidly alert—hunger, thirst, the desire for warmth, and to cut a smart figure in the world. The astute sergeant, though no professor of psychology, understands the case thoroughly, as he marks down his man. He greets him heartily with a 'good day' that sends a glow through him, even before the drink at the *Goat and Compasses*, or *Green Dragon* has been tossed off, and the King's shilling accepted.

Not that there is any need for pity or regret. These young men with empty bellies, and no very obvious way of filling them, except by violence—these lads with gloom at their hearts, in many cases with a burden of shame weighing on them at having come into such a forlorn pass—in nine cases out of ten enlistment saves them; perhaps in more even than that.

But talk about compulsion and the voluntary principle! What strikes the observer most about such a scene as this is certainly not anything which can be truly termed 'voluntary.' If one chooses to put things into ugly words—which is sometimes useful, in order to give a shock to good people who are tending towards self-righteousness in their worship of phrases—this is the compulsion of hunger and

CHAPTER VII.

Perversities of the anti-militarist spirit.

misery. It might even be contended that it was not only compulsion, but a mean, sniggling kind of compulsion, taking advantage of a starving man.

The law is very chary of enforcing promises made under duress. If a man dying of thirst signs his birthright away, or binds himself in service for a term of years, in exchange for a glass of water, the ink and paper have no validity. But the recruit is firmly bound. He has made a contract to give his labour, and to risk his life for a long period of years, at a wage which is certainly below the market rate; and he is held to it. Things much more 'voluntary' than this have been dubbed 'slavery,' and denounced as 'tainted with servile conditions.' And the loudest denunciators have been precisely those anti-militarists, who uphold our 'voluntary' system with the hottest fervour, while reprobating 'compulsion' with the utmost horror.

We have heard much caustic abuse of the National Service League. It has been accused of talking 'the cant of compulsion'; by which has been meant that certain of its members have put in the forefront of their argument the moral and physical advantages which they imagine universal military training would confer upon the nation. Some may possibly have gone too far, and lost sight of the need of the nation, in their enthusiasm for the improvement of the individual. But if occasionally their arguments assume the form of cant, can their lapse be compared with the cant which tells the world smugly that the British Army is recruited on the voluntary principle?

The 'economic argument,' as it is called, is another example. The country would be faced with

CHAPTER VII.

Perversities of the anti-militarist spirit.

ruin, we are told, if every able-bodied man had to give 'two of the best years of his life,'[1] and a week or two out of each of the ensuing seven, to 'unproductive' labour. Sums have been worked out to hundreds of millions sterling, with the object of showing that the national loss, during a single generation, would make the national debt appear insignificant. How could Britain maintain her industrial pre-eminence weighted with such a handicap?

One answer is that Britain, buoyed up though she has been by her voluntary system, has not lately been outstripping those of her competitors who carried this very handicap which it is now proposed that she should carry; that she has not even been maintaining her relative position in the industrial world in comparison, for example, with Germany.

But there is also another answer. If you take a youth at the plastic age when he has reached manhood, feed him on wholesome food, subject him to vigorous and varied exercise, mainly in the open air, discipline him, train him to co-operation with his fellows, make him smart and swift in falling-to at whatever work comes under his hand, you are thereby giving him precisely what, for his own sake and that of the country, is most needed at the present time. You are giving him the chance of developing his bodily strength under healthy conditions, and you are giving him a general education and moral training which, in the great majority of cases, will be of great value to him in all his after life.

It is the regret of every one, who has studied our industrial system from within, that men wear out too

[1] This was the German period of training for infantry. The National Service League proposal was four months.

Perversities of the anti-militarist spirit.

soon. By the time a man reaches his fortieth year—often earlier—he is too apt, in many vocations, to be an old man; and for that reason he is in danger of being shoved out of his place by a younger generation.

This premature and, for the most part, unnecessary ageing is the real economic loss. If by taking two years out of a man's life as he enters manhood, if by improving his physique and helping him to form healthy habits, you can thereby add on ten or fifteen years to his industrial efficiency, you are not only contributing to his own happiness, but are also adding enormously to the wealth and prosperity of the country. Any one indeed, who chooses to work out sums upon this hypothesis, will hardly regard the national debt as a large enough unit for comparison.

The kernel of this matter is, that men wear out in the working classes earlier than in others, mainly because they have no break, no rest, no change, from the day they leave school to take up a trade, till the day when they have to hand in their checks for good and all. It is not effort, but drudgery, which most quickly ages a man. It is the rut—straight, dark, narrow, with no horizons, and no general view of the outside world—which is the greatest of social dangers. More than anything else it tends to narrowness of sympathy and bitterness of heart.

It would be cant to claim that universal military training will get rid of this secular evil; but to say that it will help to diminish it is merely the truth. The real 'cant' is to talk about the economic loss under conscription; for there would undoubtedly be an immense economic gain.

But indeed the advocacy of the voluntary system

Perversities of the anti-militarist spirit.

is stuffed full of cant. . . . We are all proud of our army; and rightly so. But the opponents of universal military service go much further in this direction than the soldiers themselves. They contrast our army, to its enormous advantage, with the conscript armies of the continent, which they regard as consisting of vastly inferior fighting men—of men, in a sense despicable, inasmuch as their meek spirits have submitted tamely to conscription.

Colonel Seely, who, when he touches arithmetic soars at once into the region of poetry, has pronounced confidently that one of our voluntary soldiers is worth ten men whom the law compels to serve. Sir John Simon was still of opinion—even after several months of war—that one of our volunteers was worth at least three conscripts; and he was convinced that the Kaiser himself already knew it. What a splendid thing if Colonel Seely were right, or even if Sir John Simon were right!

But is either of them right? So far as our voluntary army is superior—and it was undoubtedly superior in certain respects at the beginning of the war—it was surely not because it was a 'voluntary' army; but because, on the average, it had undergone a longer and more thorough course of training than the troops against which it was called upon to fight. Fine as its spirit was, and high as were both its courage and its intelligence, who has ever heard a single soldier maintain that—measured through and through—it was in those respects superior to the troops alongside which, or against which it fought?

As the war has continued month after month, and men with only a few months' training have been

CHAPTER VII.

Perversities of the anti-militarist spirit.

drafted across the Channel to supply the British wastage of war, even this initial superiority which came of longer and more thorough training has gradually been worn away. A time will come, no doubt—possibly it has already come—when Germany, having used up her trained soldiers of sound physique, has to fall back upon an inferior quality. But that is merely exhaustion. It does not prove the superiority of the voluntary system. It does not affect the comparison between men of equal stamina and spirit—one set of whom has been trained beforehand in arms—the other not put into training until war began.

Possibly Colonel Seely spoke somewhat lightly and thoughtlessly in those serene days before the war-cloud burst; but Sir John Simon spoke deliberately—his was the voice of the Cabinet, after months of grim warfare. To describe his utterances as cant does not seem unjust, though possibly it is inadequate.

We are proud of our army, not merely because of its fine qualities, but for the very fact that it is what we choose to call a 'voluntary' army. But what do they say of it in foreign countries? What did the whole of Europe say of it during the South African War? What are the Germans saying of it now?

Naturally prejudice has led them to view the facts at a different angle. They have seldom referred to the 'voluntary' character of our army. That was not the aspect which attracted their attention, so much as the other aspect, that our soldiers received pay, and therefore, according to German notions, 'fought for hire.' At the time of the South African War all continental nations said of our army what

CHAPTER VII.

the Germans still say—not that it was a 'voluntary' army, but that it was a 'mercenary' army; and this is a much less pleasant-sounding term.[1]

Perversities of the anti-militarist spirit.

In this accusation we find the other kind of cant—the cant of militarism. For if ours is a mercenary army, so is their own, in so far as the officers and non-commissioned officers are concerned. But as a matter of fact no part, either of our army or the existing German army, can with any truth be described as 'mercenaries'; for this is a term applicable only to armies—much more common in the past in Germany than anywhere else—who were hired out to fight abroad in quarrels which were not their own.

But although this German accusation against the character of our troops is pure cant, it would not be wholly so were it levelled against the British people. Not our army, but we ourselves, are the true mercenaries; because we pay others to do for us what other nations do for themselves. In German eyes—and perhaps in other eyes as well, which are less willing to see our faults—this charge against the British people appears maintainable. It is incomprehensible to other nations, why we should refuse to recognise that it is any part of our duty, *as a people*, to defend our country; why we will not admit the obligation either to train ourselves to arms in time of peace, or to risk our lives in time of war; why we hold obstinately to it that such things are no part of

[1] The pay of the French private soldier is, I understand, about a sou—a halfpenny—a day. In his eyes the British soldier in the next trench, who receives from a shilling to eighteenpence a day—and in the case of married men a separation allowance as well—must appear as a kind of millionaire. During the South African War the pay of certain volunteer regiments reached the preposterous figure of five shilings a day for privates. Men serving with our army as motor drivers—in comparative safety—receive something like six shillings or seven and sixpence a day.

CHAPTER VII.

Perversities of the anti-militarist spirit.

our duty as a people, but are only the duty of private individuals who love fighting, or who are endowed with more than the average sense of duty.

"As for you, the great British People," writes Hexenküchen contemptuously, "you merely fold your 'hands, and say self-righteously, that your duty begins 'and ends with paying certain individuals to fight 'for you—individuals whose personal interest can be 'tempted with rewards; whose weakness of character 'can be influenced by taunts, and jeers, and threats 'of dismissal; or who happen to see their duty in a 'different light from the great majority which calls 'itself (and is *par excellence*) the British People. . . ." This may be a very prejudiced view of the matter, but it is the German view. What they really mean when they say that England is to be despised because she relies upon a mercenary army, is that England is to be despised because, being mercenary, she relies upon a professional army. The taunt, when we come to analyse it, is found to be levelled, not against the hired, but against the hirers; and although we may be very indignant, it is not easy to disprove its justice.

The British nation, if not actually the richest, is at any rate one of the richest in the world. It has elected to depend for its safety upon an army which cannot with justice be called either 'voluntary' or 'mercenary,' but which it is fairly near the truth to describe as 'professional.' The theory of our arrangement is that we must somehow, and at the cheapest rate, contrive to tempt enough men to become professional soldiers to ensure national safety. Accordingly we offer such inducements to take up

Perversities of the anti-militarist spirit.

the career of arms—instead of the trades of farm labourer, miner, carpenter, dock hand, shopkeeper, lawyer, physician, or stockbroker—as custom and the circumstances of the moment appear to require.

In an emergency we offer high pay and generous separation allowances to the private soldier. In normal times we give him less than the market rate of wages.

The pay of junior or subaltern officers is so meagre that it cannot, by any possibility, cover the expenses which Government insists upon their incurring. Captains, majors, and lieutenant-colonels are paid much less than the wages of foremen or sub-managers in any important industrial undertaking. Even for those who attain the most brilliant success in their careers, there are no prizes which will stand comparison for a moment with a very moderate degree of prosperity in the world of trade or finance. They cannot even be compared with the prizes open to the bar or the medical profession.

Hitherto we have obtained our officers largely owing to a firmly rooted tradition among the country gentlemen and the military families—neither as a rule rich men, or even very easy in their circumstances as things go nowadays—many of them very poor—a tradition so strong that it is not cant, but plain truth, to call it sense of duty. There are other motives, of course, which may lead a boy to choose this profession—love of adventure, comparative freedom from indoor life, pleasant comradeship, and in the case of the middle classes, recently risen to affluence, social aspirations. But even in the last there is far more good than harm; though in anti-militarist circles it is the unworthy aim which is usually dwelt upon with

CHAPTER VII.

Perversities of the anti-militarist spirit.

a sneering emphasis. For very often, when a man has risen from humble circumstances to a fortune, he rejoices that his sons should serve the state, since it is in his power to make provision. The example of his neighbours, whose ancestors have been living on their acres since the days of the Plantagenets or the Tudors, is a noble example; and he is wise to follow it.

In the case of the rank and file of our army, a contract for a term of years (with obligations continuing for a further term of years) is entered into, and signed, under the circumstances which have already been considered. We are faced here with a phenomenon which seems strange in an Age which has conceded the right to 'down tools,' even though by so doing a solemn engagement is broken—in an Age which has become very fastidious about hiring agreements of most kinds, very suspicious of anything suggestive of 'servile conditions' or 'forced labour,' and which deprecates the idea of penalising breach of contract, on the part of a workman, even by process in the civil courts.

As regards a private soldier in the British army, however, the Age apparently has no such compunctions. His contract has been made under duress. Its obligations last for a long period of years. The pay is below the ordinary market rates. Everything in fact which, in equity, would favour a revision, pleads in favour of the soldier who demands to be released. But let him plead and threaten as he please, he is not released. It is not a case of suing him for damages in the civil courts, but of dealing with him under discipline and mutiny acts, the terms of which are simple and drastic—

Perversities of the anti-militarist spirit.

in peace time imprisonment, in war time death. Without these means of enforcing the 'voluntary' system the British people would not feel themselves safe.

This phenomenon seems even stranger, when we remember that a large and influential part of the British people is not only very fastidious as to the terms of all other sorts of hiring agreements, as to rates of pay, and as to the conditions under which such contracts have been entered into—that it is not only most tender in dealing with the breach of such agreements—but that it also regards the object of the agreement for military service with particular suspicion. This section of the British people is anti-militarist on conscientious grounds. One would have thought, therefore, that it might have been more than usually careful to allow the man, who hires himself out for lethal purposes, to have the benefit of second thoughts; or even of third, fourth, and fifth thoughts. For he, too, may develop a conscience when his belly is no longer empty. But no: to do this would endanger the 'voluntary' system.

This anti-militarist section of the British people is composed of citizens who, if we are to believe their own professions, love peace more than other men love it, and hate violence as a deadly sin. They are determined not to commit this deadly sin themselves; but being unable to continue in pursuit of their material and spiritual affairs, unless others will sin in their behalf, they reluctantly agree to hire—at as low a price as possible—a number of wild fellows from the upper classes and wastrels from the lower classes—both of whom they regard as approximating to the reprobate type—to defend their property, to keep

Perversities of the anti-militarist spirit.

their lives safe, to enforce their Will as it is declared by ballot papers and House of Commons divisions, and to allow them to continue their careers of beneficent self-interest undisturbed.

But for all that, we are puzzled by the rigour with which the contract for military service is enforced, even to the last ounce of the pound of flesh. Not a murmur of protest comes from this section of the British people, although it has professed to take the rights of the poorer classes as its special province. The explanation probably is that, like King Charles I., they have made a mental reservation, and are thus enabled to distinguish the case of the soldier from that of his brother who engages in a civil occupation.

Roughly speaking, they choose to regard the civilian as virtuous, while the soldier, on the other hand, cannot safely be presumed to be anything of the sort. Sometimes indeed—perhaps more often than not—he appears to them to be distinctly unvirtuous. The presumption is against him; for if he were really virtuous, how could he ever have agreed to become a soldier, even under pressure of want? For regulating the service of such men as these force is a regrettable, but necessary, instrument. The unvirtuous man has agreed to sin, and the virtuous man acts justly in holding him to his bargain. If a soldier develops a conscience, and insists on 'downing tools' it is right to imprison him; even in certain circumstances to put him against a wall and shoot him.

These ideas wear an odd appearance when we come to examine them closely, and yet not only did they exist, but they were actually very prevalent down to the outbreak of the present war. They

Perversities of the anti-militarist spirit.

seem to be somewhat prevalent, even now, in various quarters. But surely it is strange that virtuous citizens should need the protection of unvirtuous ones; that they should underpay; that they should adopt the methods of 'forced labour' as a necessary part of the 'voluntary system'; that they should imprison and shoot men for breach of hiring agreements—hiring agreements for long periods of years, entered into under pressure of circumstances.

But there is a thing even stranger than any of these. Considering how jealous the great anti-militarist section of our fellow-countrymen is of anything which places the army in a position to encroach upon, or overawe, the civil power, it seems very remarkable that they should nevertheless have taken a large number of men—whose morals, in their view, were below rather than above the average—should have armed them with rifles and bayonets, and spent large sums of money in making them as efficient as possible for lethal purposes, while refusing firmly to arm *themselves* with anything but ballot-boxes, or to make themselves fit for any form of self-defence.

It seems never to have crossed the minds of the anti-militarist section that those whom they thus regard—if not actually with moral reprehension, at any rate somewhat askance—might perhaps some day discover that there were advantages in being armed, and in having become lethally efficient; that having studied the phenomena of strikes, and having there seen force of various kinds at work—hiring agreements broken, combinations to bring pressure on society successful, rather black things occasionally hushed up and forgiven—soldiers might draw their own conclusions. Having grown tired of pay lower

CHAPTER VII.

Perversities of the anti-militarist spirit.

than the market rate, still more tired of moral lectures about the wickedness of their particular trade, and of tiresome old-fashioned phrases about the subordination of the military to the civil power—what if they, like other trades and classes, should begin to consider the propriety of putting pressure on society, since such pressure appears nowadays to be one of the recognised instruments for redress of wrongs? . . . Have not professional soldiers the power to put pressure on society in the twentieth century, just as they have done, again and again, in past times in other kingdoms and democracies, where personal freedom was so highly esteemed, that even the freedom to abstain from defending your country was respected by public opinion and the laws of the land?

But nonsense! In Germany, France, Russia, Austria, Italy, and other conscript countries armies are hundreds of times stronger than our own, while the soldiers in these cases are hardly paid enough to keep a smoker in pipe-tobacco. And yet they do not think of putting pressure on society, or of anything so horrible. This of course is true; but then, in these instances, the Army is only Society itself passing, as it were, like a may-fly, through a certain stage in its life-history. Army and Society in the conscript countries are one and the same. A man does not think of putting undue pressure upon himself. But in our case the Army and Society are not one and the same. Their relations are those of employer and employed, as they were in Rome long ago; and as between employer and employed, there are always apt to be questions of pay and position.

It is useful in this connection to think a little of Rome with its 'voluntary' or 'mercenary' or

Perversities of the anti-militarist spirit.

'professional' army — an army underpaid at first, afterwards perhaps somewhat overpaid, when it occurred to its mind to put pressure on society.

But Rome in the first century was a very different place from England in the twentieth. Very different indeed! The art and rules of war were considerably less of an expert's business than they are to-day. Two thousand years ago—weapons being still somewhat elementary—gunpowder not yet discovered—no railway trains and tubes, and outer and inner circles, which now are as necessary for feeding great cities as arteries and veins for keeping the human heart going — private citizens, moreover, being not altogether unused to acting with violence in self-defence—it might have taken, perhaps, 100,000 disciplined and well-led reprobates a week or more to hold the six millions of Greater London by the throat. To-day 10,000 could do this with ease between breakfast and dinner-time. Certainly a considerable difference — but somehow not a difference which seems altogether reassuring.

Since the days of Oliver Cromwell the confidence of the anti-militarists in the docility of the British Army has never experienced any serious shock. But yet, according to the theories of this particular school, why should our army alone, of all trades and professions, be expected not to place its own class interests before those of the country?

When professional armies make their first entry into practical politics it is almost always in the rôle of liberators and defenders of justice. An instance might easily occur if one or other set of politicians, in a fit of madness or presumption, were to ask, or order, the British Army to undertake certain opera-

Perversities of the anti-militarist spirit.

tions against a section of their fellow-countrymen, which the soldiers themselves judged to be contrary to justice and their own honour.

Something of this kind very nearly came to pass in March 1914. The Curragh incident, as it was called, showed in a flash what a perilous gulf opens, when a professional army is mishandled. Politicians, who have come by degrees to regard the army—not as a national force, or microcosm of the people, but as an instrument which electoral success has placed temporarily in their hands, and which may therefore be used legitimately for forwarding their own party ends — have ever been liable to blunder in this direction.

Whatever may have been the merits of the Curragh case, the part which the British Army was asked and expected to play on that occasion, was one which no democratic Government would have dared to order a conscript army to undertake, until it had been ascertained, beyond any possibility of doubt, that the country as a whole believed extreme measures to be necessary for the national safety.

If professional soldiers, however high and patriotic their spirit, be treated as mercenaries—as if, in their dealings with their fellow-countrymen, they had neither souls nor consciences—it can be no matter for surprise if they should come by insensible degrees to think and act as mercenaries. . . . One set or other of party politicians—the occurrence is quite as conceivable in the case of a Unionist Government as in that of a Liberal—issues certain orders, which it would never dare to issue to a conscript army, and these orders, to its immense surprise, are not obeyed. Thereupon a Government, which only the day before

Perversities of the anti-militarist spirit.

seemed to be established securely on a House of Commons majority and the rock of tradition, is seen to be powerless. The army in its own eyes—possibly in that of public opinion also—has stood between the people and injustice. It has refused to be made the instrument for performing an act of tyranny and oppression. Possibly in sorrow and disgust it dissolves itself and ceases to exist. Possibly, on the other hand, it glows with the approbation of its own conscience; begins to admire its own strength, and not improbably to wonder, if it might not be good for the country were soldiers to put forth their strong arm rather more often, in order to restrain the politicians from following evil courses. This of course is the end of democracy and the beginning of militarism.

An army which starts by playing the popular rôle of benefactor, or liberator, will end very speedily by becoming the instrument of a military despotism. We need look no farther back than Cromwell and his major-generals for an example. We have been in the habit of regarding such contingencies as remote and mediaeval; none the less we had all but started on this fatal course in the spring and summer of last year. We were then saved, not by the wisdom of statesmen—for these only increased the danger by the spectacle which they afforded of timidity, temper, and equivocation—but solely by the present war which, though it has brought us many horrors, has averted, for a time at least, what is infinitely the worst of all.

The conclusion is plain. A democracy which asserts the right of manhood suffrage, while denying the duty of manhood service, is living in a fool's paradise.

CHAPTER VII.

Perversities of the anti-militarist spirit.

A democracy which does not fully identify itself with its army, which does not treat its army with honour and as an equal, but which treats it, on the contrary, as ill-bred and ill-tempered people treat their servants—with a mixture, that is, of fault-finding and condescension—is following a very perilous path.

An army which does not receive the treatment it deserves, and which at the same time is ordered by the politicians to perform services which, upon occasions, it may hold to be inconsistent with its honour, is a danger to the state.

A democracy which, having refused to train itself for its own defence, thinks nevertheless that it can safely raise the issue of 'the Army *versus* the People,' is mad.

CHAPTER VIII

SOME HISTORICAL REFLECTIONS

Chapter VIII.

Some historical reflections.

Prior to the present war the chief bugbears encountered by Lord Roberts, and indeed by all others whose aim it was to provide this country with an army numerically fit to support its policy, were the objections, real or imaginary, of the British race to compulsory service, and more particularly to compulsory service in foreign lands. These prejudices were true types of the bugbear; for they were born out of opinion and not out of the facts.

The smaller fry of politicians, whose fears—like those of the monkeys—are more easily excited by the front-row of things which are visible, than by the real dangers which lurk behind in the shadow, are always much more terrified of opinion than of the facts. This is precisely why most politicians remain all their lives more unfit than any other class of man for governing a country. Give one of these his choice—ask him whether he will prefer to support a cause where the facts are with him, but opinion is likely for many years to be running hard against him, or another cause where these conditions are reversed—of course he will never hesitate a moment about choosing the latter. And very probably his manner of answering will indicate, that he thinks you insult his intelligence by asking such a question.

Some historical reflections.

It is only the very rare type of big, patient politician, who realises that the facts cannot be changed by opinion, and that in the end opinion must be changed by the facts, if the two happen to be opposed. Such a one chooses accordingly, to follow the facts in spite of unpopularity.

The little fellows, on the contrary, with their large ears glued anxiously to the ground, keep ever muttering to themselves, and chaunting in a sort of rhythmical chorus, the most despicable incantation in the whole political vocabulary :—" We who aspire ' to be leaders of the People must see to it that we are ' never in advance of the People. . . . The People ' will never stand this : the People will never stand ' that. . . . Away with it therefore ; and if possible ' attach it like a mill-stone round the necks of our ' enemies."

Of course they are quite wrong. The People will stand anything which is necessary for the national welfare, if the matter is explained to them by a big enough man in accents of sincerity.

A defensive force which will on no account cross the frontier is no defensive force at all. It is only a laughing-stock.

A frontier is sometimes an arbitrary line drawn across meadow and plough ; sometimes a river ; sometimes a mountain range ; sometimes, as with ourselves, it is a narrow strip of sea—a ' great ditch,' as Cromwell called it contemptuously.

The awful significance, however, of the word ' frontier ' seems to deepen and darken as we pass

Some historical reflections.

from the first example to the fourth. And there is apparently something more in this feeling than the terrors of the channel crossing or of a foreign language. Territorials may be taken to Ireland, which is a longer sea-journey than from Dover to Calais; but to be 'butchered abroad'—horrible!

It is horrible enough to be butchered anywhere, but why more horrible in the valley of the Rhine than in that of the Thames? If national safety demands butchery, as it has often done in the past, surely the butchery of 50,000 brave men on the borders of Luxemburg is a less evil than the butchery of twice that number in the vicinity of Norwich? And if we are to consider national comfort as well as safety, it is surely wise to follow the German example and fight in any man's country rather than in our own. The only question of real importance is this:—At what place will the sacrifice of life be most effective for the defence of the country? If we can answer that we shall know also where it will be lightest.[1]

The school of political thought which remained predominant throughout the great industrial epoch (1832–1886) bitterly resented the assumption, made by certain classes, that the profession of arms was more honourable in its nature, than commerce and other peaceful pursuits. The destruction of this supposed fallacy produced a great literature, and even a considerable amount of poetry. It was a frequent theme at the opening of literary institutes and technical colleges, and also at festivals of chambers of commerce

[1] Once more it is desirable to correct the erroneous impression that the conscript armies of continental powers are under no liability to serve outside their own territories or overseas.

CHAPTER VIII.

Some historical reflections.

and municipalities. Professors of Political Economy expounded the true doctrine with great vehemence, and sermons were preached without number upon the well-worn text about the victories of peace.

This reaction was salutary up to a point. It swept away a vast quantity of superannuated rubbish. International relations were at this time just as much cumbered with old meaningless phrases of a certain sort, in which vainglory was the chief ingredient, as they have recently been cumbered with others of a different sort in which indolence was the chief ingredient. Inefficiency, indifference, idleness, trifling, and extravagance were a standing charge against soldiers as a class; and though they were never true charges against the class, they were true, for two generations following after Waterloo, against a large number of individuals. But this reaction, like most other reactions, swept away too much.

A mercenary soldiery which looks to enrich itself by pay and plunder is an ignoble institution. It has no right to give itself airs of honour, and must be judged like company promotion, trusts, or any of the many other predatory professions of modern times. It is also a national danger, inasmuch as its personal interest is to foment wars. The British Army has never been open to this charge in any period of its history.

A profession in which it is only possible, by the most severe self-denial and economy, for an officer—even after he has arrived at success—to live on his pay, to marry, and to bring up a family, can hardly be ranked as a money-making career. Pecuniary motives, indeed, were never the charge against 'the military' except among the stump-orator class. But pro-

Some historical reflections.

fessional indifference and inefficiency were, at that particular time, not only seriously alleged, but were also not infrequently true. It was a good thing that slackness should be swept away. That it has been swept away pretty thoroughly, every one who has known anything about the Army for a generation past, is well aware.

But the much-resented claim to a superiority in the matter of honour is well founded, and no amount of philosophising or political-economising will ever shake it. Clearly it is more honourable for a man to risk his life, and what is infinitely more important —his reputation and his whole future career—in defence of his country, than it is merely to build up a competency or a fortune. The soldier's profession is beset by other and greater dangers than the physical. Money-making pursuits are not only safer for the skin, but in them a blunder, or even a series of blunders, does not banish the hope of ultimate success. The man of business has chances of retrieving his position. Many bankrupts have died in affluence. In politics, a man with a plausible tongue and a certain quality of courage, will usually succeed in eluding the consequences of his mistakes, by laying the blame on other people's shoulders. But the soldier is rarely given a second chance; and he may easily come down at the first chance, through sheer ill-luck, and not through any fault of his own. Such a profession confers honour upon its members.

Law, trade, and finance are not in themselves, as was at one time thought, dishonourable pursuits; but neither are they in themselves honourable. They are neither the one nor the other. It casts no slur upon a man to be a lawyer, a tradesman, or a banker;

Some historical reflections.

but neither does it confer upon him any honour. But military service does confer an honour. The devotion, hardship, and danger of the soldier's life are not rewarded upon a commercial basis, or reckoned in that currency.

Some people are inclined to mock at the respect—exaggerated as they think—which is paid by conscript countries to their armies. For all its excesses and absurdities, this respect is founded upon a true principle—a truer principle of conduct than our own. In countries where most of the able-bodied men have given some years of their lives gratuitously to the service of their country, the fact is brought home to them, that such service is of a different character from the benefits which they subsequently confer upon the State by their industry and thrift, or by growing rich.

From the national point of view, it is ennobling that at some period of their lives the great majority of citizens should have served the commonwealth disinterestedly. This after all is the only principle which will support a commonwealth. For a commonwealth will not stand against the shocks, which history teaches us to beware of, merely by dropping papers, marked with a cross, into a ballot-box once every five years, or even oftener. It will not stand merely by taking an intelligent interest in events, by attending meetings and reading the newspapers, and by indulging in outbursts of indignation or enthusiasm. It will only stand by virtue of personal service, and by the readiness of the whole people, generation by generation, to give their lives and—what is much harder to face—the time and irksome preparation which are necessary for making the sacrifice of their lives—should it be called for—effective for its purpose.

Some historical reflections.

If the mass of the people, even when they have realised the need, will not accept the obligation of national service they must be prepared to see their institutions perish, to lose control of their own destinies, and to welcome another master than Democracy, who it may well be, will not put them to the trouble of dropping papers, marked with a cross, into ballot-boxes once in five years, or indeed at all. For a State may continue to exist even if deprived of ballot-boxes; but it is doomed if its citizens will not in time prepare themselves to defend it with their lives.

The memories of the press-gang and the militia ballot are dim. Both belong to a past which it is the custom to refer to with reprobation. Both were inconsistent with equal comradeship between classes; with justice, dignity, honour, and the unity of the nation; and on these grounds they are rightly condemned.

But the press-gang and the militia ballot have been condemned, and are still condemned, upon other grounds which do not seem so firm. Both have been condemned as contravening that great and laudable principle of British freedom which lays it down that those who like fighting, or prefer it to other evils—like starvation and imprisonment—or who can be bribed, or in some other way persuaded to fight, should enjoy the monopoly of being 'butchered,' both abroad and at home. And it has been further maintained by those who held these views, that people who do not like fighting, but choose rather to stay at home talking, criticising, enjoying

CHAPTER VIII.

Some historical reflections.

fine thrills of patriotism, making money, and sleeping under cover, have some kind of divine right to go on enjoying that form of existence undisturbed. Since the Wars of the Roses the latter class has usually been in a great majority in England. Even during the Cromwellian Civil War the numbers of men, capable of bearing arms, who actually bore them, was only a smallish fraction of the entire population.

The moral ideals of any community, like other things, are apt to be settled by numbers. With the extension of popular government, and the increase of the electorate, this tendency will assert itself more and more. But providing the people are dealt with plainly and frankly, without flattery or deceit—like men and not as if they were greedy children—the moral sense of a democracy will probably be sounder and stronger than that of any other form of State.

Even in England, however, there have been lapses, during which the people have not been so treated, and the popular spirit has sunk, owing to mean leadership, into degradation. During the whole of the industrial epoch the idea steadily gained in strength, that those whose battles were fought for them by others, approached more nearly to the type of the perfect citizen than those others who actually fought the battles; that the protected were worthier than the protectors.

According to this view the true meaning of 'freedom' was exemption from personal service. The whole duty of the virtuous citizen with regard to the defence of his country began and ended with paying a policeman. With the disappearance of imminent and visible danger, the reprobate qualities of the soldier became speedily a pain and a scandal

Some historical reflections.

to godly men. In time of peace he was apt to be sneered at and decried as an idler and a spendthrift, who would not stand well in a moral comparison with those steady fellows, who had remained at home, working hard at their vocations and investing their savings.

The soldier, moreover, according to Political Economy, was occupied in a non-productive trade, and therefore it was contrary to the principles of that science to waste more money upon him than could be avoided. Also it was prudent not to show too much gratitude to those who had done the fighting, lest they should become presumptuous and formidable.

This conception of the relations between the army and the civilian population has been specially marked at several periods in our history—after the Cromwellian wars; after the Marlborough wars; after 1757; but during the half century which followed Waterloo it seemed to have established itself permanently as an article of our political creed.

After 1815 there was an utter weariness of fighting, following upon nearly a quarter of a century of war. The heroism of Wellington's armies was still tainted in the popular memory by the fact that the prisons had been opened to find him recruits. The industrial expansion and prodigious growth of material wealth absorbed men's minds. Middle-class ideals, middle-class prosperity, middle-class irritation against a military caste which, in spite of its comparative poverty, continued with some success to assert its social superiority, combined against the army in popular discussions. The honest belief that wars were an anachronism, and that the world was now

Some historical reflections.

launched upon an interminable era of peace, clothed the nakedness of class prejudice with some kind of philosophic raiment. Soldiers were no longer needed; why then should they continue to claim the lion's share of honourable recognition?

Up to August 1914 the chief difficulties in the way of army reformers were how to overcome the firmly-rooted ideas that preparations for war upon a great scale were not really necessary to security, and that, on those rare occasions when fighting might be necessary, it should not be undertaken by the most virtuous class of citizens, but by others whose lives had a lower value. If the citizen paid it was enough; and he claimed the right to grumble even at paying. This was the old Liberal faith of the eighteen-fifties, and it remained the faith of the straitest Radical sect, until German guns began to batter down the forts of Liége.

But any one who remembers the state of public opinion between 1870 and 1890, or who has read the political memoirs of that time, will realise that a change has been, very slowly and gradually, stealing over public opinion ever since the end of that epoch. In those earlier times the only danger which disturbed our national equanimity, and that only very slightly, was the approach of Russia towards the north-western frontier of India. The volunteer movement came to be regarded more and more by ordinary people in the light of a healthy and manly recreation, rather than as a duty. A lad would make his choice, very much as if volunteering were on a par with rowing, sailing, hunting, or polo. It is probably no exaggeration to say that nine volunteers out of every ten, who

Some historical reflections.

enrolled themselves between 1870 and 1890, never believed for a single moment that there was a chance of the country having need of their services. Consequently, except in the case of a few extreme enthusiasts, it never appeared that there was anything unpatriotic in *not* joining the volunteers.

One has only to compare this with the attitude which has prevailed since the Territorial Army came into existence, to realise that there has been a stirring of the waters, and that in certain quarters a change had taken place in the national mood. With regard to the Territorials the attitude of those who joined, of those who did not join, of the politicians, of the press, of public opinion generally was markedly different from the old attitude. It was significant that a man who did not join was often disposed to excuse and to justify his abstention. The conditions of his calling, or competing duties made it impossible for him; or the lowness of his health, or the highness of his principles in some way interfered. There was a tendency now to explain what previously would never have called for any explanation.

The causes of this change are not less obvious than its symptoms. It is an interesting coincidence that Lord Kitchener had a good deal to do with it. The destruction of the bloodthirsty tyranny of the Khalifa (1898), and the rescue of a fertile province from waste, misery, and massacre, caused many people to look with less disapproving eyes than formerly upon the profession of the soldier. The long anxieties of the South African War, and the levies of volunteers from all parts of the Empire, who went out to take a share in it, forced men to think not only more kindly of soldiers, but also to think

CHAPTER VIII.

of war itself no longer as an illusion but as a reality.[1]

Some historical reflections.

The events which happened during the last decade—the creation of the German Navy—the attempt and failure of the British Government to abate the rivalry in armaments—the naval panic and the hastily summoned Defence Conference in 1909—the Russo-Japanese war—the Agadir crisis—the two Balkan wars—the military competition between Germany and France—all these combined to sharpen the consciousness of danger and to draw attention to the need for being prepared against it.

These events, which crowded the beginning of the twentieth century, stirred and troubled public opinion in a manner which not only Mr. Cobden, who died in 1865, but almost equally Mr. Gladstone, who survived him by more than thirty years, would have utterly refused to credit. Both these statesmen had been convinced that the world was moving steadily towards a settled peace, and that before another century had passed away—possibly even in a single generation—their dreams of general disarmament would be approaching fulfilment.

And to a certain extent our own generation remains still affected by the same notions. Amid the thunders of more than a thousand miles of battle we still find ourselves clinging tenaciously to the belief, that the world has entered suddenly, and unexpectedly, upon an abnormal period which, from

[1] Influences of another kind altogether had much to do with the cleansing of public opinion—the writings of Henley, of Mahan, and of Mr. Rudyard Kipling. Though not so well known as the works of these, Henderson's *Life of Stonewall Jackson* has nevertheless changed many courses of thought, and its indirect effect in removing false standards has been very great. I can never sufficiently acknowledge my personal debt to these four.

its very nature, can only be of very brief duration. This comforting conviction does not appear to rest upon solid grounds. In the light of history it would not seem so certain that we have not passed out of an abnormal period into the normal—if lamentable—condition when a nation, in order to maintain its independence, must be prepared at any moment to fight for its life.

Some historical reflections.

It would be profitless to pursue these speculations. It is enough for our own generation that we now find ourselves in a situation of the gravest danger; and that it depends upon the efforts which we *as a nation* put forth, more than upon anything else, whether the danger will pass away or settle down and become chronic.

Although we failed to perceive or acknowledge the danger until some nine months ago, it had been there for at least fifteen years, probably for twice that number.

German antagonism to England has been compounded of envy of our possessions, contempt for our character, and hatred of our good fortune. What galled our rival more than anything else, was the fact that we enjoyed our prosperity, and held our vast Empire, upon too easy terms. The German people had made, and were continuing to make, sacrifices to maintain their position in the world, while the British people in their view were making none. And if we measure national sacrifices by personal service, and not merely in money payments, it is difficult to see what answer is to be given to this charge.

It is clear that unless the result of this war be to

Some historical reflections.

crush Germany as completely as she herself hoped at the beginning of it, to crush France, our own danger will remain, unless Germany's chief grievance against us is meanwhile removed. It is not a paradox, but merely a statement of plain fact, to say that Germany's chief grievance against ourselves was, that we were not prepared to withstand her attack. Her hatred, which has caused, and still causes us so much amazement, was founded upon the surest of foundations—a want of respect. The Germans despised a nation which refused to recognise that any obligation rested on its citizens, to fit themselves, by serious training, for defence of their inheritance. And they will continue to despise us when this war is over if we should still fail to recognise this obligation. Despising us, they will continue also to hate us; the peace of the world will still be endangered; and we shall not, after all our sacrifices, have reached the security at which we aimed.

We may end this war without winning it, and at the same time without being defeated. And although it appears to be still believed by some persons that we can win, in some sort of fashion, without accepting the principle of national service, even those who entertain this dangerous confidence will hardly dare to deny that, after a war which ends without a crowning victory, we shall have to accept conscription at once upon the signature of peace.

For it should be remembered that we have other things to take into account besides the mood of Germany. If we stave off defeat, only with the assistance of allies — all of whom have long ago adopted universal military service in its most rigorous

Some historical reflections.

form—we shall have to reckon with their appraisement of the value of our assistance. If we are to judge by Germany's indomitable enterprise during the past two generations, she is likely to recover from the effects of this war at least as rapidly as ourselves. And when she has recovered, will she not hunger again for our possessions, as eagerly as before, if she sees them still inadequately guarded? And maybe, when that time comes, there may be some difficulty in finding allies. For a Power which declines to recognise the obligation of equal sacrifices, which refuses to make preparations in time of peace, and which accordingly, when war occurs, is ever found unready, is not the most eligible of comrades in arms.

In a recent letter the Freiherr von Hexenküchen refers, in his sour way, to some of the matters which have been discussed in this chapter. . . . "The 'British People," he writes, "appear to be mightily 'exercised just now about their own and their neigh- 'bours' consciences; about what they may or may 'not do with decency; about whether or no football 'matches are right; or race-meetings; or plays, 'music-hall entertainments, concerts, the purchase 'of new clothes, and the drinking of alcohol; whether 'indeed any form of enjoyment or cheerfulness ought 'to be tolerated in present circumstances.

"But although you vex yourselves over these 'and other problems of a similar kind, you never 'seem to vex yourselves about the abscess at the 'root of the tooth.

"The Holy Roman Empire, which was not holy, 'nor Roman, nor yet an empire, reminds me not a 'little of your so-called voluntary military system,

Some historical reflections.

'which is not voluntary, nor military, nor yet a 'system. It is only a chaos, a paradox, and a 'laughing-stock to us Germans.

"It is *our* army, and not yours, which really rests 'on a voluntary basis. Our whole people for a 'century past have voluntarily accepted the obliga-'tion of universal military service. Those amongst 'us who have raised objections to this system are 'but an inconsiderable fraction; negligible at any 'time, but in this or any other great crisis, not merely 'negligible, but altogether invisible and inaudible.

"Our people desire their army to be as it is, 'otherwise it would not be as it is. No Kaiser, or 'Bureaucracy, or General Staff could impose such 'a system against the public will and conscience. 'Your people, on the other hand, have refused *as* '*a people* to accept the military obligation. By 'various devices they endeavour to fix the burden 'on the shoulders of individuals. Is this the true 'meaning of the word 'voluntary'—*to refuse*? . . . 'Sir, I desire to be civil; but was there ever a more 'conspicuous instance of cant in the whole history 'of the world, than your self-righteous boastings about 'your 'voluntary' military system?

"You may wonder why I bracket these two things 'together—your soul-searchings about amusements 'of all kinds, and your nonsensical panegyrics on the ''voluntary' principle. . . . To my eyes they are 'very closely connected.

"Cheerfulness is a duty in time of war. Every 'man or woman who smiles, and keeps a good heart, 'and goes about his or her day's work gaily, helps 'by so much to sustain the national spirit. Not 'good, but harm, is done to the conduct of the war,

CHAPTER VIII.

Some historical reflections.

'by moping and brooding over casualty lists, and 'by speculations as to disasters which have occurred, 'or are thought to be imminent. But there is one 'essential preliminary to national cheerfulness— 'before a nation can be cheerful it must have a good 'conscience; and it cannot have a good conscience 'unless it has done its duty.

"Your nation has a bad conscience. The reason 'is that, *as a nation*, it has not done its duty. This 'may be the fault of the leaders who have not dared 'to speak the word of command. But the fact 'remains, that you well know—or at any rate suspect 'in your hearts—that you have not done your whole 'duty. And consequently you cannot be really 'cheerful about anything. As you go about your 'daily work or recreations, you are all the while 'looking back over your shoulders with misgiving. '*As a nation* you have not—even yet—dedicated 'yourselves to this war. When you have done so— 'if ever you do—your burden of gloom and mistrust 'will fall from your back, like that of *Christian* as he 'passed along the highway, which is fenced on either 'side with the *Wall* that is called *Salvation*."

In the great American Civil War, the Southern States, which aimed at breaking away from the Union, adopted conscription within a year from the beginning. They were brave fighters; but they were poor, and they were in a small minority. The Northern States — confident in their numbers and wealth — relied at first upon the voluntary system. It gave them great and gallant armies; but these was not enough; and as months went by President Lincoln realised that they were not enough.

2 E

CHAPTER VIII.

Some historical reflections.

Disregarding the entreaties of his friends, to beware of asking of the people 'what the people would never stand,' disregarding the clamours of his enemies about personal freedom, he insisted upon conscription, believing that by these means alone the Union could be saved. And what was the result? A section of the press foamed with indignation. Mobs yelled, demonstrated, and in their illogical fury, lynched negroes, seeing in these unfortunates the cause of all their troubles. But the mobs were not the American people. They were only a noisy and contemptible minority of the American people, whose importance as well as courage had been vastly over-rated. The quiet people were in deadly earnest, and they supported their President.[1]

But the task which Lincoln set himself was one of the hardest that a democratic statesman ever undertook. The demand which he determined to make, and did make, may well have tried his heart as he sat alone in the night watches. For compulsion was a violation of the habits and prejudices of the old American stock, while it was even more distasteful to new immigrants. It was contrary to the traditions and theories of the Republic, and, as many thought, to its fundamental principles. It was open to scornful attack on grounds of sentiment. Against a foe who were so weak, both in numbers and wealth, how humiliating to be driven to such desperate measures!

But most of all—outweighing all other considerations—this war of North and South was not only war, but *civil* war. Families and lifelong friendships were divided. What compulsion meant, therefore, in this case was, that brothers were to be forced to

[1] Cf. *Round Table*, March 1915, 'The Politics of War.'

Some historical reflections.

kill brothers, husbands were to be sent out to slay the kinsmen of their wives, or—as they marched with Sherman through Georgia—to set a light with their own hands to the old homesteads where they had been born. Between the warring States there were no differences of blood, tradition, or religion; or of ideas of right and wrong; no hatred against a foreign race; only an acute opposition of political ideals. Compulsion, therefore, was a great thing to ask of the American people. But the American people are a great people, and they understood. And Lincoln was a great man,—one of the greatest, noblest, and most human in the whole of history,—and he did not hesitate to ask, to insist, and to use force. What the end was does not need to be stated here; except merely this, that a lingering and bloody war was thereby greatly shortened, and that the Union was saved.

The British Government and people are faced to-day with some, but not all—and not the greatest—of Lincoln's difficulties. Our traditions and theories are the same, to a large extent, as those which prevailed in America in 1863. But unlike the North we have had recent experience of war, and also of the sacrifices which war calls for from the civilian population. By so much the shock of compulsion would find us better prepared.

But the other and much greater difficulties which beset Lincoln do not exist in the case of the British Government. We are not fighting against a foe inferior in numbers, but against one who up till now has been greatly superior in numbers—who has also been greatly superior in equipment, and preparation, and in deeply-laid plans. We are fighting against

CHAPTER VIII.

Some historical reflections.

a foe who has invaded and encroached; not against one who is standing on the defensive, demanding merely to be let go free. The family affections and friendships which would be outraged by conscription in this war against Germany are inconsiderable; mere dust in the balance. The present war is waged against a foreign nation; it is not *civil* war. It is waged against an enemy who plainly seeks, not his own freedom, but our destruction, and that of our Allies. It is waged against an enemy who by the treacherous thoroughness of his peace-time preparations, appears to our eyes to have violated good faith as between nations, as in the conduct of the campaign he has disregarded the obligations of our common humanity. We may be wrong; we may take exaggerated views owing to the bitterness of the struggle; but such is our mind upon the matter.

Lincoln's task would have been light had such been the mind of the Northern States half a century ago, and had he been faced with nothing more formidable than the conditions which prevail in England to-day. It does not need the courage of a Lincoln to demand from our people a sacrifice, upon which the safety of the British Empire depends, even more certainly, than in 1863 did that of the American Union.

CHAPTER IX

THE CRUCIBLE OF WAR

CHAPTER IX.

The crucible of war.

IF in the foregoing pages the Liberal party has come in for the larger share of criticism, the reason is, that during the ten critical years, while dangers were drawing to a head, a Liberal Government chanced to be in power. That things would have been managed better and more courageously had the Unionists been in power may be doubted; and certainly it is no part of my present task to champion any such theory.

The special type of politician whose influence has wrought so much evil of late is no peculiar product of the Liberal party. He is the product of the party system in its corrupt decadence. You find him in the ranks of the Opposition as well as in those of the Ministerialists, just as you find good and true men in both. In this last lies our hope. In our present trouble good and true men have a chance of taking things into their own hands, which has been denied to them for many generations.

This book has been written to establish the *Need* for National Service, in order that the British Empire may maintain itself securely in the present circum-

The crucible of war.

stances of the world. If this contention be true it is obvious that a corresponding *Duty* lies upon the whole nation to accept the burden of military service.

Neither need nor duty has ever been made clear to the British people by their leaders. Owing to the abuses of the party system, increasing steadily over a considerable period of years, a certain type of politician has been evolved, and has risen into great prominence—a type which does not trust the people, but only fears them. In order to maintain themselves and their parties in power, politicians of this type have darkened the eyes and drugged the spirit of the nation.

It is no part of the plan of this volume to offer criticisms upon the naval and military aspects of the present war, or upon the wisdom or unwisdom of the operations which have been undertaken by land and sea. All that need be said in this connection may be put into a very few words.

As we read and re-read British history we cannot but be impressed with the fact that our leading statesmen, misled by the very brilliancy of their intellectual endowments, have always been prone to two errors of policy, which the simpler mind of the soldier instinctively avoids. They have ever been too ready to conclude prematurely that a certain line of obstacles is so formidable that it cannot be forced ; and they have also ever been too ready to accept the notion, that there must surely be some ingenious far way round, by which they may succeed in circumventing the infinite.

The defect of brilliant brains is not necessarily a

The crucible of war.

want of courage—daring there has usually been in plenty—but they are apt to lack fortitude. They are apt to abandon the assault upon positions which are not really invulnerable, and to go off, chasing after attractive butterflies, until they fall into quagmires. Dispersion of effort has always been the besetting sin of British statesmen and the curse of British policy. There is no clearer example of this than the case of William Pitt the Younger, who went on picking up sugar islands all over the world, when he ought to have been giving his whole strength to beating Napoleon.

Very few obstacles are really insurmountable, and it is usually the shortest and the safest course to stick to what has been already begun. Especially is this the case when your resources in trained soldiers and munitions of war are painfully restricted. At the one point, where you have decided to attack, the motto is *push hard*; and at all others, where you may be compelled to defend yourselves, the motto is *hold fast*.

The peril of British war councils in the past has always been (and maybe still is) the tendency of ingenious argument to get the better of sound judgment. In the very opposite of this lies safety. We find the true type of high policy, as well as of successful campaigning, in the cool and patient inflexibility of Wellington, holding fast by one main idea, forcing his way over one obstacle after another which had been pronounced invincible—through walled cities; into the deep valleys of the Pyrenees; across the Bidassoa—till from the crests of the Great Rhune and the Little his soldiers looked down at last upon the plains of France.

CHAPTER IX.

The crucible of war.

Our most urgent problem with regard to the present war, is how we may win it most thoroughly; but, in addition to this, there are two questions which have recently engaged a good deal of public attention. There is a *Political* question—what sort of European settlement is to take place after the war? And there is also a *Criminal* question—what sort of punishment shall be meted out, if crimes, contrary to the practice of war among civilised and humane states, have been committed by our antagonists?

I have not attempted to deal with either of these. They do not seem to be of extreme urgency; for unless, and until, we win the war it is somewhat idle to discuss the ultimate fate of Europe or the penalty of evil deeds. You cannot restore stolen property until you have recovered it, and you cannot punish a malefactor, nor is it very convenient even to try him, while he is still at large. If that be true, which was said of old by a great king—*I do not make peace with barbarians but dictate the terms of their surrender*—we are still a long way from that.

I have not occupied myself therefore with what are termed 'German atrocities.' So far as this matter is concerned, I am satisfied to let it rest for the present upon the German statement of intentions before war began,[1] and upon the proclamations which

[1] "A war conducted with energy cannot be directed merely against the 'combatants of the enemy State and the positions they occupy, but it will 'and must in like manner seek to destroy the total intellectual and material 'resources of the latter. Humanitarian claims, such as the protection of 'men and their goods, can only be taken into consideration in so far as the 'nature and object of the war permit.

"International Law is in no way opposed to the exploitation of the 'crimes of third parties (assassination, incendiarism, robbery, and the like) 'to the prejudice of the enemy. . . . The necessary aim of war gives the 'belligerent the right and imposes on him the duty, according to circum-

The crucible of war.

have been issued subsequently, with the object of justifying their mode of operations by sea and land. The case against Germany on her own admission, is quite strong enough without opening a further inquistion under this heading.[1]

It is essential, however, to realise the falsities and perversities upon which the great fabric of German policy is founded; for otherwise we shall never understand either the nature of the enemy with whom we are at present engaged, or the full extent of the danger by which, not only we, but civilisation itself is now threatened. It is essential that the whole British race should understand the nature of the evils *against* which they are fighting—the ambitions of Germany—the ruthless despotism of the Prussian system—the new theories of right and wrong which have been evolved by thinkers who have been paid, promoted, and inspired by the State, in order to sanctify the imperial policy of spoliation.

It is also essential for us to realise the nature of those things *for* which we are fighting—what we shall save and secure for our posterity in case of victory; what we stand to lose in event of defeat. The preservation or ruin of our inheritance, spiritual and material—the maintenance or overthrow of our

---

'stances, the duty not to let slip the important, it may be the decisive 'advantages to be gained by such means."—*The German War Book*, issued by the Great General Staff.

[1] Clearly, however, when it comes to the discussion of terms of peace, not only the political question, but also the criminal question, will have to be remembered. Oddly enough the 'pacifist' section, which has already been clamorous for putting forward peace proposals, seems very anxious that we should forget, or at any rate ignore, the criminal question—odd, because 'humanity' is the stuff they have set up their bills to trade in.

The crucible of war.

institutions, traditions, and ideas—the triumph of these, or the supplanting of them by a wholly different order, which to our eyes wears the appearance of a vast machine under the control of savages—are the main issues of the present war. And when now at last, we face them squarely, we begin to wonder, why of late years, we have been wont to treat problems of national defence and imperial security with so much levity and indifference.

It is profitable to turn our eyes from the contemplation of German shortcomings inwards upon our own. If we have been guilty as a people during recent times of weakness, blindness, indolence, or cowardice, we should face these facts squarely, otherwise there is but a poor chance of arriving at better conditions. If we have refused to listen to unpleasant truths, and to exchange a drowsy and dangerous comfort against sacrifices which were necessary for security, it is foolish to lay the whole blame upon this or that public man, this or that government. For, after all, both public men and governments were our own creation; we chose them because we liked them; because it gave us pleasure and consolation to listen to their sayings; because their doings and their non-doings, their un-doings and their mis-doings were regarded with approval or indifference by the great bulk of our people.

It would be wise also to take to heart the lesson, plainly written across the record of the last nine months, that the present confusion of our political system is responsible, as much as anything—perhaps more than anything—for the depreciated currency of public character. The need is obvious for a Parliament and a Government chosen by the Empire, responsible to the Empire, and charged with the security of the Empire, and with no other task.

The crucible of war.

Why we are fighting at all is one of our problems; why we are finding it so hard to win is another. In what does the main strength of our enemies consist? And in what does our own chief weakness consist?

To say that our weakness is to be sought in our own vices, and the strength of our enemies in their virtues, is of course a commonplace. But one has only to open the average newspaper to realise the need for restating the obvious. For there the contrary doctrine is set forth daily and weekly with a lachrymose insistency—that our hands are weakened because we are so good; that the Germans fight at an enormous advantage because they are so wicked and unscrupulous.

But the things which we are finding hardest to overcome in our foes are not the immoral gibberings of professors, or the blundering cynicism of the German Foreign Office, or the methodical savagery of the General Staff, whether in Belgium or on the High Seas. These are sources of weakness and not of strength; and even at the present stage it is clear that, although they have inflicted immeasurable suffering, they have done the German cause much more harm than good.

Our real obstacles are the loyalty, the self-sacrifice, and the endurance of the German people.

The causes of British weakness are equally plain. Our indolence and factiousness; our foolish confidence in cleverness, manœuvres, and debate for overcoming obstacles which lie altogether outside that region of human endeavour; our absorption as

CHAPTER IX.

The crucible of war.

thrilled spectators in the technical game of British politics[1]—these vices and others of a similar character, which, since the beginning of the war we have been struggling—like a man awakening from a nightmare—to shake off, are still our chief difficulties. It is a hard job to get rid of them, and we are not yet anything like halfway through with it.

It must be clear to every detached observer, that the moral strength of England in the present struggle—like that of France—does not lie in Government or Opposition, but in the spirit of the people; that this spirit has drawn but little support, in the case of either country, from the leadership and example of the politicians; and that there is little cause in either case to bless or praise them for the fidelity of their previous stewardship. In the case of France this national spirit was assured at the beginning; in our own case the process of awakening has proceeded much more slowly.

It is essential to put certain notions out of our heads and certain other notions into them. From the beginning of the war, a large part of the press—acting, we are entitled to suppose, in patriotic obedience to the directions of the Press Bureau—has fostered ideas which do not correspond with the facts. Information has been doled out and presented in such a way as to destroy all sense of proportion in the public mind.

It is not an uncommon belief,[2] for example, that we with our Allies—ever since the first onset, when,

[1] In reality, as regards party politics, we have been for years past very like those shouting, cigarette-smoking, Saturday crowds at football matches whom we have lately been engaged in reproving so virtuously.

[2] Certainly up to April 1915 it *was* not an uncommon belief.

The crucible of war.

being virtuously unprepared, we were pushed back some little distance—have been doing much better than the Germans; that for months past our adversaries have been in a desperate plight — lacking ammunition, on the verge of bankruptcy and starvation, and thoroughly discouraged.

There is also a tendency to assume—despite Lord Kitchener's grave and repeated warnings to the contrary—that the war is drawing rapidly to a conclusion, and that, even if we may have to submit to some interruption of our usual summer holidays, at any rate we shall eat our Christmas dinners in an atmosphere of peace and goodwill.

The magnitude of the German victories, both in the East and West, during the earlier stages of the war, is not realised even now by the great majority of our fellow-countrymen; while the ruinous consequences of these victories to our Allies—the occupation of Belgium, of a large part of northern France, and of Western Poland—is dwelt on far too lightly. Nor is it understood by one man in a hundred, that up to the end of last year, British troops were never holding more than thirty miles, out of that line of nearly five hundred which winds, like a great snake, from Nieuport to the Swiss frontier. On the contrary, it is quite commonly believed that we have been doing our fair share of the fighting—or even more—by land as well as sea.

A misleading emphasis of type and comment, together with a dangerous selection of items of news, are responsible for these illusions; while the prevalence of these illusions is largely responsible for many of our labour difficulties.

Such dreams of inevitable and speedy victory

CHAPTER IX.

The crucible of war.

are no doubt very soothing to indolent and timid minds, but they do not make for a vigorous and resolute spirit in the nation, upon which, more than upon anything else, the winning of this war depends.

In some quarters there appears still to linger a ridiculous idea that we went into this war, out of pure chivalry, to defend Belgium.[1] We went into it to defend our own existence, and for no other reason. We made common cause with Allies who were menaced by the same danger as ourselves; but these, most fortunately, had made their preparations with greater foresight than we had done. The actual fighting has taken place, so far, in their territories and not in ours; but the issue of this war is not one whit less a matter of life-or-death for us, than it is for them.

Quite recently I have seen our present situation described glowingly and self-complacently as the 'triumph of the voluntary system.' I must be blind of both eyes, for I can perceive no 'triumph' and no 'voluntary' system. I have seen the territories of our Allies seized, wasted, and held fast by an undefeated enemy. I have seen our small army driven back; fighting with as much skill and bravery as ever in its history; suffering losses unparalleled in its history; holding its own in the end, but against what overwhelming numbers and by what sacrifices! The human triumph is apparent enough; but not that of any system, voluntary or otherwise. Neither in this record of nine months' 'hard and hot fighting' on land, nor in

[1] Mr. Lloyd George, *Pearson's Magazine*, March 1915.

the state of things which now exists at the end of it all, is there a triumph for anything, or any one, save for a few thousands of brave men, who were left to hold fast as best they could against intolerable odds.

The crucible of war.

Certain contemporary writers appear to claim more for that form of representative government, which we are in the habit of calling 'democracy,' than it is either safe to count on, or true to assert. In their eyes democracy seems to possess a superiority in all the higher virtuous qualities—'freedom,' in particular—and also an inherent strength which—whatever may be the result of the present war—makes the final predominance of British institutions only a matter of time.[1]

I do not hold with either of these doctrines. Universal superiority in virtue and strength is too wide a claim to put forward for any system of government. And 'freedom' is a very hard thing to define.

It is not merely that the form of constitution, which we call 'democracy,' is obviously not the best fitted for governing an uncivilised or half-civilised people. There are considerations which go much deeper than that — considerations of race, religion, temperament, and tradition. As it has been in the past, so conceivably it may be again in the future, that a people, which is in the highest degree civilised and humane, will seek to realise its ideals of freedom in some other sphere than the control of policy and legislation according to the electoral verdicts of its

[1] These views are very prevalent among Liberal writers, and they are clearly implied, if not quite so openly expressed, by Conservatives. They seem to be assumed in one of the ablest articles which has yet been written upon the causes of the present war—'The Schism of Europe' (*Round Table*, March 1915).

CHAPTER IX.

The crucible of war.

citizens. It is even possible that its national aspirations may regard some other end as a higher good even than freedom. We cannot speak with certainty as to the whole human race, but only with regard to ourselves and certain others, who have been bred in the same traditions.

If a personal and autocratic government — the German for example—is able to arouse and maintain among its people a more ardent loyalty, a firmer confidence, a more constant spirit of self-sacrifice (in time of peace as well as war), I can see no good reason for the hope, that democracy, merely because, in our eyes, it approaches more nearly to the ideal of the Christian Commonwealth, will be able to maintain itself against the other. A highly centralised system of government has great natural advantages both for attack and defence; and if in addition it be supported by a more enduring fortitude, and a more self-denying devotion, on the part of the people, it seems almost incredible that, in the end, it will not prevail over other forms of government which have failed to enlist the same support.

The strength of all forms of government alike, whether against foreign attack or internal disintegration, must depend in the long last upon the spirit of the people; upon their determination to maintain their own institutions; upon their willingness to undertake beforehand, as well as during the excitement of war, those labours and sacrifices which are necessary for security. The spirit is everything. And in the end that spirit which is strongest is likely to become predominant, and to impose its own forms, systems, and ideas upon civilised and uncivilised nations alike.

A considerable part of the world—though it may have adopted patterns of government which are either avowedly democratic or else are monarchies of the constitutional sort (in essence the same)—is by no means wedded to popular institutions; has no deep-rooted traditions to give them support; could easily, therefore, and without much loss of self-respect, abandon them and submit to follow new fashions. But with the United Kingdom, the self-governing Dominions, and the United States it is altogether different.

CHAPTER IX.

The crucible of war.

To exchange voluntarily, merely because circumstances rendered it expedient to do so, a system which is the only one consistent with our notions of freedom would be an apostasy. It would mean our immediate spiritual ruin, and for that reason also our ultimate material ruin. On the other hand, to continue to exist on sufferance, without a voice in the destinies of the world, would be an even deeper degradation. To be conquered outright, and absorbed, would be an infinitely preferable fate to either of these.

The nations of the world have one need in common—Leadership. The spirit of the people can do much, but it cannot do everything. In the end that form of government is likely to prevail which produces the best and most constant supply of leaders. On its own theories, democracy of the modern type ought to out-distance all competitors; under this system capacity, probity, and vigour should rise most easily to the top.

In practice, however, democracy has come under the thumb of the Party System, and the Party System has reached a very high point of efficiency. It has

CHAPTER IX.

The crucible of war.

bettered the example of the hugest mammoth store in existence. It has elaborated machinery for crushing out independent opinion and for cramping the characters of public men. In commending its wares it has become as regardless of truth as a vendor of quack medicines. It pursues corruption as an end, and it freely uses corruption—both direct and indirect—as the means by which it may attain its end. If the Party System continues to develop along its present lines, it may ultimately prove as fatal to the principle of democracy as the ivy which covers and strangles the elm-trees in our hedgerows.

Leadership is our greatest present need, and it is there that the Party System has played us false. To manipulate its vast and intricate machinery there arose a great demand for expert mechanicians, and these have been evolved in a rich profusion. But in a crisis like the present, mechanicians will not serve our purpose. The real need is a Man, who by the example of his own courage, vigour, certainty, and stedfastness will draw out the highest qualities of the people; whose resolute sense of duty will brush opportunism aside; whose sympathy and truthfulness will stir the heart and hold fast the conscience of the nation. Leadership of this sort we have lacked.

The Newcastle speech with its soft words and soothing optimism was not leadership. It does not give confidence to a horse to know that he has a rider on his back who is afraid of him.

It is idle at this stage to forecast the issue of the present war. Nevertheless we seem at last to have begun to understand that there is but a poor chance of winning it under rulers who are content to wait and see if by some miracle the war will win itself;

CHAPTER IX.

The crucible of war.

or if by another miracle our resources of men and material will organise themselves. Since the battle of the Marne many sanguine expectations of a speedy and victorious peace have fallen to the ground. The constant burden of letters from soldiers at the front is that the war—so far as England is concerned—is only just beginning. And yet, in spite of all these disappointments and warnings, the predominant opinion in official circles is still, apparently, as determined as ever to wait and see *what the people will stand*, although it is transparently clear what they ought to stand, and must stand, if they are to remain a people.

We cannot forecast with certainty the issue of the present war, but hope nevertheless refuses to be bound. There is a false hope and a true one. There may be consolation for certain minds, but there is no safety for the nation, in the simple faith that democracy is in its nature invincible. Democracy is by no means invincible. On the contrary, it fights at a disadvantage, both by reason of its inferiority in central control, and because it shrinks from ruthlessness. Nevertheless we may believe as firmly as those who hold this other opinion that in the end it will conquer. Before this can happen it must find a leader who is worthy of its trust.

Since August 1914 we have learned many things from experience which we previously refused to credit upon any human authority. We are not altogether done with the past; for it contains lessons and warnings—about men as well as things—which it would be wasteful to forget. But our main concern is with the present. And we are also treading very

The crucible of war.

close on the heels of the future, when—as we trust—the resistance of our enemies will be beginning to flag; when the war will be drawing to an end; afterwards through anxious years (how many we cannot guess) when the war has ended, and when the object of our policy will be to keep the peace which has been so dearly bought.

Lord Roberts was right in his forecast of the danger; nor was he less right in his perception of England's military weakness and general unpreparedness for war. But was he also right as to the principle of the remedy which he proposed? And even if he were right as things stood when he uttered his warnings, is his former counsel still right in our present circumstances, and as we look forward into the future? Is it now necessary for us to accept in practice what has always been admitted in the vague region of theory—that an obligation lies upon every citizen, during the vigour of his age, to place his services, and if need be his life, at the disposal of that state under whose shelter he and all those who are most dear to him have lived?

There is always danger in treating a free people like children; in humouring them, and coaxing them, and wheedling them with half-truths; in asking for something less than is really needed, from fear that to ask for the whole would alarm them too much; with the foolish hope that when the first demand has been granted it will then be easy enough to make them understand how much more is still necessary to complete the fabric of security; that having deceived them once, it will be all the easier to deceive them again.

As we look back over our country's history we

CHAPTER IX.

The crucible of war.

find that it was those men who told the people the whole truth—or what, at least, they themselves honestly believed to be the whole truth—who most often succeeded in carrying their proposals through. In these matters, which touch the very life and soul of the nation, all artifice is out of place. The power of persuasion lies in the truthfulness of the advocate, no less than in the truth of his plea. If the would-be reformer is only half sincere, if from timidity or regard for popular opinion he chooses to tell but half his tale—selecting this, suppressing that, postponing the other to a more propitious season—he loses by his misplaced caution far more than half his strength. When there is a case to be laid before the British People it is folly to do it piecemeal, by astute stages of pleading, and with subtle reservations. If the whole case can be put unflinchingly it is not the People who will flinch. The issue may be left with safety to a tribunal which has never yet failed in its duty, when rulers have had the courage to say where its duty lay.

THE END

Printed by R. & R. CLARK, LIMITED, *Edinburgh.*

ORDEAL BY BATTLE.

SOME PRESS OPINIONS.

THE TIMES LITERARY SUPPLEMENT.—"The book is a plea for national service in its widest sense, the complete organisation of Britain with a view to victory. 'Under conditions of modern warfare it is not only armies which need to be disciplined, but whole nations.' The moral is brilliantly pointed, and we may be sure that Mr. Oliver will not lack disciples to emphasise it. But the book is more than an argument in favour of a special policy. It is a storehouse of political thought, set out with a precision and an eloquence which have long been absent from the literature of politics. . . . A rare eloquence and a wealth of illustration which recalls Burke. Mr. Oliver is incapable of taking a bad point, and he has the most scrupulous intellectual honesty. Every page is lit up by some memorable phrase. Mr. Oliver never fulminates, but his irony is as merciless as it is urbane and delicate. . . . The war has produced a crop of analyses of German aims and the modern German temperament. The chapter on the subject in this volume seems to us to surpass in insight and fairness anything else written on the subject."

OBSERVER.—"Mr. Oliver's book is one which no honest mind can read without receiving deep impressions, and which no patriotic pen can discuss just now without considerable restraint."

GLOBE.—"We have long known Mr. Oliver as a writer of immense force, and one who, while he holds his opinions with tenacious strength, has shown himself ripe in judgment and scrupulously fair in argument. . . . There is not a chapter in this searching analysis of our national strength and weakness which is not informed by high patriotism and statesmanlike grasp of causes."

STANDARD.—"Mr. F. S. Oliver has produced the most notable book concerning the war that has yet appeared. The style is lucid and distinguished, and there is thought in every page. . . . The book should be read by every serious man. It is not only thoughtful, but stimulates thought."

SUNDAY TIMES.—"Everybody ought to read Mr. Frederick Scott Oliver's *Ordeal by Battle*. That compliment it deserves because so much earnestness and conviction and solid thought have gone to the making of the book, because its author handles candidly and fearlessly the subject which is of paramount interest to us all."

GLASGOW HERALD.—"It is a brilliantly written treatise. . . . Controversial certainly; but in a large and eloquent way; strong, sincere, and moving."

ORDEAL BY BATTLE.

SOME PRESS OPINIONS.

THE TIMES.—"Some ten years ago Mr. F. S. Oliver published his *Life of Alexander Hamilton*, a book which has probably had more influence than any political work of the decade. . . . The book which he publishes to-day is not less opportune in its moment of appearance, and it is likely that its influence will be still greater. For it deals with the most urgent problem which has ever faced our nation. . . . Some of the things in the book have been said before, but we do not think they have ever been said so well. . . . Mr. Oliver is scrupulously just, and his chapters are amply documented. He has no party bias. . . . To those who desire a brilliant survey of recent domestic history and character studies done with the clean precision of Swift, we recommend these chapters."

MORNING POST.—"Both for statesmanship and for style (style which is the shadow of personality) Mr. F. S. Oliver's book on the causes and conditions of the war is by far the best that has yet appeared. . . . It is not easy to say anything new and true on the growth, scope, and intention of German policy. . . . The most and best Mr. Oliver can do . . . is to give us a lucid and coherent survey of the subject. His survey is excellent; it contains the gist of hundreds of books, new and old, and now and again opens up new vistas of speculation."

DAILY TELEGRAPH.—"It may be said at once that Mr. Oliver's book is one which invites the closest and most respectful consideration. . . . Mr. Oliver is eloquent, fearless, and, in the truest sense of the word, ardently patriotic. He believes eagerly in getting his fellow-countrymen to face the truth; he is confident in their capacity to realise it. This strong, manly, and determined appeal to the nation's manhood and common-sense is bound to do good. It is not improbable that it may even prove one of the most effective literary weapons in the opening campaign on behalf of enlightenment and prompt action."

SATURDAY REVIEW.—"Already a myriad pages have been published on the War and its causes, but now at last a sequence of pages grows into a genuine Book, a great and necessary adventure in difficult truth-telling. With a courage that never for a moment tires, Mr. F. S. Oliver anticipates the verdicts that our grandchildren will write and speak; and his qualities as a good historian—his wit and humour, his searching irony, his wide knowledge and unbiased candour—have won for him the right to speak for posterity. . . . It has taken us five days to read Mr. Oliver's *Ordeal by Battle*; and if all books claimed and merited the same careful study, reviewers would be ruined and the country would be educated and secure."